Advance Praise For *Do I Stay or Do I Go?*

"A clear understanding of the conflicts couples face in deciding to end relationships comes through clearly and with compassion in this volume. The author's wise counsel, as she explores the issues, makes a special contribution to the literature. Her use of personal stories and case histories is especially welcome making the book both insightful and enjoyable reading."

Marcia Lasswell, Ph.D.
Professor of Psychology/Clinical Professor of Marriage and Family
Past President of The American Association for Marriage and Family

"As a practicing psychiatrist and psychiatric researcher, I am confronted multiple times a day with men and women struggling with relationships. They may be concerned about romantic involvements, family relationships, or even career related decisions. The key question that has them in conflict of such a profound dimension that it produces both psychological and biological distress is "Do I stay or do I go?" Dr. Occhetti has skillfully woven practical clinical wisdom into an entertaining and instructive book. I cannot imagine readers or concerned friends and family of readers who are in the midst of such a dilemma not benefiting immensely from the years of knowledge that Dr. Occhetti has shared in this book. Once people understand what makes them tick and what motivates their partners, most are able to make more intelligent decisions about the most important thing in our lives – meaningful relationships. *Do I Stay or Do I Go?* is a must read book for mental health professionals and healthcare professionals who see countless patients each day in emotional distress from relationship crises. Regrettably, it is not just the two parties involved that are torn apart by the dilemma of whether to end relationships. Children, stepchildren, parents, grandparents, co-workers, and society all suffer from the emotional drain and anger that occurs when relationships are struggling, flawed or ending.

Congratulations to Dr. Occhetti for a masterful and entertaining book, dealing with one of life's greatest problems."

Richard H. Weisler, M.D.
Psychiatric Research/Private Practice
Duke University/Department of Psychiatry
Raleigh, NC

"I found *Do I Stay or Do I Go?* rich in its practical information…warm and personal. The stories were riveting. The realness of the cases made the interventions more real, reasonable and workable."

Joan Read, Ph.D.
Fielding Institute, Santa Barbara, CA

"I look forward to recommending this book to my patients and colleagues."

> *Rich Adelman, M.D.*
> *Family practice physician*
> *Raleigh, NC*

"Dianne Reavis Occhetti does not live in a black and white world. Her clear and colorful writing style in *Do I Stay or Do I Go?* reflects the complexities of human relationships, especially the role of self-knowledge, an imaginative use of resources, and spirituality in the growth process. This highly readable book is full of useful exercises, case studies rendered dramatically, and other recommended resources. Wonderfully, the author shows us a skilled and creative therapist at work, one who believes that people know more about their lives than they know they know. And she knows how to get them to realize it."

> *Sister Evelyn Mattern*
> *Author of Blessed Are You: The Beatitudes and Our Survival and Why Not Become Fire? Encounters with Women Mystics*

"I can hardly wait to recommend this rich resource to my clients."

> *Louise Coggins, MSW, CCSW*
> *Private practice*
> *Raleigh, NC*

"...interesting, easily read, and very valuable to anyone wondering whether to stay or go. The book is fair, unbiased, and stimulates readers to take responsibility for their own choices, whatever they may be."

> *Mary Goulding, MSW*
> *Co-founder, Western Institute for Group and Family Therapy, Watsonville, CA*
> *Author of "Sweet Love Remembered" and "A Time to Say Good Bye"; Co-author, "Changing Lives Through Redecision Therapy," "The Power is in the Patient," "Not to Worry."*

"This is a must read for those with relationship troubles."

> *Rev. Denny Blake*
> *Lutheran pastor*
> *Raleigh, NC*

Do I Stay

OR

Do I Go?

How to Make a Wise Decision About Your Relationship

by

DIANNE OCCHETTI, Ph.D.

Health
Access
PRESS

InSync Communications LLC and Health Access Press
2445 River Tree Circle
Sanford, Florida 32771
http://www.insynchronicity.com

ISBN: 0-9673439-1-7
Library of Congress Catalog Number: 99-65269
Occhetti, Dianne
Do I Stay or Do I Go?/Dianne Occhetti

First Health Access Press Edition
10 9 8 7 6 5 4 3 2

All clients mentioned in this work are composite characters drawn from the clinical work and life experiences of the author. Names and details have been changed to protect confidentiality.

This publication was designed to provide information in regard to the subject matter covered. It is sold and distributed with the understanding that the publisher is not engaged in rendering legal, medical, or counseling services. If appropriate expert assistance is required, the services of a qualified and competent professional should be sought. —This statement is adapted from a Declaration of Principals jointly adopted by a Committee of the American Bar Association and a Committee of Publishers and Associations.

InSync Press books are available at special discounts when purchased in bulk for use in seminars, as premiums or in sales promotions. Special editions or book excerpts can also be created to specification. For details, contact InSync Communications LLC at the address above.

Cover Design by Jonathan Pennell
Book Design/Typesetting by Stephanie Murphy

Printed in the United States of America

Leonard R. Clark

To Lynne,
may you find what you want
and what is right for you.

Leonard

the difficulty in life is the choice

...George Moore

table of contents

Publisher's Foreword

Health care has become a buzz word or buzz phrase for our culture. As the 21st Century becomes a reality, there are few Americans, few members of the entire Blue-Marble Community for that matter, who aren't conscious of their own health care needs to one degree or another. Many of these people cannot afford the quality of health care they require, while many have coverage through a variety of HMO and PPO organizations – which, like health care itself, remain mysterious to most.

Our children know more about health care today than most adults did twenty – no ten years ago. While they may not have the expertise to go beyond a minor discussion on a topic, most have heard of the various cancers that plague humanity. They have heard of mononucleosis, anorexia nervosa, AIDS, hepatitis, epilepsy, and cardiac arrest. Our society has bombarded them with a litany of monologues on the evils of caffeine, nicotine, alcohol, and drugs from A to Z – not that the message has been understood or ingested and digested completely. But nevertheless, we can praise ourselves in the knowledge that we are the generation who bombarded our children with the truth.

Now, what is the truth? Well, I suspect that often depends on who's dispensing it. One man's truth is another's lie – just as one man's trash is another man's treasure. We have parents who preach of the ills of drug consumption but allow their children to witness their "social drinking" and "recreational pharmaceutical utilization." We are torn on how to teach our children about sex. And we're equally torn on who should teach our children about sex. Should it be total and complete abstinence? Should it be a combination of "just say no" coupled with weak parental explanations of what's going on inside a young person's body? Do we hand out condoms in public schools? Do we abort "mistakes?" The debate rages on.

And in and around the search for answers to one's own health care sits, in a well-lighted part of the room, one of the greatest health care tragedies of modern America: the rising dissolution of marriages and long-term relationships.

As Dianne Occhetti points out in her pivotal work, there are nearly 6,000 marriages that take place in this country each and every day of the year. And the truly sad part of the equation is that there are nearly 3,000 divorces granted in this nation on a daily basis. Numbers to be proud of? Numbers to cry over? Or numbers that should provide a wake-up call to men and women, spouses, parents, counselors, educators, theologians, and the general network of health care providers that this as much a disease of epidemic proportions as any of the cancers killing off human life.

How does face the myriad of challenges and potential problems in a relationship? Who should take the lead – the responsibility – for recognizing stumbling blocks and pitfalls and speak up when a couple falls prey to what appear to be insurmountable obstacles? Where does one go for sincere and useful help? Who can you trust when evaluating your options? Well, just as in other forms of health care maintenance, one must choose carefully and with forethought the professionals they seek help and comfort from. One of the purposes of this book is to empower (not enable) the reader in assessing their life, the relationships they are in, in making decisions, and being prepared to fight the good fight to save an important relationship, or know when to accept the path that is leading nowhere.

Do I Stay or Do I Go? is a book that fits into the philosophy of Health Access Press very nicely. It is written in an understandable fashion and can be appreciated equally by the lay reader as much as by the health care professional. The book offers its readers an opportunity to see that the problems they face aren't unique to them and offers opportunities for the reader to become informed and take charge of their situation (just as a cancer patient can take charge of some of their own health care destiny through becoming more informed.) Knowledge is power. There's little argument with that. But it's more important that you put that knowledge to use. Dr. Occhetti provides the reader with tools that can inform and motivate. But the key to making any of this work is the reader themselves. There's nothing magical to making a relationship work, just as there's nothing magical (or evil) in what goes into what makes relationships disintegrate.

What makes for a good relationship is a function of genetics, family history, emotional stability, the ability to be intimate, how one faces the inevitable crises of life, attitudes on finances as well as sex, one's level of humor and seriousness, occupational compatibility, health, attitudes on romance, how passive or active one is, one's ability to nurture is, and a few hundred other factors – including ones yet unidentified. The human animal is a complex entity. When it combines, combined with another human animal, the results can be amazing. Sometimes they are not compatible combinations and like chemicals in a science lab, there can be explosions.

As George Moore said, "the difficulty in life is the choice." As Occhetti might say, "wise assessment and decision making can make those choices more rewarding and healthier."

Dennis N. McClellan
Publisher, Health Access Press

About the Author

Dianne Reavis Occhetti, Ph.D., LMFT, LCSW, is a family psychologist, marital and family therapist, and clinical social worker, who is in private practice in Raleigh, North Carolina. She often appears on television and radio in the Raleigh-Durham area. She can be reached at www.occhetti.com.

Acknowledgments

This book is dedicated to Dr. A. Shamim, who helped me find hope again, my mother, who consistently showed faith in me and my persistence, and all the clients who shared their stories.

Thanks Billie (Hedberg), for connecting me with Dennis McClellan, publisher. (You're the best ex-sister-in-law a person could have.) And Dennis, thanks for providing that spark of enthusiasm for my work at just the right time which gave me the fuel to finish it.

The seeds for the book were planted early in my doctoral program at The Fielding Institute. At the Admissions Contract Workshop, I was asked to envision where I would be 10 years post-doctorate. One goal was to have written the book about extramarital affairs that my clients kept requesting. Later, at a Fielding alumni publishing workshop, I wrote a very sketchy outline of this book. Another Fielding alum, Lynn Luckow, led the workshop and encouraged me by saying that my work was like a "breath of fresh air" if I would write like I talked.

I am appreciative of all the Fielding faculty who helped with my dissertation. Special thanks to Dr. Inge Broverman (Inge, I wish you were here to see this book since you deleted so much from my dissertation, and told me to save it and write a book). And thanks to my husband, Arm, for all your help with my data collection.

Kudos to my lunch bunch group from Raleigh Professional Women's Forum for being supportive and helping me to keep my sense of humor.

Cathy Breeden, thank you for your insightful comments, enthusiasm, and helpful support. Judith Appelbaum and Florence Janovic, thanks for your help with the foreign land of publishing. Clare Ainni, my guardian angel, thanks for getting me to Dr. Shamim. Tawny, (my cat), thanks for not deleting the book more than once or twice.

Words are insufficient to express my thanks to Rich for your technical know-how, and to Jennifer and DLW for your professional expertise at just the right time.

This has been a journey; my family has experienced all the emotions along with me, and I am extraordinarily appreciative that you were behind me.

And gratitude to all who offered encouragement in thought, word, or deed.

Author's Foreword

Litte did I realize years ago when I said I wanted to write a book about affairs in 10 years, that our nation would be in the midst of a scandalous liaison between the President and a young woman his daughter's age. My book turned out to be about more than extramarital liaisons, just as I believe our nation's preoccupation with this scandal is about more than extramarital affairs.

Professional self-esteem and personal self-esteem play important roles in relationships. Reflecting on the Clinton scandal and my ongoing work with couples in the areas of marital dissatisfaction and extramarital affairs, I am struck by how much personal unhappiness is related to the difference between professional self-esteem and personal self-esteem. High professional self-esteem does not automatically equal high personal self-esteem. When a person is very successful professionally, it is hard for others to understand when unexplained behavior occurs on the personal level.

Self-esteem and accountability are, I believe, the two most important ingredients in a person's relationship choices. This is also true for the tragic Clinton/Monica liaison. In many extramarital relationships, I believe there is a sharp dichotomy between professional self-esteem and personal self-esteem. Solid professional identity does not equal solid personal self-esteem. And when personal self-esteem is low, choices are limited and consequences can be grave.

This book is about themes in relationships—the themes of professional and personal self-esteem, accountability, and responsibility, and how these issues relate to relationship choices.

Never has the time been more ripe for our nation and our people to examine and reflect upon the concerns presented in this book.

introduction

Help With a Hard Choice

The question *"Do I Stay or Do I Go?"* may sound as though it has a simple answer but if it's a question you are asking yourself – and if you are like millions of other people struggling with troubled relationships – you are probably going through a round of agony and uncertainty that may last for months or even years.

This book shows you how to get unstuck and come to a wise decision.

The first step is understanding that it's normal to be confused. "I feel so guilty because I don't know what to do," clients tell me when they begin therapy. The guilty feeling sets up a "should" – I should know whether to stay or go and something is wrong with me because I don't. Too often, the "should" is reinforced by well-meaning friends. In *her* case, they say, "Leave the bastard." In *his* case, they say, "Ditch the witch."

But of course the easy answers aren't what you really need. What you need is a way to come to the conclusion that's right for you, and that is what you will find in this book.

There are always more choices than just staying or leaving the relationship. Becoming aware of all the available alternatives and the consequences associated with each choice is an essential step. This book will show you how to see what they are.

When you are struggling with the question of *Do I Stay or Do I Go?* your journey is likely to go through passive and active stages. When a trigger event occurs, you may go into a frenzy of activity being sure that you will go. As the dust settles, and your partner improves or your perspective changes, it becomes easier to go back to the status quo. However, the state of unrest does not go away; it merely goes underground to reemerge with the next trigger.

When are your feelings of discontent due to a natural occurrence in the development of a relationship, a fit of anger, and when do they reflect more serious troubles that need to be addressed? You may be stuck in a cycle of negative emotions. For example, you may feel angry, resentful, and antagonistic. Could your negative feelings be due to the arrival of a child, or becoming part of a stepfamily? Are you or your partner having a midlife crisis, or has one of you been involved in an affair? Are there sexual problems in the relationship?

"When will I know if I 'should' stay or go?" is probably one of the most frequently asked questions in marital and relationship therapy. Two factors play an especially important role: self-esteem and accountability. When your self-esteem is on solid ground, you can begin to trust your responses. And when you can be accountable to yourself for your choice, you are well on your way to accepting your choice.

Why is self-esteem so important? First, it takes a certain level of self-esteem to even believe that you have a choice. And even after you acknowledge that life offers choices, your self-esteem often determines whether or not you take an active role in making a decision versus a passive role in just letting life happen. Whether you are active or passive will not be determined in an instant. An active journey, which is indicative of a certain amount of self-esteem, involves asking the questions appropriate to your life circumstance. For example, if you are in midlife as represented by Billy Joel's song, "River of Dreams," the questions that need to be asked are different from the questions that a new parent or a stepparent must address. The passive reality is that life's events keep revolving around you creating deeper and deeper layers of unrest.

How you address the unrest depends upon the level of "re-lationship self-esteem" you possess. Self-esteem in other areas of your life does not automatically equal relationship self-es-teem. Many complex emotional factors come into play in rela-tionships which often make the journey confusing. Ambivalent feelings often predominate. This book offers a probing look at some of the typical life situations, and encourages you to take an active role in asking the questions that are needed to help you in formulating an answer.

The accountability factor is also important. Accountability means not blaming other people or certain life events for your choice(s). Intellectually, you may know that it is not a good idea to place responsibility elsewhere; but, emotionally, the ten-dency to blame others is usually high, particularly, when you are hurting. Life events, whether illness, aging parents, job loss, or an unfair economy, can be used to avoid addressing those painful, but necessary questions.

When you can be accountable to yourself for your choice, you are well on your way to accepting your choice. Part of that accountability means leaving no stone unturned in the journey to identify your specific dilemma, your choices, and the ques-tions that need to be addressed relevant to your situation. Tak-ing responsibility for your choice, and being accountable to yourself is part of the difficulty of life. The stories in this book show how real, live people have worked their way to good deci-sions. You can too, with the tools presented in this book.

one

i should be happy but...

Susan

I wondered why I had given a third appointment time to Susan. My policy was that if a person cancelled two first appointment times, I did not offer a third unless there were extremely good reasons for the previous cancellations, like a death in the family, illness, etc. And it did matter who the referral source was, too. Even though Susan was referred by a former client, I usually did not see a cancellation of two first appointments as an indication that someone was ready to work on their issues.

On the voice-mail message, there was not even an emotional catch in her voice. It was a very businesslike request for another appointment. We played voice-mail tag until an appointment was set. And I still didn't know why I had given her a third appointment time.

Susan did make the third appointment. When I greeted her, she was busy conducting business on her cell phone. Upon entering my office, she stated she would have to leave our 45 minute appointment time 10 minutes early. I made the observation that it must be hard for her to be here. She shrugged. When I inquired what brought her to therapy, she said "I don't know, I'm just not happy." And I remembered earlier phone conversations when I asked about what she wanted help with, the response was pretty much the same. And then I had a clue as to why I continued to offer her appointments. There was an unspoken "should" about her dilemma – "I should be happy, but…." And that unspoken phrase had hooked me.

Susan continued to talk and stayed for her full appointment time, an event that neither of us addressed. She spoke of a life filled with all the "right" things: great careers for herself and her husband, a beautiful home, European vacations, and a faithful husband. I asked "faithful?" with a perplexed tone that she would use that word as the first descriptive word for her husband. "Utterly, boringly faithful and responsible," she said. "Is he aware that you see him that way?" I said. Again, she shrugged.

She continued talking, "Our conversations are perfunctory, like 'how was your day', 'do you want to eat out or order in,' 'what do you want to do this weekend'." When I inquired about the typical vegetative symptoms of depression, like eating and sleeping patterns, and mood changes, she knew what I was asking, and said "I had my doctor prescribe me Prozac, but it did not really help."

Over the next several weeks Susan continued to keep her therapy appointments, and she disclosed more. The precipitating factor that brought her in for the first appointment was that she had begun having sexual fantasies about the men she worked with, an event that jarred her. In fact, the reason she was supposed to leave 10 minutes early during that first therapy appointment was for a business meeting with the man about whom she had been having intense sexual fantasies. It was a relief to her that she had stayed the entire appointment time, and could tell her business colleague that she had been at the doctor's, and would have to reschedule.

She had begun gaining weight the unhappier she became, and she said "I don't really think of myself as sexual anymore. How can I be having these bothersome sexual fantasies with these men in my workaday world???" She and her husband had stopped having sex for about the last year. She said, "It was not a deliberate decision, the sex just withered away, or at least the interest did." When I asked about how he felt, she reflected a moment, and commented that sex was something they did not talk about anymore. It was not that they couldn't talk about it, they just didn't. "We are always tired," she said and "there is always one more project to do, or one more phone call to make, and the other person is usually asleep by the time the task-driven partner finishes for the evening." And she admitted that it alternated as to who came to bed first.

Upon further exploration, Susan's history revealed she was the "good girl" doing what her family expected, and she had followed in her father's footsteps with the corporate big company career. She married after college at just the expected time. And at every right moment they had acquired the next "thing" like the Lexus, the perfect house, the right furnishings, and the nice vacations. These "things" were OK for awhile, but then they were passe as time passed.

She said, "I felt so in charge of my career. I was alive at work. And now, I am unhappy everywhere. My friends ask me what has happened?"

I noticed that Susan throughout the sessions had said very little about her mother, responding only briefly to my direct questions. When I made this observation, Susan acknowledged that her fear was that she was going to be as unhappy as she knew her mother to be. With gentle prodding, Susan continued by saying that she knew her mother had always been unfulfilled. Her mother had stayed home, like mothers did then, and did all the right things such as volunteer and make social contacts for the family. She described her mother as being very intelligent, but even as a little girl, she always knew something was missing in her mother's marriage. She had thought by pursuing the high power career, she was avoiding what her mother had experienced.

As the subject of her mother came up she showed emotion beneath the cool controlled exterior. She vehemently said, "I will not end up as unhappy as my mother, and I will leave this marriage before I do. I must have more in my marriage than she did." I asked Susan if she thought this only had to do with her marriage. She said, "That is why I am here. You work with people on their marriages." I acknowledged, "Yes, I specialize in several areas, marriage being one of them. And sometimes what looks like a *"Do I Stay or Do I Go"* issue in marriage becomes a much broader issue and encompasses one's whole life. Are you ready to look at the broader issues, Susan?"

The Dilemma

Susan is struggling with a common pattern in marriage and relationships. She has denied her need for intimacy and sharing to the point that her body has to express symptoms to get her attention. Her marriage sounds like two strangers who live in the same house. Financial goals, material accumulations, and social obligations are mutually shared endeavors. What makes them strangers is what is not shared. Wishes, hopes, dreams, thoughts, and feelings are not mutually shared. An emotional void exists that carries over into the sexual relationship.

The Choices

Unlike her mother, Susan has financial independence to make it on her own. Would life be easier without him? At times, she thinks so. And yet, she stays. Choices are not always easy or clear cut. Her expectations are that she is supposed to be fulfilled and relatively happy. Those expectations are not being met.

Is there a chance her marriage could be modified so that more of her expectations could be met? Possibly. How much effort and how long would that take? Can she emotionally survive for much longer now that she has acknowledged the degree of her unhappiness and unfulfillment? That leads to more questions:

The Questions

The first item Susan must address is the extent of her self knowledge. She has already made some links between her parents' marriage and her own. She admits that she has repeated a pattern. What is the link between what she wants and the behaviors she chooses? She is slowly becoming aware of what she really wants. Her behaviors have not been in sync with this new level of awareness. How could she communicate about things that were not in her conscious awareness? Probably, she could not communicate in a direct manner. Her desires may have been expressed in many indirect ways. For example, her sexual fantasies about other men certainly indicate her libido is not dried up, and yet, she does not talk about sex with her husband. She has basically ignored in a direct manner that she and her husband have not had sex for about a year.

So, is Susan supposed to lower her expectations and live happily ever after? Is she supposed to accept a sexless marriage? Is it a loveless marriage, too? In her quest for self knowledge, Susan needs to probe deeper and ask what have those early family of origin dynamics got to do with her life now? Her bodily symptoms, i.e.; the weight and the sexual cravings demanded attention in a way she could not ignore. Likewise, her sexual fantasies compelled her to seek out therapy to understand these "bothersome" thoughts. The professional "in charge" Susan cannot understand the personal Susan who is "floundering" in understanding why she is so unhappy.

In many ways, Susan is still the "good girl," doing what is expected at work and at home. While she knows and understands the expectations at work, her home environment has become a nemesis. Will Susan have to leave her marriage to confront the reality of her unhappiness?

These kind of questions really do not demand a yes or no, a black or white response. And yet, it seems so easy to respond in that manner. The first part of the process is to ask the questions. This process usually takes place over time, as it has for Susan.

Increased awareness leads to the ability to know what one wants. Susan is at this stage of the process. She knows more of what she does not want, unhappiness and unfulfillment like her mother, than she knows of what she does want. And thus begins her journey of self-knowledge.

the "personal self" vs. the "professional self"

Professionally, Susan feels self-assured, competent, in charge, and she knows her career goals for the next ten years. Personally, her life is in shambles. Her relationship with her husband is unfulfilling; she is really lonely; she feels insecure. And what is her constant eating all about? And the depression? Can her self-esteem be in such a sharp dichotomy between her professional self and her personal self?

This issue is not confined to women. In a couples therapy group that I led recently, several men raised the vulnerable issue of feeling so inadequate and inferior in their personal relationships when they were the epitome of success in their professional life. Some even commented that they would be ashamed for their colleagues to see how they behaved in their personal relationships, and that they doubted they would even be recognized as the same person. These men were well- respected professionals who were in positions of authority.

Is this a self-esteem issue? Is this a self-knowledge issue? ·Yes. But how can it be that a person has self-esteem on the job, but feels so insecure and sometimes worthless in intimate relationships? The clearest way to state it is to examine the link between what Susan wants and the behavior she chooses. On the job Susan is decisive, and very much acts in the role of leader.

Susan chooses behaviors that reflect her sense of self-confidence and belief in her leadership abilities. Susan states she wants more closeness in her marital relationship; yet, she does not directly initiate intimate risk-taking behaviors. She expresses her wants and needs indirectly as she did when she planned the "perfect romantic weekend getaway" after being in therapy for a month. What was perfect in her eyes remained unexpressed to her husband. If Susan was having difficulty with a colleague at work, she would address the person and the problem pronto. How can Susan enhance her self-knowledge about this discrepancy?

1. Examination of her family patterns with Mom and Dad can help her identify what behaviors she may be unconsciously continuing in her own marriage. As Susan does so, she is struck by several factors. Her identification as an independent woman is very strongly connected to her Dad. She even followed in Dad's footsteps by working in the same company. Professionally, Dad has always been her role model.

Susan sees herself repeating the role of her mother in her marriage. Her mother was always lonely for more intimate companionship. And it did not happen in her marriage, and Susan sees it not happening in her relationship.

So, the models we live our lives by affect our choices. The values of our models may fit our lives today or they may not. How do we know if we do not engage in a reexamination of what is important and what contributes to a fulfilling life?

> A limited image of heroism, based on hand-me-down values, often discourages people from what they *could* do because it is not what they have been taught they *should* do. Stuck with untimely models, they are unable to conceive of currently useful behaviors. To counter defeating interjections takes courage because each individual must rework what she or he has been taught and construct a fresh, distinctive perspective on life. *(Polster, 1992, pg. xvi)*.

This quote is not to be interpreted as "yep, that's it, I must go, leave the relationship." The answer is not to be found in a black or white response. If our past models encouraged defeating behaviors, it is only natural that such defeating behaviors continue until one really breaks the cycle by asking different questions to gain the opportunity to see other available choices.

Easier said than done. The ways in which Susan has incorporated the values her father taught her has worked well for her in her career. Other behaviors she learned from him relationship-wise have not worked as well. For her father work and home were completely separate arenas. While he was highly involved at work, he was minimally active in the home life. In fact, Susan did not begin to have a semblance of a relationship with him until she was old enough to go with him to work on the weekends. And, once again, the interaction centered around what project he was doing. At a young age, Susan learned that to get her Dad's attention all she had to do was feign interest in the real estate dealings. And before too long, Susan found that what she liked was what her Dad liked.

From her mother, Susan learned to value intimacy, even if she could not define it consciously. She observed her mother sharing many different parts of her life with people other than her father. Her parents seemed to share only the mundane tasks of everyday life with each other. Just as her mother settled for a marriage with little intimacy, Susan saw herself repeating the empty pattern in her own relationship. Unquestionably, Susan knew that her people skills on the job were honed by the interactions with her mother and her mother's support network of friends.

But what is this intimacy jargon? Susan would have a hard time defining intimacy with her husband. If pressed to say what intimacy is to her, she would respond with an example of what it is like to talk with her college roommate. They can see each other very infrequently, maybe once a year; and yet, they can pick up the phone and never skip a beat from their last conversation. Susan can share her thoughts, feelings, wishes, and wants with her friend. She can talk with her friend about the most insignificant trivia as well as her pain and loss. They can share with each other a sense of humor about the changes in their lives and listen to one another with sensitivity and acceptance.

With her increased self-awareness, Susan knows she wants intimacy in her marriage. So? How is she going to get it? This brings us to the second major area of work in the journey for self-knowledge: RESPONSIBILITY.

2. Self-responsibility and accountability for the choices one makes is probably the most difficult challenge one has in the decision journey to *"Do I Stay or Do I Go?"* For Susan, accountability at work is no problem. She is used to dealing with "the buck stops here". She can cut through layers of communication to dissect what the problem is, identify what needs to be done, and follow through on the resolution.

Her communication in her personal relationship is another matter. She describes herself as "walking on eggshells." Is Susan afraid of being held accountable? And what is her depression about? And the "eating out of control" bit? Depression is often defined as "resentment in disguise." And could the eating disorder be due to internalized anger? Yes, depression can be a biochemical imbalance. Sometimes it is due to other things. And sometimes it is a combination of a chemical imbalance and the way in which an individual interprets events and feelings. Susan took the Prozac with the expectation that it would solve all her problems. Wishful thinking!

So, what is that "walking on eggshells" all about? If it were a work situation, Susan would "break the eggshell," directly confront the issue, and get on with it. In her marriage, Susan hears a small voice in the back of her head, her father's voice, saying "you do not hurt members of your family". With this realization, Susan knows she is afraid of saying out loud what the eggshell is all about. The eggshell is like a metaphor for the

covering that protects her husband from being hurt. Susan
doesn't want to be the one to break the shell by saying what she
knows will hurt him. With her girlfriend, Susan can say things
that she knows will temporarily hurt her friend. TEMPORARY?
The light clicks on for Susan as she realizes that she views her
words to her husband as a "permanent" hurt, not a temporary
one.

Thus, "breaking eggshells" is the next step in Susan's journey towards self-knowledge. What this will mean to her marriage is unknown at this point. But this helps Susan become less
stuck and offers her guidance in the decision-making process.

Being Stuck

The very nature of being "stuck" usually means that past
models have not provided the help one needs now to get
"unstuck." So often, when an individual comes into my office
struggling with what to do about a relationship and says, "Help
me, I'm stuck", the person cannot identify any currently useful
behavior pertaining to the relationship.

However, almost always, the same individual with a little
help (like Susan) can identify useful behaviors in other areas of
his or her life. What is needed is help in identifying useful behaviors to get unstuck in their relationship mess. The following
two exercises offer you a way to examine the models you live
your life by and help in assessing if that perspective is working
for you.

Who Is Your Hero?

This may seem like a strange question to ask to help you get
unstuck. And yet, the models we pattern our lives by determine
much of what we believe is possible. Is your hero a John Wayne,
a Clint Eastwood or a Michael Jordan type? Is your hero a

Barbara Bush, a Hillary Clinton, or a Helen Keller type? Or is your hero much closer to home, perhaps a close relative?

How does your choice of hero determine what you see as possible, and what you see as possible choices in your life? Most famous people when asked do say who their hero is. For example, President Clinton often shares about his meeting with President Kennedy on the White House grounds when he was just a youth. What that meeting gave him was a vision of hope, perhaps not at that moment, but certainly as he went through life. Hope is perhaps the greatest motivator of all.

Mariah Carey sings "the hero lies within you" from the song "Hero." As is often the case, our needs and desires as a culture are expressed via song. But where does this hero within you come from? What strengths, values, and courage are represented within you? The hero within you usually comes from the values of the models in your past and present life.

A poignant illustration of the values and influences of the previous generations is the movie "The Joy Luck Club." Generations of mothers and daughters portray the complex emotions, values, and pathos that are transmitted from one generation to the next. In the movie the daughters are not aware of the power of the past until traumatic events occur in their own lives. It is only when the daughters and mothers confront the present in the context of the past and ask questions of themselves and each other that they gain a new perspective on life and their relationships. "...no matter how revolutionary a period of change may seem on the surface, the old myths continue to whisper to us. Consciously derogated, unconsciously avoided and denied, they continue to speak with a power and persistence that will not be dismissed." (Rubin, 1983, p. 3).

As Susan began asking questions of herself and reflecting on her earlier relationship with Mom and Dad, certain voices began rumbling around in her head. The voice of her Dad, in particular, kept reverberating about not hurting other family members. And Susan recognized that what she heard as a powerful message kept her from expressing herself to her husband. She interpreted what she heard as a child as one "should" never hurt another family member at any cost. Susan had not really been consciously aware that this comment was playing such an active part in her life at the moment. It certainly helped explain the difference in her demeanor at the office and at home. Internally, through her bodily symptoms, she was expressing what she was not allowing herself to emotionally express to her husband.

Susan had to ask herself different questions in order to see other available choices. Let's go back to our earlier quote: "The difficulty in life is the choice" (George Moore). What we intend to do is often predicated upon what we see as available choices. So often the difficulties we experience with the question *"Do I Stay or Do I Go?"* is that the answer be either black or white, yes or no, either I stay or I go. Such limited choices. So often what we see as available choices in our personal relationships comes from the models we live our lives by, consciously and unconsciously.

"What Do I Want?" Exercise

Slowly, as Susan addresses the models of her past, mainly her parents, she recognizes that there are other choices beyond staying or leaving, but how does she go about answering the question "what do I want?" Although a seemingly innocent question, the response to this question requires far more than a surface answer. Often in therapy, she or he says to me through a haze of tears "I really don't know what I want." Not knowing what you want contributes to a feeling of being stuck in a rut. As one client explained it to me, "It is like driving your car on ice, then the car slips and your back tire spins and spins, going around and around, and you go nowhere."

Until you have a road map of where to go, it is perhaps inevitable that you will be stuck in indecisions. Identifying clearly what you want provides a signpost as to where to begin the journey. The following exercise can help you with the process of clarifying what you are currently doing, and what you want to choose to do. (Do the exercise before reading further)

1. **Identify your hero.** Write down the values, traits, and any special qualities of your hero.
2. **Identify the values, traits, and any special qualities of the family you grew up with.** Write down the positive and negative influences you experienced in the family you grew up with.
3. **Identify which values and influences are working for you now, and which ones are not working.** Differentiating between the pulls of the past and the present helps you to begin to formulate useful behaviors that you want to continue, and helps you to be more aware of behaviors that you need to change.

Let's follow Betty as she goes through this exercise. Betty identified her hero as the Wizard in "The Wizard of Oz." The Wizard, she said, was a wise person who helped everyone have what they needed; i.e., the tin man got a heart, and Dorothy got home.

When Betty began the second part of the exercise about the qualities and values of the family she grew up in, she became teary-eyed. Her father was an alcoholic and her mother worked all the time. Memories of her family life were unpleasant and mostly sad. She felt embarrassed and ashamed most of the time. The values she received as a child came from others outside the family. The one saying she heard over and over from her parents was "It's a dog-eat-dog world." Betty continued crying as she said she was like the Wizard with her husband, children, and just about everybody else in her life. She tried to give everyone what they needed like a great caretaker. She never received what she needed as a child, and her mission was to give her children what she never had.

When I asked Betty to look at what the Wizard wanted and how the Wizard got it, she said it was too frightening. She stated that she was terrified of identifying what she wanted. I commented that perhaps she was terrified of giving herself permission to say what she wanted. But, she said if she could say what she wanted, she would have to make a decision about her marriage. She was not ready for such a decision.

The exercise provided Betty a clearer roadmap of how she was stuck. No, she will not immediately become unstuck, but she is closer to dealing with the issues that keep her stuck.

Let's listen to how Pete does the exercise. Pete's hero is UNC-Chapel Hill basketball coach, Dean Smith. Pete likes Coach Smith's steadiness, emphasis on team work, and attention to possibilities in the most difficult game situations. Pete says maybe Coach Smith isn't really hero status, but Coach Smith is the closest thing to a personal hero that he can identify.

Pete said he definitely did not have a June and Ward Cleaver type family. His father left his mother and did not maintain contact with the family. He never had the opportunity to get to know his biological father before his father died in an accident. His mother married twice more; the stepfathers had very little to offer Pete.

What Pete remembers about his family life is that relationships were not to be counted on; love was something that came and went. Surface things like personal appearance and going along with the crowd became more important in determining how he felt about himself than anything his mother or the men in her life might say or do.

When Pete looks at what he admires about his hero, it comes as no surprise that he identifies stability, being part of a team (like being part of a family), and knowing what to do in a crisis situation. And yet, when he sees what he is doing in his current life, he acknowledges that his relationship problems are more like those of the family he grew up in. He just did not think about it in that way.

In his relationship, Pete desires love, loyalty, and trust; however, he really does not know how to give it himself. The hero exercise helps Pete to more quickly clarify what he wants and what may stand in the way of getting it. Pete can relate to this exercise partially because it is from his own experience. He commented that he did not realize that sharing his hero could say so much about himself.

Let us return to how Susan did this exercise. Not surprisingly, Susan identified her hero as her father. Qualities that she admired in her dad included ambition, independence, persistence, assertiveness with a touch of aggression, problem-solver, conscientiousness, and responsibleness.

Susan believed the positive influences in her family included all of the traits above of her father, her mother's people skills and lovingness, and their belief in her ability to accomplish whatever she wanted. Ironically, she thought the only area she had taken that to heart was in her career. She really had not known how to live that out in her relationship. And she had not had a model of how to do that.

The negative influences were mostly due to the lack of an intimate marriage model. Her mother accepted the emotionally distant breadwinner. She got her emotional needs met elsewhere through a network of friends. Her father emphasized that one did not say anything which might be hurtful to another family member. Boy, how Susan had bought into that in her own marriage.

Susan will take her new knowledge about herself with her as she breathes deeply and attempts to break the eggshell of protective covering she has placed around her husband. Where this will take her is unknown; and yet, the roadmap feels right as she pursues her new and fresh perspective on her marriage and what she wants.

Self-Esteem and Gender Differences

I certainly see discrepancies in professional self-esteem and personal self-esteem in both my female and male clients. Cultural and environmental influences on each sex are somewhat different.

The national preoccupation with the President Clinton scandal is not really so different from what I deal with on an every day basis in my work as a family psychologist and marital and family therapist. The stakes professionally for Clinton are certainly very great, and the climate for the country is very much affected by the uncertainty of what is true and what is not true. But as I reflect on these events and my work with couples in the areas of marital dissatisfaction and extramarital affairs, I am struck by how much personal unhappiness is related to the difference between professional self-esteem and personal self-esteem. When a person is very successful professionally, it is hard for others to understand when unexplained behavior occurs on the personal level. How can a person risk so much? Sometimes such behavior involves affairs; sometimes it is related to passive behavior in a marriage; at times, the behavior may include poor judgment in one's personal life in marked contrast to one's professional life.

I believe the development of such a gap in professional and personal self-esteem is due to several factors that is true for both men and women. There are three areas that I consider to be the most important in the consideration of personal self-esteem: family of origin issues and role models, unmet attachment needs, and the cultural interplay of media messages and gender differences. And there are times when excessive behavior may be due to an emotional disorder such as a bipolar (manic-depressive) illness.

I have noticed in many highly successful men that I have treated that there is a pattern in the family of origin dynamics.

Oftentimes, there is abandonment by one parent, physically or emotionally, or both, early messages of "you are not good enough, a strong desire for approval, and a need for achievement to hide the personal hurt and pain from childhood.

Attachment needs — the human desire to bond and maintain contact — are often unmet in distressed marriages, continuing a pattern of being unmet in interaction with past role models. Extramarital affairs are symptoms of larger unresolved issues. When professional crises arise, problem-solving behavior goes into high gear, with data gathering, networking, delegation, and decisive action bringing resolution. With personal crises erupting, the same road-map does not work. Being stuck in the same personal patterns without understanding the emotions underneath makes the acceptance of responsibility for such behavior less likely, and the continuation of these patterns more likely. Emotions around self-esteem, intimacy, and boundaries of the couple, are ripe for exploration and are the keys for future change.

The media and cultural interplay of the last 50 years has certainly sent forth different messages for men and women. "Boys will be boys" in the sexual arena has been played out on the national scene with prominent and powerful men. Such behavior has often been accepted, overlooked, or condoned by lack of assertive action otherwise. This is beginning to change, slowly, and usually at great cost to those who come forward. For women to be desirable, just look at the image of women in magazines, ads, commercials, etc., and you will see that the emphasis is on being young, beautiful, sexy, and thin. Eating disorders are so common among young females. Fear and insecurity are often present. "How do I look? Will I be pretty enough? Will I be accepted? Will I know how to act?" Media messages in our culture say that the woman who is sexy, beautiful, thin, and young gets ahead. Such a combination makes what is happening nationally more understandable if less palatable.

two

---

i've been betrayed

Frank

Frank stormed into my office and paced back and forth like a raging bull. He remained in an upright position, and it was very clear that he had no intention of sitting down on the sofa or in a chair. He ranted and raved, "How dare her?! I could murder her with my bare hands. And right under my nose... I win the award for fool of the year."

My administrative assistant was perceptive in allowing Frank to fill out the paperwork after the session. She said, "He was what you would call agitated in one of your reports." That was an understatement as she well knew.

Just when I thought he was calming down, the pace would quicken again, and the verbal threats would ensue as he strode back and forth. "I will throw her ass out of the house. She can be on the street for all I care," he yelled.

And then he turned that bitter anger on me:

"My doctor sends me to a woman to talk about my wife screwing my friend? How in the hell are you going to help me?"

"Have you finished?" I asked.

"Finished what, with this so-called interview?"

"Have you finished expressing your feelings about what happened?" I queried.

"Hell, no."

"Well, continue to do so," I said.

19

He stopped pacing long enough to really look at me. "You think this is easy?"

"No, I believe the intensity of your feelings indicates that you care a great deal about what has happened," I reasoned.

Surprisingly, Frank sat down, and looked haggard and drawn. He sighed, "I haven't slept in over 24 hours. That's why my doctor friend insisted that I come here."

"So tell me what happened," I softly said.

In an anguished voice, he related that the other man was his friend. "The betrayal is doubled. My feelings can never be the same for either one of them again. I couldn't sleep last night, so I went over to his house and parked outside. I wanted to go in and kill him, but I stayed in my vehicle. I couldn't trust what I would do if I broke in, or even if I knocked on the door and he opened it. I'm actually a mild kind of guy, but I guess you find that hard to believe."

I smiled. "I do not know you well, but I know that passions and emotions run pretty high in betrayal situations. You wanted to go in and kill your friend, but the important thing is that you did not."

He cringed, "Every time I close my eyes I see the two of them in each other's arms. I cannot stop that vision. When I am in my bedroom, I wonder if they were in my bed."

Frank continued to ventilate, staying with the obsession of his friend and his wife being together. He kept repeating, "What does he have that I do not? What does Faye (his wife) want?" Painfully and angrily he would alternate between saying he was leaving the marriage and asking can I give her what she wants.

I asked Frank to come back again for a second session that same week. He was gruff about saying yes, but he actually sounded relieved.

On the second visit, Frank did not storm into my office, and he did not pace. His body posture did not hold the same kind of anger on this visit. As I checked in with him, I also asked if he and Faye had talked yet. He acknowledged, "a little."

As if he could not hold it in any longer, he blurted out, "All I could talk about was revenge, and having an affair of my own."

"You want to hurt her like she hurt you", I said, and "your anger is masking an awful lot of hurt."

He sarcastically said, "My hurt doesn't matter."

"Is that really true?," I asked.

He gave his infamous grunt.

By the third visit, Frank began talking about when he was going to leave the marriage. I asked him if this was a decision to be made in isolation.

He asked me "well, who else is going to make it?"

As we continued to talk, I asked if he had invited Faye to come with him to our session.

"Yea, she said she would," he hesitantly said.

The Dilemma

Dealing with the pain and betrayal caused by knowledge of a spouse's affair requires healing time, self reflection, and an evaluation of the marriage. One question that Frank finally asked himself is very important: "Is it possible to be who I am and give her what she wants?" Affairs tend to set up a comparison game between the spouse and "the other." Frank, like many others who have walked in his shoes, wonders what this man has that he doesn't. He believes his wife rejected who he is in the worst kind of betrayal.

But did his wife reject who he is? In his present frame of mind, Frank, of course, concludes yes, "she rejected me." Over time, this question will continue to haunt Frank until he can answer it without the background of the betrayal noise.

This pattern of questioning by Frank assumes that he is the only one responsible for whether or not his marriage makes it. The affair is but a symptom of a failing marriage. Both Frank and his wife share the burden of what has happened to their marriage.

What led to the current state of the marriage? This requires that there be an open discussion between Frank and his wife. How much sharing has occurred? If talking about what each wanted, thought, and felt ceased, when did it stop? If problems occurred, how come they were glossed over? If thoughts and feelings were expressed, did both partners really listen instead of preparing their defense as one partner spoke his or her mind?

At this point in time, Frank must answer the painful question of what his wife wants to do about the marriage. Does she want out? Does she want to work on the relationship? Frank is sorting out his own responses to these same questions; however, his responses cannot be made in isolation.

The Choices

Frank has already made one choice at this point because he is still in the marriage. Although he is not sure he will stay; for the moment, he has chosen not to leave.

Frank believes he wants to work on the relationship. If his wife agrees, they will need to examine the options. A third party to help mediate the differences may be one choice. Frank never had the vision of a marriage counselor in his future, but maybe that would help. With their tendency to cover things up, Frank is not optimistic that they could do the repair work on their own.

The choice of letting the issues just lie is not a choice at all for Frank. He knows something has to change. The status quo does not cut it anymore. If the relationship continues to deteriorate in spite of their best efforts at repair, the choice remains that either spouse may leave the marriage.

The Questions

The depth of self-reflection required by this crisis is new to Frank. He sees himself as a major income contributor, a hard working and loyal husband, and a practical sort of guy. Some things one just doesn't question. He never questioned his marriage or his commitment to the relationship. And now he is hearing all kinds of things about what he has not brought to the marriage. Passion? Excitement? Communication?

First Frank has to hear the words without reacting to them immediately. Easier said than done. He has to ask himself: What have I done to create passion? What is my responsibility? What has she done to create passion? What is her responsibility? Frank knows he is not a Victorian era guy. But what is acceptable to him? A little communication might go a long way.

Oh, this is hard. Frank sees himself as a doer, not a talker. Actions speak louder than words. Or so he thought. Words seem superfluous, and yet, "everyone" says he must "talk" to her.

What does "talking" consist of? Frank is not sure. His temptation is to treat this crisis like another business problem to be solved. Define the problem, seek alternatives, network to find out what has been tried, and proceed until there's resolution. Just talk? What is the purpose?

Frank thinks in terms of a purpose. The purpose in this instance is to share and get to know his own thoughts, feelings, wishes, wants, desires, as well as the thoughts, feelings, wishes, wants and desires of his wife. Awkward at first? Of course!

Sharing at this level creates the basis for Frank to begin unraveling the mystery of what has happened to his marriage.

alternatives to the marital status quo

When struggling with the question of *"Do I Stay or Do I Go?,"* it is natural to consider alternatives. "...consciously or not, people compare their current relationships to alternate ones" (Levinger, 1979, p. 58). When an affair occurs in the relationship, as Frank experienced in *"I've Been Betrayed,"* it is so easy to wonder about the "comparison" being made. Frank agonized about how he compared to the "other man." Would his wife choose the "other man" over him? Would she leave the marriage to be with the "other man"?

Even though Faye said she would come to the session, Frank continued to be ambivalent about entering marital therapy. I gave Frank the name of a marital therapist, and he scoffed at that idea. "We will come here when I am ready," he flatly stated. Frank had rather quickly recognized that saying what you will do if faced with such a decision is quite different from what you may do if actually confronted with the real-life dilemma. Frank did not want to see the marriage end; yet, he was so ambivalent about entering marital therapy.

Inwardly, I smiled at Frank controlling what he could. So I wasn't too surprised when he and Faye came to the first session, and Frank stated rather proudly in front of Faye, that he wanted to know what my "success rate" was with the couples I had worked with. I am often asked this question by partners who feel the most threatened in a relationship.

My initial observations did not make Frank too happy; if anything, they increased his anxiety. I shared that what I view as "success" may differ from his definition of success. And furthermore, I commented that I do not measure success by whether or not the marriage remains intact. (I could see Frank's huge gulp as I said this.) I stated that I believe that the growth of each individual in assessing if the marriage is able to meet both individuals' needs now and in the future, is a more viable definition of success. In some cases that will translate into a renewed commitment to the marriage or the relationship. In other situations, the couples will decide to go their separate ways.

I knew my response would make Frank want to bolt out of the door. At the same time, I knew I had to bring Faye on board, and I did not know her at all. The timing of sharing my beliefs needed to be now. I hoped my relationship with Frank would help him tolerate hearing what he did not want to hear.

Frank, in his gruff manner, told me that his purpose in being in marriage (strongly emphasizing the word marriage) counseling was to see if his marriage could work. Faye said she feels "stuck", and "paralyzed," unable to make any decision. I shared with them that they are stuck in different ways. Frank sees Faye having to choose between him and the "other man." Yes, the difficulty in life is the choice; however, Faye can be faced with other alternatives besides either staying in the marriage or leaving to be with the "other man." And, even though he doesn't recognize it, Frank also has more choices than passively accepting what she does. (I did not use the word "passive" in the session because I knew the embarrassment and humiliation it would cause Frank.) Yet, neither one of them can clearly envision a direction in which they can go to resolve what they can do about their damaged marriage.

To actively get UNSTUCK requires confronting the alternatives. I share with them that the more clearly they can identify the available options, the more realistic the choices may be, and the less it is likely that the "grass is greener on the other side of the fence" mentality will reign. Frank liked that comment. It made up a little bit for the earlier success rate stuff. I explain that some years back, I did research with couples who were in marital therapy struggling with the question of *"Do I Stay or Do I Go?"*. As a result of that original research, I developed an instrument to help couples clarify what their options really are.

Marriage and relationships are a complex entity; recognition of this fact is included in the three level examination of each alternative in the MOPS (Marital Options and Possibilities Scale): how easy or difficult it would be to choose that alternative, how desirable or undesirable that alternative would be for you to choose, and how likely or unlikely it is that you would choose this alternative. The point in taking the survey is to stimulate your thinking and help you come up with alternatives that fit your situation. There is no either/or response. Being actively aware of your relationship alternatives will help you as you deal with the common patterns and themes that individuals and couples face in being stuck in indecision.

Frank was quite hesitant about taking this scale. Faye embraced it eagerly, saying she would do anything to get unstuck. Living in limbo land was not acceptable to her. I arranged individual interviews with them to discuss the results, and then a joint session to decide on a course of action over the next year. Even if Frank and Faye decided on a separation, under NC law, a divorce could not take place for one year.

Following is the scale that both took home to complete:

Marital Options and Possibilities Survey (MOPS)

A. When your marriage is troubled, it's natural to consider alternatives. Below are some alternatives which people typically consider at such times. For each of the following alternatives, please indicate how easy or difficult it would be for you to choose that alternative.

(Please circle your response)

1. PHYSICALLY MOVE OUT OF THE HOME YOURSELF

1	2	3	4	5	6	7
Extremely Difficult			Neither Difficult Nor Easy			Extremely Easy

2. HAVE SPOUSE PHYSICALLY MOVE OUT OF HOME

1	2	3	4	5	6	7
Extremely Difficult			Neither Difficult Nor Easy			Extremely Easy

3. GET A DIVORCE

1	2	3	4	5	6	7

Extremely
Difficult

Neither
Difficult
Nor Easy

Extremely
Easy

4. WORK ON THE RELATIONSHIP BY GIVING MORE OF
    MY TIME AND ENERGY TO THE RELATIONSHIP

1	2	3	4	5	6	7

Extremely
Difficult

Neither
Difficult
Nor Easy

Extremely
Easy

5. GET SEX OUTSIDE OF THE MARRIAGE

1	2	3	4	5	6	7

Extremely
Difficult

Neither
Difficult
Nor Easy

Extremely
Easy

6. GET EMOTIONAL NEEDS MET OUTSIDE OF THE MAR-
    RIAGE

1	2	3	4	5	6	7

Extremely
Difficult

Neither
Difficult
Nor Easy

Extremely
Easy

7. KEEP THINGS THE WAY THEY ARE AND NOT MAKE
    MAJOR CHANGES

1	2	3	4	5	6	7

Extremely
Difficult

Neither
Difficult
Nor Easy

Extremely
Easy

8. PUT MORE TIME/ENERGY IN WORK

1	2	3	4	5	6	7

Extremely
Difficult

Neither
Difficult
Nor Easy

Extremely
Easy

9. SPEND MORE TIME/ENERGY WITH FRIENDS
    1   2   3   4   5   6   7
Extremely   Neither   Extremely
Difficult   Difficult   Easy
                                Nor Easy

10. STAY IN MARRIAGE UNTIL CHILDREN ARE GROWN
    1   2   3   4   5   6   7
Extremely   Neither   Extremely
Difficult   Difficult   Easy
                                Nor Easy

11. PUT THE SITUATION IN GOD'S HANDS
    1   2   3   4   5   6   7
Extremely   Neither   Extremely
Difficult   Difficult   Easy
                                Nor Easy

B. You are now going to be given the same set of alternatives, only this time please indicate how *desirable* or *undesirable* that alternative would be for you to choose.

1. PHYSICALLY MOVE OUT THE HOME YOURSELF
    1   2   3   4   5   6   7
Extremely   Neither   Extremely
Undesirable   Undesirable   Desirable
                                Nor Desirable

2. HAVE SPOUSE PHYSICALLY MOVE OUT OF HOME
    1   2   3   4   5   6   7
Extremely   Neither   Extremely
Undesirable   Undesirable   Desirable
                                Nor Desirable

3. GET A DIVORCE

| 1 | 2 | 3 | 4 | 5 | 6 | 7 |

Extremely
Undesirable

Neither
Undesirable
Nor Desirable

Extremely
Desirable

4. WORK ON THE RELATIONSHIP BY GIVING MORE OF MY TIME AND ENERGY TO THE RELATIONSHIP

| 1 | 2 | 3 | 4 | 5 | 6 | 7 |

Extremely
Undesirable

Neither
Undesirable
Nor Desirable

Extremely
Desirable

5. GET SEX OUTSIDE OF THE MARRIAGE

| 1 | 2 | 3 | 4 | 5 | 6 | 7 |

Extremely
Undesirable

Neither
Undesirable
Nor Desirable

Extremely
Desirable

6. GET EMOTIONAL NEEDS MET OUTSIDE OF THE MARRIAGE

| 1 | 2 | 3 | 4 | 5 | 6 | 7 |

Extremely
Undesirable

Neither
Undesirable
Nor Desirable

Extremely
Desirable

7. KEEP THINGS THE WAY THEY ARE AND NOT MAKE MAJOR CHANGES

| 1 | 2 | 3 | 4 | 5 | 6 | 7 |

Extremely
Undesirable

Neither
Undesirable
Nor Desirable

Extremely
Desirable

8. PUT MORE TIME/ENERGY IN WORK

| 1 | 2 | 3 | 4 | 5 | 6 | 7 |

Extremely
Undesirable

Neither
Undesirable
Nor Desirable

Extremely
Desirable

9. SPEND MORE TIME/ENERGY WITH FRIENDS

1	2	3	4	5	6	7
Extremely			Neither			Extremely
Undesirable			Undesirable			Desirable
			Nor Desirable			

10. STAY IN MARRIAGE UNTIL THE CHILDREN ARE
    GROWN

1	2	3	4	5	6	7
Extremely			Neither			Extremely
Undesirable			Undesirable			Desirable
			Nor Desirable			

11. PUT THE SITUATION IN GOD'S HANDS

1	2	3	4	5	6	7
Extremely			Neither			Extremely
Undesirable			Undesirable			Desirable
			Nor Desirable			

C. Finally, go through these same alternatives once more, and indicate this time how *likely* or *unlikely* it is that you would choose this alternative.

1. PHYSICALLY MOVE OUT OF THE HOME YOURSELF

1	2	3	4	5	6	7
Extremely			Neither			Extremely
Unlikely			Unlikely			Likely
			Nor Likely			

2. HAVE SPOUSE PHYSICALLY MOVE OUT OF HOME

1	2	3	4	5	6	7
Extremely			Neither			Extremely
Unlikely			Unlikely			Likely
			Nor Likely			

3. GET A DIVORCE

1	2	3	4	5	6	7
Extremely Unlikely			Neither Unlikely Nor Likely			Extremely Likely

4. WORK ON THE RELATIONSHIP BY GIVING MORE OF MY TIME AND ENERGY TO THE RELATIONSHIP

1	2	3	4	5	6	7
Extremely Unlikely			Neither Unlikely Nor Likely			Extremely Likely

5. GET SEX OUTSIDE OF THE MARRIAGE

1	2	3	4	5	6	7
Extremely Unlikely			Neither Unlikely Nor Likely			Extremely Likely

6. GET EMOTIONAL NEEDS MET OUTSIDE OF THE MAR-RIAGE

1	2	3	4	5	6	7
Extremely Unlikely			Neither Unlikely Nor Likely			Extremely Likely

7. KEEP THINGS THE WAY THEY ARE AND NOT MAKE MAJOR CHANGES

1	2	3	4	5	6	7
Extremely Unlikely			Neither Unlikely Nor Likely			Extremely Likely

8. PUT MORE TIME/ENERGY IN WORK

1	2	3	4	5	6	7
Extremely Unlikely			Neither Unlikely Nor Likely			Extremely Likely

9. SPEND MORE TIME/ENERGY WITH FRIENDS

   1   2   3   4   5   6   7

Extremely   Neither   Extremely

Unlikely   Unlikely   Likely

                    Nor Likely

10. STAY IN MARRIAGE UNTIL CHILDREN ARE GROWN

   1   2   3   4   5   6   7

Extremely   Neither   Extremely

Unlikely   Unlikely   Likely

                    Nor Likely

11. PUT THE SITUATION IN GOD'S HANDS

   1   2   3   4   5   6   7

Extremely   Neither   Extremely

Unlikely   Unlikely   Likely

                    Nor Likely

When Frank and Faye returned for their individual sessions, I did not start out with the results of what they had answered. After checking in with how they were emotionally, I used the questions on the scales as stems – sentence completion forms. I will select out some of the items and give examples of how Frank and Faye completed them. The instructions were for them to give as many responses as came to mind for each stem (each item on the scale).

Frank came in first, probably because he was in the most pain. How I asked the question, and Frank's responses to some of the items follows:

To physically move out of the home yourself is ......

    -simply making room for "him" to move in

    -unthinkable

    -reminds me of when my Dad left us (at this point Frank

       began crying)

-hurts beyond anything I could ever imagine

-an admission that I failed, just like Dad, only I would not
    be the one ending the marriage

To get a divorce is ....

-wrong

-immoral, according to my religious upbringing

-like saying that Faye and I never loved each other

-the easy answer

-something I just can't accept now

To work on the relationship by giving more of my time and
energy to the relationship is ....

-something I never thought I would agree to if my wife had
    an affair

-what I want now

-scary, because I don't know what she wants or what has
    been missing

-what will I do if it doesn't work?

-will I ever be able to forget that she had sex with another
    man?

To get sex outside of the marriage is ....

-wrong, wrong, wrong

-part of me thinks I ought to do it for revenge

-is it ever "just sex"

-not the answer, and I do not want to admit that it could be
    a warning that something is very wrong in the marriage

-an act that may be unforgivable

-so very, very hurtful to the other partner

To put more time/energy in work is ....

-easier, simply because I know what is expected and I can
    do it

-what I have always done when home life was painful

-not the answer now

-not really what I want either

-what my Mom said that my Dad always did

To put the situation in God's hands ....
    -would be so easy if I really believed in God
    -is desirable, so someone else can take responsibility for this
        unholy mess
    -is what my Mother did, and I cannot forgive her for doing
        that
    -I don't like what this stirs up in me

A very powerful therapy session with Frank ensued. Connections between his parents' divorce and what was happening
in his marriage became painfully obvious. Although Faye knew
his parents had divorced, he had never shared his feelings and
hurt with her. He realized that he had closed himself off emotionally since that time, and that, maybe, some of what Faye
wanted from him, he had never given her. He was prepared to
share his newly discovered self-knowledge with her in the joint
session.

Faye's first question to me when she came for her individual
session was "what did you do to Frank?" When I inquired as to
what she meant, she said he cried like a baby when he came
home, and he had never cried through their entire marriage. As
a result, she wasn't sure whether she wanted to come to the
session. I shared with her that I was very glad she had decided
to participate, and hopefully, she would better understand
Frank's pain in the joint session. She quickly told me "I don't
need any more guilt."

I suggested we proceed, and I explained the stems to her.
Some of her responses to a few of the items follow:

To have your spouse physically move out of the home is ....
    -what I would like
    -really not possible because of my guilt

-something he would never do anyway
-probably economically unfeasible
-not addressing the real problem in the marriage

To get a divorce would be ....
-what my "friend" wants
-something I have so many feelings about both ways
-typical in my family
-so hard for me to actually do
-I don't know if it is what I really want

To work on the relationship by giving more of my time and
energy to the relationship is ....
-so tiring to me, because I have genuinely tried
-questionable – what would it accomplish?
-not possible if it is one-sided
-all I want is someone who can give of himself

To get sex outside of the marriage is ....
-not the answer
-was not my intention
-not just sex, it was more the closeness, somebody caring
    about me
-a red flag
-saying I want more than I have in my marriage

Getting emotional needs met outside of the marriage ....
-is how I have survived my relationship with Frank
-is not what I want – not in total
-became easier and easier when I got nothing from Frank
-on an ongoing basis means the end of the relationship
-leaves me feeling lonely and empty

Keeping things the way they are and not making major changes......
-is absolutely impossible

-I would simply wither away

-or I would have another affair

-now I understand some of why I am stuck - I can't just
    keep having affairs

-is what I am afraid that Frank wants or what he will do if
    we stay married

-I just can't

Putting the situation in God's hands means ....

    -my interpretation is that I have been praying for I don't
        know what

    -getting in touch with my spiritual side which has been lost
        for awhile

    -God will not decide my life or make my troubles go away;
        yet, I need something bigger than me to get through
        this

Faye became very thoughtful during her individual session. She said she was looking forward to the joint session. She reported that she had gained some understanding of her own behavior beyond the "guilt" that she felt.

The much awaited joint session began with Frank asking Faye if he could have her time and attention while he shared some of his past with her. Faye nodded, and Frank proceeded to tell her what it was like for him when his father left the family. His hurt and pain unfolded, and Faye responded. She told him this was the first time that she felt he had given her something of himself. The session progressed with a great deal of sharing from both. At the end of the time, I asked them where they wanted to go from here. My question brought smiles, and they said practically in unison that they had a lot of work to do.

In this instance, Frank and Faye made a decision to work on their marriage. At the moment they are hopeful, but recognize much work is ahead. Sometimes, one spouse has already made up his or her mind before the therapy has even begun. In my business, marital therapists often call this the "doorstep deposit." The partner planning to leave "deposits" the one to be left with the therapist so the leaver can let go easier and with a clearer conscience since there is someone to take care of the "mess." Confronting the alternatives makes the departing partner a little more honest, and interferes with any charade or false hope that may be given to the other partner.

Whatever the state of the relationship, confronting the reality of "what is" and exploring the meaning of each alternative helps couples become unstuck. As you explore your situation, be creative and add alternatives that fit your circumstances.

three

and then the kids came...

Stephanie and Bob

Stephanie was casually dressed; she would have been attractive except for the sullen expression on her face which permeated her entire body. Bob was nattily attired with an indifferent and withdrawn air about him. I looked at them and thought this is going to be an interesting session. I also knew that I would have to watch that I didn't work harder than they did. They had been in therapy with a colleague of mine for three months. She referred them to me when she decided to leave the therapy field due to managed care.

Bob finally spoke asking me how I could be a marriage counselor with the hours I kept? I ignored the hostile tone and said, "Perhaps I can be one because of the hours I don't keep. I know it is difficult for people who want evening hours , but I stop at 6 p.m., so my last appointment is 5:15 p.m. Can you work within that?"

Before he could answer, Stephanie almost shrieked, "He always does that – he accuses you, and then he always wants more than what you can offer." "So this touches a nerve with you?," I said to Stephanie. With that acknowledgment on my part came an outpouring of feelings from Stephanie.

In a softer, more vulnerable voice, she said, "I feel so betrayed by motherhood. I don't know. Maybe I thought it was more environmental or something. I talk to them, I nurture them, and then I expect it to work, and it doesn't. For God's sake, I managed 40 adults in a high tech business, and I did fine, no, I was excellent. And now I need help on what to do with my kids, and my marriage sucks. It doesn't matter anymore if I take a shower, if I get dressed. Motherhood is so degrading."

"You'd think I forced her to be a 'stay-at-home mom'. It was a joint decision all the way around." Bob's comments had a biting tone. Stephanie retaliated with "But you aren't the one who had to give up the career. Your life hasn't changed that much, and mine has changed totally."

"Oh, my life has changed alright – I don't have a wife anymore," Bob said bitterly. The ensuing silence filled the room as unspoken accusations bounced back and forth between them.

I decided to break the silence in an effort to bring the dialogue into the open. I commented, "Expectations that each of you have had for this transition have not matched reality. You each have experienced losses that were not in the game plan. Stephanie, you've lost the identity you had in your job and career. Bob, you believe you've lost your wife as a sexual partner".

Another long silence followed. Stephanie began to cry softly. Bob said sarcastically, "A little sex would go a long way." Stephanie raised her chin defiantly and choked out the words, "How do you have sex with someone you resent every morning when they leave for a world that used to be yours, too?"

"This is good," I said. Bob raised his eyebrow at me quizzically, and Stephanie's mouth dropped open. "It takes life and energy to express your feelings, and bring the real issues into the fray," I continued.

Stephanie and Bob were responding to bringing the dialogue into the open, much more quickly than I thought possible at the beginning of the session.

The next week I received a telephone call from Bob asking for an individual session. I told him I would be happy to see him, but I would also need to see Stephanie for an individual session. He said he had not told her that he called. I suggested that he tell her he thought it would be a good idea for each of them to come in and see me individually for a session. Reluctantly, he agreed.

When Bob came in the first words out of his mouth were "I want a divorce." He continued by saying he was tired of a sexless marriage. "I can have affairs; I have surely been tempted, but if I am going to do that, I might as well get a divorce. What are the effects on the kids, and how can I minimize that?" I reflected that in talking with his previous therapist, I learned that both partners had been satisfied with the marriage prior to the arrival of their daughter, Susie, age 4. Bob conceded that that was the case, however; he added that sex had practically stopped after Susie's birth, and it had totally stopped after Andy's birth. And that was not the case with friends he knew who had children. He added that he was tired of thinking about sex nonstop which he attributed to not getting any. When the nonsexual begins to look sexual, he realized that change was in order.

At the end of the session, I stated that I would address the "effects on the kids" question with both he and Stephanie in a joint session. Bob said, "You can tell her I want a divorce." I said, "Not likely. That is your responsibility, and I would suggest that you give some thought to the amount of rage you both demonstrate toward each other. Would there be such fireworks if you did not care about each other?"

The individual session with Stephanie proceeded according to plan. She seemed a bit freer to express her anger, hurt, and sense of loss. "I don't know who I am anymore. Who I was and who I am is lost for now. Bob wants sex all the time, and I am not interested. I realize that our arguments are often because I am tired, and he wants something – SEX – that I cannot give him at the time. I want to just go away and disappear."

I explored further with Stephanie the postpartum depression that she experienced after Andy was born. Her gynecologist had recognized her symptoms and prescribed Prozac. Her energy level had improved, but not her sex drive. I talked with her about the sexual side effects of some antidepressants. I elaborated on the fact that sex is truly just another form of communication, and obviously, with the present communication pattern, sex was unlikely to take place.

The Dilemma

Stephanie and Bob, and then Susie (age 4) and Andy (age 2), and then the marriage is over??? Life is not supposed to be like this. Whatever happened to the perfect family – two adults, two children, a boy and a girl? The media tells us this is the perfect family. What happens when this "mix" does not bring happiness?

The themes that Stephanie and Bob share are common in many, many marriages. When couples say "I do," expectations of what it will be like with kids are unclear, vague and filled with fantasies. Magically, the belief is that life as a couple will continue and that the children will just complete the picture of the family.

But how that life as a couple will continue after the arrival of children is often marred by reality factors that the couple may have never considered. The physical and hormonal changes that the female experiences during pregnancy and after the birth is not usually discussed when the couple makes the decision to have children. The management of time and tasks is one of those mundane issues that doesn't quite get discussed. What is a LOSS, such as a career path or a certain job, and what is GAINED, such as increased economic pressure, is often unexplored beforehand.

What, specifically, will be the reality of who does what after the arrival of children? Will Stephanie and Bob each do what their parents did? What will Stephanie expect Bob to do? What will Bob expect Stephanie to do? Will these expectations be clearly stated?

And what about the bundle of intense feelings each spouse experiences? Will these feelings be shared only in the heat of the battle? Can these feelings be shared with each other at a calmer time?

This most difficult phase of a marriage redefines the amount of closeness and distance a couple can expect from each other. Negotiating this phase is indeed the dilemma.

The Choices

Physically, Stephanie's fatigue and general feeling of being "down" could be monitored with her gynecologist and therapist. The media is now reporting that it may take one to two years or longer for a woman's body to recover from the hormonal changes caused by pregnancy. Emotionally, Stephanie's sense of loss of identity needs to be TALKED ABOUT with friends, a support group, and/or a therapist.

Bob's transition to fatherhood could be helped by educational classes on such subjects as becoming a father, how to parent, the use of discipline, and communication skills. Bob *and* Stephanie could meet with a marriage counselor to address their respective feelings about the lack of sex in the marriage. It is not unusual that when Stephanie can't get what she wants in the way of HELP, Bob can't get what he wants, more SEX.

Of course, the status quo could continue. But the more choices open to Stephanie and Bob, the more likely that the status quo will change.

The Questions

Perhaps the biggest question relates to whether or not this is merely a difficult phase in the life cycle of this couple, or if the problems are signs of deeper and more complex issues. Bob and Stephanie can answer that only if they begin to act upon some of the choices that do not entail leaving the marriage immediately. The option of leaving is always there; therefore, it seems more sensible to try the other available choices first.

How much closeness and how much distance is needed by Stephanie and Bob at this time? Stephanie wants time just for Stephanie, which means she needs some distance from Bob *and* the children. Bob wants companion time with Stephanie as a *couple*, which means he needs more closeness. Negotiating these different wants and needs require that Stephanie and Bob TALK with each other and learn how to resolve this issue.

Inevitably, if these closeness and distance issues are left unresolved the distance factor will increase. What then happens to the marriage is indeed a question of the unhappy status quo versus the breakup of the marriage.

what happens to sex after kids?

Whether I am working with a couple married in the 1950's, the 70's, or the 90's, an extremely common complaint that I hear is that sex is NEVER the same after the children are born. "We had a great sex life before the kids, and it has been downhill ever since." What happens in Hollywood is often an exaggeration of what is happening in our culture in general. And look at what is happening today to Hollywood marriages after the birth of children. Christie Brinkley separates from second husband 7 weeks after the birth of her son; Dudley Moore divorces six weeks after the birth of his child; Val Kilmer separates two months after the birth of his second child. Am I saying that the arrival of children is responsible for the break-up of the marriages? Not exactly. I am saying that the arrival of children marks a critical transition time in the life of the couple. And that critical transition time usually includes a change in the sex life.

The Meaning of *Sexuality*

When couples come in to see me about sexual problems at any stage of their development as a couple, I want to know far more than the specific sexual problem of the moment. Not only do I want a thorough history of their sexual development, but I also want them to share what sex means to them individually, and as a couple. And how has sex evolved in the relationship?

In our culture, sexual development and sexuality often remain stuck at the adolescent stage. The opening paragraph is one example of how the media portrays sex and marriage. It certainly looks as if the two cannot coexist when kids arrive. What does this really say about sex? I think about adolescents when I think of the confusing messages in the media. Adolescence is a developmental time of extremes. Earlier generations, particularly the females, were taught that the body is "dirty," and parts of the body were to be hidden, and certainly not to be enjoyed. Today, the culture is at the other extreme - no holds barred in what is shown of the female body, and sex is to be blatantly enjoyed as a physical craving and fulfillment of the physical desire.

In my clinical work with adolescents, I find that in spite of the raging hormones, what is often expressed to me in sexual terms is really a craving for closeness. Sex is often substituted for closeness in both females and males. Adolescents often crave closeness, but haven't been taught other ways to feel close; therefore, when the hormones rage, sexual activity increases with all the unhealthy patterns that go with it. For example, adolescent girls who crave connection and closeness with their peers, and who have not experienced closeness with their family, are particularly vulnerable to much sexual activity and unwanted pregnancies. And, so often upon my questioning, I learn that not only have they never experienced orgasm, but they just wanted to either be "close" or were afraid the guy would leave the relationship ("abandonment"). Adolescent males sometimes say "I have to change sexual partners frequently because the girls will take over my life if I stay in the relationship." Again, the fear of getting close is another misrepresentation of what sexuality is; to that adolescent male, sex with the same partner more than a few times means too much closeness.

And so it becomes essential to sort out the sexual developmental history from the crisis of the relationship stage. Sex after the arrival of kids will mean very different things to different people based on the sexual developmental history. Let us look at Stephanie and Bob from this perspective.

Stephanie and Bob

When Stephanie and Bob came into my office, Bob was emphatic that either he would be able to get more sex in the marriage or he wanted out. Stephanie was very angry, and her emotions raged across her face. Obviously, communication between them was at an impasse. By the end of a few sessions, I had heard about the current crisis from each of them. When I began to explain what I wanted in the way of a sexual developmental history, both were quick to rule that out as a complete waste of time and effort when neither had time nor energy to spare.

I responded that we could proceed with a quick review of the developmental stage they were experiencing, some negotiation exercises for them to use regarding time and energy, and discussion of closeness and intimacy. I matter of factly said that they could use their internal resources to help them proceed in their own way and at their own pace. That was fine with them, and Bob stated that they would be quick to resolve this matter. Stephanie agreed, and said she didn't have the energy or desire to drag anything out.

What I did not say to Stephanie and Bob was that the above tasks would define their sexual developmental history quite explicitly. When couples come in to see me about their troubled relationships, I often discover that they date the beginning of the relationship demise to after the birth of the first child. And when I inquire about how they negotiated the separate and different needs for closeness and distance, it becomes obvious that such needs have never been fully negotiated. And to be able to negotiate such differences requires great compatibility or the awareness of what their sexual development means to the current state of or lack of intimacy.

How we develop sexually beyond the academic overview in school is not a topic of conversation in public or private. When I ask couples at what point they experienced or became aware of differences in the male and female body, I often hear giggles and uncomfortable noises. Sometimes the response is a very dry intellectual rendering of facts. Less often, but occasionally, I receive a humorous anecdote of a childhood experience.

Since Stephanie and Bob were seemingly more comfortable with just examining the issue of sex in the marriage that is where we started. It goes without saying that sex can never be quite the same with the presence of children. But that is not due merely to their presence. The emotional demands and physical requirements made upon both parents, especially the mother in most cases, changes the priorities in the relationship. For example, Stephanie is saying that all she wants is SLEEP and not to be bothered sexually. Sex is not the uppermost factor in her mind, and sexual desire is not alive and blooming. The change in Stephanie's sexuality prompts an increased need for sex for Bob. In his mind, the lack of sex and a sexual partner renders sex a much needed priority.

How can Stephanie and Bob address these conflicting needs in this time of transition to their parenting roles? Having the opportunity to express their needs to each other is a beginning. It is not enough for each to merely state his/her thoughts and feelings. If Stephanie decides she wishes to share, she must first get acknowledgment from Bob that he is willing to listen at this time. If this happens not to be a good time for Bob, Stephanie needs to ask "when will be a good time"? Once joint acknowledgment of this time as OK has been made, Stephanie, as the initiator, may express what is on her mind. Bob's role, as the listener, is to put his reactions on hold, and to listen as intently as he can, being careful not to engage in planning his defense while Stephanie is talking. When Stephanie has completed her say, Bob needs to repeat back in his own words what Stephanie has just said. Stephanie can confirm that he heard what she said, or let him know that he did not hear part of her message, and repeat that part (hopefully, without adding to her message). It is often a temptation to add to one's message, after hearing it repeated back. Although seemingly simplistic, this process is quite hard to do with a relationship partner. The importance of this exercise lies in the fact that it is the only way that Stephanie can be absolutely sure that Bob heard everything that she said. Once Stephanie has confirmed that Bob heard her statements, Bob may wish to send his own message about his thoughts and feelings, while Stephanie assumes the role of listener.

Practice with exercises like the above helped Stephanie and Bob begin talking and listening to one another. Stephanie identified that something was still missing for her. After the birth of her first child, she acknowledged that something changed within her. She could not identify what it was. She had nightmares of a black hole – and she had never shared these nightmares with anyone. How could she tell anyone about such horrible dreams when this was supposed to be a time of joy for her? I shared with Stephanie that bringing a child into the world often intensifies one's own childhood experiences and fears. What may be unresolved in her own past can become highlighted as she enters the mother role. That is different from saying she doesn't want to be a mother.

As Stephanie continued to share about her past, the tears flowed freely as her story unfolded. Her family was crazy as she put it - my words were that she was from an alcoholic family. The yelling and screaming about sex was a nightly affair. She often lay awake after the fights had subsided. She tried to be the best child possible in hopes that the fights would stop. Nothing ever worked, and she felt more and more worthless. Emotionally, she felt empty and needy at the same time. That is what scared her about the "black hole" nightmare after Susie was born – it was the same feelings she had as a child. And she said that somehow in her mind, even after her body healed from the first pregnancy, she equated sex with the horrible memories of her childhood which she could not shake, even though she had thoroughly enjoyed sex with Bob previously.

Now Bob's reaction to all of the sharing by Stephanie was interesting. He appeared to be extremely uncomfortable, and at moments acted as though he would rather be anywhere but in this room. I observed that patterns from each of them made sharing most difficult – Stephanie's avoidance of reliving the pain of her past and Bob's great discomfort with the vulnerable sharing by Stephanie. That particular session Bob was unable to share anything about what was going on inside him.

I reached out to Bob individually, and asked him to come in for a session alone. I explained to Stephanie that I wanted to see Bob alone, and she was fine with that. She indicated that she could use some time "off the hook." Bob did come in, and said he was in knots after the last session. He knew about Stephanie's alcoholic family when he married her, but he didn't know all that she shared in the session. I gently said to Bob that, today, I was more interested in hearing about him and his family. Ever so slowly, his wall began to come down. There was nothing abnormal about his family, he said. Everyone did what they were supposed to do. His father was the breadwinner, his mother was the homemaker, and his childhood was uneventful. I listened. He began to talk about his sexual experiences as a teenager. His first sexual experience was with a girl whom he deeply loved. When she left him, he was devastated. She ended the relationship after they had a deep talk about closeness - how much was enough and how much they should be with other friends. Other relationships had faltered whenever these issues were discussed. Bob became very effective at making sure these subjects did not come up in his relationships. Now, he felt horrible guilt at knowing he had sent strong, deep messages not to talk about these issues. I shared with Bob that part of his sexual development had stopped in adolescence. The cutoff occurred when he equated the ending of his first sexual relationships with discussions of closeness and distance.

In the next joint session, Stephanie and Bob began their painful discovery journey together. In relationships, the recognition of conflicting needs must be treated as a caution signal. It is a warning sign that if ignored, can lead to increased havoc in the relationship. In the case of Stephanie and Bob, if the wants and desires of each remain unexpressed in a direct manner, they will continue to go their separate ways and become increasingly distant. Their feelings will most likely be expressed in indirect ways, which will probably be destructive to the relationship. Bob may "fall into" an affair. Stephanie may devote all of her time to the kids and "fall into" a depression.

The Pleasuring Technique

The next step in the negotiation process is for Stephanie and Bob to make the time (not find the time – it will never happen) to engage in what is known as the pleasuring exercise. I often use this technique when I am treating couples experiencing a variety of sexual problems.

Couplehood's frequent enemy is lack of time. What Stephanie and Bob must first do is make at least 30 minutes available 2 or 3 times per week. The goal of pleasuring is to take the pressure off of having to be in the sexual act. This is accomplished by saying that sexual intercourse is off limits; no touching of the breasts or genitals is allowed during the pleasuring exercise. A part of the exercise is that sexual intercourse is not allowed at all during the four weeks (or whatever time frame works for the couple) of the pleasuring technique. The idea is to get to know each other's bodies in a relaxed, completely non-threatening way.

I often ask couples to take turns setting the atmosphere. It can be romantic with soft music and candlelight. Wine and fruit may be on a table nearby. Aromatic massage oil and lotion can be available for use. I ask that the couple use their imagination and creativity in designing a relaxing background.

Who will be the giver and who will be the receiver can be determined ahead of time, or it can be flexible, depending upon the needs of the individuals at the time. Flexibility will only work if there is equality in the number of times one is the receiver and the giver. Perhaps the most important part of the exercise is that each individual must tune into his/her own sensations, thoughts, and feelings without regard to what the other is experiencing at the time. This may sound selfish, but it heightens awareness of one's body both as a giver and receiver. In order to maintain the internal focus, talking is not allowed. If a particular kind of touch is unpleasant, communicate nonverbally by taking the giver's hand and placing it elsewhere on the body.

Human nature being what it is, it often happens that by requesting no sex, the opposite transpires. Couples sometimes come back rather sheepishly, admitting that they had sex, and that it was enjoyable. I tease them by saying I need to get out my ruler and swat them on the hands. Having "forbidden sex" is often just what the doctor ordered.

No matter what stage of the life cycle a couple is experiencing, the pleasuring exercise can be utilized to help resurrect a dead sex life. Occasionally, one partner believes he/she is less articulate than the other partner. The nonverbal way of communicating while pleasuring helps place two people on an equal footing. Feeling "equal" often brings about improved communication. "Talking" about sex verbally or nonverbally opens a window of opportunity for an improved relationship.

There are times when other issues are so prominent and so unresolved, that even considering sex in any way, shape, or form is unlikely. In these relationships sex is indeed dead for the moment, and other issues must first be addressed before a sexual resurrection can take place. Until Stephanie and Bob began talking, such an exercise would have been fruitless for them. Another example of this is when a yours, mine, and ours stepfamily has allowed boundaries to fade, and an all-out war between a stepparent and stepchild emerges to take center stage. The couple is enmeshed in their respective positions, and war is declared. Sex is not likely until there is some change. Likewise, immediately after an affair is discovered is not the time to begin the pleasuring exercise.

Sex As Communication

Sex, after all is said and done, is simply another way to communicate. Transitions in life, of which the shift to parenting is one, cause growing pains and insecurities to be manifested at full speed. Modern life does not allow a leisurely look at what is happening. To be informed about what is likely to happen in each transition phase can give one a starting point in which to examine the intense feelings that emerge.

The building block for every transition is TALK, TALK, TALK. Infamous mind-reading must take a back seat. Life is about change – it is inevitable. Making a decision in the dark about whether to stay or go is not wise. Unfinished business will continue to follow you. Talking with your partner, even if the partner does not respond, will help you. Clarity comes from many different directions.

CHECKLIST FOR SEX AFTER THE ARRIVAL OF KIDS

Complete the following phrases and make a sentence:

During the day, my thoughts are mainly about _____ .

If I could have anything I wanted, it would be_____ .

Since the arrival of kids, I have gained _____ .

Since the arrival of kids, I have lost _____ .

What I most need from my partner is _____ .

What I least need from my partner is _____ .

When I think about sex, I _____ .

Five years from now, my life will be _____ .

My fantasy about my sex life in the future is _____ .

Now, for the checklist, check off each item that you have shared with your partner.

This will give you a barometer of how much closeness and distance exists within your relationship. Sometimes, simply sharing your responses with your partner will open previously shut doors. If it does not, more work in the area of intimacy may need to be explored (see the chapter on intimacy) prior to making a decision on whether you stay or go.

four

---

mirror, mirror on the wall, who's that walking down my hall?

Barbara

At the end of a long day, I was listening to my last voice mail message. "You may not remember me, but you saw my husband and I about 15 years ago. You were at a different location, but I saw you on TV, and I know that is you. I need an appointment for me..." She only left her first name which irritated me greatly. I knew now was not the time to return the call.

Realistically, I knew that I had seen a great number of people in the intervening years; nonetheless, I prided myself on my memory. And I could not place that voice. And then it hit me – this message from the past made me feel old. I did not like that. I wondered how she looked 15 years later, and knew that I was asking myself the same question. Therapists are not immune from all the things our clients deal with, and this was another reminder for me. Awareness of self is as important for the therapist as it is for the client. I placed the voice-mail message in my book, and knew I would return the call the next day.

I did feel better the next day, and returned the call. An appointment was set two weeks away, and I still could not place her even after she had given me her last name.

When Barbara arrived for her appointment, I began to have faint recollections of a naïve young couple struggling with in-law issues. She said that one of the things she remembered that I suggested was for her to keep a journal. Although she had never done so for most of the years, she still remembered it, and it nagged at her. About a year ago, she said she had begun a journal, and she wanted to share some of it with me. This obviously meant a great deal to her, and I wanted to respect and honor the request. "Please, go ahead. Sharing your innermost thoughts will bring me on board with your concerns. Why don't you read it aloud?" I said.

Journal entry # 1: Rumblings of unease have been with me since the beginning of the marriage. I knew we were from different backgrounds, but I thought we could work it out. Our arguments reflect the different ways we grew up. Our spending philosophies, our choice of recreation, our discipline of the children, and our gift-giving are as different as day and night. He is a hoarder; I believe in spending money on needs and occasionally a luxury. His idea of recreation is to watch sports on the boob tube. I want to travel and experience different cultures. He believes in "spare the rod and spoil the child." I do not think spanking serves any purpose other than to say violence is OK. My family always gives thoughtful gifts; his family buys K-Mart specials.

Journal entry # 2: How did we ever get together? Young love is blind, but middle-aged love is "20/20." Life is not over at age 45, and yet, that is how I feel. I now truly understand the meaning of the phrase "I'm trapped." Did I marry John as an act of rebellion? How could I choose someone so opposite from me in every way? And when I see who my daughter is dating, I think "Oh, no – the pattern is repeating itself".

Journal entry # 3: I feel just like Francesca in *The Bridges of Madison County*. I am so ripe for some unknown stranger to walk into my life. And unfortunately, my ending would probably be like hers. Staying in this marriage is the right thing to do for my children and for John. It is the worst thing for me.

Journal entry # 4: I ask myself: "What has happened to us over the years?" Have our backgrounds influenced us so much that we have become our parents? I know certain behaviors became pronounced when we started having children. How many times did I tell my own mother that I would never say or do that to my children? And, of course, lo and behold, I would say the same things my mother said. And when I say to my husband, John, "You are just like your father" he has an epileptic fit. That is what I see, more so with every passing year. I am not like his mother. I cannot adapt to whatever he wants like John's mother does for his father. I cannot be a passive, submissive wife.

Barbara looked up from her reading, and said with a great deal of sadness, "If I am leaving this marriage, I know I had best be prepared to go. John will never leave the house except in a casket. He has told me that on numerous occasions. The house means nothing to me. I want it because the children see it as their home, and I do not want them to lose it."

I asked Barbara, "How long have you felt this sad?" She said, "For a long time, but especially since I turned 40. Do you know what my own mother said to me? "Work it out, Barbara — he is the main breadwinner. We haven't had a divorce in our family." She also says, "Think of the children." My mother always was good with the guilt-inducing comments. And to top it all off, she ends with "remember what Ann Landers says: Are you better off with him or without him? — And you are better off with John." I can write off any emotional or financial support from my family."

"Barbara," I asked, "did anything in particular trigger your phone call to me?"

"What sets me off now is every mannerism and phrase that John uses that is just like his Dad. The authoritarian tone is the worst. John even has that pregnant pause just before he delivers his edict. I can't stand the sound or sight of him at times."

"Is there anything happening right now?" I queried.

"Well, it is vacation planning time. John assumes that we will be going to visit his family. He says his parents are getting old. I will not use my precious vacation time visiting his family. He can take the kids and go. I had rather be alone than put up with his mother," she said coldly.

"In-law issues have been a source of pain in your marriage," I commented. "I also hear some scared feelings when you look in the mirror," I added.

"Why do we think we are so immune?" Barbara asked. "I hate getting older, I hate seeing my mother's face when I look in the mirror, I hate feeling guilty about my parents and in-laws getting older and needing care-takers in the near future. Have you ever felt any of this?" she asked in exasperation.

I laughed, and asked her if she would like to hear a funny story. I shared with her all the thoughts that went through my mind when her phone call came in. She laughed, too, and told me that she had one advantage – she had seen me briefly on the news, but had not studied my looks in detail. We continued to laugh together, and it lightened the mood.

Barbara ended the session with these comments and questions: " The tugs of leaving my marriage are so strong. I daydream and fantasize a lot. Will any of these daydreams become reality? Will I be able to handle the guilt? Or will I be dealing with the question of *Do I Stay or Do I Go?* for a long time to come?"

The Dilemma

Barbara is struggling with that age-old dilemma of how do you live with an "opposite" after the initial attraction wears off? Years of marriage have reinforced the differences between Barbara and John. With hindsight, Barbara finds it difficult to believe that she chose John.

At midlife, Barbara cannot ignore the pull of the past. She sees John becoming more and more like his father. In certain ways, she acknowledges the influence of her mother. Her fears about what kind of marriage she has and will have overwhelm her. It is difficult to accept that she may be repeating a pattern; and yet, she sees a pattern when she observes who her daughter chooses to date.

How can the past be such an influence on Barbara's life now? Her parents and her in-laws ain't what she thought they were – entities completely separate from her life and her marriage. Establishing her independence from her family of origin and establishing an independent tone in her marriage has not really worked to free her of their influence. It is almost as if the more she fights the past, the more influential the past becomes in her life.

The Choices

Within the framework of remaining in her marriage, Barbara faces many possible choices. She and John have not learned how to negotiate their differences – a must for opposites who wish to maintain a healthy relationship. Seeking out ways to learn this skill as a couple is one available option. Even if John chooses not to participate, it is important that Barbara recognize she can do so on her own. Building communication skills that include negotiation tasks increases the likelihood of greater satisfaction being experienced in this relationship. Barbara can check out community offerings and seminars on communication, reading material on the subject, and she can talk with her religious leader, or choose marriage counseling or psychotherapy.

Barbara is becoming aware of behaviors in her family that she sees in her parents and in-laws. She seems to hunger for an exploration of how her past influences the dynamics of her present life. What would happen if Barbara began doing her autobiography as well as keeping a journal? She might become aware of more patterns and behaviors that she could choose to change, modify or keep the same. And she might begin to understand the origins of more of her feelings.

Another choice involves the exploration of Barbara's own external life. While her inner life is an area ripe for exploration based on her musings about her marriage, it is also important that she not ignore resources and opportunities to further pursue her individual interests outside of her family life. Continued development of her own identity and support system outside the family will help Barbara wherever her ultimate choice takes her.

As Barbara struggles with the option of leaving her marriage, she also confronts the practicalities of the economic choices. She can always utilize legal consultation, perhaps checking out more than one attorney, to help her get a grip on what is possible or likely to occur. She can chart her LOSSES and GAINS to help her with the reality of what she can live with and what she can live without.

The Questions

At midlife, Barbara is grappling with some very existential questions: 1) What is the meaning of my marriage?, and 2) What is the meaning of my life? As Barbara has entered this questioning phase of her life, she mentions the influence of the past and her fear of the future. How does she put the pieces together?

First, Barbara needs to address some very basic questions about herself. "Who is Barbara?" is still a largely unknown entity. She must have a clearer perspective on this question before she can answer "What is it that Barbara wants?" Barbara appears to be ready for a challenging self-journey.

Barbara states she is not like her mother-in-law; i.e., she can never be passive and submissive. This is a comment about who she is not – she needs affirmations about who she is. It may be just a matter of Barbara clarifying the things she already knows about herself. Or the probe for self-knowledge may extend to a shake-up of her idea of who she is as defined by her parents and her husband and her children.

As who she is becomes clearer, Barbara can more realistically grapple with what she wants, including what she wants from her marriage. Barbara's story is symbolic of what she does not want in her marriage; the reader may assume that she wants the opposite of what she gets. That may not be accurate. Barbara may have a need(s) for some of what is in her marriage. She must ask herself the hard question of what she will do if certain things are no longer in her marriage. Does she really want all of her husband's behaviors to change? Are there some comfortable, familiar behaviors that she needs, or are there familiar patterns that she knows she wants to change?

The next phase involves how Barbara communicates what she discovers to her husband. The self-discovery phase takes place over time. It will be interesting for Barbara to observe if changes in her behavior lead to any modification in her husband's behavior. Clarity about what she wants will help Barbara be able to share her feelings, wants, and needs with her husband.

Also over time Barbara will assess her husband's response or lack of response. Since she stated she will in all probability be struggling with the question of *"Do I Stay or Do I Go?"* over the next several years, the above questions provide an alternative of one possible self-journey.

negotiating differences

When opposites attract like Barbara and her husband in *"Mirror, Mirror On The Wall, Who's That Walking Down My Hall?"* the initial attraction can become a cauldron of resentment if the couple does not learn how to negotiate. But before negotiation even becomes a viable option, the focus needs to be on understanding the differences between each other. Easier said than done when one partner wants to relax on the beach and the other partner wants to see the sights and go, go, go, while on vacation. Or when the couple engages in a joint project, and one is task-oriented while the other likes to think through the whole process before beginning with any portion.

Needless to say, with opposites even the most mundane event can become fraught with "perfect misunderstandings." Our comic strips would have to search for other material if life were not so full of differences. Classic movie fights strike a universal chord because each of us has some experience with similar themes. Comedians with words and gestures portray our foibles about our differences. So, we read the comics, watch the movies, and listen to the comedians, but when it comes to OUR RELATIONSHIP, suddenly, it is not so funny. What can we do about our differences?

Myers-Briggs Type Indicator

A most helpful tool that I use to help couples deal with their differences is the *Myers-Briggs Type Indicator* (MBTI). The instrument basically identifies your preference for responding to the environment around you in terms of:

"I" Introversion   or   "E" Extroversion
"S" Sensing   or   "N" Intuition
"T" Thinking   or   "F" Feeling
"J" Judging   or   "P" Perceiving

This instrument is based on Carl Jung's theory of psychological type. Katharine Briggs and Isabel Briggs Myers developed the instrument as an application of Jung's theory. A popularized short version has been completed by Keirsey and Bates in the book, *Please Understand Me* (1984).

Your type refers to which of the four letters describes your preference for relating to the world. Pick out the following cue words that depict you from each type, and you will have a beginning understanding of what your type might be if you take the Myers-Briggs Type Indicator.

E (75% of population)   versus   I (25% of population)

Sociability .... Territoriality
Interaction .... Concentration
External .... Internal
Breadth .... Depth
Extensive.. Intensive
Multiplicity of relationships .... Limited relationships
Expenditure of energies .... Conservation of energies
Interest in external events .... Interest in internal reaction

S (75% of population)   versus   N (25% of population)

Experience .... Hunches
Past .... Future
Realistic .... Speculative
Perspiration... Inspiration
Actual .... Possible
Down-to-earth ....Head-in-clouds
Utility .... Fantasy
Fact .... Fiction
Practicality .... Ingenuity
Sensible .... Imaginative

T (50% of population)   versus   **F** (50% of population)

Objective .... Subjective
Principles .... Values
Policy .... Social values
Laws .... Extenuating circumstances
Criterion .... Intimacy
Firmness .... Persuasion
Impersonal .... Personal
Justice .... Humane
Categories .... Harmony
Standards .... Good or bad
Critique .... Appreciate
Analysis .... Sympathy
Allocation .... Devotion

J (50% of population)   versus   **P** (50% of population)

Settled .... Pending
Decided .... Gather more data
Fixed .... Flexible
Plan ahead .... Adapt as you go
Run one's life .... Let life happen
Closure .... Open options
Decision-making................................... Treasure hunting
Planned.. Open ended
Completed .... Emergent
Decisive .... Tentative
Wrap it up .... Something will turn up
Urgency .... There's plenty of time
Deadline .... What deadline?
Get show on road................................ Let's wait and see

From Keirsey and Bates, *Please Understand Me*, 1984, pp. 25-26.

From these cue words you can select what you think your type may be from a choice of 16 types. I am an INFJ; my husband is an ISTJ. We are definitely different from each other on the intuitive and sensing modes, and on the feeling and thinking modes. We are alike on the introversion and the judging modes.

Understanding your type and your partner's type can decrease the arguments and increase the humor in the relationship. For example, if you can see that each person is reacting to an event according to type rather than doing something to deliberately irritate the other, feelings often abate. A "J" wants a decision made now; a "P" wants more time to think about it. Harry, a "J," used to almost always end up in a fight with Kay, a "P," over insignificant issues, like always being early so as not to be late. Now, Harry jokes with Kay about her "P" showing. Yes, they still have fights, but not as many, and the fights are reserved for more meaningful issues instead of ordinary daily events.

If you are an ENFJ, that does not mean that you are not capable of being or acting with the qualities of the other types. Your type simply refers to your preference, in this instance, for being sociable , acting on your hunches, being subjective, and needing closure. At times you may also exhibit characteristics such as being very practical and analyzing something in depth.

Jung's theory also proposes that in midlife, one often becomes more in touch with the "shadow" side of self; in type terms that means realizing your least preferred dimension. As an INFJ, my least preferred dimension is "S." And at midlife, I have become much more in touch with health and body issues rather than just taking them for granted.

Nuances of Communication

Let's examine an end of the day interaction according to type. Jeff comes home and says, "What did you do today?" Alice hears this question as "What did you DO today?" and is immediately irritated. If she says she relaxed, she believes he will not see that as a "worthwhile endeavor." Jeff is an ESTJ, and his question is oriented toward his S and J. Alice is an ENFP and she resents his emphasis on productivity and activity. Jeff asks "What did you do today?" much as Alice would ask "How was your day?." Feelings are set into motion with the way the question is asked. A fight ensues and sometimes the partners cannot identify how or why it started. The mood is set at the beginning of an interaction.

How can such unfruitful encounters be prevented? Understanding the differences in the nuances of communication is a first step. How often have you witnessed an exchange between two people, especially spouses, and shook your head in disbelief at the angry response that seemed to come out of nowhere? Of course, there is a history of interaction in the relationship that you may know nothing of, and yet, it is still difficult to understand how such words could engender this incredible response. Often the confusion is cleared up when you look at the interaction in type terms. Those nuances often set the stage for the forthcoming response.

Understanding that there are differences in people which often create certain nuances in communication is not enough. The *validation* of those differences is what is needed. Validating the differences is not the same thing as complaining about them or playing the game of "if only." For example, the game of "if only you were like my girlfriend," does not *validate* the difference because there is not the effort to understand the difference. Validation is more than mere acknowledgment that such differences exist. Validation leads to acceptance that, yes a "T" and "F" are quite different; however, there is no value judgment placed upon the idea that a "T" is right and the "F" wrong, or that being an "F" is better than being a "T."

In the example of Jeff and Alice, Jeff becomes impatient with Alice's "N" – her hunches and love of fantasy. He deals with the actual and the practical, true to his "S" and sometimes states his impatience with the nuance of what Alice hears as he is right and she is wrong. Jeff and Alice react to the world around them and organize that data in very different ways. Jeff's impatience is also due to his need for closure – his "J." He processes information in terms of the practicality and usefulness of what is being said. He doesn't organize his world according to hunches and what might be possible in the future.

Alice reacts to the "nuance" she hears rather than identifying Jeff as being in a typical S mode. She's hurt by what she perceives as a judgment of her whole being. Meanwhile, Jeff scratches his head in disbelief and mutters "women, I'll never understand them." Alice believes her ability to look at the "whole," the "Gestalt," and what is possible in the future is very much unappreciated.

And so Alice and Jeff dance to the nuances, and their interactions become steeped in trigger-like reactions and assumptions about what is forthcoming. Misunderstandings multiply, and hostilities increase.

One of the most popular T.V. shows, "Home Improvement," illustrates some common nuances in communication. Tim, the tool man, operates out of his "S" and "T" mode, and Jill expresses her "N" and "F" side. In a typical sequence when Tim turns "40," he is preoccupied with his bodily functions and health, expressed in a typical "S" fashion. In one of the humorous moments Tim takes two mirrors to examine that supposed imperfection on his back which could be something serious. Tim must "see" it for the mark to be real. Meanwhile, Jill is intuitively reacting to Tim's preoccupation with turning "40," as she reflects and speculates on his midlife crisis. Tim, of course, is not amused. He wishes to deal in the present – the actuality

of the knot on his throat and the mark on his back. Jill's specu-
lations irritate him. And Tim's antics seem foolish to Jill. According to their type, they react to nuances in their interactions
and "perfect misunderstandings" occur in every show.

Thus, the first step in preventing unfruitful encounters is
understanding the differences in type which lead to certain
nuances of communication. So, you have identified your type
and your partner's type – what is next? Communication must
still take place. And, regardless of your type, certain communication skills provide that important bridge in helping you express your perceptions and asking what you need to know in
order to understand your partner's point of view.

A Note About Barbara

Barbara's story is what initiated this chapter on negotiating
differences. Barbara decided to go into therapy and invited her
husband to go with her. He refused, and continued to refuse
even after her therapist also invited him. Nonetheless, Barbara
decided to continue with individual therapy. She kept a daily
journal and began working on herself. Understanding the differences between herself and her husband helped make daily
life more bearable. She increased her support network, and began following her own dreams.

An intelligent woman, Barbara believes that ultimately, she
will obtain a divorce. She is not there yet, and that is more OK
with her now than it used to be. She is busy exploring who she
is and what she wants to do with the rest of her life. What that
will mean to her marriage is not yet clear. She is slowly becoming more at peace with who she is.

five

the little red Porsche – my river of dreams

Ted

"Well, Ted," I stated trying hard not to laugh over the telephone line, "you are indeed right about the referral. I have never before received a referral based on a rock concert I attended."

Ted continued with his sales job, "As I said, my attorney said you were the therapist to see because you would understand my restlessness. He saw you at the Billy Joel concert. I believe you have seen my attorney friend. How else would I have known when to call you to reach you instead of your infamous voice mail?"

Warning bells began to go off in my head. I maintained a light tone of voice, and said, "If this is a fishing expedition, I don't fish. If you wish to make an appointment, we can do that." He began laughing and said, "The confidentiality thing, right?" I said, "You are astute." With that, he then made an appointment.

It was the end of the day before I could check with my support staff. I learned that he had charmed them with calling to ask when I would be free, and calling every few minutes at that time. When I would run late, he apologized to them for interrupting them with his calls, and enlisted their cooperation as to when I would be free. I thought he is quite the charmer, and I remembered that he had never disclosed the name of the supposed referral source.

His appointment day arrived, and he did not show for his appointment. I was not completely surprised, but thought no more of it. The next day, my staff received by Federal Express mail full payment for the session he did not attend with a note asking could he please reschedule. With that bit of dramatic flair, he had the support staff asking me if I had yet called him and made another appointment. I told them they would see it on my schedule when I did.

I did not know quite what to make of Ted. I decided to withhold judgment until I had a little more information. He had charmed the support staff – instead of hearing complaints about this and that, he had peaked their interest, and I knew that he knew they would respond to his phone calls more readily.

His second appointment day arrived. The staff had taken bets on whether or not he would show. It wasn't the most professional thing to do, but they were having fun with it. I hesitated to stop it, even though I wasn't supposed to know about it, since he had not yet officially become a client.

For this appointment Ted arrived right on time, filled out his paperwork, and acted like the model client. He entered my office, and as the most gracious Southern gentleman, stood standing until I was seated. (I thought it had been awhile since I had seen that. Of course, my family would remind me that I had married not one, but two men who were reared north of the Mason-Dixon line.)

Ted began, "It is not often that I begin an acquaintance, much less a professional relationship, with an apology." As I nodded, he continued, "I missed the last appointment due to unforeseen work complications. I will talk about that later. I was referred to you by an attorney that I work with occasionally on business dealings. He did not refer me to you solely because of the concert. I had researched you pretty thoroughly before coming in, and I saw you at the concert. That cinched it. That makes everything above board, now. OK?"

"So where would you like to begin?," I asked.

"At least you have a half smile, so I guess I am off the hook," he half-pleaded.

"Thanks for the explanation. I will look forward to hearing the full story later," I said.

With that, Ted's demeanor began to change ever so slightly as he talked. "Nothing captures the way I feel quite like Billy Joel's song, *The River of Dreams*. Like the song says, I don't know what I'm searching for; I'm restless, I am not satisfied at work, at home, anywhere. I have these incredible fantasies nonstop. Don't worry, I am not going to share them. I am for real, I really see myself needing help to sort this out."

"So tell me about yourself, and your life," I requested.

"There's not much to tell. I grew up in Raleigh, am a native, got married, had two kids who are in college now. I'm a Carolina fan – I see one of your degrees is from Carolina," he said.

"Now, stay on track. You are superb at sidelining; we will talk about basketball later," I said.

"Ouch!" he replied. "My wife thinks I am nuts. She laughs at me, and tells me I am going through a midlife crisis. She says talk to her when I get over it. She tells me I cannot go out and buy my little red Porsche."

"You say that 'little red Porsche' with such feeling," I said.

"I built a little red Porsche model when I was 12 years old," he said wistfully. "I daydream about driving around in the real thing, Billy Joel's song playing on my CD, and a beautiful babe by my side. When I wake up from my fantasies and daydreams, I feel empty inside."

He continued, "I feel so restless. It is expected by everyone in my life that I continue to do the same thing day after day. I want to feel alive. I'm 47 years old; in 13 years I will be 60, and where will I be then?"

"The song, *The River of Dreams*, embodies what you feel. I have a copy of the words here. Why don't we go over it line by line, and see what it triggers for you?" I suggested.

As we did that, several themes emerged. A major one involved his work. He did not make it to the first appointment because he had to tell five employees under him that they no longer had jobs. One took it especially hard, and Ted had to remain with him to assess whether or not he was likely to come back to the company and kill someone. It had happened before, so Ted took the responsibility seriously. Ted knows that in probably a year someone will be doing to him exactly what he did to those employees as the company continues to downsize. He described work as having been his mistress. He used to work all the time, loved it, and knew where he was going. Now, he no longer has the mistress of work. Because of the time he spent at work, he did not develop relationships of any depth with others. He spoke sadly of not really knowing his kids.

Another theme was a marriage assessment. He believes he and Janet, his wife, have taken each other for granted all these years. It did not bother him as long as he had the mistress of work. Without work, he knows he needs more. He described Janet as a good, decent person who assumes they will always be together. Their lovemaking pattern of sex on a certain night of the week drives Ted crazy now. She doesn't ask or even know what Ted's needs are now.

"I know I have been able to stay in this marriage because I was having an affair. Not an affair with another female, but an affair with my work. I invested my energy and time in work, especially at times when I was so unhappy at home. There, I've said it," he concluded.

"Said what exactly?" I asked.

"That I have been unhappy at home for a long time. Midlife crisis or no midlife crisis – that is still the truth. It feels like I am dying a slow death. If and when I am sacked by my company, I do believe I will break out of everything. And yet, why wait for a calamity? Why not leave my marriage now?"

The Dilemma

Ted sums up his dilemma in the phrase "I don't know what I'm searching for." Midlife!!! As Ted grapples with the inevitability of the latter half of his life, he is questioning everything about his here and now existence. He documents his unhappiness in almost every area of his life. He masks his moodiness and irritability with sometimes exaggerated Southern charm. Almost anything looks better than what is.

And what has given him his sense of identity in the past – his work – is no longer there for him in the same way. He recognizes that he has probably not given much time, attention, or thought to his marriage because he has had his work. When his identity is no longer consumed by his work, he consciously begins to address his unmet needs in the marriage.

The dilemma goes deeper than assessing his work and marriage. He, too, is struggling with existential issues such as what does he have to show for his life at this point, and what meaning will his life have at age 60? As Billy Joel says in the song *"The River of Dreams"*....

> *But now I'm tired and I don't want to walk anymore*
> *I hope it doesn't take the rest of my life*
> *Until I find what it is that I've been looking for*

And so Ted's search is a broad one. His struggle over his choice of a car reflects the typical male macho image that the car is reflective of the male's self-esteem. And that Ted has not admitted to himself. He has not identified what is impacting his self-esteem other than work.

What does his sense of restlessness mean? In one sense, the changes in his work environment forced a reassessment of his life. Would he have continued with the mistress of work if his level of satisfaction had been satisfying? Probably for awhile, but inevitably, he would have to deal with those grappling issues that come at the midpoint of one's life.

Part of Ted's reflections needs to encompass the context of meaning in the entire fabric of his life. Marriage is only one dimension. It is sometimes too easy to focus on one dimension to the exclusion of the other facets of the dilemma. That, of course, does not mean that the marriage is not to be addressed. But it is not the sole culprit causing Ted's unhappiness. When marriage is viewed as part of the whole, and not the whole itself, conclusions about the marriage can be more reflective of an honest approach to one's life.

The Choices

Ted has not attempted to reach out to others in his struggle. His jovial mask sends messages that all is well when it is clear that all is not well. Being vulnerable with others will be difficult, but it is important that Ted not give up. His feelings of aloneness will abate somewhat when he realizes he is, in fact, not alone in his anguish. Support systems do exist; Ted must search until he finds one that is right for him. Many churches, parishes, and temples offer support groups for men, not always identified as dealing with Ted's issues. However, if a group of midlife men get together, these topics usually come up. Often support groups in the larger community may form around the work issues of downsizing, job displacement, and career change.

Ted's outreach needs to be expanded to his marriage as well. How well can Janet really listen? Has Ted verbalized the extent of his suffering? When Janet pooh-poohs his midlife meanderings, is there perhaps a hidden invitation for him to share substantive thoughts with her about his fear, uncertainty, and pain? It is imperative that Ted at least try to do so. Too many relationships end with one partner saying, "if only I had known."

One of Ted's comments is interesting. He states that he wonders if he were sacked by his company if he would break out of everything, including his marriage. He views that as an option to his slow death. The metaphor he uses of "breaking" could have many meanings. One definition of breaking is to crack without separating into pieces. Another definition is to disrupt the continuity of something. The choice always exists for Ted to end his marriage. However, his comment implies much more than the marriage is at stake. It is true that growth or change in one major area of one's life often foreshadows change in another area. Ted's issues are, indeed, a classic example of the adage that the whole is greater than its parts. Whatever choices that Ted pursues, it would be unfortunate if he did so without attention to his whole being; his intellectual, emotional, spiritual, and physical sides. Examining his marriage, career, children, fears and uncertainties from each of these dimensions requires a wholistic approach.

The Questions

The midlife phase is full of the existential search for the meaning of Freud's two most important things in life – work and love. How does one go about such a challenge? It is not easy. I am reminded of Jung's work on temperament at midlife. At midlife our shadow side often becomes more pronounced, and can actually be developed if we pay attention. In regard to Ted, the very things he has ignored in life while paying homage to his mistress, may be the areas in his life ripe for development.

Meaningful personal relationships were not, in all likelihood, high on Ted's priority list previously. This is one area ripe for exploration. His tentative reaching out to others indicates that this could be a timely intervention. Personal growth in this domain will probably lead to other undeveloped interests. A question he needs to ask himself as he practices developing substantive personal relationships is does he feel greater satisfaction?

Men have frequently denied themselves the time and energy it takes to develop a relationship with other men as well as women. It is considered a luxury! When confronted with a drastic change around the mistress of work, men do begin to question what can bring meaning to their life. Support systems have traditionally been much greater for women than men. Another question is how can I develop a support system to enhance the quality of my life?

At midlife, the spirituality dimension may emerge as an undeveloped area that men like Ted wish to examine. In Billy Joel's song, *"The River of Dreams,"*

> *I'm not sure about a life after this*
> *God knows I've never been a spiritual man*
> *Baptized by the fire, I wade into the river*
> *That runs to the promised land*

the issue of spirituality is tied in with the existential search for meaning. Religion per se may have never been in Ted's background; but, now, it could be filled with unanswered questions and ruminations.

While Ted's issues may seem superficial as he relates his vignette, it is crucial that the questions raised in his story be examined in some depth. Ted did not reach this time in his life in one year, and he will not emerge from his struggles in one year. Asking himself in depth questions could make his a more enlightened journey of self-growth that encompasses far more than the question of *"Do I Stay or Do I Go?".*

when "it" is larger than "i" or "we"

Developmental stages of one's life and one's relationship heavily influence the themes of "*Do I Stay or Do I Go?*". In the vignette "*The Little Red Porsche – My River of Dreams,*" Ted's *midlife passage* colors his feelings and reactions to everything and everyone in his path. THE POWER OF THE PASSAGE THROUGH THE LIFE CYCLE CANNOT BE IGNORED.

Likewise, in the vignette "*And Then The Kids Came,*" Stephanie and Bob are experiencing one of the most difficult stages of a marriage. When children are between the ages of birth and 6 years old, the strains and stresses on the marriage are enormous. This time in a marriage strongly affects the levels of dissatisfaction on the part of both partners. Yes, there can still be individual and couple issues, but it is imperative that the issues be placed in the context of the life cycle.

Barbara, in the vignette "*Mirror, Mirror on the Wall, Who's That Walking Down My Hall?*" is also experiencing the midlife pull. She struggles with wondering if the last half of her marriage has the potential of being satisfying, or if it will deteriorate even further. She questions the patterns of the past, and in some ways Barbara is an example of a little knowledge is a dangerous thing. She needs to find out who she is, and she has just begun. Her conclusions about her life are scaring her. It will be helpful to her if she can put her concerns in the framework of the midlife cycle. Her fear of the future and her new-found knowledge of the influence of the past are normal discoveries for this period of one's life. It is not strange or unusual for Barbara to be striving to deal with these issues.

If the stages of the life cycle had a voice, it might go something like this: "GIVE ME MY DUE." Do not ignore me or pretend that I do not exist. I will be a factor in your quest to answer the question "*Do I Stay or Do I Go?*".If I am ignored, you may make a decision that you will regret.

Midlife Themes

Midlife is like adolescence in many ways. It can be a time of extremes. The jokes about the change in hairstyle, whether male or female, the sudden need to diet, the urge to exercise, and the almost immediate change in lifestyle and interests reflects a different vitality. As one midlife male said to me, I feel "reborn" and "my creative juices are flowing." In adolescence, the need to be an adult and a unique adult - separate from one's parents, is the strong motivating force behind all the "crazy" behavior. In midlife, there is often the fear of getting old, and not having done important things yet. There is also often a shift in values, and questioning what is really important, after all. Midlife is like looking at the world through rose-colored glasses that focus on "me, me, me."

Just as in adolescence, some of the behavior in midlife brings about exciting discoveries for self and others. New careers are born, lives are refocused, and a new passion for life can emerge. The "shadow" side of one's personality, as Jung calls it, arises with zest. The part of one's self that has so been ignored , the shadow – can emerge with new meaning. As with any of life's transitions, the time of midlife can indeed be a rejuvenating force, or it can be a time filled with calamity and painful disaster. Our comedians and humorists have focused on the midlife phase of life with great gusto. And even with such open public viewing of this phase of life, it is still too easy to ignore that one may be in the throes of midlife. As the adolescent says, "it can't happen to me." The invincible theme, the I'll live forever theme, and the impulsive live life now theme, are all common to both adolescence and midlife.

The developmental themes throughout this book simply cry out "please notice me, know what normally happens during this time, look at your life in the context of the phase you are in, and then, and only then, make the important decisions." Life is hard; decisions are hard. Recognition of the themes in each life transition can help you make responsible decisions that you will be able to accept and live with now and in the future. What happens when a midlife male suddenly decides to divorce his wife and remarries a twenty-something female as soon as his divorce is final? In his search for happiness, the midlife male may have ignored his current stage of the life cycle. Dissatisfaction is rampant at this time of life, and may be due to a marriage in shreds, or it may be due to unanswered existential issues at this time of life.

The Hunger for Connection

Ted, in "*The Little Red Porsche – My River of Dreams*," comments that he, like Billy Joel in his song, is searching for something and he doesn't know what it is. Everything in his life seems empty and meaningless. While the search for meaning can take place at any developmental stage, midlife is especially prone to a questioning stance. And what is missing at this time of life? There is often an existential loneliness, a painful angst, and an often denied need for connection. When the mistress of work is no longer providing the satisfaction or driving challenge, when friends or family seem distant, there exists a hunger to be connected emotionally to another human being(s).

Acknowledgment of this need can be scary. Knowledge implies that you will then know what to do to fulfill the need. What is connection, exactly? And how will you get it? For a moment, let's go back to Billy Joel's song, *The River of Dreams: "God knows I've never been a spiritual man....."* Yet, the very fact that "spiritual" emerges suggests that it can be a midlife awakening in some way. A spiritual connection, a human connection, and a family connection are all usually important during this time of life. That does not imply that one has these connections.

Indeed, Fred, a client in the throes of midlife, said to me that he had found his "soulmate" in another female whom he could talk with for hours about what made the universe go 'round. Such conversation was totally alien to Fred prior to his search for a midlife identity. Is this connection? Perhaps, of a shallow kind. It is not what I would refer to as *authentic connection*. A substantive connection is sharing based on all the personal learning and growth that has gone on before in your development. Recognition of what you have taken and learned from each stage of your development, as well as what you have given (not the easiest task in midlife) provides a depth to your sharing with another person. Of course, this kind of self-knowledge is sometimes feared, and sometimes not valued. But the hunger for connection is so strong, that sometimes the fear is overcome.

Clients enter my office with many different problems; yet, a common link is the need for human connection. How they have connected or not connected is part of their human story. Every story is significant, full of hopes, dreams, rejections, acceptance, and often pain. At midlife, self-reflection on one's own human story is quite common. In assessing that story, it is so important to let it unfold without judgment. Trust that your story will guide you in your hunger for human connection.

Ted, from *"The Little Red Porsche - My River of Dreams,"* entered therapy with me in a skeptical state of mind. He was very skeptical that his life story could tell him anything he didn't already know or that would be helpful to him now. I said he might be right, and if he was, he would know soon enough. And so he began.

As Ted shared about his family, it was obvious that two very important people in his life were his father and sister. Yet, he stated he had no memories of childhood. Ted was so uptight and anxious when dealing with his family of origin that I worked with him first on relaxing every muscle in his body, and every thought in his brain. Gently, I encouraged him to find in his memory the safest, most secure, most comfortable, and most pleasant place in his childhood. As Ted did so, I allowed him to experience this place without asking anything of him or suggesting that he ask anything of himself. He reported experiencing an incredible calm after the session.

As we returned to this place in ongoing sessions, Ted's memories began to emerge. Many childhood memories of activities with his father came forth. His father seemed the perfect man and father in Ted's eyes. Ted admired his father immensely, and wanted to be just like him as a child. His sister, on the other hand, was a wild and wanton sibling. Ted struggled with these memories, but eventually, what came forth was a great deal of sexual play with his sister and other kids. His sister was three years older, and her appetite for sexual touching continued into latency age. The most vivid memory occurred when Ted was 10 and his sister was 13 years old. Ted could recall every nuance in the setting where it happened, from the smells to the temperature to the external sounds. His sister had another male friend, and she attempted to get Ted to have sex with her in front of the other boy. It made Ted so sick that he ran out of the building. He didn't really understand everything that was going on, but could to this day hear his sister cackling with laughter. I reminded Ted that he was to share his story without judgment – it was what happened to him and there would be a message in the story that could help him now.

From this point on, Ted's life was filled with becoming like his father, and never straying from the straight and narrow. Even in adolescence, Ted rebelled very little. He simply did what was expected of him. His level of risk-taking was practically nil. He went to college, played sports, took a job with a then stable big company, got married, had the two kids, and now was miserable at midlife.

So what is Ted struggling with? So what if there was a little sex play with his sister in his past? Big deal! The big deal is how Ted experienced this memory, both then and now, and how this experience as well as his many other life experiences, affects Ted's ability to be close and connect with other people. The hunger for connection has really never been fulfilled for Ted. His shameful feelings from that early sexual play left him afraid to get "too close" to anyone, although he could never really define why. It was just who he was. Accepting that that experience happened, and redefining it for himself now opens the way for more fruitful encounters with others.

Now everyone cannot remember a detailed specific event in their past that has affected every event in one's life. Nonetheless, preparing for such self-reflection is one way of putting midlife in perspective. And since marriages and relationships at midlife are often questioned, it is especially important to have a handle on what the transition is saying about you, and what the transition is saying about your relationships.

Self-esteem is still an ever present issue. All of your life experiences play a part in shaping who you are. Emotional self-esteem is crucial in the ability to connect with others. Your whole being, physical, sexual, emotional, and spiritual, all are part of your story. Playing out in your own mind, if nowhere else, all of your story, offers opportunities of understanding and ongoing growth.

The following exercise is one way of beginning the journey of telling your own story; however, a cautionary note is in order: Memory is imperfect, and research has shown that there is no guarantee that what is remembered is factually accurate. With that knowledge in mind, decide if you wish to do the following exercise.

1. Create a relaxed frame of mind in whatever way works best for you. Take at least 15 or 20 minutes to do so.
2. When you are ready, find the safest, most secure, most comfortable, and most pleasant place from your childhood, and allow yourself to experience the peacefulness of this place.
3. Later in the day, or the next day, repeat this experience.

4. After several experiences of just being in this place, allow any memories from childhood that wish to emerge, to do so.

5. Write these memories down in a special journal. As your story emerges, allow yourself to make emotional connections in whatever way you wish with your memories and the people in your life now.

Spirituality at Midlife

Authentic connection embraces spirituality in whatever form works for you. The existential musings of what gives life meaning, and is there a God, and who is God, usually have a more defined form than in adolescence. Ted, as do many at midlife, returned to the organized religion of his childhood. But what he did not return to was the rote participation of ritual. Instead, he followed through on the urge to become involved, to connect with the "body of Christ" in his community of believers. And, in this way, Ted strived to become more connected.

Two important themes in the spiritual journey are healing and forgiveness. By midlife, most, if not all of us, have done things we regret, have made mistakes – some which affect other people, and have made very uninformed choices with painful consequences. Whatever our story is at midlife, healing is often needed to prepare ourselves for the remainder of the journey. Forgiveness comes before healing begins. We may wish to jump to the healing, but the hard first part is forgiveness.

Many books have been written on the subject of forgiveness. One of the best is *Forgive and Forget: Healing the Hurts We Don't Deserve* by Lewis Smedes. The point to forgiveness is to not only prepare the way for healing, but also to accept our life story up to this point. When we try to run away from or deny what has gone before, we lose sight of how to impact that story in a positive, healthful, and healing way.

So, how does this help the book's question of *"Do I Stay or Do I Go"*? By giving the phase of the lifecycle its due, in this instance, midlife, the question can be addressed in a more honest manner without the background noise of midlife. Yes, the background noise needs to be considered, but in the context of your life story. The decision you make is one you wish to be able to live with beyond midlife.

six

i thought she would grow out of it

Peter and Jane

I received a phone call from a Catholic priest our practice had evaluated when he was a candidate for priesthood. He was visiting our area again when he ran into an old childhood friend. He met his friend's wife and spent an evening with them. The purpose for his call besides to say "Hello" was to let me know he had referred the couple to me for marriage counseling. They are "good Catholics," he told me jokingly, with the usual guilt and over-responsibility issues. He also shared with them I was not Catholic, but Lutheran, and still a person that would be sensitive to religious issues. "And P.S.," he said, "I didn't tell them you evaluated me. If I had done that, they might not come!"

I heard from Peter the following week, and an appointment was scheduled for the couple for marriage counseling.

When I went to greet the couple, I saw only a tall, lanky man dressed in a business suit with a briefcase open with papers everywhere. Peter explained that Jane, his wife, was home with their sick daughter.

"Jane was going to call you earlier today, but I told her I would handle it. I thought about canceling, but I got very busy at work and didn't call, so I decided to come alone," he hurriedly said as we walked to my office. Peter then proceeded to tell me that he didn't really know why he was here. "I was talking to my friend, John, you know the priest who referred us, and he expressed a great deal of concern about my marriage being in trouble."

"Do you think your marriage is in trouble?" I asked.

"Yes and no," he reflected. "When I think of trouble, I immediately think of how to solve the problems, and proceed with testing out the options. That's not possible with marriage. I was raised Catholic, and marriage is supposed to be f.o.r.e.v.e.r."

"And yet, I hear ambivalence in your yes and no," I commented.

"Well, I am responsible for the welfare of my family," he said in a dull tone.

"Totally responsible?" I queried.

"That's part of the problem. I would *love* to have *a partner* and not another child that I have to take care of," he stated emphatically.

"Can you give me an example of what you mean?" I asked.

"Sure. Take this week, for instance. We had a problem in the house, and Jane couldn't even hire a handyman on her own. She had to call me three times at work and interrupt me in the midst of some important meetings. And even when I said go ahead, she asked me time I walked in the door if what she did was OK. And as if that wasn't enough, when I asked where she wanted to go for dinner, she said as she inevitably always does, 'wherever you want to go is fine with me.' We had a huge fight because I refused to leave the house until she chose the restaurant."

"So how would you describe the feeling tone between the two of you now?" I explored.

"The magic just isn't there anymore. What I used to find so cute and adorable about Jane, I now find repulsive. She is so immature. I know I stay at the office longer and longer," he responded.

For a moment he was quiet, and then quickly, he began backpedaling, "Now, please don't get the wrong idea, Jane is great and all that, and you will see that when you meet her."

I smiled, and shared that there are always two sides, and sometimes more, to issues between partners. I explained that I needed to hear his perspective on the issues, and that I would also hear Jane's views. It is not a matter of one partner being right and the other wrong, but rather a sharing of one's point of view. I also added that relationships get into trouble when the personal stories (each partner's perspective) are not shared.

At the end of the session I requested that Jane call me for an individual session before we met together again. I suspected a great deal more was going on with Peter than he had shared. I believed he would be able to go a bit deeper as trust was built.

I found Jane to be a bubbly outgoing warm person. She was very much wrapped up in her children's activities, excited about field trips, church events, and seemingly content. When I asked about what brought them to marriage counseling at this time, she became quiet for the first time since she had entered my office, and looked down at the carpet.

"I know Peter is not happy," she began. "He is always talking about the bright women he meets on the job. He says I am not stimulating enough. He will not admit it, but I believe he is ashamed of the fact that I didn't go to college. When we met, he was the big man around campus, and it didn't bother him then that I was working and did not have the desire to go to college. Peter wants me to be someone I am not."

"And have you talked about this with each other?" I probed.

"A little," she said. "He doesn't seem attracted to me physically anymore. We seldom have sex, and when we do, Peter doesn't seem to be into it at all. I talk with my friends – please don't tell Peter – and know that some of them have similar problems."

She continued, "We went to Marriage Encounter, do you know about that, good, and I thought it was wonderful. Peter's comment was 'why do I have to be the center of your world?' I was hurt, and we ignored each other for over a week. I want you to help us. We loved each other at first. I have always loved Peter, and still do. But I am not sure if he loves me."

I shared that I looked forward to our joint session.

The Dilemma

The parent-child behavior in this relationship precludes sexual attraction by one partner to another. Peter and Jane are more like roommates and will probably remain so unless a more equal/equal relationship is achieved. Peter laments his blindness to early signs of inequality in the relationship. Jane acknowledges his early need to be the big man on campus type which seemingly included taking care of everything involving her.

At what point Peter recognized his need for more in the marriage is unclear. And how much he has specifically shared with Jane is also unclear. Over-responsibility for the tasks and business of the marriage make Peter "a very dull boy." Even his words have a leaden quality about them. Just as Peter is not the same person he was at the beginning of the marriage, neither is Jane. The roles assumed in this marriage have become very unrewarding.

Additional difficulties for Peter include turmoil over religious values and moral feelings of guilt and responsibility. It is one of life's paradoxes that the very ways in which he wants to be different, such as the area of responsibility, contribute to him remaining at the status quo in the relationship. A great deal of the dilemma seems to be that growth in the relationship for whatever reason has been stymied.

Part of Peter's struggle needs to be to address his own desire to be in the parental role apart from the early diagnosis of a big ego. He has become enmeshed in this role in his marriage which creates much unhappiness for him. What changes in his own behavior are required to change this role will be a formidable task. This will be a fruitful journey for him to take regardless of his decision to stay or go.

The Choices

The parent/child interaction that Peter describes places him in an untenable position if he attempts to change the status quo. He sees himself as being the caretaker of the family although it appears that Jane has assumed the responsibilities of raising the children. If he decides to leave, he will harbor enormous guilt. If he remains where he is, his resentment will continue to grow and his daydreams may lead to undesirable behavior according to his value system.

Fortunately, there is always more than a black or white choice. Peter and Jane's fights end up unresolved; therefore, it is doubtful that simply talking to one another will invite the needed changes. Nonetheless, Peter may choose to start discussing with Jane his unhappiness and invite her input as to what they can begin to do to help the relationship. If Peter truly invites Jane to give her input, he may be in for a pleasant surprise. Sometimes it is so easy to become entrenched in a role, that one can lose perspective on how the other person may want out of his/her assumed role. Even if Jane behaves as Peter would predict, it is still important for Peter to begin a dialogue on what they can do to change the relationship. By addressing the issue, Peter is making a statement that the status quo is no longer acceptable.

Since religious values are a significant part of Peter's past, Peter may consider consulting his priest for help with understanding the role of guilt in his interaction with his family. It would likewise be helpful for Peter to discuss his struggle and feelings about divorce with a priest. If he is uncomfortable addressing the subject with his own priest, his friend could refer him to another priest in the area. Outside consultation seems to be a very needed ingredient to help this relationship become unstuck.

Another consideration for Peter may be to remember that a change in one cog of the wheel often precipitates change in the remainder of the wheel. If he makes a concerted effort to take himself out of the parental role with Jane and allows her space to make decisions AND mistakes, she may change in response to his change.

Regardless of his final decision, the above possibilities represent necessary parts of a process that Peter will need to walk through in order to have peace of mind about his ultimate destination in life. Underlying his words are feelings of agony. This is not an easy decision for someone who sees himself as the caretaker of the family.

The Questions

Perhaps the beginning question for Peter to ask himself is what behavior has he observed in his life that may have been a model for his parent/child relationship with Jane? Many possibilities exist, including the relationship of his own parents. Or did Peter find himself in a position in his family where he had to be the caretaker for one or more family members? Such a role would prepare him for assuming the parent role in a relationship even if he were not aware of doing so.

Although his words indicate with certainty that he wants Jane to change, another question he must ask himself is does he REALLY desire her to engage in different behavior? If he still says, "without a doubt," he must prepare himself that he may not like the changes, and the changes may not be what he thought they would be. It is sometimes a rude awakening to get what one asks for. Somehow in our fantasyland, it was supposed to be one way, and then reality brings something that was not in the bargain to the fantasy.

There will likely be GAINS and LOSSES experienced by Peter if he is able to receive what he desires in the relationship. How he handles these will also determine if he must dig deeper in understanding what is wrong about his relationship.

If, after all his efforts, Jane's behavior remains childlike, Peter must address his own stuck behavior. Whether or not he leaves the relationship, he still must take stock of what he needs to do to continue his own growth. Becoming unstuck will be the beginning of that growth process.

dependency and intimacy

In the movie, *Days of Wine and Roses,* starring Jack Lemmon and Lee Remick, the intimate relationship becomes intertwined with an alcohol dependency on the part of both partners. Where does the intimacy begin and the dependency end? This is a tragic story which strongly makes the point that true intimacy cannot begin until the dependency upon alcohol has ended.

But what about relationships where dependency and intimacy do not revolve around another substance such as alcohol? Let's start at the beginning of the relationship. There is a symbolic lighting of one candle from two candles in many traditional weddings. Two people are now joined as one. What does that really mean? Does it signify one organism has been formed? What happens to the two individuals and personalities when a union takes place?

Many couples are now leaving the two candles representing the two individuals lighted, and lighting a third candle as a symbol of the union. The symbolism is that each individual with separate personalities and interests comes together in a committed relationship without losing who he/she is as an individual.

Intimacy can become confused with dependency. When a union has been formed by two people, it does not mean that the union always speaks with one voice or one opinion. It is interesting to listen to a couple when sentences begin with "We." Is a joint opinion being expressed that has been discussed by the two individuals, or is one person speaking for the union? When the "We" represents one voice, it is an example of over-responsibility which often occurs in parent/child unions. And it can also be an easy habit to slip into without really being aware that one is doing it.

Parent/Child Union

Peter, in the vignette "*I Thought She Would Grow Out of It*," represents a classic example of an overdeveloped "parent" marrying an underdeveloped "child." But is it really that simple? Peter is the "parent" and "breadwinner" in the relationship. Jane is clearly the "parent" with the children and maybe even around the home. If both spouses agree to their respective roles who is to say that it needs to be different? However, Peter is clearly unhappy with what he defines as a lack of equality in his interaction with Jane. He does not desire a dependent spouse.

Peter, the "parent," is unhappy. It is not unusual for the "child" in some relationships to want to break out of his/her role and flex some independence. The "parent" in such a relationship may have difficulty letting go of the dominant role. Change may become the order of the day in many parent/child pairings.

When Peter and Jane entered therapy with me, he claimed Jane was too dependent upon him. When I inquired as to what was too dependent, I heard some vague mutterings. So I decided to read the following fable to them with the instructions to think about how their relationship was similar or different than the one depicted in this fable:

> "I want you out," said the Bacterium to its Virus.
> "What are you talking about?" the Virus responded.
> "Out," repeated the Bacterium, "out of my space."
> "All the way?"
> "Beyond my limits," said the Bacterium.
> "Why?" asked the Virus.
> "I no longer want to share my existence with you."

"Things don't happen that way."

"I know," said the Bacterium.

"We've lived together a long time," the Virus added.

"Nonetheless," said the Bacterium, "it's my space and I no longer want to share it with you."

"You don't know what you are doing," responded the Virus.

"I was never more determined."

"But after all this time?"

"I want to be myself," answered the Bacterium.

"But you can't be without me."

"I can't be because of you."

"You are going against your nature," said the Virus.

"Only against my past behavior."

"What's the difference?"

"That's what I want to find out."

"You're considering a different Virus, then?" asked the Virus.

"Not right now," said the Bacterium.

"You would try it on your own?"

"At the beginning, anyway."

"I've done my best. I was always benign."

"It has to do with me, not with you."

"But what were you before I came along?"

"Much the same as I am now."

"Before we came together you weren't near what you are now."

"That's not what I meant," said the Bacterium.

"I don't understand."

"I haven't really changed."

"But you have, greatly."

"No, I still depend on you in order to be me."

"What's wrong with that?"

"That's transformation, not change."

"What's the difference?"

"In change, something remains the same."

"I made you you," said the Virus.

"You helped greatly."

"Helped? We need one another."

"We don't actually know that."

"How could you doubt it?"

"It's just a new thought."

"We became one organism," said the Virus.

"That's why I want you out," responded the Bacterium.

"You'll regress."

"For a while."

"For a while? Forever."

"I am determined."

"How will you function without me?" asked the Virus.

"I no longer need you to turn me on."

(Friedman, 1990, pp 113-115)

When Peter and Jane heard this fable, their reactions were strong and vocal. Peter said, "That's exactly how I feel – it is like we became one organism. And I find myself wanting my own space." Jane had a different perspective. She doesn't see herself as that dependent. If she exerts change, not transformation, in any area of their life together, he ignores her and makes no comment. He always acts in charge and does not include her in major decisions. And this makes Jane conclude that he talks a good game, but she questions his ability to remain independent without her to organize their life.

Further exploration of this issue led to a discussion of Peter's and Jane's family of origin. Peter is from an alcoholic family. As the eldest child, he was often in the role of caretaker due to his father's alcoholism. And so, when he first met Jane, it was ever so natural for him to take care of her, too. Peter began to recognize that for his entire life, he had been in the role of caretaker. No other role was familiar to him. He knew he wanted something different now, but, he wasn't sure how to get it, or how to act once he did get what he thought he wanted.

For Jane, this was a most welcome discussion. She acknowledged that early on in the relationship, she did, indeed, want to be taken care of; after all, she was the youngest child in her family, and her brothers had always been there to do most things for her. But, she increasingly wanted to do things on her own in the marriage, and felt thwarted by Peter.

Sometimes it is easier to identify patterns of interaction when you are actually involved in doing an activity rather than merely talking about it. For this reason, I asked Peter and Jane to do the following exercise:

Dependency Exercise

Do this exercise first as a couple, and then as an individual.

1. Take an atlas. Choose someplace in the U.S. that neither of you have ever visited.
2. Plan the trip; first the means of transportation, and then the activities and itinerary.

Please take note if this is the usual way such trips are planned. Who does what? Sometimes one person has a particularly strong suit, for example, a sense of direction. It makes sense for that person to be in charge of geographically plotting the way. However, is there a dominant role that is always played by one person? Does it seem like there is always the same person in charge? What does this say about the relationship?

What happens when you do the exercise as an individual? Are you quite capable of completing both parts of the exercise? Is one part easier than the other? How different is it when you do the exercise as an individual as compared to doing the task as a couple?

Peter's and Jane's observations were interesting. Peter engaged in all the major decision-making, but Jane did all the research and gathered all the information to present it to Peter for his decision. Now Peter did not realize that their planning went this way – he just saw himself making all the decisions. Jane said her way of getting input was to select and deselect the material prior to giving it to Peter. She was responding to his need to be in charge, and Peter expected to make the decisions, and thought that the least she could do was gather material.

Peter was surprised at the efficient manner in which she handled doing the exercise all by herself. Jane joked with him and said, "I haven't lived around you all these years for nothing".

Peter and Jane began a journey to uncover their dependency and intimacy issues. Alcoholic families (and other chemically dependent families) have a difficult time with dependency and intimacy. The legacy, as Peter knows, continues with adult children of alcoholics, as the book, *Struggle for Intimacy,* (Woititz, 1985) illustrates. Peter had a superordinate need to be over-responsible in his marriage and in his other relationships as well. Identifying what the dependency is associated with is often the first step forward for alcoholic and nonalcoholic individuals.

A healthy interdependency occurs when the "I" is still a solid "I" when the "We" interacts. Recognizing when and how the "I" is weak will give clues to an unhealthy dependency. Likewise, when the "I" is over-responsible, dependency is fostered, sometimes unknowingly, in the relationship.

There are parent/child unions that remain stuck in an unhealthy dependency. And sometimes, "partners separate because they were unable to separate" (Friedman, 1990, p. 17). Growth by one partner that is not shared verbally with the other partner signals trouble in the relationship. Partial or incomplete sharing means that one partner is engaged in game-playing, even if unintentionally. When a partner withholds information about self out of fear of how the partner will respond, or out of lack of concern about the feelings of the partner, the relationship is in trouble. Unfortunately, such trouble does not just go away; rather, it grows exponentially.

Jane and Peter are now talking, and Jane is no longer playing to Peter's need to be in charge and to be the one making all the decisions. If they were not talking, Peter may have continued on his journey to try and leave the marriage. This would not have been an easy journey for Peter considering his religious background. And Peter may have proceeded to leave the relationship and enter the single life. And guess what? In all probability, Peter would have chosen another "Jane-like" figure because he did not understand his own part in the marital dynamics with Jane.

Even if Peter and Jane eventually decide that their marriage does not meet their needs, this particular issue will be understood, and will not be the misunderstood reason for ending their relationship. And having explored this issue, hopefully, other issues within the marriage will be addressed before a decision on staying or leaving the marriage is made. Sometimes, the decision to separate is the one to be made. Such a decision is never one to be made lightly.

seven

---

the second time around
is a charm – oh yeah!"?

Amy

The first words out of Amy's mouth were, "You are a fake!"

I was definitely taken aback. I looked at her in surprise, probably with my jaw hanging open. It was clear that she was seething, and I waited to see if more was forthcoming.

When I didn't immediately respond, she projected in a challenging tone, "Do I strike you as crazy?"

I said in an even tone, "You strike me as very angry, and I am not sure what your anger is about."

"Well, I think I am crazy to land in this insane stepfamily land mine," she elaborated. "Jim and I were at the presentation at Holly Hill Hospital that you and your stepdaughter did, you know, from the point of view of the stepparent and the stepchild. Watching the two of you together, and hearing that her real mother was also there listening, made it seem possible that this stepfamily thing could really work. So I thought it could work. I know better now. P.S. I don't believe that yours works, either."

"And yet, you are here," I observed.

"So now I know I am crazy," she announced.

"My Aimee and I did that presentation several years ago. Were you and Jim married then?" I asked.

"We were dating and in 'la 'la land'. We felt so good after hearing you and your stepdaughter. I thought for you to include your stepdaughter in a talk meant that these kind of families could work," she protested.

"So now you feel betrayed, perhaps?" I questioned.

"It doesn't matter what I do, what I say, what I don't do, what I don't say – it is always fucking wrong!" she yelled. In a paradoxical way, she then became apologetic, "Before trying to avoid these stepfamily land mines, I never used to use such language. This whole second marriage thing is a farce. My first marriage may not have made me happy, but I didn't have to deal with bloody fights over kids. It is like, what is that stress thing that Vietnam Vets have?"

"PTSD, post traumatic stress disorder," I responded.

"Yea, that is it," she concurred. "I wish he would hit me, so I could leave immediately with cause. I want out. I would rather be alone than stay shellshocked."

"So, it is like you are constantly in a war zone," I remarked. "Who are the players in this war?"

Amy slowly related, "Myself and Jim – supposedly, the commanders; Audrey, my 16 year-old daughter, and Andy, Jim's 14 year old son, the enlisted ones who go AWOL all the time."

"And what about ex-spouses, grandparents, etc." I probed.

"The infantry is always trailing making messes and interfering with the best laid plans," she declared. "Just when I think something might work, enter the fighting infantry ensuring that the battle is lost before the fighting begins. Jim's ex is the supreme battle-ax."

"Are the commanders in unison about when to attack and when to withdraw?" I canvassed.

For the first time Amy laughed, "The only thing we are in unison about is the existence of blood and guts with every battle."

"It would be nice if the commanders could come together for a little war strategy. I invite both commanders if that is acceptable to you. And maybe down the road the rest of the military can enter the fray if the commanders so deem," I offered.

"Maybe," she affirmed.

The session stayed with me throughout the day. I thought about her words "you are a fake," and remembered that the transition and adjustment to stepfamily land was not easy or immediate. The presentation with my stepdaughter occurred about 12 years after I had been in a stepfamily. I routinely share with my clients that stepfamily adjustment takes a minimum of 2 years, and oftentimes more. Of course, Aimee and I shared many stories in our presentation about the difficult times. However, I also recollected other stories and comments after the presentation, both then and later, that clearly showed that people heard certain parts depending upon where they were at the time in their own lives.

Also, what I said during that presentation and later in various forms was that so much of the stepparent/stepchild relationship initially depends upon how the biological parents handle the break-up with the children. I was indeed, very fortunate, that my husband and his ex-wife did not use the children as pawns in their communications with each other. After a very brief time, the children's mother embraced me as their stepmom. Likewise, my husband allowed the children to interact freely with their stepdad without encouraging guilt, which is often the case in newly formed stepfamilies. In fact, Aimee's mother was at the presentation, and was very supportive of our comments. Neither Aimee nor I knew that she was coming, but we looked at each other and didn't change a thing in our talk.

Not having children of my own, the adjustment to kids alone was more than I could have imagined. And like everything else in life, some days were good, and some days and weekends were not so good. But I know that the children have enriched my life, and hopefully, I have enriched their lives. So, am I a fake? If I say that adjustment occurs naturally by joining a stepfamily, then I am a fake. When I say that adjustment takes years, I know that I am not a fake.

The Dilemma

The metaphor of stepfamily land as a war zone accurately describes what often occurs after the second marriage honeymoon has ended, and life with the stepfamily begins. Couples often say to me that during the dating period, everyone got along famously. Then, they cringe, and ask "what happened after the marriage?"

Expectations do not equal reality, and the myths of stepfamily life emerge full force. Amy expected the adjustment to stepfamily life to take place quickly; she expected what is referred to as "instant love;" she expected her authority and discipline style to be immediately accepted; she expected the spaces in her home to be used as they had been; she expected the division of labor and of possessions to work out smoothly; she expected the comings and goings of children and stepchildren to work as if this were an ordinary family. None of these matters flowed as Amy had expected or desired.

Communication with her spouse was laced and edged with the latest altercation with "her child" and "his child" differences. What had seemed like such a good idea (marriage) now teemed with second thoughts and high emotional tension. The explanation that "we only fight over the kids" was wearing thin and becoming untrue. The entire fabric of the relationship had been affected by the alliances and comings and goings of the members of the stepfamily.

Amy can no longer sort out what is normal adolescent development from the chaos of the stepfamily interaction. She is tired of struggling with what is fair, and very dejected in feeling that whatever she does, it is wrong in everyone's eyes. Amy is weary of being consumed with her own emotions and everyone else's feelings.

The Choices

Wanting out of the marriage, as Amy verbalizes, is becoming more and more of a conscious choice as she handles the bedlam. But Amy is acting on another possible choice by entering therapy, albeit reluctantly. She comes to therapy alone, not as a couple, and not as a family. At this time she wants something for herself; she is not yet ready to include part or all of the stepfamily in the therapy. It is one thing to talk about the possibility of the family's involvement in a safe way; however, it is another undertaking to have the whole crew in a room together for self and group examination.

Amy desires a choice that will help her feel and believe it is not her fault when cacophony breaks out in the family. The only option she can verbalize out loud is that she wants out. What she is really wanting out of is the strife and turmoil. That can be achieved in more than a black or white, in or out kind of choice.

The turbulence of adolescence for any family, much less a stepfamily, is a bottomless challenge. Support networks are essential for parents of adolescents. Amy can scour her community for opportunities to become part of such groups. The Stepfamily Association of America, Inc., often has local chapters which provide quarterly publications, informational resources, and news about the annual stepfamily conference. Groups will send Amy the message that she is not alone, will give recognition of others who may be at a different level of development, and provide Amy with a "listening ear" at times when she most needs it.

And if there is not a local chapter of the Stepfamily Association of America, Inc., Amy can start a local chapter. If she connects with other stepfamilies in the community, there may be group interest in establishing a local chapter.

The personal sense of failure Amy carries around can best be handled by providing herself with opportunities to tackle the difficulties in creative ways so that she can feel better about herself regardless of the outcome of her marriage. And as she feels better about herself, her perspective on the stepfamily may change.

The Questions

How much of what is happening in this stepfamily is due to the sense of loss and the function of change? Every family member has experienced loss whether or not it is acknowledged. Synonyms for the word loss include misfortune, deficit, dispossession, depletion, and disappearance. Strong emotions usually accompany each of those words. Homage is usually given to children who encounter the break-up of their nuclear family. That loss continues when change in the form of a stepfamily enters the picture. When the "new" is experienced, the loss of "what used to be" is heightened. It is also true for adults who must cope with the unfamiliar patterns, routines, and decision-making of this new kind of family structure.

Change is never easy when one is also dealing with loss. The daily grind of stepfamily living takes a toll on all members at a time when it can be the least tolerated. Taking this into account, it is not so surprising that many second marriages end in divorce due to "conflicts with the children".

What about that couple covenant? I am reminded of a story about my stepdaughter, Aimee, who was eight years old at the time. She and her younger brother, Bud, were playing with a group of other children, some of whom were dealing with the break-up of their parents' marriages, and the introduction of the "other person" in their parent's life. Aimee, in her all-knowing way, assured the other children that when their parent first met the new person, all the interest and attention went to this new person in the 'kissie time', but not to worry, they would get tired of each other, and then the kids would see them again.

In the eyes of a child the couple covenant is one matter. How is it defined between the two adults? Is there sufficient "alone time"? How does the couple replenish each other after the strains of daily living? Is there commitment to a long-term relationship? Are money issues worked out in an acceptable fashion? What is agreed upon with regard to different disciplining and parenting styles? Is there a mechanism in place for agreeing to disagree?

When there is a breakdown in the above litany, the turmoils intensify, and the adults may find themselves asking "is this better than being alone?"

is this better than being alone?

Masks are often worn when expectations do not equal reality. Do you really admit to friends and family how bad it is? Do you wear a stiff upper lip and pretend that all is well, or that only a few things are not working out? Coming down from the high of 'romantic love' to the here and now interaction of the stepfamily is more than a rude awakening. It is like an awakening every morning, every day, that goes on and on. Do you escape to your work, do you get lost in a flurry of activities, or do you become depressed and morose?

Amy is experiencing cascading emotions which are often the norm in stepfamily life. She portrays a tough exterior which belies the myriad of feelings underneath. However, the only type of feelings that she is comfortable admitting are the angry and frustrating ones. Remember her tone in the early part of this chapter?

I believed Amy needed to be more accepting of herself and her negative emotions before she could become unstuck and engage in forward moment in the stepfamily land mine. Also, it was too early to reintroduce the idea of the entire family coming to therapy. The only member of the family who had reached out for help was Amy, and I needed to have a strong ally to help the family move toward coming in for treatment as a family. Enhancing Amy's self-acceptance was a way to help Amy feel better about herself.

As a way to reinforce the normality of negative feelings in stepfamily life, and as a way to flood her with many negative emotions, I asked Amy at the beginning of each session to circle emotions on the following list that she had experienced within the last week:

pissed off	extremely mad	annoyed	bitter
enraged	exasperated	antagonized	fuming
fiery	hateful	indignant	irritable
offended	sulky	uptight	aggravated
hissy fit	miffed	resentful	slow burn
agitated	boiling over	displeased	steamed up

Of course, Amy complained vehemently when she saw this list asking what good was it to circle the obvious, but she did proceed with it and circled every feeling. I nodded and kept the list.

The next week and the week after that, etc., I gave her the same list, and asked her once again to circle the feelings she had experienced within the last week. She would begin the session by saying "let's get the cheat sheet over with." As the weeks went by, a pattern emerged. I asked Amy to look at the pattern and tell me what was happening. The intense feelings rose a notch when her stepson returned home from visitation weekends with his mother. The most pleasant weeks were when Jim and Andy were both away, leaving Amy and her daughter, Audrey having the house to themselves. When there were no comings and goings of adults or children, Amy had even starting writing in a few positive words every now and then. Once again, I raised the possibility of the whole family coming in; Amy said, "Audrey and myself?" I gave her a thoughtful look and told her to let me know when the whole family could come to a session.

This cataloguing on a weekly basis provided a far more accurate self-analysis for Amy than anything I could say. It certainly identified the trigger points in the family. There were still hostile feelings felt, if not expressed, but they were evolving in a pattern that Amy could see which pointed toward the need for entire family involvement.

At times I use this method with a different twist depending upon the resources and interests of the client. A watercolor artist in a stepfamily entered therapy with me. When I was about to give her the "feeling sheet," I hesitated, and instead, asked her to give me a five minute painting of her feelings each week. She did so, and years later I received a letter in the mail from her. She had moved to another part of the country and said as a lark she had entered one of those "feeling" paintings she had done when she was in therapy in a contest. She won a prize and sold the artwork for a nice sum of money. In her letter she asked me why she hadn't done this sooner. Although her tone was one of jest, I responded and wrote back that I thought she was now able to show her vulnerability because she was in a better place emotionally.

Yes, it can take years for emotional resonance to come together in a person's life, especially in stepfamily land mines. Knowledge of this fact helps individuals, like Amy, be more accepting of what they are feeling and reduces the finger-pointing and blaming which is typical of stepfamily interaction. I encourage my clients to re-read the stepfamily books and literature as they continue to go through different phases of the evolving stepfamily land. As with most things, our attention is immediately drawn to that which resonates with us at the moment. To say, "oh, I have already read that," does not begin to do justice to the help available when sources are re-read at a different time. I have illustrated this at times with clients with reading a passage with the source unidentified. When the comment is "yes, I feel exactly that way," and that is followed by "where is that written? I need to get it," I share that I believe they may have the source already.

Teenage Angst

I received an emergency call from Amy one weekend. She was screaming into the phone that everything was over - the marriage, the mother-in-law, the fucking teenagers, the dogs, the neighbors. When she calmed down enough to hear me, I asked what had brought this on. She gave a litany of what was wrong. I said to her that I had heard everything she said before, and I knew that an emergency phone call on the weekend was something she had never done before, and I wondered what that meant.

Finally, Amy related that her mother-in-law was in town staying with them. She paused and said her mother-in-law's room was next door to her stepson's and that battle-ax had "overheard" some remarks, and walked in on him finding him at a pornography site on the Internet. In the exchange following the discovery, Andy related to his grandmother that Audrey called the 900 sex lines – and just wait until that phone bill came in. Of course, to make matters worse, Audrey called Andy a liar, Jim said his son didn't lie, and Amy said her daughter didn't lie, and battle-ax said maybe it was time for this family to see the handwriting on the wall. Battle-lines were drawn, positions were etched in stone, and no one was moving an inch.

The stepfamily research literature states that the most difficult time for a stepfamily to form is when the children are between ages nine and fifteen. Some sex differences have been noted as well, with stepdaughters coming out as more difficult. Problems arise with stepsons, but the early literature reports that adjustments tend to take place at a quicker pace for the boys. The reasoning used to explain the statistical differences is that a tighter bond forms between daughter and mother after divorce while sons after divorce tend to be very angry with mom for driving dad away.

My own experience, both personal and professional, tends to be that adjustment is more readily linked to how the biological parents handle the transition with the children. Sex of the child becomes more of an issue when that transition is problematic. An issue often mentioned with stepdaughters is the aura of competition between stepmother and stepdaughter for dad's attention, particularly when the adjustment between the adult couple is good. What I would be interested in, though, is how is the adjustment between the biological parents. I believe most problems can be worked through if the biological parents have their act together. When they do not, sometimes the odds are insurmountable.

Amy was now ready to encourage the family to come for a session. If battle-ax was going to still be in town, I wanted her to come for the session as well. Amy spewed and puffed about that possibility, but in the end agreed. I knew that Amy was also worried that how I saw her might change when the other characters in this family drama were in full life form. So, I thanked Amy for her courage and willingness to bring this family in to support change.

All of the family, including mother-in-law, came in for a session. Mother-in-law's first observation was that she understood I was a stepparent, and therefore, I was probably biased and would be unable to see the point of view of the parent; i.e., her son. She shared this just as everyone was getting seated, so "I," the therapist would not be beginning the session. (Inside, I thought to myself that mother-in-law had just told me more about herself in the opening moments than she had imagined.)

I began the session by enlisting mother-in-law's help in understanding the recent chain of events. I asked her to physically place the family in the respective positions in my office that would tell this story best. I told her anywhere in my office was fair game. She acknowledged that it was good that I had a large office. She proceeded to place Andy at my computer center, Audrey lying down on my "pink" leather sofa, as she called it (Amy interrupting her to say it was camellia, not pink!), Jim in the executive chair, and she was struggling with where to put Amy. I did not offer to help, but waited. Finally, she placed Amy at my back office exit with her hands on the doorknob. She hastened to add that her placement of the family was only to aid in the telling of the story.

As events proceeded to unfold in the session with the telling of the "story," I paused and asked mother-in-law if she would help me once again. She said "yes" in a tone that conveyed that she didn't think too much of what was happening in this supposed "therapy." I explained that since it was such a beautiful day outside, I wanted her to walk around the complex with Andy and Audrey devising the ideal homework assignment that would help this family. I didn't have time to worry about her response because both Andy and Audrey jumped up and pulled grandmother to her feet and said "let's go".

When they had gone, Jim looked at me, and said, "That was as masterful maneuvering as I have ever seen with my mother." "Oh?" I said in feigned surprise. "But it will not last," he said assuredly, "and how is that going to help with this mess?"

I thought about Jim's question and decided to respond about another matter. "I am so glad you agreed to come. For change to take place, I need the executive committee on board and ready to tackle the issues," I entreated.

It was obvious that Jim was about to launch into more questions about the problems at hand when Amy spoke up, "Jim, I am lost as a partner with you. I am hanging on for dear life as a parent, and I believe you are, too. But, if we cannot deal with these issues as a team, then I know I will have to leave the marriage. It is not a threat, it is just the truth."

Jim turned to me and angrily and accusingly stated, "So that is what these so called therapy sessions have been about." It was again Amy who responded, "No, Jim, these therapy sessions have enabled me to stay in the marriage thus far. We couldn't talk, I have had so many feelings, and I want a place where you can express your feelings, too. I am just trying to let you know how seriously I believe that our marriage is in danger."

I shared with both of them, "Stepfamilies are a little like trying to achieve the impossible with every distraction thrown in for good measure. You are bringing together different value sets, different parenting and disciplining styles, different histories, different ex's, all in a boiler plate of a new marriage with adolescent children. Throw in the distractions of technology via the Internet, the culture with emphasis on adolescent sexuality with accessible phone sex, and a mother (turning to Jim) and mother-in-law (turning to Amy) who thinks things were better the way they used to be. And you two are the team who is supposed to solve all this."

"Easier said than done," commented Jim. "And you deal with these issues all the time?"

"I try. Sometimes what I think and what you think may not work, but there are usually lots of other choices to explore, " I added.

Amy said, "To come full circle, it is like one land mine after another, but you build resources and do not give up trying to find the resources."

"I couldn't have said it better, Amy," I answered.

Stepfamily Challenges

Stepfamilies are increasing with every divorce and remarriage. And remarriages are on the rise, so a child may be in more than one stepfamily. I encourage families entering stepfamily land to try and do the following tasks as soon as possible, and to repeat them on a regular basis throughout the journey:

1. Build a stepfamily support network with different support systems for each family member, and a support frame of reference for the family as a whole. Examples can be school friends, church or synagogue or religious institution, extra-curricular activities, stepfamily clubs, stepfamily groups, support groups and affiliations, and time for each family member to have access to support in whatever form works best for the individual.

2. Read everything you can on the subject, and share what "hits home" with the rest of the family. Review from time to time what the family has gathered on its reading list.

3. Respect the need for pairings. The couple is the backbone pairing, and need time together to act as a couple. If neglected, everything and everyone else suffers. Parent/child pairings are also important, and activities that include such pairings need to be fostered.

4. Be patient. Rome wasn't built in a day, and stepfamilies are not made when the members come together.

5. Ask for help when needed. Try not to expect to know everything about what happens; try not to expect to understand every feeling, said or unsaid.

eight

---

those "highs and lows"

Dean

A psychiatrist I work with regularly called and wanted to refer a client that he said would be interesting and challenging. Briefly, he related that Dean's fiancee was bipolar, had been so since she was an adolescent, and that Dean was extremely skeptical of doctors and of medication. For the moment, he wanted to refer Dean with the idea that couple involvement at a later time would be appropriate. He described Dean as highly intelligent, highly questioning, and sometimes a "pain in the neck".

This "pain in the neck" person began his questioning of me on the phone call to set up the appointment. At the end of the phone conversation I told him he gave me the most thorough interview of my credentials since graduate school and the licensing board. He related that he had heard that before from other professionals.

Considering his fiancee's diagnosis and his questioning manner I prepared for the interview with material on the illness he could read and a list of resources he might explore if he so chose. Even if I did not use it, I felt better having it with this person.

Even to this day, I don't think I could ever have prepared for the shock I received when I entered the waiting room to greet this client. It was like seeing a ghost. I felt the blood drain out of my face. I must have looked pretty sick because a woman that I hadn't even noticed right beside me touched my arm and asked if I was OK. At the moment I didn't think so, but I said yes and thanked her for her concern. Only then did I recognize her as a regular client who saw one of my colleagues. My thoughts were I must make it through this initial interview and transfer this client.

Dean looked exactly like my father, so close it shook me up. Right after dad died 18 years ago, I went through that normal stage where you see people with a slight resemblance and think it is your loved one. I had never met anyone who physically looked so much like him. Intellectually, I knew that I "should" be able to get beyond the physical characteristics once I knew this person, but at the moment all I wanted to do was be alone with my memories.

Just as I was debating what to do, Dean came forward and introduced himself, asking if I was really OK. That put me back on track, and I escorted him into my office. I felt my color begin to return, and I turned to the business of the interview.

Dean basically gave me a quick history of his fiancee's illness. I wrote everything down because I wasn't sure I would remember it otherwise. When my pen had stopped moving, Dean said tentatively, "I would really like to know what happened to you in the waiting room. You were fine until you looked at me."

There were many things I could have said, but what I said was, "You are the same age my father was when he died, and you look incredibly like him. For that reason, at the end of our session, I will give you the names of two other therapists."

"Did you like your father?" he asked.

"I loved my father very much, and was very sad when he died," I softly related. (What I did not say to him was that I was also saddened by the circumstances of his death.)

I was taken off guard by his next question, "Do you believe in karma?" he pried. "Are you Buddhist?" I responded.

Dean elaborated, "Perhaps that was a bit unfair of me. I do believe in karma, and I believe you are the therapist to work with me. You answered my question honestly when I asked what happened to you in the waiting room. You could have made something up. I have interviewed six therapists, and I know you are the one that can help me."

Inside, I was groaning. What do I have here – a Zen Buddhist, a person who believes his karma says to work with me, and I am doing nothing this interview but handling my own feelings.

At the end of the interview when I gave him the names of other therapists, he asked me to please think about it. To top it all off, his history said his father was a psychiatrist in another state. I thought, yep, that is what I need alright, a malpractice suit for treating someone that I have so much positive transference for based on his physical looks alone.

Later, all I could think about was parallel processes. What was this client bringing to me that was touching so much inside me? Gee, I must be developing hypomania, I thought. I didn't want to deal with highs and lows at the moment.

Needless to say, I was most affected by this encounter. I knew I needed to call the referring psychiatrist and tell him I could not see Dean. What I did do was go see my mentor. His question to me was "Are you in this work because you need to get something back from your clients, too?" I told him he already knew the answer to that question for me. "Well," he continued, "take the weekend and play with the possibilities of what seeing this client might do to enhance your own self-understanding, your own personal growth work, and remember I can be here to walk with you on this one."

I inundated myself with theory, ethics, and philosophy of doing therapy over the weekend. I realized that I was probing in the wrong area. I had to take care of personal unfinished business with ghosts of my family of origin.

And so I began. As a therapist, I have always known that clients trigger certain reactions and feelings within one's soul. The key is the therapist's own self-awareness. Feelings, those expressed and those unexpressed, are the guideposts to maintaining the therapist's objectivity, and paradoxically, the human connection with the client.

For reasons unclear to me at the time, I called the referring psychiatrist and stated what had happened, and added that I was thinking about working with the client. The psychiatrist responded with humor that I could always blame my father if this didn't work out.

I called Dean as I had promised I would after two weeks, and inquired if he had followed through with the therapist recommendations I made. "No," he said, "there was no need."

I had already made the decision to talk with Dean again, based mainly on the fact that I had an excellent support network to look back over my shoulder and make sure that I did no harm to the client, Dean. He responded to my news with joy and restraint. At least I could notice that I was back into him rather than into myself, a good sign, I thought. I wasn't sure what the restraint on Dean's part meant, but believed I would find out in the next session.

On the second visit, Dean related that there had been a crisis with Jean, and that he needed to talk about it first. He stated he truly loved her, but knew he had to be realistic about her bipolar illness. She had been hospitalized several times with emphasis on depression once, and on mania the second time. This would be a second marriage for both of them. She had children by her first marriage, both out of the home at this time. One adult child was already displaying depressive symptoms. Dean had no children by his first marriage.

He readily acknowledged that he had no love of medication, and wondered about all the medications Jean took. I asked what he had read about the illness, both serious and pop style. In actuality, he had read very little. I talked with him about the author William Styron (1990) and his book, *Darkness Visible*, an autobiography of his own bouts with depression. I shared that William Styron had visited NCSU and made a talk in honor of his father who was an NCSU graduate. Bill Styron revealed that his father also suffered from depression that went untreated at the time. I told him that I attended the talk and offered my impressions of the man and his management of his illness.

Other resources were offered, including the local chapter of the National Manic/Depressive Society. I gave him the names of the two leaders, Sheila Singleton and Charlie Hinton, and suggested he visit the office and examine the wealth of resources. Dean indicated that he would do so.

I noticed that I was now aware of how different Dean was in many ways from my father. As I got into Dean, I thought of my dad less and less. That is how I knew it was supposed to be. Yet, I knew that I would continue to struggle with the meaning of this client in my life at this time.

Dean began to share how torn he was in dealing with Jean's highs and lows. "She is irrational and accusatory at times. She was in one of those moods when you called to say you would see me again. It saps my energy to have to deal with it. I find myself asking when will it ever stop? And then, there is the sleep pattern, or I should say, no sleep. I never know all that she does in the wee hours of the morning. At times when she is up, she has the most boundless energy of anyone I know. She is absolutely delightful to be around. There is a sharpness about her mind that I find so attractive and enticing, and even a little eerie. She can tune right into your most vulnerable spot."

He continued, "Her depressed moods actually make it easier for me to relate to her. She is so much more mellow, yet sad. She says the medicine keeps her from going deeply into the black hole. But then come the crises that she seems to need to create. These crises "rev" her up, but everyone else down."

"Have you been around manic or depressed people before?" I inquired.

"My father is retired now, but I think he is what your literature calls hypomanic," said Dean. "His moods were and are not as severe as Jean's; obviously, I grew up in such a household, compounded by the fact that my father was a psychiatrist."

"Did the two of you or anyone in the family ever talk about this?" I asked.

"Ours was not a talking family, you understand," he declared. "Dad went off to work, Mom handled home life, and that was it. I was never close to my father as I told you when you were taking my history."

"Dean, how would you describe yourself?" I questioned.

He responded, "I am even, consistent, and persistent. I will get things done, just not on Jean's timetable. What I haven't shared with you is the hurt, the pain, the numbness I feel after one of her "episodes." When I think life with her is getting better, boom – it was the quiet before the storm. I remain depleted so much of the time. You may not understand this, but it takes energy just to be around her. I have really developed a mask that I wear before the world."

"Dean, you seem so different from that first telephone call you made to me. Is that part of this mask?" I asked.

"That first phone call to you was my father talking through me," he conveyed. "The person you see now is me. My father wore a mask all his life and very well, at that. The reason I wanted to see you is that you were professional, but real. I had to see someone who did not wear a mask."

"What are you working out in this relationship with Jean?" I enjoined.

"That is why I am here," he affirmed. "My perceptions are so colored by my family that I cannot be sure that I am giving Jean a fair shake. I have been so close to leaving this relationship, and yet, I stay. I do not understand myself."

The Dilemma

There exists a double dilemma here, one for the client, and one for the therapist-client relationship. For Dean, he is battling whether or not to remain in a partnership with a woman who has a bipolar disorder. He finds it difficult to understand why he has not made the choice to leave when they are not even married yet. He realizes that his family background plays a part in his stuckness. He is unsure of how to pursue the unfamiliar world of a bipolar diagnosis, a drug regimen, and the maintenance factor of living with someone who copes with depression and mania.

And I, the therapist, wrestle with my initial transference factor with Dean due to his strong physical resemblance to my deceased father. The strength of my reaction upon seeing Dean resonates with me. It has personal meaning for me that I do not yet fully understand. I must cope with what meaning this transference will have on the therapist- client relationship.

On the other hand, I appreciate Dean's difficulty with his "mask." The dramatic spectacle of my shock upon seeing him represented a metaphor of "uncovering" my professional mask to Dean making me "real" to him. His ability to relate to others without the mask is a dilemma for him that crosses over to the therapist/client relationship. His bonding to the therapist based on what he perceives as a removal of a mask, can also be used as a positive leverage to recommend appropriate treatment that may facilitate movement out of his stuckness.

The Choices

Exploring self-understanding is an extremely viable choice for Dean. Until he identifies what motivates his behavior, it will be troublesome to capture how he may become unstuck. His mask protects him from being vulnerable in his interactions with others. Dean has acted on the decision to check out therapy. Interviewing six therapists and finding none that are a "match" does raise some argument about whether he intends to pursue this avenue. Nonetheless, individual therapy remains a possible choice.

I visualize another component of therapy being crucial to this mix. Whether he is in individual treatment with me or someone else, I recommend as an additional choice, group therapy. The appropriate "match" between Dean and the "right as rain" group could bring big dividends in facilitating the removal of Dean's mask in a protected and secure milieu. The "realness" he professes to desire happens in group therapy. I know several ongoing groups that my colleagues in the Carolina Group Psychotherapy Association lead which would be a "match" for Dean.

Educational offerings on bipolar illness are also encouraged. Knowledge opens up more choices, and enhances one's ability to act upon the choices. This geographic area is rich in support groups, and as mentioned earlier, there is the local chapter of the National Society for Manic Depression which offers ongoing education and support for the families, recognizing that dealing with manic/depression is a family affair.

I, as the therapist, also have choices. The most obvious one is to see Dean individually in treatment or refer him out to other therapists. Referral to a specific ongoing psychotherapy group for individuals is also an appropriate alternative.

Being clear about what I, the therapist, see as the viable options is very important. Sharing the options and ultimate choice with Dean is part of the ongoing uncovering metaphor of the therapist mask.

The Questions

A very important question for Dean to ask himself is "why now?" He is seeking treatment in a methodical manner, interviewing therapists and asking questions of his fiance's psychiatrist. His entry into the world of "highs and lows" has taken place over a period of time. At this point, commitment has been made to Jean; however, it is now after the promise has been given, that Dean is seeking professional help. Perhaps the reality has hit home, and he has gotten cold feet, or that he is rethinking the responsibility.

His thoughtful probing on his own indicates that he knows he has ghosts from his family of origin to explore, pursue, and claim. I, the therapist, also raise the question of ghosts from my own family of origin that require attention. The physical resemblance of Dean to my father raises questions for me; likewise, the pull of the "father" rings true for Dean's history as well. And this brings me back to my earlier question of "why is this particular client in my life at this special time?"

navigating depression and hypomania

When you or your loved one are experiencing even a mild depression, it affects the life of everyone around you. I disclosed that I wondered why this client, Dean, came into my life at this time. I have treated depressive and bipolar clients and their families for over 20 years. I believe I now know. Just as clients pay attention to life events that immediately affect them in the media, in magazines and books, and with people, so did I. And I am approaching the age my father was when he had a sudden heart attack. Just last month I called a cardiologist I know because I was having unexplained chest pains. I said to him and to myself, "Oh, it is because I have been under so much stress due to major practice changes." He walked me through what I needed to watch out for, and referred me to someone he thought would work well with me. I did call, but I never scheduled an appointment. I talked with one of my brothers, who is three years younger, and we bemoaned together our family's physical history.

All of this is to say I had been focusing on my father. What I now realize is that I sincerely believe my father suffered from depressions, probably of a moderate nature. He was never treated for it. I knew my father had low self-esteem, but I never attributed any of his passivity to depression. He was marvelous with people and that is the way I wanted to remember him. But as I look back now, the signs were there.

How many times have I gone over the litany of depressed symptoms with clients, with managed care companies, etc. – too numerous to recite. And I ignored the pull of looking at my family. Sure, I have been in personal therapy, but I never touched or talked about my father as a depressed man.

Do I believe in karma? Perhaps, in some way. I have often asserted that there are no coincidences. But did I really believe it? That is another matter. I guess my verdict is still out. I do have a skeptical nature.

Recognizing the Signs/Symptoms of Depression

I remember as a child Sunday afternoons in particular. That is the time I learned that if I wanted to feel down, Sunday afternoons were a good time to do it. My dad often felt "blue" on Sundays, for reasons I only later thought of as part of his depression and part of his reaction to life around him.

My own case of the "blues" when I was in college always occurred on Sunday afternoons. I was a perfectionist and always worried about that next exam, but particularly on Sundays.

Depression takes many forms:

1. Examine the daily habits of yourself and your loved ones.
2. Notice changes in the routine and specify the changes.
3. Ask questions about the changes.
4. Are there fluctuations in the mood, eating habits, or sleep patterns?
5. How about changes in the ability to enjoy life, to explore passions previously enjoyed?
6. Is there constant unexplained irritability?
7. Is there a need to withdraw, to escape from life?

Mania

Just as there are many levels of depression, there are degrees of mania. Some of our most talented leaders have suffered bouts of depression and mania. In Ronald Fieve's book, *Moodswing*, many of our past political leaders and outstanding trailblazers in varied disciplines who have been identified as depressed and/ or manic are featured. The incredible highs and ongoing boundless energy are often associated with high levels of creativity. The downside is the massive depression that may follow.

It is natural to enjoy the benefits of the mania from a distance. Living with a family member with a bipolar disorder is a challenge that often takes its toll. Help, professionally and personally, is as important for the family member or loved one as it is for the individual with the disorder, a fact that is now beginning to be recognized more and more. I often wonder what may have occurred in some client relationships that I saw in therapy if ongoing professional and personal support had been accessed by the family member throughout the troubled time of the relationship. Saying "it is all I can do to manage my life, career, and my partner's hospitalization," for example, is not good enough.

I often find myself saying to family members, "try not to take it personally." I remember one male client whose wife had been engaging in one sexual indiscretion after another looking incredulously at me when I made a similar statement. When an individual experiences mania, they will often say to me, "but I can't stand it when the edge is off. I am left with none of the great highs, only the lows and that horrible neutrality." In addition, the high creativity is often stymied with medication. Often the individual will discontinue the medication and highs return along with sometimes irresponsible behavior such as sexual indiscretions.

What is the difference between sexual addictions and manic-like sexual indiscretions? This topic has received increased attention due to high profile personalities being accused of numerous sexual indiscretions. Mania creates excesses, whether it be in the arena of compulsive spending, gambling, or risk-taking. Addictions can certainly be a part of the mania; however, addictions can also occur without the presence of a bipolar disorder. Other personality disorders may be a more accurate diagnosis in the case of some sexual acting out or other excesses.

Remembering that there are degrees of mania just as there are of depression, here are some signs and/or symptoms of mania:

1. Racing thoughts
2. Rapid-fire speech, excessive talking
3. Inability to sleep
4. Sense of grandiosity
5. Poor judgment after excessive forays into risk-taking behaviors such as sexual indiscretions, buying sprees, poor business investments
6. High distractibility
7. Increase in creative or goal-directed pursuits

Accessing the Help

What William Styron's father and my father did not have was cultural acceptance and availability of treatment. "Treatment for nerves" in my family of origin, was reserved for those family members who suffered from PTSD (post traumatic stress disorder) as a result of being in one of our country's wars. If, however, the individual is functioning in a job or career, it does not matter to the public how the individual may be feeling. The job is getting done. Mike Wallace, of CBS's *60 Minutes* fame, has talked openly about the public perception vs. the private hell.

Accessing help is easier today than when my father was alive; nonetheless, many myths and stereotypes still prevail. But perhaps the biggest obstacle to identifying the need for help is that of denial; if I had asked my father if he were depressed at any time along the way, he would have denied it. Denial is a common reaction when the subject of depression and/or mania is addressed. Family members often talk about it long before the individual is willing to get help. Sometimes a specific life event helps the cause. I spent the afternoon with my father before he died in the early morning hours. He insisted that I return home, but did agree to get some professional help because my mother had left him. Would he have agreed if a marital separation had not occurred? I doubt it.

Educating the Public

The number one FACT: THERE IS HELP. Disseminating information to the public must continue to be a high priority. I will list the nonmedical options to try first which may work for mild and moderate disorders, and build up to the choices for more severe disorders including medications:

1. Complete physical work- up, most especially having the thyroid checked. Hypothyroidism causes depression. We had a U.S. senator from NC commit suicide, only to find out that his thyroid had not been checked during recent physicals, and his autopsy revealed he was suffering from hypothyroidism. Do not assume that your thyroid has been checked. ASK in a proactive way that it be checked.

2. Change in life-style: Appropriate amount of exercise, low-fat diet, and *moderation* in eating and drinking habits. This alone, sometimes results in the lifting of depression. Besides, these changes are always a help and not a hindrance to one's life.

3. Change in thinking: The cognitive behavioral approach to depression recognizes that the stimulus triggers feelings of

low self-esteem which leads to black or white thinking and negative conclusions. The cognitive behavioral way of addressing this issue is to focus on *changing* the thinking which can, in turn, change the feelings. Numerous resources exist which explore this method. Two prominent authors are Aaron Beck (1988) and David Burns (1980, 1990).

4. Psychological and psychiatric evaluation to determine if medication is appropriate. Natural herbs, such as St. John's Wort, are a possibility for mild and moderate depression. Research has shown that the best treatment is a combination of psychological therapy and medication for the treatment of the "highs and lows."
   For severe ongoing depression and bipolar disorder consult a psychiatrist.

A Note about Dean

I referred Dean for ongoing group therapy, and continued to see him individually about twice a month. I also referred he and his fiance for couple counseling to a colleague. Dean could not commit to marriage. Eventually, the fiance broke the engagement. They still see each other at this time, but less and less frequently.

nine

---

cybersex

Adam and Ellen

"If it weren't for the kids, I'd be gone," Adam yelled into the phone. "Now, I have to be the responsible one, and get this show on the road. Give me your first available time, so I can get this over with."

When I asked for more information, Adam, still yelling said, "I don't have time to talk about it now."

"I assume this involves you and your partner," I stated.

He yelled back sarcastically, "No, it involves the dog."

I calmly said that I would like to see both partners if possible. His response was, "We'll see."

When the couple arrived for the interview, Adam and Ellen sat as far apart as possible in my office – one at the end on one sofa and the other at the opposite end on another sofa. It was quite clear that Adam's anger had not abated. On Ellen's part, she held her chin in a defiant manner.

Looking at Adam, I said, "I spoke with you on the phone, but it was very brief. I would like to hear from each of you, (looking at both), what brings you in today."

A long silence followed. I waited.

Angrily, Adam began, the whole time looking at me with nary a glance towards Ellen, "Ellen is leaving Friday to see the man from cyberspace she has been e-mailing behind my back. I learned this from my son. When she returns, the kids and I will be gone."

Ellen pitched forward and said in a deadly tone, "They are my kids, too, and if you try and kidnap them, it will be the last breath you take."

Adam slowly turned to Ellen and stated just as deadly, "I don't have to kidnap them – any judge will award me custody based on your behavior."

Ellen slumped on the sofa.

I commented, "There are many more pieces to this puzzle than what I know at this point. In order for me to help you, I need both of you to fill in the pieces now."

What followed was one angry exchange after the other. I let them go at it in an effort to get more of the story. When there was a silence, I intervened and stated that I would like to summarize what I had heard to this point. When I had finished, they could ask any questions or make corrections.

I reiterated, "You have been in Raleigh for eight months due to Adam's company transfer. As a result of the move, Ellen gave up a job she loved, and has been a homemaker since the geographic transplant. Ellen doesn't like Raleigh, has been very lonely, and met a man in a chat room on the Internet. She has been corresponding with this man for the last six months, and decided to visit him at his home. Ellen has never informed Adam of any of this exchange. Adam was in the car with your son taking him to T-ball practice when he heard his son saying 'Mom is going away with a man she met on the Internet.' Confrontation between the two of you occurred, and intense verbal exchanges have been practically nonstop."

"What you said is fine, but what you left out is that Ellen stopped cooking, the clothes piled up, and the house was a terrific mess and sex stopped," Adam complained.

Not to be outdone, Ellen replied, " You were so wrapped up in your great new position, that you never asked how my day went, or showed that you gave a damn about what I had given up for your career."

"I thought this was a joint decision we made, and not one that I would hear about forever," Adam responded.

I intervened here, and communicated, "Beginnings and endings are always hard. This transition has taken a toll on this family. I have heard declarations from each of you about this move, but where I want to move is to have you express your feelings on this subject."

"What do you think I have been doing?" yelled Adam.

"Tell me the feelings you have expressed," I asked.

"She'll get the kids over my dead body. How's that?" Adam answered impatiently.

I announced, "That's a clear thought, Adam. The message still does not convey your feelings about this move."

"OK," Adam continued, "I feel that Ellen ought to start being a wife and mother."

Responding to his impatience with patience, I suggested, "Try substituting the words 'I believe' for 'feel', and see if the sentence makes sense."

Adam did so, and related, "Yes, it does, so???"

"Most of the time when you substitute 'I believe' for 'I feel' and the sentence makes sense, you have expressed a thought, not a feeling. Now, go back to that same sentence, and, here, let me give you a feeling list of words, and choose one that fits, one that describes your emotion of the moment," I added.

Adam perfunctorily took the list and chose a word, and said, "I am livid that Ellen is not acting like a wife and mother." He went on, "Now, tell me what the big deal is about changing a word."

I answered, "First, I like the fact that you started the sentence with "I" which says you take ownership of the feeling 'livid'. It is important in communication to identify the specific feeling and take ownership of that feeling. Just expressing thoughts is incomplete communication. And part of what has been happening in this marriage is incomplete communication."

I turned to Ellen, and affirmed, "Now, it is your turn to express a feeling."

"Can I have the list?" she requested. I gave her her own copy and waited.

With surprise in her voice, she said, "Out of all the words, here, the one that best describes how I feel every day is 'neglected'. Yes, I am angry, hurt, and livid too, but neglected is where it is at for me."

As the session came to a close, I asked Ellen if she were taking the trip to meet her on-line pal this Friday or if it would be later. She responded that she was not sure at this point. She agreed to let me know before the next appointment.

The voice-mail message came the next week. Ellen explained that she decided to delay her trip to see her on-line pal, but that she had a "bombshell" on Mr. Adam that she was going to deliver to him in my office. Her message, of course, heightened my curiosity. But I had learned a long time ago that truth is always stranger than fiction. When a marriage is in trouble, one partner alone seldom has all the culpable behavior.

When I entered the waiting room to greet them for the second appointment, I was immediately met with apologies from Ellen about the children being present. She explained that the babysitter didn't show up after school, and she couldn't leave them home alone. She had brought toys, etc., to keep them occupied and hoped that would be OK. I allayed her fears, met the children myself and introduced the children to the support staff, and shared with the parents that I would like to see all of them together towards the end of the session. I considered their presence a plus.

Ellen was exuberant; Adam was strangely quiet. I waited for them to begin. Ellen's tone rang out strong and clear, "It seems that I am not the only one with an e-mail fetish. And mine is all verbal, no pictorials anywhere. I can't say the same for my pure and clean husband."

Adam remained silent. I asked, "And how did this come out?"

Ellen asserted, "My daughter came to me and wanted to know what daddy was doing at night on the computer. So I caught him the next night. Pure, dirty PORNO!"

Finally, Adam spoke, "When a man gets no sex from his wife, he can have an affair or see to his needs otherwise. I will not have an affair."

"What do you call your porno bunnies with their perfect little fake bodies?" Ellen exclaimed.

"What do you call your infamous e-mail chatrooms?" Adam yelled back.

After two or three more such exchanges, I stopped them cold with "Has it ever entered your minds that what has been going on has permeated all the way down to your children who are taking sides as they try to sort this all out. You, Adam, were told by your son what mommy was doing. Ellen, you were told by your daughter what daddy was doing. Whatever is going on between the two of you has now evolved into children taking messages back and forth. This is what can happen in bad divorces, and you two are still together. I can't wait to see what happens if you divorce."

Both Adam and Ellen looked sheepish and ashamed. I asked, "By the way, what did you tell the children about coming here today?"

Ellen answered, "I explained that mommy and daddy had appointments at the doctor's, and that they would be coming with us to wait in the waiting room."

"Do either of you have problems with what I would like to say to them, which is, 'the family is coming to see me to talk about feelings in the family. Everyone has feelings in a family, and it is important that feelings be talked about'," I concluded.

Adam angrily stated, "Some things are not appropriate for children to hear. I will not have my children used as pawns."

I emphasized, "I will not play a part in the children being used as pawns. On that, we agree. However, the children have already been used as messengers in this family. Some corrective work must be done. Focusing on feelings in the family can be a way to do that corrective work."

Grudgingly, both parents agreed that the children could participate in such a focus at the end of the session. I reminded them that their work was far from over, and that I hoped the goal of connectedness would be uppermost in their minds as the work continued with each other and with the family.

The Dilemma

Transitions can foster disconnectedness in families. Adam and Ellen both have many unexpressed feelings about this change in their lives. Today's technology brings with it anonymity that I believe interferes with ownership of feelings, thoughts, wishes, wants, and even actions. Our culture has not been one of small communities for several decades now. How does an individual and/or family moving to a new area become less anonymous? It is certainly not with obsessive or excessive use of the Internet. As with many tools, the Internet can be a pool of positive resources, and also, it can be used to fuel anonymous addictions, whether they be emotional or sexual.

For the last five years of my practice, I have seen a steady rise in the problems that Adam and Ellen represent in their story. I believe these problems will continue as our culture struggles with disconnectedness. Adam and Ellen are normal people that are caught up in unhealthy ways to handle their feelings. Yes, some of these problems become full-blown addictions if left unaddressed.

Ellen has chosen the anonymous route to handling her lonely feelings. Can she reach out to the community, the neighborhood, the religious community, and any of the numerous support groups to get her needs met? Chatrooms on the Internet can be a fun enjoyable way to connect with other people, but if it is the only connection one is making in a new city, trouble lies ahead. It is safe (as long as it is in the chat-room only), it is easy (one does not have to get dressed to go out), and it is anonymous (one can say anything and disclose innermost feelings without worrying about seeing the person on the street or anywhere else).

Adam is not alone in using the Internet to watch the porno babes. I have received referrals from executives wanting help for male employees engaging in the porno web sites on the job. The executives are worried about sexual harassment lawsuits that women may file who enter the offices of men engaged in porno at their desk. When is it harmless and when is it an addiction? As with any addiction, when the activity begins to interfere with normal daily life on the job or at home, the activity must be evaluated. What purpose is it serving? Is it a cover-up for serious unaddressed problems at home or at work?

Clearly, in the case of Adam and Ellen, problems from the geographical move have not been pried into in a concerted way. Their marriage is in a dilemma; furthermore, their family life is in trouble with young children already choosing parental sides.

The Choices

If the issue is disconnectedness in this family, an obvious choice is whether or not Adam and Ellen choose to reconnect with each other and their community. Adam has sexual needs that are going unmet – he did make reference to them before his Internet porno was disclosed. Sexual needs usually mean emotional needs are also going unattended, even if not verbalized as such. Adam can choose to address these unmet needs more directly. He did reach out for help for the marriage when he became aware of Ellen's involvement in cyberspace. Continued disclosure on his part in the marriage counseling would be one choice.

If Adam chooses to leave the marriage, the issue of the kids becomes paramount for him and the family. In all likelihood, the marriage has not seen smooth sailing for sometime. The use of the kids as messengers will continue if changes are not made in the way Adam and Ellen communicate. Deterioration in the family functioning will continue if changes are not made in the status quo.

Ellen also may choose the status quo, or hope for her knight in shining armor on the Internet to take her away from all her troubles. If not, she may choose ongoing involvement with the community and her family. What were her interests in her previous locale? Has she pursued these interests in Raleigh? Has she gotten out and investigated what the city may offer, or has she taken the easy way out on the computer?

As a couple, what have Adam and Ellen chosen to do that defines them as a couple, not parents, not homemaker, not business executive? This identity, if there previously, has been lost in the geographic transition. Redefining themselves is a possible choice. In therapy, I will be bringing up another choice – taking Couple Communication, a group course that teaches communication skills with other couples.

The Questions

Perhaps the most important question was asked earlier: What purpose does the Internet activity of each serve in their functioning as individuals, as a couple, and as a family? My viewpoint is that the human need to connect is the basis for much of their Internet involvement. As mentioned earlier, it is safer, easier, and anonymous.

When family and friends are no longer nearby, how does one share and communicate about daily events? How does one let off steam to individuals who will still accept you after you ventilate? How does one develop the freedom to share when opinions may change as events unfold?

What support systems exist to help this couple and this family? Is there access to community support, to religious community support, to specialized interests support? In other words, how can these individuals singly, and as a family, find ways to connect not only with each other, but with the community?

the spiritual and intimacy void

When there is a lack of connection in people's lives, there usually exists a spiritual and intimacy void. Look at the books on the bestseller list today. There is an emphasis on topics such as conversations with God, angels, spiritual inspiration, re-awakening, second chances, and hope for more holistic approaches to mind, body, and spirit. Such themes illustrate the public craving for spiritual nourishment. *Touched by an Angel* is a hit TV sitcom.

The adage *reach out and touch someone* appeals to the human need for intimacy. But that safe, vulnerable, trusting space called intimacy is not a given part of life. The brokenness of relationships often means the human touch is not present. Pets play a significant role in our lives – as a nonjudgmental accepting source of love and affection. There are sayings on mugs and placards, etc., like *we are staying together for the sake of the dog* or *our cat doesn't understand joint custody.* The anonymity of the Internet conveys a false sense of nonjudmental acceptance in the online chatrooms. It is not known if he or she is who they say they are online, so who really knows what is real and what is fake? Vulnerable self-disclosing does take place in chatrooms, but how safe and trusting that space is remains questionable.

I am often asked "does any marriage have enough sustenance in the areas of intimacy and spirituality to make it?" I share that the answer often lies in how one defines the traits of a good marriage. As fodder for discussion, I also may share what Judith Wallerstein calls the nine tasks a good marriage processes over and over if necessary:

1. To separate emotionally from the family of one's childhood so as to invest fully in the marriage and, at the same time, to redefine the lines of connection with both families of origin.
2. To build togetherness by creating the intimacy that supports it while carving out each partner's autonomy. These issues are central throughout the marriage but loom especially large at the outset, at midlife, and at retirement.
3. To embrace the daunting roles of parents and to absorb the impact of Her Majesty the Baby's dramatic entrance. At the same time the couple must work to protect their own privacy.
4. To confront and master the inevitable crises of life, maintaining the strength of the bond in the face of adversity.
5. To create a safe haven for the expression of differences, anger, and conflict.
6. To establish a rich and pleasurable sexual relationship and protect it from the incursions of the workplace and family obligations.
7. To use laughter and humor to keep things in perspective and to avoid boredom by sharing fun, interests, and friends.
8. To provide nurturance and comfort to each other, satisfying each partner's needs for dependency and offering continuing encouragement and support.
9. To keep alive the early romantic, idealized images of falling in love while facing the sober realities of the changes wrought by time.

From Wallerstein and Blakeslee, The Good Marriage, 1995, pp. 27-28.

Another observation that Wallerstein makes in regard to the good marriages is that violence stops the flow and is intolerable. Arguing, fighting, and conflict are part of the mix as long as there is no physical violence.

When I shared this information about the good enough marriage with Adam and Ellen, their reactions were interesting and revealing. Ellen's initial comment was that so there is no physical violence, but what about *intense verbal abuse?* When asked to elaborate, Ellen stated that she believed such verbal abuse had been present in her marriage for a very long time. And as a result, she had withdrawn more and more until she found a sympathetic ear on the Internet. She was quick to add that she did not paint Adam as a vicious scroundel with her e-mail pal; rather, she tuned in to her on-line pal's intuitive responses to her comments. Needless to say, there were no examples of verbal abuse in their e-mail chat.

Adam found the accusations of verbal abuse hard to fathom. He acknowledged being direct, having a quick temper, and being sarcastic. He related the verbal carping to the discovery of her secretive relationship with the e-mail guy. Ellen quickly chastised Adam's interpretation, reminding him of how he could never be wrong, how he always blamed her or someone else for things going wrong. Ellen further described how humiliated she was when he harped on her incessantly in front of other people, blaming her for things over which she had no control.

As he listened to Ellen, Adam attempted to gloss over her statements, and tried to move on to other things. Ellen was angry enough that she did not allow that at this time. She told him he was going to listen and she was going to finish in spite of his interruptions. Ellen gave him examples of his behavior that had occurred throughout their marriage.

When there was a break in the exchange, Adam queried if he could now have a turn. Without waiting for a response, he began by asserting that Ellen was still tied to the umbilical cord of her mother, even if her mother now lived in another state. This lack of separation, he thought, had caused a great many problems in their marriage.

I commented that they had already focused on two areas that needed working and reworking. In the weeks that followed

Adam and Ellen continued to talk out some of their issues. During a session, Ellen asked for an individual session. I was curious about the timing, but stated that now would be a good space to check in with each of them individually. Adam was OK with that. I believed I was accurate in picking up vibes that had I not agreed to see them both individually, Adam would have bolted or sabotaged the therapy quickly and efficiently.

Ellen began her individual session poignantly, "I know that I am bright, but I cannot understand why I nibble around this problem like a timid mouse, never getting to the bottom of it. I want to be a lion for my needs, aggressively and ferociously taking what I need. I feel frozen. What is wrong with me?"

"And what will happen if you are a lion and attack this problem?" I softy asked.

"Let's say I leave the marriage, and I am still unhappy," hypothesized Ellen. "Then, what is left is me. There will be no more excuses. I am so afraid of being, I don't know…, worthless."

"You are expressing an underlying dissatisfaction with your life," I observed. "And I surmise that this has been an undercurrent for a long time. Your needs were not addressed in your childhood family, and you seem to punish yourself for relationships you had in your adolescence."

"I know that is true," Ellen acquiesced, "but does my past have to follow me forever? The relationship with my mother is so confusing. She wasn't there when I was young, but as I got older, at times I was the mother and she was the daughter. My moving here has been very hard on her. It is hell to be so aware of what I want, and so tortured about my lack of a meaningful existence that I seek it out with my anonymous on-line pal."

Ellen used her individual time to further explore her individual history and the links to her current unhappiness. I encouraged Ellen to seek some individual therapy, and provided her with names of people with whom I thought she could relate.

In his usual sarcastic form, Adam began, "So, the only reason you are seeing me alone is because she asked to see you alone, right?"

"Not quite," I responded. "There are issues I want to discuss with you first without the presence of Ellen."

"You think I beat her up with words, don't you?" Adam hammered out.

"That is what she says, but I believe we are addressing that in your couple sessions," I explained. "Tell me about what drew you to the porno sites on the Internet."

"Look, you're a female," Adam shrugged, "how on earth can you get it?"

"Well, I know that males tend to be more turned on by the visual, and instant nude females on the Internet can accomplish that," I answered.

"If you're after if I am addicted, I can tell you no," Adam said disdainfully. "There is a guy I work with, and he is on the Internet porno sites at work, at home, and probably on the boat if he could have a connection. I know he is addicted, which is a sign of a much larger problem. Hell, if I could have sex with my wife, I wouldn't need to look at female bodies on the Internet."

"What did happen to sex between you and Ellen?" I queried.

His response was quite delayed, but I waited. "It was a long time ago," Adam related, "but I think it began with the abortion. We were both in school, and a baby then just wasn't in the picture. It was a mutual decision, but I do not know if Ellen has ever forgiven herself or me."

"And when was the last time you both talked about this?" I questioned.

"It has been years," he sighed. "I think it was when she was pregnant with our daughter. I remember something you said during one of our sessions – guilt is the gift that keeps on giving – and it fits here."

Ellen had not shared specifically about the abortion, only that her past history with men had been troublesome. Slowly, a picture begins to unfold that provides clues to Ellen's feelings of worthlessness and Adam's constant anger. For this couple, the manifestations of their feelings were played out in the crisis of the cyberspace usage. The unresolved concerns about the abortion and the likely lack of forgiveness are issues of substance. The lack of intimacy between Adam and Ellen along with decreased spiritual renewal contributes to further alienation. Such a relationship is prime for Internet exploitation.

The ties between Adam and Ellen remain tenuous. Their difficulties are complex. Movement has been made in the clearer identification of the sources of the problem areas. That may be all that is possible at the moment.

ten

---

how to deal with those
patterns of inertia

People who are struggling with the question, *"Do I Stay or Do I Go?"* are not making a rash, impulsive decision to leave the relationship. Nonetheless, the underlying relationship dissatisfaction often leads to the refrain of "help me, I'm stuck," and "I do not know what to do." There are common themes in the stuckness problem just as there have been mileposts in the crises presented in the vignettes. This chapter will address some of the more frequent roadblocks.

Personal Worksheet

When I am doing a workshop on the topic of, *"Do I Stay or Do I Go?"*, I ask each participant to write down reflections on these questions:

1. _____ (your age)

What are the issues that come to mind when you think about this age?

What is your own personal statement about where you are at this age?

2. _____(age of your partner)

What are the issues that come to mind when you think about this age?

What is your personal statement about where your partner is at this age?

3. _____(# of years in marriage/relationship)
    _____(# of marriages)
    _____(# of your children by this relationship)
    _____(# of your children by previous relationship(s)
    _____(# of partner's children by previous relationship(s)

What are the issues/struggles common to this stage of the marriage/relationship?

What is your personal statement about your view of the relationship at the present time?

Not knowing what the problem truly is, is not uncommon. Sometimes all that can be said is "I'm unhappy." Susan, in the vignette, *I Should Be Happy But...*, did not initially understand what her unhappiness was about. What these questions can do is to get the mind moving in addressing possible causes for one's dissatisfaction.

Confronting the relationship alternatives will be the next step. In the vignette, *I've Been Betrayed*, Frank and Faye did that by completing the Marital Options and Possibilities Scale (MOPS). I request that workshop participants also give their responses to this scale as truthfully as possible.

In the workshop format, I use the questions on the scale as stems and ask for volunteers to complete the sentences with as many responses as come to mind. You, the reader, can do so by finishing the stems that apply to your situation.

1. To physically move out of the home myself is ...

2. To have spouse/partner physically move out of the home is ...

3. To get a divorce is ...

4. To work on the relationship by giving more of my time and energy to the relationship is ...

5. To get sex outside of the marriage is ...

6. To get emotional needs met outside of the marriage is ...

7. To keep things the way they are and not make major changes
    is ...

8. To put more time/energy in work is ...

9. To spend more time/energy with friends is ...

10. To stay in the marriage until children are grown is ...

11. To put the situation in God's hands is ...

If the above alternatives do not fit your particular situation, add ones that do and complete the unfinished sentences with as many responses as come to mind.

The initial exercises help outline the common themes that exist at a certain age and at a certain stage in the relationship. What the MOPS scale often points out is that there is a reluctance to becoming unstuck. The ensuing dilemma is to isolate the hurdles that contribute to the pattern of inertia. Some of the more universal barriers that often play a part in keeping people "stuck" will now be examined.

Misplaced Hope

Getting unstuck requires examining preconceived assumptions. Perhaps one of the most common is what I call "misplaced hope" that the partner will change. This hope colors everything that happens in the relationship, and makes it easier for the partner with the hope to excuse unacceptable behavior. Still, there is a niggling doubt in the partner's mind that all is not as it needs to be, and so the partner with the hope remains stuck while holding on to the hope that the other partner will indeed change. Such hope does not die a natural death easily. There are many false starts and stops. Individuals are not black and white, and so it is not unusual for some appropriate behavior to occur just at the moment that the partner with the hope is ready to call it quits.

It is not enough for a relationship to hinge on whether or not one partner changes. Barbara, in *Mirror, Mirror, on the Wall, Who's That Walking Down My Hall?*, acknowledges that the opposites attract theory has worn thin in her marriage. Of course, there are many things in her wishful thinking that she hopes will change in her husband. As she uncovers the twists and turns in her relationship, she also begins to address the changes she can begin in her own life. Her decision is not to leave her marriage at this time, though she certainly leaves the question open. Rather, she will focus on what she can do now to further her own development. Barbara gradually turned from what was wrong with her husband to how she could move forth with her own growth.

Another old saying is be careful what you wish for, you may get it. Peter, in *I Thought She Would Grow Out Of It*, wanted an equal partner in his relationship. What he had not examined were his own needs in always being the one in control. Giving up control, even though he said it would be a welcome relief, is never easy, especially when he does not understand his own need to be in charge. Initially, Peter zoomed in on his wife's need to change for the marriage to be better. These changes were clear to him; if she became what he wanted in the way of an equal partner, then he could be fulfilled.

Dialogue with Jane, Peter's wife, presented the other side of the story. She did not believe that Peter really wanted her to be more in control. If Jane becomes a "true partner" as Peter says he desires, she may not look or act like he expected. So not only can hope be misplaced, hope can also wear a certain "halo" of preconceived expectations. Examining and exploring the reality of what a "partner" is with both Peter and Jane may be the beginning of becoming unstuck. When confronted with the actual reality of how life might change with a "true partner," Peter has a clearer choice of what is congruent with what he says he desires.

Assessing how realistic the hope is involves several steps:

1. Identify "realistic" expectations as opposed to fantasyland expectations.
2. Identify any patterns of misplaced hope in your childhood family.
3. Identify individual growth strivings and pursue them while you remain hopeful about the relationship.
4. Reevaluate the above steps every six months.

The Masking of Self

Very early on in my career, I learned that how a partner is in an individual session *vis a vis* a couple session can be quite different. Later on in my work, I also saw distinct differences between the personal self and the professional self. Sometimes this helped account for the changes in the presentation of self as an individual and as part of a couple.

When the professional self is so unlike the personal self, I want to challenge the partner to begin the work of uncovering the *real self.* What are the childhood hurts that need to be masked by incredible achievement, perfectionism, and the incredibly strong desire for approval? Can the ability to take risks in the human attachment arena be developed?

I worked with one CEO who often used a metaphor to describe how he viewed life from the *personal self.* He characterized his approach to life like being in a fox hole. Slowly, the perimeter would be surveyed through the lenses of the periscope peering over the top. Movement would be from one tunnel to the next tunnel as though he were a rat scampering through life hidden in his foxhole. Others ventured out of the foxhole, but he did not. Fear was always with him as he had to exert great effort to remain hidden in the foxhole. If he emerged, he would be "found out."

This CEO's employees would ridicule any portrait of their head guy as being in a fox hole. And yet, on a personal level, that is how he portrayed his activity. Slowly, over time, he began to unveil himself to his wife in marital therapy. That meant unmasking his façade to himself as well as to others. That meant stating his honest opinion when he was in situations outside of his work venue, including when he was with his wife.

It takes an incredible amount of energy to maintain a mask. The "gruff" professional mask may sap one's strength leaving little life for the personal camouflage. Dean, the character in the vignette, *Those Highs and Lows* also had to fight wearing a mask. Dean had grown up in a home that was devoid of much emotional displays. His search for a therapist included the directive that this person be real. Before he could deal with the *Do I Stay or Do I Go?* question, Dean knew he had to see if he could let go of his protective armor.

When the real self is exposed, vulnerability is high. Fear of humiliation, shame, and rejection is rampant. The CEO mentioned earlier defended against his fear of shame through expressions of rage, contempt, and transferring the blame. What he was really avoiding was any chance for connection. His in-

terpretation of his behavior was that he was not allowing himself to be shamed. For him, vulnerability equalled shame and
rejection.

During one of his therapy sessions, he quietly talked about
gauging everything he did personally on how another person
was going to approve or disapprove of what he did. He acknowledged that he feared change and the unknown. The overwhelm-
ing sense of responsibility for everything around him defined
his sense of self. He found himself constantly looking for escapes.

It is not unusual for men in power to choose extramarital
affairs to show their vulnerability. With this supposed "safe person," the male can often display emotional connection in a way
he cannot with his public partner. And so, such emotional connection is often weighed in an inappropriate manner. When he
is with his partner after being with his "safe female," internal
withdrawal is his modus operandi. This withdrawal then leads
to an increased urge to disclose with the "safe female," thus
creating a vicious cycle. If the male does not allow himself to
pursue emotional connection with his partner, he cannot truly
know whether or not it is possible. Camouflage becomes a way
of life.

As women continue to rise in the traditional male hierar-
chy, they often do so with a mask. Culturally, women have been
conditioned to accept shame more readily, but most know that
it is not synonymous with power. Always on guard, and shielding themselves from the possibilities of rejection, women become less in touch with their emotional selves. There are exceptions in both male and female leadership roles; however, the
trend strongly favors the "masked" leadership.

Guilt: The Gift That Keeps On Giving

I often make the comment that "guilt is the gift that keeps
on giving" when clients are struggling with this obstacle. I first

heard this statement from my pastor as he was describing his own personal dilemma with the use of time. Where does all this guilt start? When does guilt become excessive? Is guilt ever a part of a healthy relationship?

Clients frequently say: *I have felt guilty all my life, guilt is about making it right, guilt is the should and ought of life, I was guilty coming out of the womb because my mother said I was a terrible delivery, and I could make this decision about my relationship this moment if I didn't have to feel so guilty.* In the skirmish to reach a decision about *Do I Stay or Do I Go?*, guilt can be ever present. The guilt clients speak of usually goes back to an earlier time before the current relationship dilemma.

Religion was one of my undergraduate majors. I remember one religion professor who had a gift for engaging the young naïve student. To this day, I can see him writing on the blackboard the word sin with a little s, a very large I, and a little n. The message was that whenever the I was engaged and placed above anything else, sin was involved. Guilt, of course, was the result of sin. Interestingly, as my religious curiosity grew, and I began questioning more and more, this particular professor became unhappy with me. He wanted his students, me included, to spout back what he said as he said it. Thankfully, there were other religion professors who encouraged my critical thinking. But whenever I think of guilt, I remember him standing at the blackboard in a very animated way talking about **s** I **n**.

Most of us have early memories about how guilt was used in our families. Peter, in the vignette *I Thought She Would Grow Out Of It*, expresses his responsibility to his family in a heavy guilt-ridden way as though he had a ball and chain around his neck. Now Peter is from an alcoholic family where his role was the caretaker. If Peter is not taking care of others, he feels guilty. He *should* take care of his childhood family, and now that same *should* feeling is present in his marriage.

In the vignette *I've Been Betrayed*, Frank's wife, Faye, states that she can't have Frank physically move out of the house because of the guilt. Faye had the affair, and she feels guilty because of the choice that she made. The crisis of the affair brought Frank, and then Faye, to counseling. As they examined their issues, Faye was able to better understand the behavior that led to the feeling of guilt. Confronting the alternatives in the marriage honestly led to a give and take between Faye and Frank as Frank shared childhood hurts for the first time with Faye.

With the issue of guilt it is important to do the following:

1. Identify which definition of guilt is more typical for you: remorseful awareness of having done something wrong; self-reproach for supposed inadequacy or wrongdoing; the fact of being responsible for some breach of conduct.

2. Identify early childhood memories of how guilt was played out in your childhood family.

3. Identify similarities between the theme of guilt in your childhood family, and in your current relationship.

4. Identify what guilt is acceptable for you now. Let go of the excessive guilt.

Forgiveness

Guilt is not the only issue associated with religious teachings. "Turning the other cheek" and "making amends" and "repairing relationships" is a part of rich religious history. Like many clients, Kathy yelled out her frustration with this forgiveness problem: "forgiving does not equal no consequences," "forgiving does not mean I wipe the slate clean," "saying I'm sorry does not mean you are forgiven," "to forgive and forget is not human." When there is an affair, an ugly secret, or even an unresolved hot issue, feelings are raw and exposed.

And yet, love and respect and forgiveness are all about human connection. The journey to get or return to human connection is a complicated passage. Whenever I am dealing with the subject of forgiveness in relationships, I remember Carl Jung's words about marriage being the most complex of all human relationships. Paths from betrayal, harsh words, verbal abuse, dishonesty, horrendous behavior, and deceit back to the relationship are difficult.

Forgiveness of Self

Sometimes, forgiveness needs to start with forgiveness of self. In the vignette *CYBERSEX*, Adam shared that he believed their sexual problems could be traced back to an abortion early in their relationship. Ellen disclosed much of her unhappiness, but she had not mentioned the abortion. I will now share what happened during individual sessions.

"Adam said he told you about the abortion," Ellen began. "I guess I need to talk about it."

"When you are ready, let me know," I responded.

"It's funny. I will be driving our daughter to practice, and I see a bumper sticker saying 'abortion is murder'. I cringe throughout the day. And inside myself, I say it was murder. My spirit is broken, and I feel I don't deserve to heal. A voice inside me says I don't deserve what I want," Ellen said, the pain evident in her voice.

I remained quiet, allowing Ellen to continue at her own pace.

After a few minutes of silence, Ellen continued, "I remember every single thing about that day, every sound, every smell." She sighed heavily.

Continuing the sigh that was almost a moan, she said, " How do you forgive carelessness that results in murder? I don't deserve to be happy. I feel judged by the bumper stickers, the church, people's opinions, and my parents. It hasn't done any good not thinking about it."

"Have you felt this way since the abortion?" I asked.

"No," Ellen replied. "I was footloose and fancy-free right afterwards. I seldom thought about it. I got married, and it changed a little, then. When I became pregnant, the thoughts were relentless and unbearable. I resent what I did; I resent Adam for encouraging it. The "committee" thought it was the best decision. I beg to differ. I was in no emotional state to be making such a monumental decision that I would carry with me for life."

"Choices sometimes seem unfair," I added. "When you became pregnant, the meaning of what happened earlier became clearer. Did you ever name your unborn baby?"

A look of utter shock came over Ellen as I asked the question. Very softly, she moaned, "I always knew she was a girl, and I couldn't give my first child her name. She is 'Trish'."

The flood of tears commenced. When there was finally a break, I said, "Have you considered a service, a ritual where Trish forgives you, and petitions you to let her go in peace?"

"Forgiveness," she gingerly entreated, "is really between Trish and me, isn't it?"

I nodded.

In subsequent sessions, Ellen continued her work and devised a service that was right for her. Through the open acknowledgment of Trish's being, Ellen was able to move forward with forgiving herself as Trish forgave her.

In the first individual session I had with Ellen, before I knew about the abortion, she said the following: "I know that I am bright, but I cannot understand why I nibble around this problem like a timid mouse, never getting to the bottom of it. I want to be a lion for my needs, aggressively and ferociously taking what I need. I feel frozen. What is wrong with me?"

These words, this passage, takes on new meaning after the disclosure of the abortion. This is an example of forgiving self as an initial step to forgiving relationship deeds.

Forgiving the Partner

What occurs when a partner has been forgiven for deeds such as an affair and the deceit and betrayal that goes along with the affair, and then repeats the offensive behavior again, and sometimes again? Husbands in certain professions have ample opportunity to continually engage in such self-destructive and relationship destructive acts. Women in the workplace tend to use that venue for their extramarital liaisons.

Is forgiveness wiping the slate clean each time? Bill offered the following metaphor for this relationship pickle. Two countries border each other. Both have relatively passive, respectful leaders, and the people are happy. Then the leadership changes, and one country restricts trade, and begins encroaching on its neighbor's territory. If the neighbor doesn't stand up for itself, the one country continues to invade. If the neighbor asserts its boundaries and sets limits, tension between the two countries increases. Negotiations take place until boundaries are clearly established; and subsequently, tensions decrease. Or, if negotiations fail, war is declared.

Bill's wife has had several affairs. Bill is a passive, easygoing guy who has not laid down the law about where the "crossover" line is for him with regard to his wife's behavior. Tonya, his wife, does not respect him, and his passivity triggers greater aggressiveness in her.

As Bill bit the bullet and stood up for himself, the dynamics changed. He separated, and as a result, Tonya "requested," not demanded marriage counseling. Bill told her forgiveness did not mean wiping the slate clean. Her repeated affairs were no longer acceptable to him. He expressed his intense feelings of bitterness, anger, and resentment. The wounds from these agonizing feelings were too raw for him to be able to offer forgiveness at this time.

For Bill, his emotions were in the war zone. The red hot pain was ruling his life. This happens in many relationships when there has been betrayal and verbal abuse. As the pain slowly subsided, it became possible for Bill to lessen the "punishment" meted out to Tonya. As long as the pain was consuming his every movement, forgiveness was not in the cards for Bill. With time and ventilation, Bill may approach the point when he lets go of the intense negative feelings. Bill does not know if he reaches the point of forgiveness, if that can equal restoration of the relationship.

Jay was caught in an affair by his wife whom he described as not even a geek. Jay elaborabated, "I see that you are on a (computer) network here at your office. Let's say you are on a network consisting of two computers. You and the other computer are communicating with each other over the network. These computers are capable of using several protocols or languages to "talk" to each other. Obviously, they need to be using the same protocol when communicating to accurately exchange information."

"You and your wife were using different protocols to communicate?" I queried.

"Yes," he said, "but it was more than that. You see, the connection also needs to be free from interference to prevent the information from coming across with pieces missing or garbled, or corrupt as we say."

"So, let's see if I have this right," I commented, "the communication between you and your wife was impacted by some outside interference."

"Well," Jay continued, " if the computers are coordinating tasks, lack of information prevents the tasks from being completed. Or the results are not an accurate reflection of all the possible information."

"Help me, Jay," I responded. "I still do not yet know what garbled the communication between the two computers; i.e., you and your wife.

"OK," he slowly said, "another computer came on the scene that could talk in my protocol."

"Yes, you mentioned an affair," I acknowledged, "but something behind the GUI, which would be the real workings taking place behind the scenes is a must for the programmer to understand."

"Yes, that's right," he said with a pleased smile. "Her parents dominate her, and us, and I can't take it anymore."

This exchange led to further discussion about Jay's situation. He had not communicated directly with his wife about his feelings about her parents' involvement in their lives. Instead, he had opted to communicate with another female. This had been the only time Jay had "cheated," as he said, and part of him wanted to be found out. Forgiveness in this marriage may be more possible than in Bill's marriage.

When two people end their relationship, forgiveness can be part of the healing process. Forgiving the injustices of the past is possible when the raw wounds of the hurts and injuries are allowed to heal, and life is permitted to go on rather than remain stuck in the past. I hear comments like "you are going to pay for this, for a long, long time," "you will never be forgiven," "I will hate you until the day I die." While such comments are understandable in the aftermath of confessions and knowledge of betrayals, the person who suffers the most is the one who hangs onto the persecuted victim theme. As hard as that is to hear, movement out of the stuckness can only begin when one can let go of the hatred and resentments. Such progress does not occur immediately; it takes time as wounds are slowly healed.

Points to remember about forgiveness:

1. Forgiveness takes place within you; it is not bestowed upon you.

2. The acts and injuries inflicted upon you represent only a part of you; they do not reflect all of you.

3. Letting go of the strong, strong negative emotions is part of the realization that what happened to you in the past does not have to happen to you in the future.

4. As you let go of the desire to punish, the path to human connection becomes possible again, if not with the person who hurt you, with others.

5. Forgiveness can take place without restoration of the relationship.

Responsibility, Accountability, and Self-Esteem

The ability to forgive, the ability to be responsible, and the ability to be accountable for one's choices are all related to the level of personal self-esteem. As noted throughout this book, professional and personal self-esteem are not necessarily synonymous. Susan in the vignette, *I Should Be Happy, But...* saw herself at work as a leader capable of making tough decisions and living with the consequences. On the personal level, she acquiesced frequently, without even knowing why on a conscious level. Through her therapy she learned that she feared "hurting" her husband; and therefore, always walked on eggshells. I regularly hear one partner not being honest with self or the partner out of fear of, or the excuse of, "hurting" the partner. This too, is a choice with consequences.

Disclosure Dilemma

The excuse of "not hurting the partner" usually refers to keeping a secret whether it be an affair or something else. Can you be responsible and accountable as long as you are shielding another from the truth? Mental health professionals vary in their position on whether or not the truth needs to be exposed. I treat many individuals who have told me about an affair, and then want to bring their partner in for joint counseling. Or the couple may have started out in joint counseling, and then for one reason or another I see one or both individually, and the secret of an affair comes out.

What do I do in such situations? Recently, I had in treatment a man and his wife whom I had seen a number of years ago. Previously, at the end of the first treatment span, the man had attended some individual therapy sessions. I had suspected an affair at that time, but such information was not shared. When they returned for treatment, the man attended one session alone when the wife was out of town. At this time, I learned that he was still involved in an ongoing affair. He couldn't bring himself to "hurt" his wife. Interestingly, his definition of hurt did not include what he could not give his wife in their relationship. What this gentleman wanted from me, although he did not directly state it as such, was for me to tell his wife about the affair. My response on this matter is loud and clear. I choose not to take responsibility for conveying this news. My experience tells me that the other partner usually already knows at some level, but is not ready to acknowledge the reality. I encouraged the man in this instance to take responsibility for the affair by sharing the news with his partner.

Does this really happen in the course of the counseling? Most of the time, yes, but sometimes, no. When the partner engaged in the affair is getting ready to leave the marriage, the news usually comes out since it will in the end, anyway. There also occurs some safety-netting; i.e., sharing the secret in the presence of the therapist/counselor sends the message that there is someone else here to help pick up the pieces.

When the person having the affair intends to remain in the marriage, the secret may not be shared. I have seen at times overt collusion on the part of both parties not to acknowledge what both know at some level has occurred. I have even offered opportunities to both partners when such news could come out in the course of therapy. I respect the decision, whichever way it goes. Above all, I recognize that the choice is not mine to

make, but rather the choice must be made by the clients I treat.
That is my gift to them. I will help them leave no stone unturned
in their journey to identify the dilemma, the choices, and the
questions relevant to their predicament. But the choice remains
theirs alone.

Sabotaging Self-Esteem

Are you sabotaging your personal self-esteem? How do you
define yourself personally? Stephanie in the vignette, *And Then
the Kids Came*, lost her sense of professional identity after having two children. This loss affected her personal self-esteem drastically. Ted in the vignette, *The Little Red Porsche – My River of
Dreams*, no longer has the mistress of work as his company continues to downsize. When professional identity is impacted for
whatever reason, personal identity needs to be fulfilling. Sometimes it is only when the professional identity is in danger from
some outside force, that attention is brought full circle to what
makes up the personal side of things, including the *relationship*.

Defining self only through work or professional interests is
limiting to the relationship. The camouflage can too easily be
stripped away in today's world. Even with a planned event like
pregnancy, the calculated loss of professional identity takes an
often unexpected toll. The *losses* and *gains* are not what was
expected, and strong feelings emerge. With companies
downsizing, and the work force advocating younger and younger
personnel, adults in midlife face special challenges.

Typecasting

Typecasting one's identity as professional only is especially
limiting in today's world. I notice that younger people are not
willing to do that as easily as the older generation.

However, typecasting does not only occur professionally; it
also is very much present personally. Examples of personal type-

casting might include: I am fat; I am a slob; I am responsible for everything and everyone around me; I must be perfect; I base everything I do dependent upon another's approval; and I always hear the negative voices repeating over and over... Such mutterings indicate low personal self-esteem.

Identification of the reasons for low personal self-esteem is very important in relationship therapy. Is the low personal self-esteem due to relationship issues, a crisis, a transition, or are there personal demons that must be examined? Dean, in the vignette, *Those "Highs and Lows,"* comes to treatment to try and understand manic depression in its various forms, both for himself and his partner. He also must explore his own childhood family as he acknowledges the hypomanic nature of his father's personality.

Always feeling over- or under- responsible in one's personal life interferes with the ability to have a fulfilling personal life. Peter in the vignette, *I Thought She Would Grow Out Of It*, took on the over-responsible role in his marriage. The vignette illustrates that other choices were possible. Identification of what those other choices were helped Peter.

When personal self-esteem is low, there is a tendency to blame self or others. Neither is a productive stance. Such a stance does not promote accountability for one's behavior or actions. I have worked for some time with a woman who is struggling with when to leave her relationship. She has made the decision that she believes she must do so; nonetheless, she blames her husband with all his crises, she blames having children to take into account, and she blames her church for making her feel guilty if she leaves.

As this woman continues her struggle, she is ever so slowly trying to become more honest with herself about how to be accountable for her choice. It is not that the other factors are not present; it is just that until she can be accountable within herself, she is unable to take the decisive action of leaving.

As an example, I asked her to tell me how she could make a responsible and accountable decision with regard to her child. What did that mean, she wanted to know. I responded that she would need to determine where she and the child would be residing (I already knew that she would have to have custody of her child, or she would not leave), what the transportation plans would be for getting her child to and from events, and what the economic downside would be. While this sounds obvious and simple, when a person is hurting a great deal, it is helpful to put predicaments in concrete terms. This implies that one can do something about a difficult issue.

Many factors can play into the ambivalence about leaving. One of the most perplexing examples I have worked with involves a young woman I will call Danielle. Professionally, she has achieved at an extraordinarily high level. Her achievements surpass those of her husband. She was diagnosed with breast cancer a few years ago. Needless to say, this event changed her life in many ways. She was and is a fighter, and maintained her professional job throughout her illness. Her research of the medical profession about her treatment was one of the most thorough I have ever seen.

The illness affects her still, but not very much on the outside. She struggled with whether or not to leave her relationship with her husband even before the diagnosis of breast cancer. Her husband, according to her, is a complicated, intense man. She often asks "why can't he be an alcoholic or a domestic abuser?" At this point, I joke with her and say, "because that would make your decision easy."

Danielle endeavors to figure out her personal demons that keep her in the never, never land of indecision. She also is continuing to work individually on her fear of change, her fear of loss of control over her health, and the fear of the unknown. Her family background has themes which play into her ambivalence. Dealing with accountability also requires Danielle to seriously consider marital therapy. I long ago gave her referral names, but her husband was unwilling, and then she was un-willing. I have had a long relationship with her, and therefore, recommended that they see someone else for ongoing marital therapy. She is an example of a woman with very high professional self-esteem who battles low personal self-esteem due to many factors.

Those Internal Resources

Being responsible and accountable for one's choice often calls for tapping into one's internal resources. This entire book is a prod to stimulate *your internal resources* as you struggle with your own dilemma.

Write your own vignette that describes your struggle. If you can plug in some of the exercises in this book that may fit your dilemma, do so. If none fit your situation, take your cue from some of the ones in this book, and design your own. Go back to the personal worksheet and review what you wrote. Do the worksheet again in a week, in a month, and see if anything has changed.

Know what the obstacles to your decision- making are. Alone time to think and be with yourself has to be a priority. Our lives today do not lend themselves to such time. This means you must make time, even if it is when you are in the bathroom, in a meeting when you can zone out, or any other place you can create in your mind.

Trusting your decision means you have left no stone unturned in this journey. It means further that you can state with clarity whether this quandary is due to a relationship is-sue, a developmental crisis typical in this stage of the relation-ship, a transition time for one or both partners, personal child-hood family issues that have resurfaced at this particular time, or individual personal demons like illness, depression, or per-sonality disorders. Such demons may also be bourne by the part-ner.

I use the word "demon" in the sense that it is a persistently, tormenting force. Events like illness and depression are persistent, and can also be tormenting for individuals. Giving demons like these their due is part of the process in struggling with the accountability and responsibility factor.

When Is It About Suffering and When Is It About Being Right?

Living in the Tobacco Belt and the Bible Belt, I am never bored by what comes out of the media about this area. I am a native so my perspective is reflective of my cultural tradition in that I can usually see the sides *not* portrayed in the media. I had to laugh at my reaction to the recent quote by Paige Patterson, leader of the Southern Baptist Convention. He is president of Wake Forest Seminary, formerly a moderate theological institution, now extremely conservative. The seminary is located in Wake Forest, NC, next-door to Raleigh, the city in which I live. His quote, widely disseminated and ridiculed in the media was that "women graciously submit to their husbands." I was working on the section about suffering and being right when the quote appeared, and all I could think about was how perfect his timing was. After all, if he had to be *right*, then his woman could sweetly *suffer*, right?! P.S. The wife has a Ph.D. in theology, too. That point is not picked up very often in the media, though.

Seriously, suffering is oftentimes done in the name of holding on to a past resentment or grudge. "Being miserable makes me right" has been said to me more than once during the course of therapy. Sadly, the person being hurt the most is the one holding onto the grudge.

Suffering means there is pain and hurt and frequently disguised resentment. Letting go of the pain, hurt, and resentment is not easy, and I do not know of a quick fix. But such festering is detrimental to one's health. The choice can be made not to suffer on an ongoing basis. Review the points at the end of the forgiveness section.

Examine the "need to be right." What is that really about? Ending the suffering is about not being right? Logically, it does not make sense. Emotionally, the matter is another animal. Injustices cause all kinds of reactions. Initial emotional reactions do not have to be the ongoing reactions. Life is about change, movement, and hopefully, moving ahead rather than living in the past.

The Role of Acceptance

"Acceptance equals sainthood, and I will not be a saint!" exclaimed one of my clients. When I think of acceptance, I do not equate it with sainthood. Martydom is not something I encourage. On the other hand, I believe it is healthy to reach a point of acceptance of the decision one is ready to make at the moment. For example, if you have read this book and done the exercises, you may be on a journey to resolving your dilemma with regard to the question, *"Do I Stay or Do I Go?"*

At some point along that journey you are ready to make a decision based upon the roads you have traveled in your quest. The decision may be to leave the relationship, to recommit to the relationship, to review staying on a regular basis, to work on yourself while remaining in the relationship, etc. Identification of your specific dilemma, the choices, and the questions, enables you to thoughtfully and reflectively reach a conclusion that is not rash or impulsive. The idea is to reach a decision that your internal resources say is right for you at this time.

Allow the necessary reflective time in this struggle. Doing so is part of taking care of yourself. The job of the reflection is to get the mind moving in a problem-solving fashion. Learning to trust your internal resources develops both professional and personal self-esteem.

May both your professional and personal self-esteem continue to grow.

eleven

resources

Choosing a Therapist

Talk to someone who can help is the slogan for the American Psychological Association's national public education campaign to inform the public about how to seek help for emotional problems. I am the media chair on a state-wide public relations campaign of the North Carolina Psychological Foundation to promote this educational message. As a psychologist, marital and family therapist, and clinical social worker, I know there are professionals who can help.

There are many helpful guides published by professional associations about how to choose a therapist. I will be giving a list of some of the professional associations in this chapter.

Rule #1 is to find someone with whom you can connect who has appropriate credentials. Notice I did not say comfortable because therapy is not necessarily comfortable.

Rule #2 is to ask questions. A competent professional will be happy to share information with you.

Rule #3 is if you not believe you can work with the professional after 3 sessions, ask for a referral to someone else. If you do not feel comfortable doing that, ask friends or health professionals or call the local chapters of the organizations I will list below:

American Association for Marriage and Family Therapy (AAMFT)
Telephone: 202-452-0109
E-mail: central@aamft.org
web site:www.aamft.org
Document on request (toll-free fax service): 1 (888) AAMFT 99
1133 15th St., NW
Suite 300
Washington, DC 20005

American Psychological Association
750 First Street, NE
Washington, DC 20002-4242
(202) 336-5913
(202) 336-5797 Fax
APA's Help Center on World Wide Web: http://helping.apa.org
New info brochure free of charge by calling 1 (800) 964-2000 or
Internet site

National Association of Social Workers
750 First Street, NE
Suite 700
Washington, DC 20002-4241
1 (800) 638-8799
centennial@naswdc.org

Other Helpful Resources

National Depressive and Manic-Depressive Association (National
DMDA)
1 (800) 826-3632
web site: www.ndmda.org
730 North Franklin St.
Suite 501
Chicago, IL 60610-3526

National Mental Health Association
(703) 684-7722
Information Line: (800) 969-NMHA
e-mail: nmhainfo@aol.com
web site: www.nmha.org
1021 Prince Street
Alexandria, VA 22314

Stepfamily Association of America
650 J. Street, Suite 205
Lincoln, NE 68508
(800) 735-0329
(402) 477-7837
http://www.stepfam.org

notes

Introduction

Page xiv
For a thorough discussion of emotions from different theoretical perspectives, see S. Johnson and L. Greenberg, (eds.), *The Heart of the Matter: Perspectives on Emotions in Marital Therapy* (New York: Brunner/Mazel, 1994).

Chapter One

Page 7
M. Polster, **Eve's Daughters: The Forbidden Heroism of Women** (San Francisco: Jossey-Bass Publishers, 1992), p. xvi.

Page 11
The movie, *The Joy Luck Club* is adapted from Amy Tan's book, *The Joy Luck Club* (New York: G. P. Putnam's Sons, 1989).

L. Rubin, *Intimate Strangers* (New York: Harper & Row, 1983), p. 3.

Chapter Two

Page 23
G. Levinger, "A Social –Psychological Perspective on Marital Dissolution" in G. Levinger and O. Moles (eds.) *Divorce and Separation: Context, Causes, and Consequences* (New York: Basic Books, 1979), p. 58.

Recommended reading on the topic of alternatives to the marital status quo:

G. Levinger, "Marital Cohesiveness and Dissolution: An Integrative Review" *Journal of Marriage and the Family,* 1965, 27, 19-28.

G. Spanier and R. Margolin, "Marital separation and extramarital sexual behavior" *Journal of Sex Research,* 1983, 19, 23-48.

T. McGinnis, *More Than Just a Friend: The Joys and Disappointments of Extramarital Affairs* (Englewood Cliffs, New Jersey: Prentice-Hall, 1981).

Page 25
D. Occhetti, *Marital Options and Possibilities Survey: A Preliminary analysis.* Unpublished raw data (Santa Barbara, CA: The Fielding Institute, 1986).

D. Occhetti, *Marital Satisfaction, Gender, and Children: The Perceived Attractiveness of Alternatives to the Marital Status Quo.* Doctoral Dissertation (Santa Barbara, CA: The Fielding Institute, 1988).

For a further examination of the literature on the topic of attractiveness of the alternatives and the decision to divorce, please refer to:

R. Green and M. Sporakowski, "The Dynamics of Divorce: Marital Quality, Alternative Attractions and External Pressures" *Journal of Divorce,* 1983, 7, 77-78.

R. Carson, *Interaction Concepts of Personality* (Chicago:Aldine, 1969).

M. Kalb, "The conception of the alternative and the decision to divorce" *American Journal of Psychotherapy,* 1983, 27 (3), 346-356.

V. Pestrak, D. Martin, and M. Martin, "Extramarital sex: An Examination of the Literature" *International Journal of Family Therapy,* 1985, 7, 107-115.

Page 34
Recommended reading on the subject of affairs:

F. Pittman, *Private Lies: Infidelity and the Betrayal of Intimacy* (New York: W.W. Norton & Co., 1989).

R. Brzeczek, E. Brzeczek, and S. DeVito, *Addicted to Adultery* (New York: Bantam Books, 1989)

E. Brown, *Patterns of Infidelity and Their Treatment* (New York: Brunner/Mazel, 1991).

Chapter Three

This chapter is about closeness and distance in relationships. Recommended reading includes:

H. Lerner, *The Dance of Anger* (New York: Harper & Row, 1985).

H. Lerner, *The Dance of Intimacy* (New York: Harper & Row, 1989).

Communication and sexuality are two other themes in this chapter. The author with her husband has taught the Minnesota Couple Communication Course for twenty years. Both are certified instructors. The author did postgraduate study at the Masters and Johnson Institute in St. Louis, Missouri and discussed the pleasuring techniques personally with Masters and Johnson. References on these topics include:

S. Miller, P. Miller, E. Nunnally, and D. Wackman, *Talking and Listening Together* (Littleton, Colorado: Interpersonal Communication Programs, Inc., 1991).

W. Masters and V. Johnson, *Human Sexual Inadequacy* (Boston: Little, Brown, & Co., 1970).

J. LoPiccolo and L. LoPiccolo, (Eds.) *Handbook of Sex Therapy* (New York: Plenum Press, 1978).

C. Botwin, *Is There Sex After Marriage?* (Boston: Little, Brown, & Co., 1985).

Chapter Four

Page 64
D. Keirsey and M. Bates, *Please Understand Me*, (Del Mar, CA: Prometheus Nemesis Book Co., 1984) pp.25-26.

Two other helpful references for type talk include:

J. Campbell (Ed.), *The Portable Jung* (New York: Penguin Books, 1971).

O Kroeger and J. Thuesen, *Type Talk* (New York: Dell Publishing, 1988).

Chapter Five

The theme of this chapter on mid-life crisis fits right in with B. Joel's song, River of Dreams, 1993. Even Jung's work is applicable to this theme in J. Campbell, op. cit., 1971.

Page 73
Joel, op.cit., 1993.

Page 76
Joel, op.cit., 1993.

Page 82
The author chose to add the cautionary note due to the controversy over false vs. true memories and the ensuing legal battles. The remainder of the chapter deals with authentic connection, forgiveness, and healing. Helpful references for this include: A. Occhetti and D. Occhetti, "Group Therapy with Married Couples", *Social Casework*, February, 1981.

J. Wallerstein with S. Blakeslee, *Second Chances: Men, Women and Children a Decade after Divorce* (New York: Ticknor and Fields, 1989).

L. Smedes, *Forgive and Forget: Healing the Hurts We Don't Deserve* (New York: Pocket Books, 1986).

L. Smedes, *Art of Forgiving: When You Need to Forgive and Don't Know How* (New York: Ballantine Books, 1996).

Chapter Six

Page 85
The following article gives specific information about how our practice has evaluated priests for the Catholic priesthood for 10 years:

D. Kravetz, A. Occhetti, D. Occhetti, and C. Zinni "Team Approach to a Comprehensive Evaluation of Priest and Religious Candidates" Horizon, *Journal of the National Religious Vocation Conference*, Summer, 1995, vol. 20, Number 4.

Page 94
E. Friedman, *Friedman's Fables* (New York: The Guilford Press, 1990) pp 113-115.

Page 96
J. Woitiz, *Struggle for Intimacy* (Pompano Beach, Florida: Health Communications, Inc., 1985).

Other helpful references for adult children of alcoholics include:

J. Woitiz, *Adult Children of Alcoholics* (Pompano Beach, Florida: Health Communications, Inc., 1983).

C. Black, *It Will Never Happen to Me* (New York: Ballantine Books, 1987).

C. Black and L. Drozel, *The Missing Piece: Solving the Puzzle of Self* (New York: Ballentine Books, 1995).
Page 96 E. Friedman, op.cit., p.17.

Chapter Seven

Page 103
See chapter on "Resources" for address and phone number of the Stepfamily Association of America.

Page 121
A long-term stepfamily research study has been done by J. Bray at the Family Medicine/Baylor College of Medicine. In his book, Bray also discusses earlier research. J. Bray and J. Kelly, *Stepfamilies: Love, Marriage and Parenting in the First Decade* (New York: Broadway Books, 1998). Also, check out the entire issue of *The Family Therapy Networker*, May/June 1994, on the Divorce Debate. Other helpful resources on stepfamilies include:

Wallerstein with Blakeslee, op. cit., 1989.

J. Gottman, *Why Marriages Succeed or Fail* (New York: Simon and Schuster, 1994).

E. Visher and J. Visher, *How to Win as a Stepfamily, Second Edition* (New York: Brunner/Mazel, 1991).

H. Coale, *All About Families the Second Time Around* (Atlanta, Ga.: Peachtree Publishing, 1980).

Chapter Eight

This chapter addresses the mood disorders. The following references are recommended for further reading:

W. Styron, *Darkness Visible* (New York: Random House, 1990).

T. Real, *I Don't Want to Talk About It* (New York: Scribner, 1997).

R. Fieve, *Moodswing* (New York: Bantam Books, 1975).

P. Whybrow, *A Mood Apart: Depression, Mania, and Other Afflictions of the Self* (New York: Basic Books, 1997).

K. Jamison, *An Unquiet Mind* (New York: Vintage Books, 1995).

A. Beck, *Love is Never Enough* (New York: Harper & Row, 1988).

D. Burns, *Feeling Good: The New Mood Therapy* (New York: William Morrow & Company, 1980).

D. Burns, *Feeling Good Handbook* (New York: William Morrow & Company, 1989).

Chapter Nine

Page 136
J. Wallerstein and S. Blakeslee, The Good Marriage (Boston: Houghton Mifflin Company, 1995), pp. 27-28.

Chapter Ten

The inertia themes of misplaced hope, wearing a mask, guilt, forgiveness, and suffering can be explored in more detail in the following references:

H. Kushner, *How Good Do We Have to Be?* (Boston: Little, Brown, and Company, 1996).

L. Smedes, *A Pretty Good Person* (New York: Harper & Row, 1990).

Smedes, op. cit., 1986.

Smedes, op.cit., 1996.

J. Tatelbaum, *You Don't Have to Suffer* (New York: Harper & Row, 1989).

Page 162
How the South and the Bible Belt are portrayed in the media is always fascinating to follow. The conservative Southern Baptist Convention fueled this discussion from the "Southern Baptist Convention's Statement of Faith", The Raleigh News and Observer, July 13, 1998.

DREAMS and SCHEMES

STEVE LOPEZ

DREAMS AND SCHEMES

(My Decade of Fun in the Sun)

Camino Books, Inc. | Philadelphia

Library of Congress Cataloging-in-Publication Data

Lopez, Steve.
Dreams and schemes: my decade of fun in the sun / Steve Lopez.
p. cm.
Author's columns originally published in the Los Angeles Times.
ISBN 978-1-933822-31-0
1. Los Angeles (Calif.)—Politics and government. 2. Los Angeles
(Calif.)—Social life and customs. 3. Los Angeles (Calif.)—Social
conditions. 4. Los Angeles (Calif.)—Biography. 5. Politicians—
California—Biography. 6. Celebrities—California—Biography.
7. Lopez, Steve. I. Los Angeles Times. II. Title.

F869.L845L67   2010
979.4'94—dc22   2010035571

INTERIOR DESIGN: KATE NICHOLS
INTERIOR PHOTOGRAPH © ZEPHERWIND | DREAMSTIME.COM

This book is available at a special discount on bulk purchases
for promotional, business, and educational use.

Publisher
Camino Books, Inc.
P.O. Box 59026
Philadelphia, PA 19102

www.caminobooks.com

33090014664884

This book is dedicated to everyone with a paid subscription to the *Los Angeles Times*, and to those who dig three quarters out of their pockets now and again.

We appreciate your support.

Contents

Politics as Usual

Why Live Anywhere Else?

Keep Them in Your Prayers

Around the Corner and the World

Grace Notes

Introduction

Coming up on 10 years of writing columns for the *Los Angeles Times*, the most common question I get from readers is: Where do you get your ideas?

Come on, folks. This is Southern California. Open your eyes.

People from around the world risk everything to get to this chaotic, cracked, tragically spectacular tract of overpriced real estate. Every strain of dreamer and schemer is here. We've got $50 million manses a short limo ride away from cardboard box colonies. Action heroes and billionaires run for office with neither a plan nor a clue. You can get a fake driver's license or a medical marijuana card faster than you can drive six blocks. We've got mudslides, the Minutemen, the marine layer. Yes, even the air is a column.

Thank you, Arnold and Antonio. And thank you, Cardinal Mahony, for reserving a crypt for me at the Rog Mahal.

Thank you, thank you, thank you, Los Angeles, for giving it up week after week after week. There's drama in each day, a story on every block.

A columnist's dream.

I have the sense, nearly 10 years and more than 1,300 columns into the courtship, that Los Angeles remains as gloriously indefinable and mysterious as ever, with the most revealing stories still hidden out there somewhere between mountain and sea, waiting to be discovered. If you stumble upon one of them, call or e-mail me, will you? I can always use the help, because no columnist works alone.

The most consistent support, feedback and guidance have always come from my wife, Alison. Here at the *L.A.Times*, I've been lucky to team with two of the most giving and talented editors in the newspaper business— Sue Horton and Sam Enriquez. I've been blessed, as well, to learn from, get help from, and be part of a team that has included hundreds of the best journalists in the country. Many times my column idea isn't my own at all, but an outgrowth of the relentless, superlative, keep 'em honest reporting of my cohorts, and the *Times* copy desk has saved me hundreds of times on deadline and produced a raft of terrific headlines. Our ranks have been reduced by global forces that are blowing through the entire news industry, but those who remain at their battle stations are as committed as ever, living by the code that we keep shooting until we run out of bullets.

Where do I get my ideas?

I wake up and roll out of bed and bump into column ideas everywhere. But many of the best ones have come from you. The column would have died long ago if it hadn't been nurtured by readers from Riverside to Redondo and Santa Barbara to San Diego. This relationship is for me a privilege, an honor, and the best part of the job. Thank you for sharing your triumphs, your victories and your unwavering contempt for the phonies and rogues. With your support, I'll continue to celebrate the good guys, backhand the bums, and take a light to the back of the cave.

THE HIGH AND MIGHTY

Playing Footsie with a
Dragon's Basic Instinct

(June 13, 2001)

All I have to say is this: If my wife were to tell me that as a special Father's Day gift, she was going to put me into a cage with a seven-foot lizard, I would start sleeping with one eye open. I might check in with the life insurance agent, too, and see if there were any recent changes in the policy.

You know the story.

San Francisco newspaper editor Phil Bronstein came to Los Angeles with his wife, actress Sharon Stone, and special arrangements were made for him to have some private time with the Komodo dragon at the L.A. Zoo. Bronstein, as I understand it, was instructed by the zookeeper to remove his white sneakers before entering the dragon's domain, so the beast would not mistake his feet for rats.

Now look. I have worked for seven newspapers and a lot of editors, and none of them came within eight yards of normal. But if you had scraped them off a barroom floor at two a.m. and asked if they'd enter a cage with an animal that might mistake their feet for rats, they would have had the sense to stand clear. They don't even like contact with readers, let alone exotic animals.

Have you seen pictures of this Komodo dragon, by the way? Its head looks like a boulder with eyeballs. The dinosaurs in *Jurassic Park* looked friendlier, and they were eating SUVs. Bronstein apparently likes these things, though. Or at least Stone managed to convince him that he would.

"No, really honey. Just scratch him behind the ears and he'll roll over on his back."

So he goes in with the lizard while Stone watches from outside the cage. The same Sharon Stone who got rich and famous playing a woman suspected of whacking her lovers with an ice pick. Not to read into this. But Stone and Bronstein hadn't been married 10 minutes when, out of the blue, he develops a heart problem. And then, with a rebuilt ticker and no note from his cardiologist, she sends him into the cage with a dragon.

Basic Instinct II: Return of the Dragon Lady.

"Of course I loved my husband, detective. Why do you ask?"

And what does this dragon do upon realizing that a member of the media has dropped by unannounced? It goes for the newspaper editor like a shark after chum. It chomps down on his big toe with the jaws of life and won't let go.

Maybe the dragon has read *The Chronicle*. Maybe it knew that Bronstein and Stone hadn't paid admission to the zoo or made a donation either, as others in the privileged and pampered set have done before getting the royal treatment.

Bronstein, having married into show business, makes like Crocodile Dundee. He manages to free himself from the Komodo dragon and escape through a trapdoor, and they run him to the hospital for foot surgery.

Happy Father's Day.

All things considered, it could have been worse than a big toe. Joe Brown, a *Chronicle* spokesman, said Bronstein was in stable condition and was doing some work Tuesday from his hospital bed. My guess is that across the country, newsroom reporters are taking up collections to send their own editors to the L.A. Zoo. It's a shame that when he visited L.A. to tell us we could take our energy problem and drop dead, no one arranged for President Bush to get a special tour.

The dragon, by the way, is doing fine, not that anyone asked. Lora LaMarca, zoo spokeswoman, described a dragon that seemed to be quite pleased with itself. Maybe this is a north-south thing with the lizard. LaMarca confirmed the dragon never bit anyone from L.A. Next time the San Francisco Giants come down to play the Dodgers, someone ought to arrange for Barry Bonds to stop by the zoo.

LaMarca says the dragon that ate Phil Bronstein is now unavailable for private viewings, but that's a big mistake, if you ask me. This thing is world-famous now, and it could be worth a fortune. I'd bet the mortgage that people would pay for a chance to tempt fate. If you have faith and your heart is pure, He'll protect you in that cage, won't He?

Bronstein must not be a believer. Or maybe there's a cosmic force for universal justice, and it says that if you're going to win Sharon Stone as your wife, at some point you're going to be attacked by a seven-foot reptile. From one hack to another, Phil, if she starts hinting at something special for Christmas, run for the hills.

Talking Philosophy with a Billionaire
Over the Combo Plate

(June 18, 2001)

East we travel in chauffeur-driven BMW luxury, our chariot gliding under Beverly Hills palms that stand as erect as palace soldiers. Eli Broad, the baron of Los Angeles, is in the front passenger seat; I'm in the back. We are going to Los Tacos for lunch.

A column under my name suggested that Broad had violated the spirit of election law by pushing $100,000 through a back door and into the campaign of mayoral candidate Antonio Villaraigosa. I said in passing that unless Broad dines at Los Tacos on Santa Monica Boulevard just west of Fairfax, we probably would never break bread. A good sport, he. Broad responded with a letter inviting me to lunch at you know where.

Why Los Tacos? you ask. Because eight years ago, I knew a young lady who lived nearby. While courting, I got hooked on both the No. 3 Combination Platter and the young lady, not necessarily in that order, and even though I kept taking her there for dinner, she said yes when I asked her to marry me. Ever since, when I'm trying to impress someone, back to this shack I go. Eli Broad is an art collector, and I haven't even told him yet that he is about to see the finest on-velvet art collection in the Western Hemisphere.

Los Tacos sits snugly between a 7-Eleven and a laundromat. As James our driver spins us into the lot, it seems a safe bet that Broad will be the first billionaire to peruse the four-to-seven-dollar offerings (rice and beans included).

The retired philanthropist, who made his fortune building homes and managing retirement accounts, is natty in a navy suit, gold silk handkerchief triangulating up from his breast pocket. He is gabbing endlessly about his passionate interest in public education, biomedical research and the reinvention of downtown L.A. All of which I may write about one day. But this is "a tale of two cities." It's Howard Hughes walking into a chapter of *Tortilla Flats*. Do you want to hear about school district governance, or do you want to know how a billionaire eats his beans?

As we walk toward the restaurant, a solitary man eyeballs us as if we were landed aliens. He is in denim and leather and looks like someone you'd want on your side in a knife fight. I notice only the briefest hesitation in Broad's gait. On my recommendation, we go with the No. 3—the cheese enchilada platter. I offer to pay, because that's the polite thing to do, even though he invited me to lunch and is worth four billion dollars. And what does he do? He lets me pay. I know exactly what my father would say.

"That's why he's a billionaire."

So here we are with our enchiladas, and Broad, a trim white-haired gent with a tan the hue of Kiwi polish, says he wants a diet soda. In so many words, I remind him this isn't spa food, so why bother? In for a dime, in for a dollar.

"Should we go with something exotic?" he asks.

We sit now with our No. 3 platters and our Jarrito strawberry sodas the color of nothing natural. Laborers are in here, speaking in Spanish about the guy in the suit. Gays and hipsters quiz us silently, me and this billionaire drinking his strawberry soda and dreaming up a new world for all of them.

The tableau is rich and crazy and as vibrant as the painting that hangs on the wall over our table. A waterfall scene in colors the same as the Jarrito sodas. Broad once bought a two-and-a-half-million-dollar Roy Lichtenstein with an American Express card so he could earn interest until the bill came due, and also so he could get two and a half million frequent flier miles. To which my father would say again: "That's why he's a billionaire."

I ask Broad the collector and connoisseur what he thinks of this painting and the others, and he says: "You won't see them in any respectable museum."

He eats around the enchiladas. Rice first, then beans, ixnay on the salsa, and then he works on the enchiladas, lobbying the whole time in his disarmingly candid way.

He pushed that money to Villaraigosa because he thought Tony was a better proposition than Jim Hahn, and if the campaign laws are a mess, it's not his fault.

He helped invent sprawl with all those tract houses he built, but the zoning commissioners allowed it and people made lives in those homes, and he has neither apology nor regret. Remaking Grand Avenue into a pedestrian attraction is not penance, he says. It's just his next project.

I start to debate the logic. No downtown is real without people living there, so why doesn't the king of residential development get to work on that? But you can't knock Eli Broad off stride. He's a Lithuanian Ross Perot, and all you can do is admire that someone 68 years old, who could disappear to a perfect place, has ego and money enough to think he can fix this broken one.

"I'm a maniac," he says, Los Tacos enchilada cheese doing a bungee jump off his chin. "I'm a workaholic."

I get the point. But next time, he buys.

Broadway Bill Bratton

(October 6, 2002)

He speaks without commas and if I were going to tell you about
my first encounter with Los Angeles police-chief-in-waiting Bill Bratton,
I wouldn't even know where to begin because he talks so fast that even I
was out of breath and amazed at his ability to segue onto the subject of the
Renaissance and the future of the American city without ever completely
answering a single question about things like whether the LAPD is going
to have a bigger gang unit and how exactly he's going to storm the streets
and bring down the crime rate immediately and into eternity without indiscriminately beating people up.

Bill Bratton is the kid you knew in school who could hold his head
underwater for three minutes. He hasn't even moved here yet and Broadway
Bill's already the biggest star who isn't in the movies, and the former Bosto-
nian also brings to Los Angeles the only accent we didn't already have.

"Two to one, he ends up hosting the Oscars next spring," says Mike Bar-
nicle, a Boston and New York newsman who's known Bratton for 30 years.

Only time will tell whether the former New York City police commis-
sioner, who clashed with Mayor Rudy Giuliani in a war of egos, can deliver.
But we know he can talk. He swaggers into a room chest first, and although
it's a little scary that he keeps talking about Sergeant Joe Friday's *Dragnet*
as if it were real, you have to admire the confidence of a man who promises
results before he's even been sworn in.

Graffiti? He's going after it fast and hard and without delay because he hates it—oh he hates it with a passion and even his wife (the *Court TV* anchor who came along with him to the editorial board meeting) hates it and they went traveling to other cities that were once beautiful and they were covered with it. It has to be eliminated.

The LAPD? It's an underperforming department and they know it and the public knows it and all of that is going to come to an immediate halt as soon as he decentralizes the centralization and takes care of the training division mess and if there's a cop out there who doesn't get with the program and realize that assertive policing is about productivity and activity and creativity (and at least several other itys) he can send in his retirement papers because, guess what folks, there's a new sheriff in town.

His relationship with the mayor? They're on a honeymoon and getting along just famously because first of all they have the same vision for what the Los Angeles Police Department should be and secondly and of course most importantly you can put the two of them in a room together and ask a question and Bratton can be relatively certain that whatever else happens he can bet his badge on one thing. Mayor Hahn will not interrupt him.

After a half hour with Bratton my ears were bleeding, and so I walked across the street to City Hall and sat down with the mayor, not just to see if he uses earplugs, but to find out how he narrowed the field to Bratton. Jim Hahn recalled a moment several months ago when his search had not yet begun and Bratton dropped by his office while working as a monitor of the LAPD.

"I was sitting there," Hahn said, pointing to the sofa, "and he was sitting there, and he said, 'I know exactly who you need to be your next police chief, but you'd never hire me.'" My guess is that Bratton went up to the front of the class in second grade, told the teacher to take a break, and never let her back in the room.

Hahn said he gave Bratton big points for doing his homework, cobbling together a detailed plan, and making it clear he badly wanted the job.

As for Bratton's Jupiter-sized ego, the mayor could only see it working to the city's advantage. When it comes to the two main goals they share—reducing crime and advancing the reform of the department—Bratton does not intend to fail. But was Hahn at all worried that Bratton only intends to be here long enough to get his own star on Hollywood Boulevard, or that he'll use too much rough stuff on the streets to get results? You're bound to be a star as police chief of the second-largest city in America, Hahn said. "Bernard Parks was one of the 50 sexiest men" in America, according to *People* magazine.

As for the rough stuff, Hahn pressed Bratton on how he intended to implement his so-called assertive policing philosophy without going too far. Bratton said, among other things, that he would get the community's "authorization," meaning he would bring law-abiding citizens in on the deal.

We'll see. It isn't going to be easy in a vast city-nation with only 9,000 officers as compared to New York's 40,000. And Bratton's success in New York can be attributed in large part to a strong national economy that also dropped the crime rate in many cities. But Bratton already has L.A. cops buzzing, some out of fear they'll have to get out of the office and work, and some out of respect. One lieutenant told me Bratton was the first LAPD chief in a while who seems to like cops.

"I am very certain I made the right decision," Hahn said. But not as certain as the man who speaks without commas and might already have made several arrests just for the exercise because he's a professional who's done the job wherever he's gone and does not intend to be parked behind a Vegas buffet table like Willie Williams or locked in his office like Bernie Parks. And if anyone has any doubts that Bratton invented modern police science, here's the shortest quote I have from him in my entire notebook: "It's what I do. I'm very good at it."

Sand Aid

(July 17, 2002)

In case you've been wondering, mega-mogul David Geffen never did return my call about using the beach at his spread in Malibu. I promised I'd be in his front door and out on the sand in no time at all, but he didn't even have the decency to call back.

The beaches of California are legally owned by the public, but Geffen and other seaside dwellers—including his DreamWorks SKG partners Steven Spielberg and Jeffrey Katzenberg—have had a "Keep Out" sign up for years. And now Geffen, a man long associated with liberal causes, has sued the state and the nonprofit group Access for All, trying to block their efforts to open the beaches to the common man.

"These Democrats are a bunch of hypocrites," said Access for All president Steve Hoye. He noted that billionaire Democratic Party fund-raisers Eli Broad and Haim Saban, neighbors of Geffen, tried to keep their digs private by buying a nearby parcel for use as a sort of "Riffraff Beach."

"It's a class issue and it's about privilege," said Hoye. "It's about these people with their money and their beach wanting to keep it to themselves and keep out ordinary people."

When I saw that Geffen and the city of Malibu had filed suit together, making the same old misleading argument that the area can't reasonably accommodate public use, I figured it was all over. Geffen has enough money to keep this thing tied up in court until Adam Sandler makes a movie I would pay to see. But then, while perusing the geffen.com Web site, I got an idea. The bands on that site include Sheryl Crow, Sting and U2. And what do those acts have in common? A social conscience. If the cause is to feed the hungry, fight injustice or save the planet in the grand tradition of Live Aid or Farm Aid, you can probably count on those artists to show up and sing their hearts out. So why not a concert to liberate the beaches of Malibu?

Geffen sold the music portion of his empire, and he has nothing to do with any of those bands. But he built his substantial fortune, in part, on the backs of socially conscious crusaders like Peter Gabriel, Jackson Browne and Joni Mitchell, who wrote the famous "Big Yellow Taxi" lyric: "They paved paradise, they put up a parking lot." Well, guess what, Joni? They stole paradise, they put up a country club. It's high time we got it back.

My plan is to hold the event on the pier in the People's Republic of Santa Monica, perhaps as early as August. Proceeds can go to the legal defense fund of Access for All, the modest for-the-people outfit that Geffen— a billionaire several times over—is attempting to crush like a cockroach.

"We'll definitely have to raise some dollars to defend ourselves," says Steve Hoye, who suggested adding Don Henley to the concert bill. Not a bad idea. The former Eagle tried to save Walden Pond, so there's a good chance he'll be interested in rescuing a public beach from the clutches of these champagne-sipping pirates. Henley is also one of countless musicians who have tangled with Geffen in bitter business feuds. Some of the details are in Tom King's *The Operator*, a book the *Los Angeles Times* called a "chronicle of greed and misanthropy." Geffen had cat fights with Bob Dylan, Elton John, Cher and Neil Young, among others. This is their chance to get back at him. I've already gotten word to representatives of Sting, Sheryl Crow, U2, Peter Gabriel, Jackson Browne and Joni Mitchell, inviting them to come together once more, for the people, in the name of equal opportunity.

In 1983, Geffen got permission to remodel his beach digs. Any idea how? He promised to create a walkway for public access to the beach. But when John Q. Public showed up with his family on a hot summer day, Mr. Liberal Do-Gooder told him to get lost. And then, when he feared he might not get his way, he did exactly what you'd expect a guy like him to do. He sued.

Where's Bono now? Isn't the U2 front man done saving Africa? It's time for Sting to put another message in a bottle. I'm going to call Los Lobos, too, and Ozomatli, a couple of L.A. bands. The latter has an activism icon on its Web site with links to 11 causes, including women in prison and the United Farm Workers. How about making it a dozen?

"We could call the concert Give Back Our Sand," said Hoye. Yes. But in the tradition of Live Aid and Farm Aid, we could also go with Sand Aid. If anyone comes up with a better name, the prize is a backstage pass. And I'll share producer credit with the person who writes the best parody of "Big Yellow Taxi." Pardon us, Joni, but instead of "Hey, farmer, farmer, put away that DDT," how about:

> Hey, mogul, mogul, put away
> that lock and key.
> You stole the best beaches,
> Fenced them off from my friends
> and from me.
> Don't it always seem to go
> That you don't know what
> you've got till it's gone.
> They stole paradise.
> They put up a country club.

A Bird in the Hand Beats
a Shot in the Tush

(February 15, 2006)

"**If you get shot** out there," Mike Raahauge said Tuesday morning as I headed out on a pheasant hunt in Norco, "don't go to the doctor. Just go lay up at home." Raahauge said an inexperienced doctor could make a mess digging lead out of my hide. The very suggestion made me wonder if the vice president would be joining us.

If Dick Cheney did shoot me, just like he plugged a 78-year-old hunting partner in Texas on Saturday, there's no telling how long he'd try to keep a lid on the story. It wasn't until Sunday that we learned he had sprayed his buddy's upper body with birdshot, and the poor guy took a turn for the worse Tuesday with a heart attack.

Of course, if you had five deferments during the Vietnam War, as Cheney did, and then went quail hunting after sending American soldiers off to risk their lives in a war that was supposed to be about weapons of mass destruction, you probably wouldn't want the world to know your buddy was picking pellets out of his teeth.

I'm no hunter, so in fairness to the vice president, I figured I should do some field research to see how easy or difficult it is to mistake a 78-year-old lawyer for a quail. I called the owner of Raahauge's Pheasant Club and said I was with the *Los Angeles Times*, and the response made it clear I was about to enter another world.

"Are you a communist?" Mike Raahauge asked.

"No," I said. "A columnist."

I don't think he figured there was much difference. But Raahauge sounded like a good sport and told me to be at his clubhouse at seven in the morning.

The rustic hideaway, near the prison in Chino, is adorned with photos of Raahauge and friends. He's posing with former NRA president Charlton Heston, and several former Los Angeles Rams and California Angels. If you hunt in Southern California, this is apparently the place to be.

Hunting is safer than people think, Raahauge said, and shotgun mishaps seldom kill anyone. But accidents do happen. Several years ago, he said, 12 attorneys and a judge went hunting on his property, and the judge came back full of buckshot. I don't know. Doesn't sound like an accident to me.

"Is there anybody in this room who hasn't been shot?" Raahauge asked before we set out on our hunting trip. Six people were in the room; three had been shot. I didn't know if I liked my odds, but I felt a little better when I put on a vest and hat the color of Mars.

My partner was Steve Foster, the brother-in-law of one of my colleagues. Foster, a realtor in southern Orange County, is a seasoned hunter and Air Force vet who flew hundreds of combat missions over Vietnam. He's the kind of guy you want in your foxhole. Foster brought along his bird dog Stormy, and we were accompanied by a top-notch guide named John Guest, whose dog Buster was in a cage with a bumper sticker that read "Sportsmen for Bush." I love how you can travel just an hour east of downtown L.A. and be in Texas.

So there we were, setting out across several acres of rolling hills with grass and low brush, looking for three pheasants that had been dropped out there for us. It doesn't seem quite fair that the birds were raised domestically and put out there for us to blast away at, but I knew the deal going in.

Not five minutes into our trek, we came upon a pheasant that sprung up about 20 feet away and took flight. Foster smoothly raised his Browning 12-gauge, wheeled smartly to his right as Guest neatly ducked out of the way, and fired. I reached up with both hands and my head was still there. The pheasant is no longer with us, but no humans were injured in the killing of the bird. I see how things can get crazy in a hurry. The bird pops up unexpectedly and the hunter quickly follows its panicked flight, finger on the trigger. But Foster put safety first, holding back until he was certain there were no heads, torsos or arms and legs in his line of fire.

It seemed like a simple enough exercise, and I began wondering if Cheney shot the guy on purpose. Would you rather have the country talking about your little hunting accident or the fact that your aide Scooter told a federal grand jury his bosses authorized a leak of highly sensitive intelligence?

After bagging his bird, Foster handed me the shotgun and gave me a few pointers, and I was ready for battle. Just between you and me, my hunting license might not have been entirely in order, but then, neither was Cheney's.

Quietly, I came upon a pheasant, waited for the dog to scare him up, and pulled the trigger. The bird looked back once, appeared to be laughing, and leisurely flew north like he was on vacation. Nobody was injured, but now the pressure was really on. Even Cheney occasionally manages to shoot a bird.

Stormy, trying to help me out, scared up another pheasant. I leveled the Browning and took aim, but the bird was flying low with Stormy giving chase, and all I could think of was New Orleans. I still get mail from people accusing me of abandoning a dog as it swam through a flooded neighborhood after Hurricane Katrina. It was bad enough that I was now trying to kill another member of the animal kingdom. If I shot Stormy, I'd be flogged by dog lovers until I was in the boneyard. So I pulled up my aim.

"I appreciate that," Foster said. Hey, safety first. Another bird will come along. And soon after there it was. I stood atop a bluff, Mt. Baldy, in the distance, a pheasant taking flight before me. I waited until everyone and everything was clear, fired once from about 30 yards, and sent the bird to the barbecue grill.

It's just not that hard to do. I suggest Cheney get some training from Foster, a man of experience who doesn't lose his cool under pressure. Or for $35, he could take the Raahauge hunter safety course. If you're vice president of the free world, you can't have people thinking you're not a straight shooter.

Going for the Look
of the Head of State

(November 5, 2006)

I called Arnold Schwarzenegger's Beverly Hills hairdresser the other day to book an appointment for a make-over.

"When can you come in?" asked the receptionist.

I was a little surprised the maestro was so available, but two hours later I parked on Canon Drive and walked to the Giuseppe Franco Salon. Schwarzenegger and I have had our differences, but there's one thing I can't deny as we close in on Tuesday's election: He's got the look of a winner.

The man has survived monumental flip-flops, blatant contradictions and scandalous accusations. Every time you think he's finally been knocked off the horse, he flashes that golden smile and comes back more invincible, high in the saddle and looking good. I wanted some of that magic that comes with knowing you look your best, and I had reason to believe Mr. Franco could handle the job.

"For more than two decades," says the salon's website, "only one man's scissors have touched the hair of the most powerful man in the state of California, Governor Arnold Schwarzenegger, and those scissors belong to Giuseppe Franco."

Franco's shop has a big Schwarzenegger poster in the window—Arnold on the cover of *Vanity Fair*. There's another *Vanity Fair* cover of him inside, larger than life. Right off the bat, I began to suspect that a salon is very different from a barbershop. A receptionist named Anita, a blond Hungarian in a leopard-pattern cowboy hat, told me Mr. Franco was in a meeting and would be with me shortly. A meeting? While waiting, I wondered if I really wanted to go through with this. Glancing in the mirror, though, I had to admit the S.Lo look was in need of some attention. The hair on top was going Joe Biden and the rest was way down the road from gray to white. Before I could decide, I heard someone calling my name.

"Steve Lopez," said the skinny, rock star-looking guy who came my way with his jet black hair sticking straight up. "Stevie!"

That's Giuseppe Franco? I was expecting someone from Italy. Franco is from Hoboken. He's got the accent and attitude to prove it, too. Al Pacino is a mummy compared to this guy. I told Franco I wanted to leave the shop looking as good as the governor, to the extent possible, even if it meant Arnold-style red highlights.

"I'm gonna make you look BETTER than the governor!" he guaranteed.

Franco recommended that we start with a major trim job on my goatee.

"You never, EVER, let your beard go ZZ Top on you," he said, referring to the blues-rock band whose members look like they've got beehives hanging off their chins. He also recommended some color. I've always prided myself on going natural, but hey, it wasn't subtlety that made Arnold a winner.

Red wouldn't work on me, said Franco. I'd look like a redhead in a black and white film. But he doesn't do the color himself. He called out to Bryan Howe, one of his color guys, and Howe, with a tie he borrowed from Yogi Bear and tattoos quilted over his arms, looked me over, along with his boss.

"You walked in here salt and pepper, and you're going to walk out with a little more pepper," Franco said after their confab. "You're gonna look like a sex pistol when I'm done with you, Steve-O."

I was beginning to see why the governor likes Franco, who stepped outside into a breezeway and pried the hard pack of Marlboro Lights out of his front pocket and lighted up while contemplating the project ahead. Inside, a stunning young blond was having her hair done and the place was a parade of eye candy and young guys in torn jeans, T-shirts and tattoos, who turned out to be hairdressers on break. Actor Gary Busey lolled about smoking a big cigar. "La Bamba" played on the sound system.

This was Arnold's World, with Caffè Roma in the same cluster of breezeway shops, along with Nazareth's Fine Cigars, where the governor has his nameplate on a humidor in the smoking lounge. I'd already been transformed from S.Lo to Steve-O, man about Beverly Hills, and Franco hadn't even reached for his scissors yet. When he returned, though, he'd had some second thoughts. If my intention was to make him or the governor look bad, he said, the deal was off. He and the governor are such pals, Franco is planning to spend election day with Schwarzenegger, knocking on doors, touching him up, whatever the governor needs. Nothing to worry about, I told him. I was there because I wanted be more like Arnold. I wanted to be able to have a bad day now and then, but still keep up appearances. His wife called and I could hear Franco's conversation with her.

"He's the one that called Arnold Woody Woodpecker," he said to her. That's the trouble with writing a column: People have long memories. "OK, I love you, pumpkin."

I guess his wife advised him to go ahead, because Franco had me shampooed and then got out his scissors. The same man who, according to his brochure, cuts Sean Penn, Joe Pesci, Drew Barrymore, Mikhail Baryshnikov, Christopher Walken, Johnny Depp, Brad Pitt, Sharon Stone, Charlie Sheen, Sylvester Stallone, Benicio Del Toro and the cast of *The Sopranos* was cutting Steve-O's hair.

"Tonight's gonna be your night, Stevie," said Franco, who told me he got into the business to meet girls. "You want espresso, pizza, anything? You sure? We have a relationship with our clients in here. It's full service. They cancel therapy sessions after coming here. Look at you, what a sex machine. This is not Supercuts, Steve-O."

These are things my barber has never said. They brought in a pepperoni pizza and passed it around. A double espresso landed in front of me and a shiatsu massage therapist named Anthony Salmon gave me a little tuneup. What a life Arnold leads. I asked Franco if he thought the governor's challenger, Phil Angelides, was in need of a makeover.

"He's got a lot of heart," Franco said, promising the Democrat a free cut after the election. The problem is the style, not the color, Franco said of Angelides' hair. And someone who loves him should tell him to ditch the glasses.

"He's 1971," Franco said. "Oklahoma weatherman. No, substitute teacher."

The color job took forever, with Howe using a brush to dab at my head. Lowlights, he explained. Pepper. It was a leap of faith, to say the least, and

I wasn't sure I was going to walk out looking my best. The color seemed a little closer to shoe polish than pepper, and I worried about the reaction from my wife, whose jaw drops at the sight of middle-aged guys who do mortifying things to their hair trying to look young. Don't worry, Franco told me. It'd look fine once they rubbed some of the gray back in.

"You can't rush color."

He said I had virgin hair, meaning it had been untouched by color or product. Now that I was deflowered, was I stuck coming back every six weeks? Did I really want t start worrying about roots along with prostate enlargement?

Before I could get an answer, Richie Palmer, New York-born owner of Mulberry Street Pizzeria across the street, walked in to tell Franco he was a nobody without the governor. Palmer insisted he had more celebrities in his pizza joint than Franco had in his salon and the two of them wrestled and goofed like schoolboys playing hooky in Little Italy. This is a Beverly Hills I never knew.

A cop named Reiner came by to pick up his daughter after a style job, and Franco asked if he could shoot the officer's gun real quick. Actor Seymour Cassel went by with a lighted cigar. Busey was still wandering around like he was lost.

Are all the talent agents in Beverly Hills blind? Give Franco a TV show, with or without the governor.

What's Palmer's story? I asked the stylist to the stars. Used to date actress Cathy Moriarty, he said. They started the pizza business together but split up. Then Palmer married Raquel Welch. I looked at Palmer, who was grinning as if he couldn't believe it either. Try going back to your high school reunion with that story, Palmer said. Yo, what's new out West, Richie? Not much. I opened a pizza parlor and married Raquel Welch.

"Steve-O, do you feel what's goin' on here?" Franco asked when he got his hands back in my hair. He ran up behind the counter, where Anita the Hungarian cowgirl works, and got on the PA system.

"We are winners, Stevie boy. Winners!"

I didn't want to say anything, but I wasn't sure about the dye job. The side of my head looked a little like Anita's leopard-skin hat, but for all I knew, that may have been the look he was going for. Franco used some gel to get the hair on top of my head standing up, and I wasn't sure about that either. Looked to me like a few charred stalks were still standing after a chaparral fire.

The whole thing took a little under three hours and cost $400, which is two years' worth of haircuts at my regular price. Franco said I looked 23 years younger than when I walked in, which would make me my son's age. He was thrilled with my new do, but let me remind you this is a man who, with all due respect, looks like Keith Richards might look after sticking his finger in a light socket.

I have to admit that I had some swagger in my step when I left the salon.

I bought a fat stogie at the place where Arnold has his humidor and strutted out to the sidewalk where I chatted up passing women, none of whom turned and ran. One of them even tossed me a compliment, and Franco called me a winner.

"You should've done this years ago," he said.

Yeah, look what the right stylist, and a winning smile, did for Schwarzenegger. Governor Steve-O. I kind of like it.

Put me down for next month, Giuseppe. We layer, we touch up the roots. Keep an open mind and think about a dash of paprika with that salt and pepper.

Polanski Backers Lose Sight
of a Real Victim

(September 30, 2009)

Q: Did you resist at that time?
A: A little bit, but not really because...
Q: Because what?
A: Because I was afraid of him.

That's Roman Polanski's 13-year-old victim testifying before a grand jury about how the famous director forced himself on her at Jack Nicholson's Mulholland Drive home in March of 1977. I'm reading this in the district attorney's office at the Los Angeles County Criminal Courts Building, digging through the Polanski file to refresh my memory of the infamous case, and my blood pressure is rising.

Is it because I'm the parent of a girl? Maybe that's part of it. But I wish the renowned legal scholars Harvey Weinstein and Debra Winger, to name just two of Polanski's defenders, were here with me now. I'd like to invite Martin Scorsese as well, along with David Lynch, who have put their names on a petition calling for Polanski to be freed immediately. What, because he won an Oscar? Would they speak up for a sex offender who hadn't?

To hear these people tell it, you'd think Polanski was the victim rather than the teenager. And then there's Woody Allen, who also has signed the petition. Woody Allen? You'd think that after marrying his longtime girlfriend's adopted daughter, he'd have the good sense to remain silent. But at least Soon-Yi Previn was a consenting adult.

I'd like to show all these great luminaries the testimony from Polanski's underage victim, as well as Polanski's admission of guilt. Then I'd like to ask whether, if the victim were their daughter, they'd be so cavalier about a crime that was originally charged as sodomy and rape before Polanski agreed to a plea bargain. Would they still support Polanski's wish to remain on the lam living the life of a king, despite the fact that he skipped the U.S. in 1977 before he was sentenced?

The Zurich Film Festival has been "unfairly exploited" by Polanski's arrest, Winger said. Thanks, Deb. And so sorry the film festival was inconvenienced by the arrest of a man who left the United States to avoid sentencing for forcing himself on a child.

Weinstein, meanwhile, issued an open letter urging "every U.S. filmmaker to lobby against any move to bring Polanski back to the U.S.," arguing that "whatever you think of the so-called crime, Polanski has served his time." So-called crime? Let's get back to the grand jury testimony.

Polanski had taken the girl to Nicholson's house to photograph her, ostensibly for a French magazine. The girl's mother, it's clear to me, should have had her head examined for allowing this to happen, but that's another matter. The girl says Polanski, who was in his 40s at the time, opened a bottle of champagne and shared it with her and with an adult woman who later left for work. That's when Polanski allegedly began taking pictures of the 13-year-old and suggested that she remove her blouse. Quoting again from the grand jury transcript, with the girl being questioned by a prosecutor:

Q: Did you take your shirt off or did Mr. Polanski?
A: No, I did.
Q: Was that at his request or did you volunteer to do that?
A: That was at his request.

She said Polanski later went into the bathroom and took part of a Quaalude pill and offered her some as well, and she accepted.

Q: Why did you take it?
A: I don't know. I think I must have been pretty drunk or else I wouldn't have.

So here she is, at 13, washing down a Quaalude with champagne, and then Polanski suggested they move out to the Jacuzzi.

Q: When you got in the Jacuzzi, what were you wearing?
A: I was going to wear my underwear, but he said for me to take them off.

She says Polanski went back in the house and returned in the nude and got into the Jacuzzi with her. When he told her to move closer to him, she resisted, saying, "No. No, I got to get out." He insisted, she testified, and so she moved closer and he put his hands around her waist. She told him she had asthma and wanted to get out, and she did. She said he followed her into the bathroom, where she told him, "I have to go home now."

Q: What did Mr. Polanski say?
A: He told me to go in the other room and lie down.

She testified that she was afraid and sat on the couch in the bedroom.

Q: What were you afraid of?
A: Him.

She testified that Polanski sat down next to her and said she'd feel better. She repeated that she had to go home.

Q: What happened then?
A: He reached over and he kissed me. And I was telling him, No, you know, keep away. But I was kind of afraid of him because there was no one else there.

She testified that he put his mouth on her vagina. "I was ready to cry," she said. "I was kind of—I was going, 'No. Come on. Stop it.' But I was afraid." She said he then pulled off her panties.

Q: What happened after that?
A: He started to have intercourse with me.

At this point, the girl testified, Polanski became concerned about the consequences and asked if she was on the pill. No, she told him. But, she claimed, Polanski had a solution. "He goes, 'Would you want me to go in through your back?' And I went, 'No.'" According to the girl, that didn't stop Polanski, who began having anal sex with her. This was when the victim was asked by the prosecutor if she resisted and she said, "Not really," because "I was afraid of him." She testified that when the ordeal had ended, Polanski told her, "Oh, don't tell your mother about this." He added: "This is our secret." But it wasn't a secret for long. When the victim got home and told her story, her mother called the police.

Now granted, we only have the girl's side of things. But an LAPD criminalist testified before the grand jury that tests of the girl's panties "strongly indicate semen." And a police officer who searched Polanski's hotel room found a Quaalude and photos of the girl.

Two weeks after the encounter on Mulholland Drive, Polanski was indicted for furnishing a controlled substance to a minor, committing a lewd or lascivious act upon a child under 14, unlawful sexual intercourse, rape by use of drugs, perversion (oral copulation) and sodomy. Three months later, a plea bargain was worked out. Court records indicate that the victim and her family had asked the district attorney's office to spare the victim the trauma of testifying at a criminal trial.

"A stigma would attach to her for a lifetime," the family's attorney argued.

Polanski pleaded guilty to just one count—unlawful sexual intercourse. The other charges were dropped. He spent 42 days in prison for pre-sentencing diagnostic tests. After his release, but before his sentencing in 1978, he skipped, boarding a plane for Europe because he feared he would be ordered to serve more time in prison. A warrant for his arrest has been in effect ever since, and Polanski was arrested this week in Switzerland. He is fighting extradition, but I hope he loses that fight, gets hustled back to California and finally gets a sentence that fits his crime.

There's little question that this case was mishandled in many ways. According to a recent documentary, the now-deceased judge inappropriately discussed sentencing with a prosecutor who wasn't working the case. And Polanski's lawyers allege that the director fled only because he believed the judge would cave under public pressure and renege on a promise that he would serve no more time. Regardless of whether there was such a deal, Polanski had not yet been sentenced, and under state law at the time, he could have been sent away for many years. Does anyone really believe 42 days was an appropriate penalty given the nature of the case?

Yes, Polanski has known great tragedy, having survived the Holocaust and having lost his wife, Sharon Tate, and their unborn son to the insanity of the Charles Manson cult. But that has no bearing on the crime in question. His victim, who settled a civil case against Polanski for an unspecified amount, said she does not want the man who forced himself on her to serve additional time. That's big-hearted of her but also irrelevant, and so is the fact that the victim had admitted to having sex with a boyfriend before meeting Polanski.

Polanski stood in a Santa Monica courtroom on August 8, 1977, admitted to having his way with a girl three decades his junior and told a judge that indeed he knew she was only 13. There may well have been judicial misconduct. But no misconduct was greater than allowing Polanski to cop a plea to the least of his charges. His crime was graphic, manipulative and heinous, and he got a pass. It's unbelievable, really, that his soft-headed apologists are rooting for him to get another one.

Can He Get to First Base?

(November 1, 2009)

Dear Jamie McCourt:

I know I'm being a bit presumptuous here, but as a risk-taker yourself, you'll appreciate what I'm about to say. I think I love you.

You may think that's a little weird, given that we haven't met. But sometimes a guy just knows. Besides, I feel like I know you just from reading the court filings in your divorce proceedings with estranged hubby Frank. And no, I'm not simply interested in the $487,634 a month you claim to need in spousal support so you can go on living in the manner to which you've become accustomed.

It's not the seven estates I'm after either, even if you did spend $14 million in home improvements on just one of them—the one with the Olympic-size indoor swimming pool, an outdoor pool, sauna, steam room, dance studio, massage room and 10 bathrooms.

As for the private jets that whisk you to exclusive resorts around the globe, honey, I'm already platinum with US Airways. And it would never be about where we go, Jamie. It would be about what happens when we're together.

You want to know what I'm really after? Glad you asked. I like a woman of substance. And I'm attracted to pioneering spirits who swing for the fences. Excuse me, Jamie McCourt, but did I just paint your portrait?

You're a law school grad, and you were the first female CEO of a Major League Baseball team, so I know you're motivated. You're standing up to hubby Frank for firing you, so I know you're a fighter. And two of your seven estates are in Malibu. I'm motivated, Jamie. I'm a fighter. And I share your love of oceanfront real estate. In short, my dear, we are two peas in a pod.

I won't deny that there's a complication or two. Yes, I'm married at the moment. But as you've demonstrated by dumping Frank and taking up with your driver, the heart wants what the heart wants. Speaking of the driver, I suggest you slow down, take a deep breath and open your eyes. Come on, Jamie. He's a classic rebound guy. How do I know this? Because he's everything your estranged husband is not, and that's a great way to poke Frank in both eyes with a hot stick. But these flings usually flame out after a few months. You're going to look in the mirror one morning, slap yourself in the face and scream: I'm dating my chauffeur?!

No, Jamie. You're not dating your chauffeur. You're biding your time, waiting for Mr. Right. The kind of guy who can stand up to Frank and say, yeah, tough guy, she went to Europe for two and a half weeks in the middle of the pennant run and dropped a small fortune. But she was scouting French relief pitchers.

You know what really irks me, Jamie? The way you're having to beg for a few bucks when Frank's living a stratospheric lifestyle himself, throwing money around like hot dog wrappers. The moron gave $45 million to Manny Ramirez for two years, and that loafer is poison in the clubhouse. Meanwhile, he lets Cleveland ace Cliff Lee get away to the Phillies, who pay him less than six million dollars and end up in the World Series. Ramirez was making $170,000 a game after his suspension, and Frank is giving you a hard time about a measly $487,634 a month? How dare he!

As for the driver, I can give you another reason I'd make a better mate:

Not only can I drive you anywhere you want to go, but I could offer invaluable counsel on how to keep the media jackals at bay. And believe me, they're out there, waiting to pounce.

I'm going through the section of your court declaration titled "Our Marital Lifestyle," and I know the idea was to shoot for the moon as a starting point in divorce proceedings. But I see numerous places where you could have toned it down.

I mean, the details about the private jet vacation to Vietnam, the clothing by Valentino, Gucci and Prada, the eight full-time housekeepers and other assistants, and the dining at Spago, Toscana, Giorgio Baldi and Nobu are liable to end up in a newspaper column.

Here's an example of where you needed a good editor: "We removed the tennis courts" at the $20 million Holmby Hills house "in order to build the indoor pool." And here: The $27 million Malibu beach house, as opposed to the $19 million Malibu beach house next door, "has a small pool, which is not suitable for long-distance swimming." Some smart-aleck pundit is going to get hold of this stuff, Jamie, and the headline will say: "Boo-Hoo."

Here's another place where you went too far: "We always stay in suites where available at the nicest of accommodations, such as the Ritz Carlton and Four Seasons hotels." Couldn't you have thrown in a Ramada or a Holiday Inn? As for the $5,000-a-night suite in Cabo, you're not getting good advice from either your lawyer or your glorified cabbie.

I would have told you in the most affectionate terms to think about all the working people who bust their hump so they can afford to take the family to Dodger Stadium. Now those poor saps are going to realize they're paying jacked-up prices for parking, tickets and refreshments so you can frolic like royalty in Baja.

You also could have done without telling the whole world that your hairstylist and makeup artist make house calls, that you have your hair colored once a month and that "the Dodgers also provide makeup and hair services." I make house calls, too, Jamie. No extra charge.

And if it doesn't work out between us? Fear not, mi amor. I'm willing to sign a pre-nup, and I've already discussed this with my current wife. She's completely on board, figuring that I'll end up scratching at the door for her to take me back. By the way, she thinks we could get by on $200,000 monthly, somewhere in that neighborhood, but I've got a better idea. I'd happily settle for one of the two beachfront properties in Malibu.

Sleep on it, Jamie, my sweet. But not with the driver.

U.S. Official's Flight of Fancy

(March 14, 2010)

On January 25, the local field director for Representative Laura Richardson (D-Long Beach) sent an e-mail to a Los Angeles County Fire Department official. He was requesting a helicopter tour for Richardson and her staff.

Her entire staff.

That's all nine employees in the D.C. office, who were being flown to California for training and field work, and all 10 employees in the district office. Richardson herself would make it 20 people, or roughly enough to invade a small island nation. She wanted the tour to take place on Sunday, January 31, with a focus on transportation corridors and homeland security issues at the port.

"I realize that this is relatively short notice," Richardson's district director, Eric Boyd, wrote to Anthony C. Marrone Jr., chief of air operations for the county fire department. "The Congresswoman understands that your department has important public safety obligations, and we apologize for the urgent nature of this request. We would be that much more grateful if this request could be accommodated."

A number of questions come to mind. Why would the entire staff need an aerial tour, including employees who do little more than answer phones? Couldn't Richardson, who had already hosted such a tour with congressional reps from other states, spread out a few maps and tell the staff what she had seen from up in the air? And was Richardson—who defaulted six times on homes she owns in Southern California and is being investigated by the House Ethics Committee regarding the foreclosure of her Sacramento home—aware that most helicopters can't accommodate 20 people?

I'll get to all of that.

County fire officials had some concerns of their own, and passed them on to district director Boyd. On January 26, Boyd e-mailed those fire officials to say he had explained their reservations to Richardson. What were those concerns? First, according to Boyd's summary in his e-mail to the fire department, it was an unusually large group, so two helicopters would be needed. Second, emergency services would be compromised. And third, "the cost to accommodate our request is estimated to be between $20,000-$25,000. This level of expenditure…possibly opens both L.A. County Fire and our office to public scrutiny…."

You think?

Yes, the public might frown on that kind of expensive joy ride, given the lousy economy, budget cuts at every level of government and the huge number of low-income residents in Richardson's district, which includes Compton and Willowbrook.

But despite all that, and the concerns of fire officials, Boyd said in his e-mail, "the Congresswoman would like to speak to someone in the department regarding this request."

That conversation turned out to be unnecessary because the fire department decided to give in. Not only did the county supply a helicopter, it got the Los Angeles Fire Department to supply a second one because part of the 37th Congressional District is in L.A., and a single helicopter wasn't enough to accommodate the entire Richardson party. Both the city and county fire departments told me they try to accommodate requests by public officials for legitimate reconnaissance flights, though no one I spoke to was aware of a time when one member of Congress flew with an entire staff.

Sometimes there are frivolous requests, and they're rejected, said John Tripp, chief of emergency operations for the L.A. County Fire Department. He wasn't involved in granting this particular request, he said, but his colleagues deemed the helicopter tour a worthwhile way to provide "the best… understanding of truly what this infrastructure is in this community."

Tripp said the cost for the county helicopter, based on 1.8 hours of flying time, was $3,000. He couldn't explain the estimate of $20,000 to

$25,000 that had been passed along earlier. But the county helicopter and its two-man crew remained out of service for six hours because of fueling, a weather delay and the fact that it had to fly from Pacoima to Long Beach and back. I'm guessing all that time and personnel—along with the need for two helicopters—produced the initial higher estimate.

Richardson told me she considered the aerial tour an excellent use of time and money, saying she's been trying to get her staff trained since she won a special election in 2007 after the death of Representative Juanita Millender-McDonald. She argued that her district's location and facilities make it a unique security risk, and that her staffers need to understand the district's complexities in order to put up a better fight for funding of local projects.

During four days in the district, Richardson said, her staff worked long hours. They also toured the area on a bus provided by Long Beach transit, and stayed at the Hotel Maya, whose website describes it as a four-star "luxury…boutique resort."

Richardson said the bill for the entire trip came to $19,028.23, not counting helicopter costs incurred by the fire departments.

I spoke to other congressional offices and was told that flying D.C. staff to the area they represent every couple of years is not uncommon, but nobody had heard of taking all 20 staffers on an aerial tour. It seems particularly indulgent to tie up two emergency-service helicopters to observe things such as how close homes are to refineries, as Richardson argued. Anybody with a computer can go to Google Earth and essentially fly anywhere, zooming in and out as if piloting a helicopter.

"I would disagree," said Richardson, who had her staff send me some photos taken from the helicopters. The pictures were unremarkable. And Google is free.

The Mayor Tries the Cheap Seats

(June 27, 2010)

It's Friday night at Dodger Stadium, and there's the Mayor of Los Angeles way, way up in the nosebleed section, almost to the moon. What's wrong with this picture?

I'll tell you what's wrong with it. Antonio Villaraigosa is a box seat, luxury suite, courtside kind of guy, always managing to get his hands on the best tickets in the house, and he doesn't pay a nickel. So I offered to take him to the Dodgers-Yankees game and let him explain himself, but the deal was that he'd have to sit with the real people for a change. His answer was cause, once more, to question his judgment.

He said yes.

As we made our way to the seats, the mayor passed Dodgers owner Frank McCourt's son, who asked if he was coming down to his usual seats about two feet from home plate. The Dodgers, in fact, seem to have been the mayor's most generous friends over the years, inviting him back again and again. No, the mayor said. He was going upstairs. The elevator took us to the top of the stadium, and I wondered if the mayor could handle the thin air at that elevation.

"Are you dizzy?" I asked. He said he was fine.

The fans up there seemed stunned to see the mayor in their company, knowing he favors the high life with the pampered set. For the record, I bought the $12 tickets, and the mayor insisted on buying the beer, hot dogs and peanuts.

We were enjoying our dogs when the New Yorker next to us realized Villaraigosa was the mayor.

"So," he asked, "how'd you get stuck with these seats?" In New York, the guy said, Mayor Michael Bloomberg, who happens to be rich, would be sitting in $2,500 seats. Villaraigosa confessed that he was usually down there himself, but this night was different.

To put Ticketgate in perspective, I should say that once upon a time in Los Angeles, we had an aggressively dull mayor who guarded his privacy, seldom emerged from his bunker and took his sister with him on the rare occasions when he stepped out. Jim Hahn was so shy I set up a service to recruit potential dates for him. In a big shakeup five years ago, the city made the switch to Villaraigosa, who seemed determined to prove that he didn't need my help.

In his five-year crusade to prove that mayors just wanna have fun, Villaraigosa has dated two TV news personalities and has been out on the town more than Lindsay Lohan. After being pressed by reporters, his staff released records saying he'd been offered free entry to roughly 100 events and attended about 85. But the recordkeeping was sloppy and incomplete, answering some questions but raising more.

It's part of his job to do the town, the mayor told me at the ballgame. And I agree with him, to a point. Boosterism isn't nearly as important as running the city well—and he's had his ups and downs in that regard—but I do agree that it's part of the job. Unfortunately for Villaraigosa, there are laws about public officials accepting freebies for themselves and friends and family, as he has done, and the city's Ethics Commission and the L.A. County district attorney's office are looking into whether the mayor violated them.

Unless a mayor is performing official or ceremonial duties, free passes are counted as gifts. And if they're gifts, you're not allowed to accept more than $420 worth in one year from a single source. And so, since Villaraigosa didn't report them as gifts, what was the official or ceremonial business at hand when he sat in $2,000 courtside seats at Lakers games with Hollywood mogul Jeffrey Katzenberg, or when he shared a luxury box at 14 or 15 Dodger games? In some of those cases, Villaraigosa said, he was there to deliver a proclamation and make a quick exit, and yeah, maybe sometimes he was back before long with another nearly identical proclamation.

"Politicians give proclamations all the time," he said. "If you can give one in front of 15,000 people, come on!" Well, that's honest, at least.

Even without a proclamation, the mayor said, being out in public is a legitimate act of boosterism and counts as official or ceremonial business. Actually, the law is not entirely clear on that, and the mayor said if the ruling is that he broke the rules, he'll pay for the tickets. But I will say that from the moment he got to Dodger Stadium, Villaraigosa was mobbed by fans who wanted to shake his hand, take pictures and get his autograph. There you go, he said. He's the city ambassador and, even at a game, he's on the job.

Maybe so. But the real concern isn't the value of the freebies, but the access they can buy. The gang that runs Staples Center and L.A. Live, for instance, has gotten millions in tax breaks from City Hall, so the free Lakers tickets they gave him are a problem, no matter how many times he flashed his smile and said, "Go, L.A."

Don't worry, the mayor said. He can't be influenced by freebies from rich and powerful friends. If he expected me to believe that, maybe the thin air was getting to him, after all.

On our way out, Villaraigosa was swarmed again and got more cheers than the Dodgers did in their 2-1 loss. If he sat in the cheap seats with the hoi polloi a little more often, maybe he wouldn't be in the fix he's in.

EXCUSE ME?

The 10 o'Clock News

(November 26, 2001)

The first story on the 10 o'clock news was about a Britney Spears concert in Anaheim.

"Come look at this," I called out to my wife, figuring there must have been a terrorist threat at Arrowhead Pond if the concert was leading the news. I was wrong. Britney topped the news all on her own, and now they were interviewing a parent who had brought her seven-year-old daughter to the concert. The child was dressed like Britney, bare midriff and all. It goes without saying, of course, that this woman should be locked up. She is clearly unfit to be a parent, and if I had caught her name, I would have called the child welfare officers myself.

The next story on KCAL 9 that night was about another concert. Jennifer Lopez this time.

"Would you come in here and look at this?" I called out to my wife again.

Jennifer was on a big swing, like a trapeze artist, hoisted over a stage in Puerto Rico. After showing a fawning montage of her career achievements—which included her infamous public appearance in a dress that was missing its dickey—KCAL broke to a live newsroom commentary from one of its anchors, who carried on as if the subject were Eleanor Roosevelt. Along the way, she kept referring to J.Lo, as the star prefers. Is my own image fresh enough? I wondered.

Steve Lopez is the old me. When my wife finally came into the room, I told her that until further notice, I wanted to be called S.Lo.

"This can't be the regular news. There's a war going on," she said. "It must be some kind of special." One would think. But no.

The third story on KCAL 9 finally mentioned Afghanistan, but not in the context you might think. This segment, which took us inside a strip club near LAX, was about efforts to stem the proliferation of such establishments. The strip club lawyer—a true credit to his profession—said with a straight face that Americans want Afghan women to come out from under the veil, but at the same time we're asking American women to cover up. Hire this attorney. Whatever jam you're in, he'll come up with something.

The fourth story of the night, switching from culture to commerce, was about shopping for lingerie.

"I don't believe this," said my wife.

Maybe it's because a Laker game just ended, I said. Maybe instead of playing to the lowest common denominator, as usual, they divide by two after a sporting event. This story took us to a lingerie shop that featured bubbly, half-naked sales clerks who seemed to have fallen into the right line of work.

"They look really smart," said my wife.

The enterprising reporter, a philosopher king himself, said that when you buy a naughty nightie for your mate, "They think they're getting the presents, but you're really the lucky one."

I took a cyanide capsule. My wife beat herself over the head with a dumbbell.

We couldn't go on.

No one in their right mind expects to be enlightened or informed by local television news. But in more ways than one, what we were watching had nothing to do with the news. We were witnessing the triumphant resurrection of bad taste. The world had changed forever, we all thought, on September 11. Irony was dead, humor would never be the same and bad taste was suddenly inappropriate. But no longer.

The fifth story was about the war in Afghanistan, but once again, not in the context you might think. It was about Operation Playmate, in which Playboy bunnies will entertain American troops. Several centerfolds were interviewed about the important mission at hand. What a perfect nightmare they must be for Islamic fundamentalists, I thought. And then a lightbulb went on. Instead of having them entertain the good guys, we could send them running through the streets of Taliban strongholds wearing nothing but bunny ears. This could draw Osama bin Laden and his men out of hiding to condemn Western values, and the war would be over.

At this point of the newscast, I found myself rooting for more trash. It was such an unabashed commitment to meaninglessness, you had to admire the conviction. (A couple days later, in fact, I rang the general manager and news director to congratulate them, but they didn't return my calls.)

Five straight wartime stories on midriffs and bosoms. Could they keep the streak alive?

Story number six: Hackers break into the Playboy website and steal credit card information. Yes! I wanted it to go on forever. Internet porn, hair removal, aging playmates entertaining Legionnaires.

But the seventh story, I'm sorry to report, ended the streak, posing a question that bordered on newsworthiness: Is it safe to send our athletes to the Winter Olympics? Before breaking to a commercial, KCAL teased an upcoming story on a traffic accident.

"Oh no," my wife said. "Maybe a Playboy bunny died."

Parking Cop Had No Empathy
on His Meter

(January 31, 2007)

Before I get to the parking ticket that pushed her over the edge in Century City, let me tell you about the long ordeal and grim prognosis that sent Shari Kahane to her attorney's office last Thursday. Kahane and her husband, Mark Baskin, are medical doctors who live in the northwest San Fernando Valley.

"I'm not certain, but I think I'm the only graduate of both the nursing and medical schools at UCLA," Kahane told me in the bedroom of her home, where she was breathing through tubes attached to an oxygen tank.

She chose nursing first because she wasn't sure she wanted to endure medical school. But she changed her mind after several years as a nurse, becoming a doctor in 1980. She worked as an emergency room physician in the San Francisco Bay Area and later at the Woodland Hills Kaiser, but a breast cancer diagnosis in 1993 turned everything upside down and started her on a fight for her life.

Since then, Shari Kahane has endured a bone marrow transplant, vaccine treatment, chemotherapy, surgery and experimental medication. She was once dropped by her health insurance company and won reinstatement only after appealing to Assemblyman Keith Richman—a physician and crusader for healthcare reform—for assistance.

In 2002, Kahane developed liver cancer, did her usual homework and located a San Francisco physician who had developed a revolutionary surgical approach. It was a success, but the return of breast cancer has kept her researching breakthroughs around the world, informing her oncologist of new options, and refusing to accept suggestions that it was time to give up the battle.

"She is a remarkable and extremely intelligent woman who inspires everyone she meets," said her husband, an ophthalmologist whose specialties include reconstructive surgery for burn victims. Through it all, Kahane told me, she has been driven by a will to squeeze out every possible minute with her husband and two sons. Her older son doesn't like to travel, but she's toured the world with the youngest, now 15, knowing each trip could be her last.

"I've been told so many times that I only have a few weeks to live," said Kahane, who is hairless and pale after the latest debilitating chemotherapy regimen. "The last time was a month ago."

Essentially, she said, she has run out of standard options and was granted permission by the pharmaceutical company Pfizer to take a drug that has not yet been approved by the FDA for use on metastatic breast cancer. Although she's hopeful that it's working, she figured it was probably wise to get her affairs in order.

So on Thursday, her husband helped her out to the Honda Accord for a trip to their attorney's office in Century City. Kahane had an appointment to revise and sign her last will and testament.

The office is on Century Park East, but after pulling into the garage and circling for 15 minutes, Kahane and Baskin found that every space reserved for disabled drivers was occupied. Kahane was feeling weak, and they had a 30-pound oxygen tank to lug. They finally left the garage, intending for Baskin to help his wife out at the red curb in front of the building and then go park the car.

"We weren't there three seconds when the officer came up behind us and started honking on his horn," Kahane said.

Baskin says he dashed around the car—which has a disabled placard—and was helping his wife with her oxygen tank when the officer, apparently not moved by their distress, insisted that Baskin move the car.

"I said, 'Officer, I know we're not supposed to be here, but I've got to get her out of the car,'" says Baskin, but he didn't get much sympathy by his account. "I can tell this guy is not going to help me out, and I've got a wife who could drop dead at any point."

Kahane had started toward the building, but returned because she didn't like the way the officer was talking to her husband.

"My husband was trying to explain the circumstances, that I had terminal cancer, that there was no place to pull off the street, and the officer said, 'I don't care about that.' People were starting to gather around who were walking on the sidewalk, telling him to leave us alone....I started crying because it was very upsetting, having to go and sign your will to begin with, and this guy was more than I could deal with."

She thought she'd seen the worst of it, but she hadn't. Cheating death is one thing, but getting the best of a traffic officer is an entirely different challenge.

"I'm five-two, and this big fella leans into my face and yells at me, 'Why are you crying? You shouldn't be crying. I'm not giving you the ticket. I'm giving the ticket to the car.'"

Baskin said the officer warned him again to move the car, but he figured that since he was getting cited anyway, he might as well help his wife up to the building. When he returned, the officer was putting a $70 ticket on the windshield.

"I said, 'You're evil, you're mean. What are you doing?' The man showed no mercy whatsoever. My husband said, 'I wonder how you sleep at night when you do things like this,' and he said, 'I sleep very well, thank you.' And then he drove off."

When a supervisor in the city's parking department told me I couldn't talk to the officer, whose name is listed on the ticket as D. Brown, I drove to Century City and parked in the very spot where Kahane and Baskin got their ticket. Yes, it's a red, clearly marked no-parking zone. But several cars were stopped there and did not appear to be obstructing the flow of traffic. So it's hard to imagine why a traffic officer would find himself incapable of allowing a disabled person two minutes to get out of the car.

I sat there for 10 minutes, 20, then 30. Where's a traffic officer when you need one? I drove around Century City looking for Officer Brown, or any other traffic officer, but struck out. I drove back to Century Park East and waited another 20 minutes. No luck.

Amir Sedadi, assistant general manager of the parking and traffic office, said an investigation is under way following a complaint by Kahane. Although it's not complete, he said the officer reported that he twice asked Baskin to move the car before writing the ticket.

"The driver refused and unfortunately the officer had no choice but to issue the citation," Sedadi said.

Hogwash.

The choice the officer had was to open his eyes, see a couple in distress, and show a little compassion.

"If there's something good that can come out of it," Sedadi added, "we'll use this to enhance our training modules....We do run one of the nation's best parking programs."

Who Has the Bread
for a $15 Hot Dog?

(March 11, 2007)

Even in Greater Los Angeles, home to Urasawa's $250 sushi dinner and Campanile's $14-and-up grilled cheese sandwiches, it does not seem possible. A $15 hot dog? A hamburger at that price would be an obscenity. But a lowly wiener? This is history in the making, if not a sure sign of the apocalypse. In the year 2007, Southern California has gone over the edge.

The home of the offending haute dog is the brand-new Trifecta Restaurant & Sports Lounge at 2nd and Hill Streets in downtown Los Angeles. Downtown boosters kept telling us a renaissance was going on downtown, but they never warned us it would lead to this.

One day an editor and I stopped in at the Trifecta to see with our own eyes if the rumor could possibly be true. We checked the menu and there it was: "BOLD VENTURE—The Big Footer." Bold venture, indeed.

The dog was described thusly: "A foot-long all-beef juicy hot dog on a toasted, buttered hot dog bun, served with sauerkraut, red cart onions (New York–style onions), brown mustard and ketchup."

Unless it came with all the beer you could drink, that still didn't explain why it was $15, and I thought it made sense to invite a team of wiener experts to join me in a taste test. So I called the Pink family.

Pink's hot dogs, at Melrose and La Brea Avenues, has been a local institution since 1939. Gloria Pink took my call, heard me out and then asked the obvious question.

"A $15 hot dog?" Yeah, it's un-American, isn't it?

Gloria, Richard and Beverly Pink gladly accepted the mission and met me at Trifecta one day last week, and see if you can guess what color they were wearing.

Yep. Richard's pink shirt had "Pink" cufflinks from the upscale London clothing and accessory store by that name, and his wife and sister wore hot dog pins and toted little hot dog purses. I wish I'd gotten there in time to see whether they arrived in a wienermobile.

Trifecta has roughly 600 TV screens, some of them bigger than the face of Half Dome. Between that and the glare off the Pinks, I could barely see the menu. When our waitress came by, we asked what she thought of the hot dog. It's excellent, she said. Kind of like the hot dogs at Costco.

Who could say no after a recommendation like that? Richard and I each ordered a dog, and Beverly and Gloria decided to split one. Meanwhile, they sent us a new waitress. I think the first one might have been locked in the freezer after the Costco comparison.

The hot dogs at Pink's start at $2.85 and go all the way up to $6.45 for the Three Dog Night—three wieners in a giant tortilla, with onions, chili, three slices of cheese, three slices of bacon, three paramedics and a defibrillator. I should point out that fries cost an extra $2.15, whereas they're included with the Trifecta dog.

Finally, the moment of truth.

"It's a beautiful-looking dog," Mr. Pink said as he surveyed the white, rectangular plates with three little cups for mustard, relish and ketchup. "Nice presentation."

Each of the Pinks poked and tasted, poked and tasted, as if they were judging duck à l'orange.

"A little spicy," Richard said approvingly, but maybe a bit too dense. A bit? The LAPD should look into replacing their batons with these things.

"It's good," said Gloria, but she couldn't hide what was really on her mind. "It doesn't have the snap," she said.

"No," Beverly said in a somber tone.

"No," Richard chimed in gravely. That's the problem with grilling dogs, he said. When you steam, as Pink's does, a dog holds its snap—a crackling burst of flavor. It's that snap, and good value at low prices, that keeps customers lined up day and night, Gloria said.

"A hot dog should be habit-forming," Richard said, doubting that many folks can afford a $15 hot dog habit. "You're really going to have to love a dog at that price."

Chef Will Gotay had gotten word that the Pinks were in the house, and he visited our table to see what they thought.

"It was good," they said simultaneously.

Gotay, who cooked previously at Mastro's and Citizen Smith, said he wants to cater to an upscale, sports-minded crowd, so he asked his meat purveyor to get him the best dog he could find. These were flown in from Chicago, Gotay said, and I almost choked on the coincidence: The *Tribune*-owned *Los Angeles Times* keeps flying wieners in from Chicago, too.

Gotay told the Pinks he's still working on the menu and the concept, and hopes to add a cigar bar and movie and dinner nights on Fridays. It's a tough business, for sure, and they wished him well.

I asked Gotay if, by chance, he'd ever eaten at Pink's. He seemed to have lost track of how many times.

"Any chef who doesn't tell you he hits Pink's or Carl's Jr. after work is lying," Gotay said.

Speaking of hamburgers, try not to fall off your chairs when I tell you what Trifecta's Kobe beef hamburger costs. Twenty-five bucks!

Are the owners of Tommy's burgers reading this? If so, let's have lunch.

Out on a Limb Over
Trimming Fiasco

(November 28, 2007)

Everybody's got a horror story about a bureaucratic nightmare, but if you can top this one, call me collect at your earliest convenience.

Ann Collard was seven months pregnant with her third child in June when an abatement notice came from the Glendale Fire Department. She and her husband, Mike, were ordered to clear some foliage and maintain five feet of "vertical clearance between roof surfaces and overhanging portions of trees." The Collards knew their oaks and sycamores needed a trim. And so they talked to neighbors, did a little research and called a recommended tree trimmer based in Orange County.

For $3,000, the guy said, he'd remove about 15 percent of the foliage and they'd be in the clear. The Collards asked if a permit was necessary. Not at all, said the licensed trimmer, who told the Collards he'd done lots of work in Glendale.

On the third day of the three-day job, the city's urban forester happened to be in the neighborhood, and noticed the tree trimmer doing his thing.

"She saw what was happening and said, 'Stop! Cease and desist!' " says Mike, a work-at-home software and computer guy.

Glendale has an indigenous tree protection ordinance that dates to the 1980s. It was enacted to discourage developers and homeowners from bulldozing or hacking trees willy-nilly. Earlier this year, because of citizen complaints that native trees were still being ruined, the city approved more restrictions and bigger fines. None of which the Collards knew about.

They now admit that had they read the fire department notice closely, they would have seen in small print that a free permit was required to trim oak and sycamore branches larger than one inch in diameter. But it was an understandable oversight.

A week after her first visit, the urban forester was back, telling the Collards an arborist would come by soon to assess the damage. The Collards recall being told they might want to hire an attorney.

"That's when we realized the gravity of the situation," says Ann. "I was pregnant and crying, but it didn't help."

In August, the Collards got a visit from the arborist. She looked at the trees, took measurements and jotted down notes. How bad could it be? The Collards began to anticipate the possibility of a fine, but it wasn't as if the trees were mauled. They looked pretty good in fact. Finally, on October 1, a letter arrived. It was from Glendale's Neighborhood Services administrator.

"Dear Owner," it began. "The city of Glendale is committed to maintaining a community with quality streetscapes that include the care and well-being of protected indigenous trees."

The letter informed them they had improperly pruned 13 trees, some of them on city property because they were near the street, and some on their own property. The fine was listed on page two, where the Collards were informed they would be charged "two times the value of the damaged tree(s)."

"Total: $347,600."

"I about passed out," says Ann. She'd been worried they might get fined as much as, say, $3,000. "But this wasn't like 'Oh no, we won't be able to go on that vacation we were planning,'" she said.

Fortunately, the city did not ask for the Collards' newborn son as part of the settlement. But the prospect of financial ruin had the former high school sweethearts wondering if they could serve jail time instead of taking out a second mortgage. The Collards began dialing City Hall for help.

"Is there somebody who could adjust the amount?" Ann recalls asking, without ever getting an answer. "But even if they met us halfway, that's $170,000. We can't pay that, either."

Ann points out that White House aide Lewis "Scooter" Libby was fined $250,000 for perjury, obstruction of justice and lying to investigators in the case of CIA operative Valerie Plame. She adds, with appropriate exasperation, that Glendale Memorial Hospital drew a $25,000 fine in October for a medical error in which "a person was killed."

The Collard home is in a relatively high danger zone for wildfire, so I can understand why the fire department told them they needed to trim back flammable plants. But if the city's going to go after anybody, they'd be better off citing the Collards' next-door neighbor, whose branches are perilously close to the house.

"It's ridiculous," said Frank Ramos, who lives across the street and can't believe City Hall could leave the Collards hanging like this. The yard looks good, he said. It's not like the trees were butchered. He said he'd have done the same thing in their shoes. "They're a nice couple."

The Collards owe $1,200 to an attorney who got hold of the arborist's report, which alleged they'd had up to 60 percent of the foliage whacked on some trees. The trimmer used spiked shoes, too. A no-no.

The Collards are sorry they didn't know about the required permit, but they dispute the 60 percent allegation and have before-and-after pictures to argue their point. The report also said some of the trees were worth as much as $100,000. I'd like to go on the record as being in favor of trees, but if the Collards really have more than a million dollars worth of trees, maybe they should declare their property a national forest and secede from Glendale entirely.

And how about that team of geniuses who bloodlessly produced a $347,600 fee notice and blithely stuck it in the mail without a single person saying, "Hey, wait a minute. Isn't this insane?"

The Collards called City Hall repeatedly to see if someone might offer them an option other than robbing a bank. When they got no satisfaction, they started a website, www.glendaletreefine.com, to lay out their case and call for revision of the tree-cutting ordinance. Glendale residents quickly weighed in, slamming City Hall.

"Absolutely ridiculous," wrote Stephen.

"Two words—common sense!" wrote Jonathan.

The Collards soon found out they weren't the only victims of excessive fines.

"I was fined $175,000 for cutting two sycamores after my architect contacted the city and was warned not to touch oak trees," says John Oppenheim, a registered nurse and single dad. "I am not a criminal, though because of a string of bad advice, I did make a mistake."

Only after the tree fine story got some attention did city officials step up. City Councilman John Drayman told me the Collards shouldn't have to pay a nickel. Councilman Frank Quintero called the whole thing a fiasco and an embarrassment.

When I got hold of Mayor Ara Najarian, he said I was the first to learn that City Attorney Scott Howard had decided to drop the case against the Collards.

So they're completely off the hook? For now, Najarian said. But they'll be called in for a conference at some point. And might they still be fined? Possibly, he said, but nowhere near $347,600.

How much, then? Maybe $10,000, maybe less, Najarian said.

And maybe the tree trimmer should get stuck with the bulk of the fine. Yeah, and maybe the city should apologize to the Collards, pay their lawyer fees, and clear the deadwood out of City Hall.

The Yard Cops
Will Not Be Deterred

(February 13, 2008)

You'd think that after fining a family $347,000 last year for trimming some overgrown trees on their property, the city of Glendale could rest on its laurels. But there is no end to the zeal of City Hall bureaucrats, who are as determined as ever to let no good deed go unpunished.

A couple of years ago, Pete Anderson and Sally Browder decided to do something about a nagging bout of guilt. Like most people in water-challenged California, they were pouring gallons of it into their yard, feeding a nice green lawn like every other resident of their block.

"It's the principle of the thing," said Browder, a recording engineer and the mother of a little girl who happens to be one of my daughter's buddies.

"Even if I had all the money in the world," said Anderson, a musician, endlessly running the sprinklers "would be wrong from an ecological point of view." So they decided to starve their lawn.

While they waited for it to die, Browder began researching drought-resistant plants and making trips to the Theodore Payne Native Plant Nursery in Sun Valley. Last August, she and Anderson removed the dead grass, ripped out the irrigation system, built a decorative dry creek bed, and paved an area along the driveway with used brick. In rich dark soil next to that, they neatly placed incensia, sage, blue-eyed grass, monkey flowers, Point Reyes manzanita and woolly blue curls, taking care not to squeeze the plants too close together.

"I like it a lot," said next-door neighbor Rachel Stull, who helped with some of the planting. "I think it adds character" on a block that otherwise looks like "a planned community."

But a City Hall emissary, working for the same Neighborhood Services department that was involved in the infamous tree-trimming fiasco, did not share this enthusiasm. He cited Anderson and Browder on August 29 for having too much paving material and too few plants.

Anderson and Browder were dumbfounded. Until they got the violation notice, they had been unaware of a city ordinance requiring that 40 percent of their lot be fully landscaped. They thought they'd done a pretty nice job, so when two months went by without more contact from the city, they assumed the matter had been dropped.

Reader alert: No one living in Glendale should ever assume that City Hall has backed off. If your fence, flagpole, trees or anything else is the least bit out of conformity, the city's good soldiers will always keep coming.

Anderson says a mix-up led to a missed appointment with an inspector. And then, before the year was out, he and his wife were slapped with another, completely unrelated violation.

"Pursuant to BSC V5.1001.8.2," said the notice, "the paint on the exterior windows, frames, sills, doors is peeling/flaking, a substandard condition."

What next, they wondered? Would their daughter be cited for riding a tricycle on the brick pavers? They had already intended to paint the house, but it was more than a little strange having City Hall order them to. Then came Anderson's call to a City Hall employee who mentioned "the photos."

"What photos?" Anderson asked.

"We took some pictures of the house," came the response.

Anderson's reaction? "It really creeped me out." He said the man told him he had "too much brick on his setback."

"I want to comply," Anderson told him, "but what am I supposed to do?"

At this point, it would have been easier to move to Burbank. But Anderson and Browder, who had now been billed $148 for city inspections, were too ticked off to back off. On January 31, they went to City Hall for a meeting with Suzana Delis, a Neighborhood Services administrative analyst. Anderson brought photos he had taken of other houses in Glendale with lots of paving out front and wondered why only his house was being targeted. He said the city asked for the photos as evidence, presumably so they could bust some more hardened criminals, but he refused to turn them over.

Browder, meanwhile, said Delis wagged a finger at them, saying she wanted their yard to have "no brown, all green" within 90 days. Browder tried to argue that the drought-tolerant plants would take some time to fill in. She says Delis told her there was no such thing as drought-tolerant plants, and Browder did her honest best not to pull out someone's hair.

Delis was out of the office Tuesday and did not call back to give me her version of events. She might have been too busy researching this crazy rumor of drought-resistant vegetation.

The upshot? Anderson and Browder have been given until April 30 to paint any rough surfaces on their house, to remove "excess paving" and to "fully landscape with live plant materials, and maintain at all times."

And what if they don't? The notice is clear on that: "Failure to make the required corrections…may result in criminal charges being filed against you." Yahoo for Glendale, the city that never disappoints.

Joy Gaines of the city's water and power department told me what I already knew: that water availability in California is always a concern. Her department encourages residents to use drought-resistant plants, and she said she would be meeting with city officials to make sure everyone's on the same page.

At City Hall, Sam Engel, the head of Neighborhood Services, said Anderson and Browder should have checked with City Hall before doing anything in their yard. I told him I didn't think people should need permission to do a socially responsible thing like conserve water. Rather than harass Anderson and Browder, I told him, the city should make them a poster family for living in harmony with the environment. All his department can do, Engel insisted, is enforce existing ordinances. If citizens want them to be changed, that's the business of the City Council. When Engel looked at the landscaping photo I borrowed from Anderson and Browder, he said he thought their plants were too small.

"That's dirt," he said of the area between the native plants. "Is it not dirt?"

Well, he's got me. There is indeed some dirt between the plants.

Anderson kissed his wife before leaving for work Tuesday morning and suggested she do her best to keep the gendarmes at bay. The family has already decided to make a concession and dig up some of the bricks. But if that doesn't satisfy City Hall, Anderson is prepared to do hard time.

I Think I See Russia

(September 21, 2008)

I wanted to see the real Alaska, and I was told that would require me to get beyond Anchorage, which is sometimes derided as Los Anchorage because of its enormous population (280,000) and sprawling suburbs. How about going to Nome?

Nome is way, way, way out west on the Bering Sea, reachable only by plane, boat or dog sled. And as vice presidential candidate and Alaska governor Sarah Palin said, in trying to put voters at ease about her foreign affairs credentials, you can see Russia from this part of the state.

So I landed on this edge-of-nowhere burg (population 3,600, give or take a few Eskimos) and headed into town expecting to find lots of Palin supporters and perhaps even a few potential foreign policy advisors in the event of a John McCain–Sarah Palin administration.

It turns out lots of people here have seen Russia, but none of them felt qualified to be vice president or take on a Cabinet position. I borrowed some binoculars and got excited when I zoomed in on a large land mass just to the west.

"That's not Russia," said Norbert Thomas, an Inupiat Eskimo who was carving a piece of driftwood near the beach on a balmy and sunny, 50-degree day. "It's Sledge Island."

I tried to talk politics, but Thomas said he wasn't interested. Besides, he said, "If I don't carve, I don't eat."

My first big surprise came when I dropped by the *Nome Nugget*, which calls itself Alaska's oldest newspaper.

"Rural Alaska is mostly Democratic," said editor and publisher Nancy McGuire.

I wondered, then, how Palin's approval ratings as governor were as high as 80 percent. That's an easy one, McGuire said. The state population is concentrated in and around Anchorage and Wasilla, where she's the hometown girl.

"Shows what they know," said McGuire, a sassy old salt whose shack of an office sits on Front Street, a saloon-studded strip that was teeming with gold-rush prospectors 100 years ago.

Sure, McGuire said, on a crystal-clear day from the nearby village of Wales or from one of the islands, you can see Big Diomede Island, which belongs to Russia, or maybe even the distant cloud cover on the Russian mainland. But it's not like you can smell the Smirnoff or wave to Vladimir Putin.

When McGuire told me that she once flew near Big Diomede for a college class and that her plane was chased away by a Russian MiG, I suggested she might be in line to become Secretary of State.

"I'll go for President," she said, noting that she has more experience with Russia than Palin. "I've seen it closer."

To be honest, I hadn't expected to find a member of the liberal media elite in the town that serves as terminus for the Iditarod mush trail. McGuire's views are not local gospel, though. Mary Knodel, who runs the Arctic Trading Post, is a Palin fan, and not just because she's selling the hot biography, *Sarah: How a Hockey Mom Turned Alaska's Political Establishment Upside Down.*

"She's a breath of fresh air," said Knodel, calling Palin unafraid to stand up to Big Oil or Alaska's GOP establishment. And don't worry about foreign affairs, Knodel said. "If McCain dropped dead tomorrow," Palin would have well-informed advisors, and she'd be able to make "common sense" decisions.

Former Nome mayor Leo Rasmussen said Palin's selection was news to cheer, in part because it promotes the great state of Alaska. But if McCain keels over, is she prepared to lead after just two years in charge of a state with roughly one-third the population of the San Fernando Valley?

"Who is prepared to lead this country?" Rasmussen asked, suggesting that the story of Palin's sudden rise from small-town obscurity was practically Lincolnesque.

OK, so I may not have agreed with everyone I met, but I kind of liked this town, whose motto is "There's no place like Nome." It's a funky, independent-minded burg where it's not uncommon to find people stumbling out of saloons midday or talking politics over coffee.

I met lots of no-nonsense people—some of whom still fish, hunt and work the mines. And most of them, whether they support Palin or not, would have preferred that Palin just be herself, rather than make the silly suggestion that she has foreign affairs insights based on geography, or "command experience" simply because her office oversees the state's National Guard.

At Milano's Pizzeria & Sushi, which is run by Koreans, a table of four was joking about Tina Fey's portrayal of Palin on *Saturday Night Live.*

"And Tina Fey said, 'I can see Russia from my house,'" one woman giggled.

Lew Tobin can't see Russia from his house, but he visited its Bering Sea town of Provideniya in the 1980s with a local envoy. "We broke the ice curtain here first," he boasted.

Lew Tobin. Remember the name. If McCain and Palin prevail, they may look to Nome for a new U.S. Ambassador to Russia. But Tobin, who teaches vocational education to villagers, is no Palin supporter.

"We've had so long a time of people who've gotten by on charisma," he said.

"We want someone who's smart again."

In her *Nugget* editorial this week, McGuire took on both the Democrats and the Republicans for their packs of lies and twisted truths in the presidential campaign. But she neatly harpooned Palin, arguing that her comments on Alaskan energy production were flat wrong and her line about Russia was embarrassing.

"Someone please whack her over the head with a geography book," McGuire wrote.

She ended the editorial with this observation: "Palin is woefully under-qualified to be anywhere near the Oval Office. It kind of makes you want to go out and find a moose and put lipstick on it."

A Stop at the Med Pot Doc

(October 28, 2009)

Oooh, there's a pinch in my lower back. My head hurts, too. And my vision is blurred from going through long lists of Southern California physicians who specialize in herbal medicine. I need relief, and I need it fast, but how does one go about choosing a medical marijuana doctor?

"I am a person first, a scientist second and a friend always," a Melrose Avenue doctor says in an ad that can be found in medical cannabis magazines.

I suppose there are advantages to having a medical marijuana doctor who is a friend always. But I wasn't really looking for a friend.

"Sadly, many of the doctors' offices in our field are shoddy at best," said an ad for a clinic in my neighborhood. "They definitely are not something to gamble on."

Good advice, I guess.

In the end, I chose a Glendale clinic because it was close to home, offered "superior professionalism" and had an appointment time that worked for me. But I was a bit nervous on my way to see the doctor. What if I got rejected? Not that I've heard of that happening to anyone. The open secret is that it's a cinch to get a marijuana "recommendation" in California. A "recommendation" isn't a prescription, but it would allow me to visit a dispensary and buy my buds. In Los Angeles, locating such a place would be no harder than locating a palm tree. The little green crosses are everywhere, with 186 dispensaries operating with city permits and an estimated 600 more that found a loophole.

Why so many? Because of the usual bungling at City Hall. An estimated 600 or so managed to open—if you can believe this—during a *moratorium* on new dispensaries, while city officials fiddled.

Neighborhood groups began complaining about proliferation, proximity to schools and rising crime. So now we've got a city attorney who wants to shut them down and a City Council that will take another whack at this thing in a week or two. But in the meantime, you can shop till you drop for "Sonoma Coma" and "Humboldt Haze."

This is what happens when you're in that murky middle between legal and illegal. I'm all for medical marijuana, and know it brings great relief to many sick people, but it doesn't take a detective to realize that recreational users are driving the industry under the guise of medical need.

As I've written before, we'd be better off legalizing pot altogether in this country, as well as regulating and taxing it. Instead, we spend a fortune on a failed fight that helps cartels and drug gangs prosper, even as bodies pile up. But let's get back to my courtship of Mary Jane.

I parked in Glendale, took the elevator to the top floor of a high-rise and was greeted by a young man in jeans and a ball cap.

"Are you here to see the doctor?" he asked.

As far as I could tell, the entire floor was abandoned but for this little operation. Nice to know there's still one part of the economy firing on all cylinders.

Three other patients were waiting, including a woman with a cane. When she stood, she walked gingerly. I could be in trouble, I thought. My back problem wasn't as obvious. Should I limp when it was my turn?

I felt like I was in a Coen brothers movie. The big empty room, the unseen doctor behind the door, the furtive glances between patients. I filled out some forms, describing the back pain that began roughly 25 years ago. Surgery was recommended in later years, but I've opted instead for stretching and occasional painkillers. Sometimes the pain crawls down my legs or up my back, sometimes it wakes me up at night, and that's the truth, so help me God.

I turned in the forms but then, on the table next to me, I saw a medical marijuana magazine called *The 420 Times*, in which the lead story was, conveniently, "Your First Doctor Visit. What to expect and know." I began to read.

"Would they take me seriously? Would I be laughed at?" the author wrote. "Turns out, I really didn't have much to be worried about. Getting medical marijuana wasn't as hard as I thought it would be." His problem was migraines, and he was in and out of the office in no time, marijuana recommendation in hand.

I was in a panic. I'd had a headache or two. Why hadn't I gone with migraines, and was it too late to switch? Before I could move, the woman with the cane exited the office 10 minutes after she entered. The doctor, wearing a white lab coat, followed behind her.

"I looked at it from across the table, and I trust you," he said to her. It sounded promising.

When it was my turn, the doctor sat at a desk in an otherwise empty room and read my papers. The only medical equipment I saw was a blood pressure cuff.

The doctor told me there were many options for treating back pain, and I told him I didn't want to risk surgery or take conventional painkillers. He wanted to know how I'm affected when back pain keeps me awake. I'm fuzzy and have trouble focusing the next day, I told him.

He seemed to be looking for a different answer. If I'm a writer, he said, did that mean I had trouble doing my job? Definitely, doctor.

I stood to show him where my back hurts. He asked me to bend down, and I demonstrated that I couldn't touch my toes, but I don't think he could see that. He hadn't moved from his seat. I pointed again to my lower back and asked if there were a disc that low. He said he knew nothing about back problems.

"I'm a gynecologist," he said. I see.

He asked if I could have my primary care doctor fax over a brief note about my back problem. Sure, I said.

"There's no rush," the doctor said.

Without having laid a hand on me, he led me back out to the receptionist with the ball cap. I paid $150 for my 10-minute exam and was given my recommendation.

"This certifies that Steve Lopez was evaluated in my office for a medical condition, which in my professional opinion, may benefit from the use of medical marijuana."

Several more patients were waiting their turn. Me? I had some shopping to do, and several hundred stores to choose from. Check back with me next week and I'll let you know how it went.

Mind Over Marauders?

(March 17, 2010)

I was sleeping lightly Tuesday morning and the shaking woke me up, but I didn't think it was an earthquake at first. I thought it was raccoons or skunks tearing up the frontyard again. I jumped off the sofa with my camera, ready to take their pictures, then realized my mistake.

Let me explain. I had been asked by an animal communicator to photograph the invaders if at all possible. Dana Miller, of the Sunland-Tujunga area, says she is better able to "connect" with animals if she's got their photos. Yes, it's come to this. Me sleeping in my clothes with one eye open, trying to take pictures of raccoons and skunks for an animal psychic. It's crazy, I know. Combat does that to you.

Please do not—repeat, DO NOT—send me your advice on how to get rid of the pests. I've tried them, trust me, and they didn't work for more than a few days with this band of marauders. I have killed worms and grubs, replaced turf with stones, soaked rags in ammonia, scattered mothballs, sprinkled coyote urine, burst hoses using motion-sensor sprinklers, and shaken out enough cayenne pepper to season all of Louisiana.

Still, raccoons and skunks tear up my yard two or three times a week. Repairing the damage has cost a small fortune the last several years, and I have nothing to show for the investment. Trapping? Nope. They'd just send in replacements. The only idea readers sent me that I didn't try was a five-foot-tall, motion-activated, singing Santa. I was game, but then Walmart discontinued the product. On the Internet, I found a possible substitute—an African American Santa who dances, sounds like James Earl Jones and sings "Jingle Bells," "Up on the Housetop" and "O Christmas Tree." But he cost $155, and the way things have been going, the raccoons will be selling tickets to concerts in my frontyard.

I was out of options until I met up with some Laurel Canyon residents who were trying to capture a coyote, and finally did so with help from Dana Miller. If Miller could talk to a coyote telepathically and help capture it, I asked her at the time, could she please tell my raccoons and skunks to leave me alone? Possibly, she said.

"I know you're a skeptic," Miller told me Tuesday morning when I met with her at Coffee Bean & Tea Leaf in Montrose.

Who, me?

OK, so I have a little trouble believing that someone can use psychic power to find lost dogs, or speak to cats who have passed to the other side, or sit in a living room in Sunland-Tujunga and talk to raccoons and skunks in Silver Lake. But I'm desperate, and what do any of us really know about normal? Miller's website, www.whatanimalstellus.com, is loaded with testimonials from satisfied customers ("Because of you, I got my sweet Lucky back," Gina of Burbank wrote about her cat). And I must say that Miller, a former medical writer and classical musician, looked and sounded pretty normal to me. I mean, she didn't say her dog was one of the Twelve Disciples, or that in an earlier life her husband was a parakeet.

Miller asked me to bring pictures of the yard if I struck out photographing the animals. She must be a fortuneteller as well, because the raccoons got the best of me again Monday night. They were wise to me lurking around the yard with a Canon Powershot and stayed away. After she looked at the photos of my yard, Miller asked me to go back through the history. For a while, I said, the motion-sensor sprinkler got rid of the varmints. They gave me a break and began digging trenches in Daisy's yard next door. But then they came back with a vengeance, and there's no apparent reason why, in the immediate neighborhood, I'm the only one who gets hit regularly.

"There's an energy there," Miller said. Meaning what, they don't like me personally? I didn't get a direct answer.

There might be a witness to the nightly mayhem, I told Miller. I'm pretty sure that Teddy, my neighbor Hilda and Emil's dog, knows more than he's telling. I suspect his silence may be because of retaliation threats by the leader of the raccoon gang. Would a photo of Teddy help in her investigation?

"It might," Miller said, but she asked me not to get my hopes up. "I can't guarantee anything," she said, explaining that her work is easier when she can focus on a single, specific animal.

If she's able to make contact with my tormentors, Miller said, she'll ask them why they're subjecting me to such suffering and whether they'd consider going elsewhere.

Instead of an up-front fee, Miller asked me to consider a donation after the fact, based on the results. Fair enough. I'll give it a few weeks, and if nothing has changed, I'm either selling the house or calling in the black Santa.

Who's Who
with Whose Funds?

(April 21, 2010)

A few weeks ago, my colleague Garrett Therolf wrote about how Los Angeles County Supervisor Mark Ridley Thomas used $25,000 in public funds to buy himself a place in *Who's Who in Black Los Angeles*. Well, it turns out he wasn't the only one. Last week I bought a copy of the $34.95 book to see what we got for our $25,000, and sure enough, Ridley Thomas is in there. But what jumped out was the "Government Spotlight" section, a six-page feature on a local utility that's been all over the news because of its arrogant rate-hike demand.

You guessed it. The Los Angeles Department of Water and Power.

• No fewer than 10 senior members of the department are featured in *Who's Who in Black Los Angeles* with nice head shots and bios. Lamar Odom of the Lakers didn't make the cut. Will Smith is nowhere to be found. But 10 DWP people you never heard of are in there?

And there's more. You'd think that after the amazing five-year package of bonuses and pay hikes DWP employees were given late last year, they'd be making enough to pay their own way into *Who's Who*. But they didn't, of course. Documents show that the DWP paid $7,500 in 2008 to be in the first edition of *Who's Who in Black Los Angeles*, and another $15,000 to be in the current edition. I guess we're lucky it's not a monthly publication. These sums aren't going to break the bank at DWP, a $4.5 billion agency. But that's ratepayer money, and not since about eighth grade have I met anyone who actually looks at a *Who's Who* of anything.

The first time I got a letter from *Who's Who* congratulating me on my selection into the club, I felt great. Until I got to the second paragraph, where they told me what it would cost. That's when I chucked the whole thing.

"I was solicited to be in there," said Earl Ofari Hutchinson, the author, columnist and commentator who is *everywhere* in Los Angeles except in *Who's Who in Black Los Angeles.* Hutchinson said the solicitation struck him as "a hustle" and he ignored it.

"I have a body of work," he said. If they wanted to include him in the publication on his merits, fine. But Hutchinson said he wasn't going to pay or look for a sponsor. It's for people who "want to promote their ego," Hutchinson said, and he didn't feel the need. When he saw the publication, he wasn't impressed, not that there aren't a lot of worthy honorees.

"I can immediately think of 10 people who have done meaningful things to contribute to the life of the city, and I dare say they're not in there."

When I called the Who's Who Publishing Company in Columbus, Ohio, I was told you don't have to pay to be in their publication. And that's true for some of those included, although DWP leaders and Ridley Thomas generously obliged, paying for packages that included some advertising.

L.A. City Councilman Bernard Parks' staffers told me they aren't sure how he ended up in the publication, but no payment was made. And Earl Paysinger, LAPD assistant chief, didn't pay and didn't know he was in the book until I called him.

Senior Editor Nathan Wylder told me *Who's Who* reads local publications for "people whose names and faces pop up in the news." That could explain why Sharon Harper was included. She made headlines for being demoted as L.A. County's second highest executive late last year after the *Los Angeles Times* reported that county auditors found she had improperly helped her son-in-law obtain a county job at inflated pay.

At DWP, spokesman Joe Ramallo said the utility was solicited by Anthony Asadullah Samad, a local author who serves as associate publisher of *Who's Who in Black Los Angeles.* (I left messages but didn't hear back from Samad.) Ramallo said the money the DWP spent on *Who's Who* wasn't just to honor its employees, but for "outreach and communication within the African American community." This year's $15,000 payment covered three pages of advertising in *Who's Who* and 25 complimentary copies of the book.

As for Mark Ridley Thomas, he told Garrett Therolf that his $25,000 was for the inclusion of 14 county officials besides himself. I've asked Ridley Thomas to explain his justification for the expense, and to update me on the plans he announced last year to spend $707,000 remodeling his office. He was busy but said he would meet with me soon.

That's good, because I can't wait to hear his explanation for spending county money to see himself and a few colleagues in a dust-collecting vanity publication. His $25,000 *Who's Who* payment came out of a discretionary fund. Each supervisor gets $3.4 million each year to spend at will, and currently the unspent total for all five supervisors is about $27 million.

That's nowhere near enough to cover the $500 million budget shortfall. But if the supes surrendered their personal stashes, they could save dozens of jobs and cover the $27 million in proposed cuts for four departments—public health, libraries, social services and the assessor's office.

They'd be heroes. Heck, they could end up in *Who's Who*.

An Award and a Pink Slip

(June 23, 2010)

Last Wednesday, Alhambra High School library technician Terry Cannon rose to a standing ovation from his peers as he was named the school's employee of the year.

Two days later, the employee of the year got laid off. And so it goes in California, home of never-ending school budget cuts. Happy summer to all.

Cannon's work was outstanding, said Alhambra Valley Unified Superintendent Donna Perez, who called budget-driven layoffs "heart-wrenching." He taught kids research skills, introduced them to great literature, catalogued books—anything that was needed.

Cannon was given the ax along with 17 other library technicians, health assistants and custodians—layoffs that were almost certain to be made official at Tuesday night's Alhambra Unified board meeting. In addition, 17 bus drivers have been told they'll lose a month's pay.

Perez said she has whacked a total of $45 million out of her budget over the last three years and could lose 80 teachers next year, when it looks like she'll have to squeeze out an additional nine million.

"I've come to terms with the loss of the job," Cannon told me Tuesday afternoon in his living room, saying he was primarily upset about the way it was handled. He was fired on the last day of school after the students had left, so he didn't get to tell them he wouldn't be there in the fall when they return.

"I guess they're afraid you'll go postal, or steal library books, or, God forbid, lower morale," said Cannon, 56. "Although, I've never seen morale as low as it is."

As we spoke, Cannon went to a living room cabinet and brought out his award—a shiny golden apple. He told me that in preparation for Tuesday's board meeting, he'd spent the morning at his computer, next to a Tommy Lasorda bobble head, writing the speech he intended to read to the board that night.

"My name is Terry Cannon, and you don't know me," begins the speech. "But within the hour you will rubber stamp the superintendent's recommendation to eliminate my position as library technical assistant at Alhambra High."

He intended to ruffle some feathers and accuse the board members of being all about numbers rather than people, with no personal knowledge of what those people do.

"I'm going to share an inscription written in my 2010 yearbook by a student," he said. "'Hi, Mr. Cannon,' it read. 'You are one of the nicest people I've met at AHS. I love how I could always just walk into the library and talk to you about anything. You are so dedicated to your work and you obviously love working with students.'"

It doesn't matter, Christine. He's gone (unless, after my deadline, the official termination was delayed by the board).

Alhambra High is a big school, with 3,000 students and a library collection Cannon pegged at about 50,000 books. Running that library will be a one-person job after Cannon's departure, and that won't be easy, admitted Donna Perez. Cannon said he decided to work in public service because he was inspired by his wife, an Alhambra High teacher. Five years ago, when he quit work as an editor in the publishing industry and applied for the library tech job, his interviewer asked him how he thought he'd like working with high school students.

"I have no idea," he answered back then. But, he told me, he ultimately found the answer. "I loved the kids. It hadn't been a cool thing for them to go to the library, so I wanted to make it a fun place where they could go to study or just hang out." He put together cultural displays, exhibited the work of artist friends and tried to motivate students to shoot for college.

"I think 50 percent of our kids qualify for school lunches," said Cannon, who believes the advantage gaps grow wider with each round of cuts. "In college, they'll need to do high-level academic research—not Internet searches, but reference-based research in scholarly journals—and they're not going to know how to do that. And that's our future. If we don't build a decent education for them, how do we get out of the morass we're in? We'll have huge unemployment and welfare and end up paying in a much greater way."

Well said. Not many of my days go by without hearing from desperate and angry parents, teachers and administrators struggling with cuts. We all know the state's got a huge budget deficit and some hard choices to make because nobody wants cuts to their pet programs and nobody wants to pay higher taxes. What frosts me is that in the midst of a crisis and in the heat of a campaign for governor, conventional wisdom says a candidate can't risk telling us how they'd get us out of this mess and what the state's priorities should be.

It's the only thing I want to hear them talk about. I don't care if Meg Whitman shoved a former colleague at EBay or Jerry Brown had a mixed record as governor 30 years ago. I want to know what they want to do, how they intend to do it, and whether they think Alhambra High School's employee of the year ought to be on the job in the library, or queuing up in the unemployment line with his résumé and shiny golden apple.

The Bleeding Bell Blues

(July 21, 2010)

In the newspaper business, when editors are asked what kinds of stories they want to go after, there's a popular two-word answer. The first word is "holy" and the second word is unprintable. Well, friends, my colleagues Ruben Vives and Jeff Gottlieb dug up a genuine "holy [cow]" story in the town of Bell, California last week, exposing the staggering, colossal, unconscionable salaries that city officials have awarded themselves under the radar of the struggling town's residents.

On Monday, I drove to Bell to see if I could make sense of how it all happened. I parked at City Hall, walked up to the counter and asked to speak to the nearly $800,000-a-year city manager, because I was dying to see what such a specimen looks like.

A clerk dutifully took my name and disappeared. On his salary, Robert Rizzo—or should I say Ratso Rizzo?—would surely want to take me out to a nice lunch. Or perhaps pay off my mortgage. He was dumb and arrogant enough, after all, to tell my colleagues that if his $787,637 salary was "a number people choke on, maybe I'm in the wrong business. I could go into private business and make that money."

When the clerk returned, she told me Mr. Humility was unavailable.

Maybe he was busy testing the waters in private business, because now that he's been exposed, I'm betting it will get a little hot for old Ratso—and his $376,288 assistant, and the city's $457,000 police chief, and the

$100,000 part-time council members. In fact, it already is. Outraged citizens descended on City Hall by the hundreds Monday night demanding that the bums be tossed out on their ears.

"They've awakened a sleeping giant," Denisse Rodarte, a lifelong Bell resident and one of the organizers of the rally, told me in her home a short distance from City Hall. But why was the giant asleep in the first place, and unaware of the plundering?

Corruption is everywhere in California and beyond, from civic centers to Wall Street. But there's a particular strain of brazen malfeasance in south and southeast Los Angeles County, with a shameful history of headlines emanating from Maywood and South Gate and Compton and Carson, to name only a few. Whether you're talking to residents or think-tank types, you hear some common themes.

Those cities have largely poor, immigrant populations that are too busy working to pay close attention to City Hall, which means they can be easily exploited. Voter turnout is low, in part because many residents are undocumented and even many legal immigrants aren't yet qualified to vote. And there's not much media presence because of cutbacks by everyone in the industry, including the *Los Angeles Times*, so the rascals are left to steal with impunity.

"It's a very predatory type of mentality," said Cristina Garcia, a Bell Gardens resident who is an adjunct professor at USC. Garcia, who is now helping organize protests in nearby Bell, said she suspects the vultures deliberately move into cities where they think it'll be easy pickings. Rizzo moved to Bell from Hesperia in 1993 at a salary of $72,000. By 2005, as Vives and Gottlieb reported, he was up to $442,000, and his contract was amended to give him 12 percent increases annually. The boobs on the City Council, meanwhile, altered the City Charter so they wouldn't have to comply with state guidelines on council salaries.

The cynic in me wonders who's rubbing whose back and what they're getting out of it. And in fact, the L.A. County district attorney is investigating Bell's exorbitant City Council paychecks. But this may merely be a case of city officials bellying up to the trough and grabbing all they can.

"People get power and it turns to greed," said South Gate mayor Henry Gonzalez, who was punched by a fellow council member and shot in the head by an unknown assailant back when his town was being ravaged by City Hall thieves in a corruption scandal 10 years ago. Jaime Regalado of the Edmund G. "Pat" Brown Institute for Public Affairs at Cal State Los Angeles said officials in southeastern L.A. County have taken advantage of the fact that many immigrant residents aren't shocked by corruption, having come from countries where it's even more blatant.

"But when it hits the press, as it has in Bell, there's the potential for an uprising," Regalado said.

In fact, no one in Bell knew about the inflated salaries before the *Los Angeles Times* blasted them across page one. But that's not because nobody was interested in local affairs, Denisse Rodarte insisted. It's because City Hall was run like the Kremlin.

"We're not ignorant," said Rodarte, a college grad who works in the nonprofit medical field.

Lots of hard-working people care about their community and how it's run, Rodarte added. But it's been impossible to get information out of City Hall, whether she was asking about how to volunteer at the food bank or about why, when there's plenty to worry about at home, Bell officials took over some services for nearby Maywood, which has its own history of rotten scoundrels.

Rodarte said residents were mocked and degraded by council members when they protested the Maywood deal, but they're not going to back down again. She's now signed on with the Bell Association to Stop the Abuse (or BASTA, which means "enough" in Spanish), and along with Cristina Garcia, her ally from Bell Gardens, she's trying to organize such a movement across southeast L.A. County. All of which brings us back to Bell's city manager, who makes twice as much as President Obama.

Are people choking on that number, Ratso? If there's justice, you'll be the first thing they spit out.

POLITICS AS USUAL

Jim Hahn in the 'Hood

(January 25, 2002)

When I saw the page one story about Mayor Jim Hahn appointing a small army of wealthy pals to city commissions, I knew exactly where I had to go. To L. Tolliver's Barber Shop at Florence and Western. Nowhere in all of Los Angeles did Slim Jim Hahn have more passionate support during his campaign than at L.T.'s clip shop, a mile east of where he grew up. The resident elders argued that Hahn's daddy had been good to the community, and the apple doesn't fall far from the tree.

But sons do not always grow up to be their fathers, and it sure looks like Jim Hahn has stiffed the very people who helped put him where he is. Of Hahn's 114 appointments to various commissions so far, the majority are campaign donors with fancy zip codes, as the *Los Angeles Times'* Matea Gold neatly documented. Would you like to know how many are from South L.A., where Hahn had practically passed himself off as another brother from the 'hood?

Five.

It's true after all. You just can't trust white people.

"The young cat was right," said a boastful Kevin Hooks, a young pup of just 30 and a regular L.T. customer. Hooks had been beaten down by the elders last year for suggesting that Hahn ought to be judged on his own merits, not his father's.

"You don't just pick up the fruit and eat it when it falls from the trée," gloated customer Tony Wafford, the only one who had sided with Hooks at the most politically tuned-in barbershop in Los Angeles. "You squeeze the fruit, you smell it. You make sure it's not rotten."

"I am appalled by this," confessed proprietor Lawrence Tolliver, dapper as always, his white beard impeccably manicured. Tolliver and his partner, Mr. Ford, had voted with pride for Jim Hahn, whose father—the late County Supervisor Kenneth Hahn—used to wave to them as he drove by the shop. "But I think it's too early to condemn the man," Tolliver added hopefully. "I still believe I rode the right horse."

"Me too," Mr. Ford said from the red-cushioned comfort of his own barber chair. Behind him is a sign that says, "Cows may come and cows may go, but the bull in this place goes on forever."

Hahn still has two-thirds of his appointments to fill, so there's time to prove he's aware that black people exist even in nonelection years. He told the *Times* that even his sister, an L.A. city councilwoman, had asked him to get on the stick.

"If he doesn't step up and support Bernard Parks, that's going to be another black eye," Tolliver promised, referring to the L.A. police chief, whose reappointment hangs in the balance.

Tony Wafford agreed, but asked a very smart question. Why doesn't Hahn quit playing games and take a stand on Parks now? Is it lack of will? General indecision? Long afternoon naps?

"The heat's on Parks now," Wafford said of a poll in which 93 percent of the force expressed no confidence in its leader. "Why would Hahn wait around except to see which way the public might go?"

"Because that's the way politicians are," Tolliver retorted.

"I'd try to fend off Parks' attackers before they got to him, not wait around and check the polls," Wafford snapped. "I thought you said he had courage like his father."

"We're not here to talk about his father," said a customer. "We're here to talk about Kenny Hahn."

He meant Jim, of course, and Wafford delighted in the mistake. Like Tolliver, Wafford's not ready to write off Jim Hahn over the snub on commission appointments. But he'd warned his buddies last year about the risks of voting for a dead man.

"If the mayor had looked ahead, this wouldn't have happened," Wafford said. "If he'd had me there, I would have said, 'Hey, Jim. Where's the brothers?' You wouldn't have had just these white boys."

"I'll tell you one thing," Mr. Ford interjected, drawing the silence that is due a man with eight decades' worth of wisdom. "You don't want to appoint some fool to one of these commissions just 'cause he's a Negro. We need someone who's got brains."

"I got a list right here," said Tolliver, who opened a drawer and produced no fewer than 90 names of community leaders he's come to know over the years. "I even got a call from Governor Davis and gave him three or four names."

Mr. Ford suggested that with a little more time, Mayor Hahn will surely pay heed to his old neighborhood, the one that trusted him with its votes. This brought Wafford out of his seat.

"If this was some redneck from the Valley, we'd be blocking his car, standing in the driveway singing 'We Shall Overcome,'" he said.

"I'm just saying we should be as aggressive with our so-called friends as we are with our enemies. He didn't have any trouble finding you when he needed the vote, and now he's hanging around in Santa Monica. You'll probably find him over at that place; what's it called? Yeah, Shutters."

What the mayor needs, all the gents agreed, is to keep company with fewer pale-faced yes-men and hangers-on, and start seeking the guidance of those who aren't in it for the money.

"He needs someone who's beholden to nothing but the truth, and that's what I've got," said Tolliver, waving his list of 90 good men Hahn overlooked.

With Slim Jim, there may be even less than meets the eye. But I think there might be enough goodwill at L. Tolliver's Barber Shop to save him.

Haircuts are $10, Jim. It'll be the smartest money you've spent in months.

Will This Grim Hospital
Saga Ever End?

(February 1, 2004)

The body count is up to five. That's how many people have died at
Martin Luther King Jr./Drew Medical Center in the last year because of
unspeakable negligence, and those are only the ones we know about so far.
I'm thumbing through the results of the latest government inquiry, which
was dug up by my colleagues Charles Ornstein and Tracy Weber, and the
44-page indictment of the Willowbrook hospital reads like a Stephen King
novel. Included are hair-raising tales of gross understaffing in critical care
units, nurses ordered to lie about the condition of patients to justify ignor-
ing them, and seriously ill patients left unattended for hours.

Twenty-year-old Oluchi McDonald, who had gangrene of the intestines,
was found dead on the floor after falling, unnoticed, into a pool of his own
vomit. In a December case, a visiting family went to a nursing station to
report that "something was wrong" with their relative, whose doctor had
ordered continuous monitoring. Nurses went to his bedside and found that
his heart monitor had flat-lined. The patient had gone into cardiopulmo-
nary arrest, and he died within hours. Later in the federal inquiry a nurse
who was questioned said she "did not feel comfortable with the use of heart
monitors." Unfortunately, reading the machines was one of her responsibilities. Two nurses at a monitoring station couldn't say whether a red X on the
screen meant an alarm was off or on.

If you find yourself feeling seriously ill while in the vicinity of King/

Drew, I suggest you take two aspirin and ask to be airlifted to any other hospital in the United States or a nearby developing nation. Public officials, of course, are shocked by revelations from King/Drew. They're always shocked, but nobody else is. We've all been reading King/Drew horror stories for years, and yet every new disaster is met with great surprise by Los Angeles County Supervisors, who wring their hands and always promise yet another cleanup—just as they're doing now—that never materializes.

"It's criminal," Supervisor Zev Yaroslavsky told the *Los Angeles Times* in response to the latest horrors. "It's just unbelievable."

Criminal, maybe. Unbelievable, no.

I'm sure King/Drew's got lots of dedicated and talented people. But it's now obvious to one and all that there's something rotten in that place. Incompetence is protected by a calcified civil service system, and a corrosive strain of racial politics has always stood in the way of a good housecleaning.

The hospital, established after the Watts riots to train African American medical professionals and serve African Americans, has had essentially the same African American administrative staff for years. As civil rights attorney Connie Rice puts it, outside input is not welcome.

"Any time it's even suggested that they create a partnership with another hospital that might help them," said Rice, who is African American, "they scream racism."

So it comes as no surprise that weak-kneed politicians have never summoned the courage to take King/Drew, turn it upside down and shake out all the bad eggs.

"There's no question there is some [racial] tension there," said Supervisor Yvonne Brathwaite Burke.

Take the January 23 rally, whose sponsors claimed that the county intended to shut down King/Drew lock, stock and barrel. Co-sponsored by the Congress of Racial Equality of California, the gathering featured fliers including a photo of a smoldering Watts and a finger-pointing Dr. King.

"Don't let it happen!" said the flier. "It's our hospital!"

The county has no intention of closing King/Drew, by the way, although it doesn't strike me as a bad idea. As for it being "our" hospital, who's "our"? The surrounding neighborhood is mostly Latino.

"We will be on top of your desk," Representative Maxine Waters warned county officials at the rally, referring to a plan to close King/Drew's neonatal intensive care unit. That unit, I should point out, was found deficient by the state. It seems to me that if you're going to make threats, maybe you should aim them at hospital administrators instead of warning county officials to back off.

And by the way, it's not about whether the place is run by blacks or whites or Latinos. It's about whether you can take your child or anyone else to the hospital with a reasonable expectation that they'll be taken care of properly, instead of ending up in the newspaper.

It was not clear to me which desk Maxine Waters intended to climb on top of, but I left a message on hers. I asked her to call back and tell me just how many people had to die before she went after the hospital, instead of defending its right to take in more victims. Waters called back to say she's not excusing anyone's incompetence, and if heads have to roll, so be it. But the hospital has to be kept open because it serves people with desperate needs and few alternatives. As for the desk-climbing threat, she said it's county health officials she's talking about. It's their job to crack down on the hospital and keep supervisors informed of problems, she said, and they've failed.

Two nursing administrators were suspended without pay over the latest deaths, and Supervisor Burke told me she thinks the county is finally on the path to reforming King/Drew.

It sounded good. Just like all the other times.

Brother, Can You Spare $500,000?

(February 6, 2004)

I'm not asking any of you to break the bank, but I have to get to New York for an Arnold Schwarzenegger fundraising dinner February 24, and I can't afford a seat at the table. Actually, maybe you will have to break the bank. Schwarzenegger is asking high rollers to help fund his bond-measure campaign, and he wants them to write a check in the amount of...wait a minute. You have to sit down for this. Are you ready?

He's asking for as much as $500,000. *Half a million dollars!*

I've never heard of a $500,000 political donation, and I have to see it in person. It's an astronomical sum, obviously, but that's only half the fun. It's being requested by the very guy who promised he would strap explosives to politics as usual and take a sledgehammer to special-interest fundraising.

Yeah, Gray Davis made treks to New York, hat in hand. He'd have flown to the moon if he thought there was a banquet hall up there. But the whole point of electing Arnold Schwarzenegger was to terminate that kind of pathetic grubbing, not to mention the pandering to donors. Now Arnold turns out to be Davis on steroids, times a thousand, and I think it's in the public interest for me to be a fly on the wall when Big Boy breaks bread in New York.

Let me make it easy on you, folks. All I need is for 500,000 readers to send me a dollar each. If that's too much to ask, my fallback is to beg 50,000 readers for a dollar apiece, because Schwarzenegger apparently will let you in the door for a suggested minimum pop of $50,000.

I think I could raise the 50 grand, but I don't want to end up shoved into a corner, talking to some sap who hasn't gotten over the Dodgers bolting Brooklyn. Get me the $500,000, which makes me a "California Recovery Team Chair," and I'll be able to whisper in Arnold's ear like all the Big Apple's high rollers.

As you might be aware, polls say a majority of Californians are turning thumbs down to Schwarzenegger's $15 billion bond proposal, which will cost us billions more in interest. But he figures if he can raise nine million for an ad campaign, we'll march to the polls like sheep and bail him out. My guess is, he's right. A lot of people have been starstruck from Day One, and gladly overlook Schwarzenegger's little inconsistencies, like his promising to end the days of borrowing our way out of debt.

If I were to bang out a column every time he was careless with the truth, I'd have to write every day and sleep on a cot in the office.

Take his current roadshow, in which the governor claims he inherited the budget gap. He inherited most of it, but he dug the hole even deeper when he rescinded a car-tax increase. During his campaign, he said he was going to square the books by ferreting out billions in waste, fraud and abuse, and then he hired finance chief Donna Arduin to do his digging. But like Punxsutawney Phil, all she brought up from the hole was her own shadow.

Now Schwarzenegger is taking his act to Broadway, and Jamie Court, of the Foundation for Taxpayer and Consumer Rights, is coming out of his shoes. First of all, Court screams, the bond and money barons are in New York, and they're all smiling like thieves as they count the loot they'll make on California's Prop. 57. (I'm asking you to please send me a dollar today, before those Wall Street jackals buy every seat at the fundraiser.)

Secondly, Court snaps, the event is being hosted at the Trump Tower home of Robert Wood Johnson IV, of the Johnson & Johnson family. That company and other pharmaceuticals are lobbying against bulk purchasing of drugs, Court says, a practice that would save taxpayers money but cost the drug companies. And Schwarzenegger declared this Consumer Protection Week in California, snarls Court, who takes the irony one step further. Pharmaceutical companies owe California $1.3 billion in rebates on drug purchases for Medi-Cal patients going back 10 years, according to a new federal audit cited by the *Orange County Register*. You'd think a governor who kept promising to audit everything in sight would have found such an obvious screw-up. But this kind of lapse is to be expected when you spend so much time at political fundraisers.

Court says if the governor cracked down on his buddies in the drug industry, he'd have that $1.3 billion in hand and could nix proposed health-care funding cuts of more than $900 million. Sure, but don't expect me to scold Arnold for every glib contradiction. As long as he sticks with the Hollywood hustle, I've got more in the bank than Donald Trump.

A judge says he illegally funded his campaign, and Schwarzenegger calls the ruling fantastic. He blows a kiss to cities, then backhands them. He plans to have himself investigated, then drops the case.

I am he as you are he as you are me and we are all together.

> I am the egg man
> I am the Walrus
> Goo goo g' joob

Supervisor Math—
They Give, You Pay

(September 29, 2004)

If you live in Los Angeles County, you're probably a far more generous person than you realized. Unbeknownst to you, your hard-earned cash has been scattered around to causes great and small, some of which you've never even heard of.

Sandbaggers Golf Club? You gave.

Daniel Murphy Catholic High School? You gave.

NAACP Holy Hip Hop? You gave.

How did this happen without your knowledge? Each year, members of the L.A. County Board of Supervisors get far more money than they need to run their offices. The extra dough—which can top a million dollars for each of the five supes—goes into discretionary funds, and the supervisors spend that money as they see fit.

When the Disney Concert Hall opened last year to great fanfare, one of the more generous donors listed in the program was Supervisor Zev Yaroslavsky, who kicked in a cool million.

His money? No. It came from Yaroslavsky's discretionary fund, so it was your money. Unfortunately, you did not get your name in the program, or on the wall, as he did. A Yaroslavsky aide argues that the boss offered that million as a challenge to private donors, who ultimately matched the amount.

Fine. But we still didn't get our names in the program. And that donation of public funds was made around the time the county was shutting down healthcare facilities. Now obviously, a million dollars is a lot of money to throw at a pet project. But it's chicken feed compared to what Supervisor Gloria Molina has been doing.

For several years, as my colleague Sue Fox pointed out this week, Molina has been stashing money from her discretionary fund for the project of her dreams—a Mexican American cultural center near Olvera Street.

How much? About $15 million. That's a lot of discretion, no?

It's hard to argue against such a project in Los Angeles, given our history. But it's fair to ask whether it's appropriate for a supervisor to squirrel away millions of tax dollars for a pet project without any input from you or me. And so on behalf of 10 million county residents, I did.

"Whether it's appropriate or not," Molina responded as we sat in her office, "is up to you to decide."

OK, thanks. I've decided it's not appropriate. I say we kill the funds, how's that? I don't want supervisors playing hero with my money, even if the cause happens to be worthwhile. We can make our own charitable contributions. The supervisors are imperial and untouchable enough without the added advantage of what East Coast wags call "walking-around money." You know, take care of friends, plant seeds for the reelection harvest.

"I don't see any challengers being given any money," says Bob Stern of the Center for Governmental Studies. "I could understand $50,000 or some small amount of money to send flowers for funerals or something like that. Maybe. But when you get to this amount of money, with no oversight...."

In the 2003-04 fiscal year, Yaroslavsky spent $3.17 million in discretionary funds. Supervisor Don Knabe handed out $1.26 million, Mike Antonovich scattered $719,828, and Yvonne Brathwaite Burke dropped $657,341.

What, you didn't get any? Call your L.A. County Supervisor today. They've got cash to burn.

Jim: Loosen Up, Lose Janice

(March 27, 2005)

Black won't do. The car has to be red. He needs a sporty red convertible. It's late in the game, and Los Angeles mayor Jim Hahn appears to be in big trouble as he tries to hold on to his job. It's time for him to loosen the tie, get some product, do a complete makeover. Hahn made a desperate attempt last week, trying to pass himself off as a maverick outsider. But given his family's 60 years in local politics, the idea didn't quite take root.

I never would have seen this coming, but I'm developing a soft spot for the guy. Challenger Antonio Villaraigosa is getting by on nothing but the fact that he isn't Jim Hahn, so I think it's only right for someone to give Hahn some advice.

First thing the mayor should do in his new convertible, top down, hair spiked, is go find his political advisors and fire them. They have no idea what they're doing, not that it's entirely their fault. Nobody has any idea how to run a campaign because nobody has any idea how to run Los Angeles. More than ever, the city is unmanageable, indefinable and not interested. Of the 2.7 million voting-age Angelenos, about 1.5 million are registered to cast ballots. Of those, three-fourths didn't show up for the mayoral primary.

"I just found out about the election last night," I overheard one guy say at Taylor's steakhouse on election night, explaining to his parents why he hadn't voted.

The guy who arguably ran the smartest campaign finished out of the running. Bob Hertzberg, despite having been Speaker of the California Assembly, suffered because nobody knew who he was. Had he been the weekend weather guy on local TV, he would have been lighting cigars by now, victory in the bag.

Institutions that hold other cities together don't exist in Los Angeles. Brown people now live where black people once lived. Westsiders know more about the Mayor of New York. Old alliances have eroded and political endorsements are meaningless, although Villaraigosa got a decent nudge last week from Congresswoman Maxine Waters in another blow to Hahn. And the most well-informed Angelenos all happen to be living in Pasadena, so they can't vote.

These realities are part of the exotic and exasperating allure of L.A., a city like no other. But it's not easy to be mayor of a laboratory experiment in which 3.7 million mice are on the loose, several hundred thousand of them still wishing they'd seceded. When Villaraigosa talks about bringing the city together, it's like saying he wants to bring the Balkans and the Middle East together. When, how and why?

But at least he knows how to play the game.

It's L.A., so we don't mind being lied to. For instance, Villaraigosa says he's going to build the world's greatest mass-transit system. There's a better chance of Keanu Reeves becoming an astronaut, but it doesn't matter. Would you rather hear about Villaraigosa's subways and trains, or Hahn's left-turn lanes and his Hal Bernson endorsement?

Listen to me, Jim. Time is running out, and desperate measures are called for. As I said, you've got to really work at it to get the city's attention. Play the bad boy, the bon vivant, the dreamer. Fall in love with a stripper, fire all the commissioners, get a shovel and fill those potholes yourself. I saw you do the Slauson shuffle at Tolliver's barber shop, so I know you've got a couple of moves the public hasn't seen.

First thing you've got to do is ditch the stealth black SUV because it's looking more and more like a hearse. Get yourself the red convertible, drive like the devil and repeat after me:

I have to stop dating my sister.
I have to stop dating my sister.
I have to stop dating my sister.

Janice is nice enough, and the family bond is heartwarming, up to a point. But you've got to bring a few other sweets to the dance. You're Mayor of Los Angeles, and you were sitting up in the rafters at the Oscars, a good-looking single lad like you. Do you have any idea how many starlets and wannabes are on the loose in this town? Lie to them if you have to. They're not going to recognize you anyway. Just say you're a producer.

Better yet, steal the convertible, if not the girl, and lead the police on a long, slow chase. For once, all of Los Angeles will be watching the mayor's every move.

Wife's Book Has
Good Tips for Gov

(April 24, 2005)

I sat down to a haircut Friday morning and began reading a book by Maria Shriver, wondering which would come first: the end of the haircut or the end of the book.

It was a horse race for a while, but I breezed through the last two chapters of *And One More Thing Before You Go...* then had nothing to do while the barber cleaned up my neck.

With time on my hands, I went back to the Acknowledgments and saw that Shriver, the First Lady of California, confessed she had her doubts about writing this "book." She didn't love the idea, she wasn't sure anyone would read such a book and she didn't think she had the time to write it. I can understand her first two concerns, but I don't quite get the third. The $13.95 book is the size of a Hallmark card, and that can't be mere coincidence. If I could read it in less time than it took to get a haircut, how much time could it have taken to write it?

The book grew out of a speech Shriver gave at a luncheon for girls who were graduating from high school and on their way to college. I don't know what high school we're talking about, but I just have a feeling it wasn't one of the California public schools with a scandalous dropout rate and more trouble ahead now that Shriver's husband, Governor Arnold Schwarzenegger, has reneged on his promise to give schools the full funding they were owed.

But thanks to this remarkable book—assuming their school libraries can afford to purchase a copy—even girls at the most crime-ridden and disadvantaged schools will learn from an American aristocrat that "Fear Can Be Your Best Teacher." I have to tell you something, though. While reading this 62-page philosophy for better living, it occurred to me that Maria's words of wisdom—"Be willing to make changes"—might be of use to someone other than teenage girls.

As you probably know, Governor Schwarzenegger's Arnold Express has dropped its transmission. With his agenda disintegrating, staff members duking it out, his popularity dipping and Maria telling Oprah she wants Arnold to come home, it looks like he could use some help.

I don't like to get in the middle of family affairs, but here's a suggestion: Why not just give Arnold a copy of *And One More Thing Before You Go...*? I would advise, however, that he skip Chapter Five: "And When You Need Courage...Think of the Women in Your Life." Enough said on that one. But I would highly recommend Chapter Two: "Be Willing to Let Go of Your Plan." At first, Shriver writes, she felt like it was the end of the world when Arnold decided to run for governor. Then her wise friends emphasized that her life had merely been altered. "Remember that phrase: Just altered. It'll come in handy in your life."

The lesson for Arnold? Maybe he should alter his strategy of bullying legislators, avoiding negotiations and throwing countless half-baked propositions onto the ballot. Reading Chapter Three—"Learn from Your Mistakes"—would point him in the right direction. As Shriver admits, she tried to commandeer a state museum in Sacramento and ticked off everyone involved. She had to then put her ego aside and make amends. Wanna guess how she did that?

"I listened, and I altered [there's that word again!] my vision." And today, Shriver's new book is for sale in the museum gift shop. That's incredible. Way to go, Maria! Sure, it was a struggle, but guess what? "It's not shameful to struggle. It's not wimpy or weak."

Everybody makes mistakes, Shriver says. "Don't panic. Do admit it." I hope Arnold reads that section carefully. It might lead him to admit that it was the height of hypocrisy to criticize former governor Gray Davis for his shameless fundraising, only to rake in a gazillion dollars more than Davis ever dreamed of getting his mitts on, much of it from corporate special interests.

Arnold could admit it wasn't nice, or politically smart, to mock and belittle hard-working nurses and teachers. This would take courage, sure. But as Maria reveals: "Along with love, courage is what you need more than anything in this life. In tough times it tells you, 'I can go through this!' Even when it feels like you can't."

You know the crazy thing about life? "It's a Balancing Act," as we learn in Chapter Six, but if you "Have a Little Gratitude" (Chapter Seven), not only can you move beyond self-pity, but, "It's good for the soul." In Arnold's case, he could say:

"Politics is harder than I thought, and I wish I hadn't broken so many of the fantastic promises that carried me to victory. But, hey, I made a bazillion dollars in Hollywood."

The governor also should study Chapter Nine, "Forget Your Mirrors," which runs all the way from page 50 to page 52. The message is to get over yourself, quit preening and do something selfless. Or as Maria puts it: "I'm challenging you today to not just join sororities in college, to not just spend your extra time in Starbucks, although I love Starbucks."

OK, so it's not quite Uncle JFK's "Ask not what your country can do for you." But politics—and publishing—aren't what they used to be.

Did These Firefighters
Truly Stand By the Gov?

(October 5, 2005)

So what was really going on last week when Governor Arnold Schwarzenegger held a news conference flanked by roughly 20 firefighters fresh off
the front lines of raging wildfires? Was it a love-in, as the governor's media
corps suggests? Or were firefighters forced to stand next to Schwarzenegger, like props, in a staged photo-op designed to boost his sagging support?
Well, I can tell you this: It's now officially campaign season, because I've
heard it both ways.

Katherine McLane of the governor's media corps was there with the
boss, and she claims Schwarzenegger was warmly greeted—cheered, even—
when he showed up to pat firefighters on the back for their brave work.

"I gotta tell you, everybody was cordial and polite, and there was no
rancor. People were glad to see the governor," McLane said, asking if I
had seen the Associated Press story on the event. No, I hadn't. So she sent
it to me.

Here's how it starts: "Thousand Oaks, Calif.—At a time when he has
been at odds with firefighters and other public employee unions, Gov. Arnold
Schwarzenegger was greeted warmly by dozens of uniformed emergency
workers Friday when he visited crews battling wildfires near Los Angeles."

It must be true, then. And yet, something rings false. The governor has
created enemies in firehouses from Eureka to Escondido. He has trashed
unions and waved his pompoms for Proposition 75, which would require

public employee union members to sign off on political uses for their monthly dues. So how did Schwarzenegger find 20 firefighters eager to pose with him?

He didn't, says Pat McOsker, president of United Firefighters of Los Angeles, who went to the command center to check on the condition of colleagues who had been on the job for three days with little sleep. He says the men and women flanking the governor were acting under duress. Some of the firefighters, he says, approached him at the command center.

"They say, 'Hey, we've been told we're going to be a part of this press conference with the governor. Can they do that? Can they make us stand with him? We're not happy about it.'"

McOsker told them to go ask their chiefs if they were required to follow such an order. The answer was yes. "It was utter hypocrisy," says McOsker, whose differences with the governor go beyond Prop. 75.

Schwarzenegger has vetoed legislation to implement the fire protections recommended by a panel he himself appointed after the deadly fires of 2003. And yet there he was, trying to pass himself off as Smokey Bear. McOsker said he began telling reporters at the news conference that the firefighters were ordered to stand up there with Schwarzenegger, and one scribe asked the governor about it. Rather than dispute the contention, Schwarzenegger said everybody is ordered to do things at one point or another. Someone was ordered to put up the podium, he said. Someone was ordered to bring in the microphone.

"I don't think we should bring politics into this," said the governor.

I wish he wouldn't always treat us like such boobs. Of course it was politics. He's got every right to show up at a fire and pat people on the back for a job well done, but the appearance can't be separated from the politics. Not that the firefighters aren't guilty of their own politicking. I only know about the controversy surrounding the photo-op because I got a note from Carroll Wills at the California Professional Firefighters, who wanted to make sure the governor didn't get away with passing himself off as their champion.

But the whole thing also raises a question that goes beyond politics and straight to the heart of voters' concerns about Schwarzenegger. Does he ever get out of makeup, or is everything show business? If firefighters were so happy to share Schwarzenegger's company, I told McLane, have one of them call me.

"Hello," said the voice on the phone. "This is Chuck Marin." Marin, a state fire battalion chief, told me he was the one who set up the news conference. "The governor's office asked, you know, for some firefighters. They asked for some fire engines to be...placed behind the podium, and to see if any firefighters were available to stand back there."

Marin said he made an announcement asking for volunteers. When they showed up, he didn't see anyone with a gun to his head. Little did he know.

"We were all in agreement amongst ourselves: Nobody wanted to do it," said Captain Wayne Ferber of the Ventura County Fire Department. "We were directed by one of our chief officers that this was something we were to do. If you were watching on the TV screen, I was to the right side of the governor, but I was sort of ducking so nobody would see me. I was doing my best to stay out of the picture."

Hmmm, I said. I was told the governor got a warm greeting.

"No, he was not greeted warmly," Ferber said. "I don't think you saw a lot of smiling faces."

Why so glum?

"My wife is a public school teacher, so we kind of get a double whammy here," Ferber said. "The governor is taking on teachers. When he came in, we all had high hopes for him."

Steve Francis, another Ventura County fire captain, said he was told his crew's participation in the news conference was voluntary, and everyone declined.

"Then at some point in the process, one of our chiefs came up and said, 'I'm ordering you guys to stand there in the backdrop,' and that was it. There was no other conversation."

"I'm a big friend of the firefighters," Schwarzenegger said once his "buddies" had gathered round. "As a matter of fact, in one of my movies, I played a firefighter."

Taxpayers Getting
Clipped By Mailings

(June 11, 2006)

Here's what I learned last week: that the Russians removed Saddam's WMDs before we could find them, that L.A. mayor Antonio Villaraigosa attended a "Marxist law college," and that there's mathematical proof of God's existence. You're wondering if I subscribe to a supermarket tabloid? Nope. I've stumbled upon some of the intelligence coming out of the office of longtime Los Angeles County Supervisor Mike Antonovich.

A county employee who didn't like being expected to help distribute these hair-raising bulletins supplied me with several inch-thick packets of clippings assembled and sent out by Antonovich. At taxpayer expense.

One of the packets, dated April 2005, was a phone book–size monster of 283 pages. The packet weighed two pounds and contained dozens of clippings, including *Wall Street Journal* editorials, religious articles and an *American Spectator* story comparing President Bush favorably to FDR and Lincoln. The bundle included a work order filled out by Antonovich's staff, requesting that the printer roll off 265 copies and return them "to Room 869 ASAP"—Antonovich's office.

So how much did it cost us for Antonovich to share his world with a wide circle of friends and like-minded citizens? Unfortunately, the answer isn't easy to come by. The costs of that and many other mass mailings from Antonovich and his fellow giants on the board are hidden in the darkest recesses of county bureaucracy, as if by design.

"Your premise is correct," county public affairs director Judy Hammond e-mailed me, "in that it is not an easy task for a member of the public or media to ascertain how much is spent by a particular supervisor on mailings." It oughta be.

To make matters worse, formal requests for public information, like mine, result in a courtesy notice to supervisors, warning them someone has come snooping. What is this, the Kremlin?

It's not breaking news that Los Angeles County Supervisors are notoriously big on power and shockingly low on accountability even though the five of them rule over more than 10 million people. But this goes beyond the pale. I was told by county employees that Antonovich is the sultan of mailings compared with other supes, but these employees were reluctant to speak up publicly, fearing they'd be exiled to Siberia—if not Norwalk.

Naturally, I wanted to find out as much as I could before placing a call to Antonovich, so I spent a couple of weeks sniffing around. With help from Hammond, I made enough progress to find that a mailing like the one mentioned above costs roughly $3,500 in printing and postage. Then you have to factor in the cost of time spent by Antonovich and his staff, plus the time of county employees involved in loading a quarter of a ton of packages onto carts and running them through the postage machines in the county administration building. I'm told Antonovich cranks up his propaganda machine every month or so.

The total expense isn't enough to break the bank, but the toll adds up over the years in a county that has seen its share of deep program cuts. Just last week, the *Los Angeles Times* reported that county officials didn't have the $30,000 necessary to print an emergency preparedness pamphlet for disabled people.

Meanwhile, Antonovich rings up thousands of dollars in costs to mail out an odd almanac of items that move across his radar screen. I don't know how many he's sent out recently, but I got my hands on three of the two-pound packets compiled this year along with the one from last year.

Some of the material is relevant to county matters, such as clippings on jail overcrowding or the latest disasters at King/Drew Medical Center, where the board's legendary ineptitude has cost lives. I even found two of my columns in the mix, one of which mentioned Antonovich's support of former Los Angeles mayor Jim Hahn. And Antonovich is big on health tips regarding, among other things, Alzheimer's prevention and prostate health.

But there's an obvious political bent to much of what he sends, with a sprinkling of Clinton-bashing, breathless reviews of books like *The Vast Left-Wing Conspiracy*, and copies of columns by Bill O'Reilly and Ann Coulter, who appear to be favorites of Antonovich's. A packet mailed just a couple of months ago includes a Coulter column that attempts to debunk reports of dwindling support for the war in Iraq and other Bush initiatives. We'll just have to wait and see if a future mailing from Supervisor Antonovich will include Coulter's recent comments about 9/11 widows, whom she referred to as "witches," accusing them of "enjoying their husbands' deaths" and using the tragedy to make a political point.

As for the startling news of Russia's absconding with Saddam's nukes, that came from a magazine called *NewsMax*. I'd never heard of *NewsMax*. I went to the website to size up the strange workings of Antonovich's mind and saw a photo of President Bush along with postings by O'Reilly and bargains galore on Coulter's books. What a surprise.

The comment about Villaraigosa was a hand-scrawled aside next to a photo caption mentioning that the mayor had gone to the Peoples College of Law. The same stack of wisdom features a political cartoon showing a skid row bus pulling into the San Fernando Valley at a "Bum Stop." Rather un-Christian, don't you think? And yet in Antonovich's world, another clipping suggests, you can begin to change your life with five simple words: "The Lord is my shepherd."

I also came upon articles saying "the unmatched power of the Israel lobby" dictates U.S. foreign policy (*Wall Street Journal Online*), a satellite "may have found Noah's Ark" (ABC News), the poor aren't really all that poor (*Wall Street Journal* commentary) and the Schwartz Report is the place for a Web listing of "books recommended by the Christian Anti-Communism Crusade."

I think Uncle Mike's been in the bunker too long. He's entitled to his peccadilloes, but I don't want him banging pots and pans at my expense any more than I'd want Supervisor Zev Yaroslavsky sending out rants by Al Franken and Michael Moore. As for Antonovich's Bible-thumping on the public dime, what about the separation of church and state?

It had occurred to me that Antonovich might be covering the printing and mailing costs out of campaign funds rather than sticking taxpayers with the tab. But a check of available files was inconclusive. And so finally, on Wednesday, I called Antonovich's office to ask for a meeting. Spokesman

Tony Bell, who already knew what I was after because the office had been notified, didn't seem all that eager for me to have a sit-down with his boss. He pooh-poohed the mailings as no big deal and wondered what there was to talk about. For starters, I said, I'd like to know who's picking up the tab.

"The county," Bell said.

I said I'd like to sit down with Antonovich, plop four of the mailings on his desk, and hear him justify them. I'd also like to know the details of where they're printed and why the billing is so conveniently obscured. Bell said they were printed in Antonovich's eighth-floor office, which didn't jibe with what I knew. He said he'd check with the boss.

I called back Thursday and Bell said there was nothing new to report, except that the packets weren't printed in Antonovich's office. They were printed downstairs somewhere and ended up going through the county mailroom. That's what I had been told all along, but neither I nor Hammond could nail it down, in part because no records are kept of mailings by individual supervisors. It just goes on the county tab, which means a supervisor can abuse the process to his heart's content and never explain what he's sending or why.

What about my meeting with Antonovich? I asked.

The Supervisor's busy, Bell said.

Doing what? Putting together another mailing? Bell eventually said Antonovich could squeeze me in on Monday.

Not soon enough, I said, asking if Bell cared to explain for his boss why taxpayers should be subsidizing these two-pound catalogs.

"The Supervisor communicates with a variety of people on a regular basis, and the mail we send to the executive office...is postage-metered there and goes out with the rest of the mail," Bell said, telling me Antonovich had long been communicating like this with other community leaders on local and world affairs. "Part of the course of doing business as a supervisor is an exchange of information and ideas." Yes, that's quite a think tank he's running.

If it's an exchange of ideas Antonovich is interested in, I've got a few. With all the problems in L.A. County, we don't need you operating a crackpot clipping service. Figure out what it has cost us over the years, dip into your own pocket, and pay us back. The public has a right to know, so open the doors from now on and get out of the way.

See you Monday?

Sharing Quality Time
with the Gov

(August 2, 2006)

The governor brought the cigars. His midnight-black Ford Excursion pulled up to Smooth's Sports Grille in downtown Long Beach, just after his get-together with British prime minister Tony Blair. I guess he saved the best for last. Governor Schwarzenegger stepped out of the car with a celebrity smile, gave a wave to patrons and hiked up the stairs to a rooftop bar. We shook hands, he handed me a stogie, and we lit up.

It all began very cordially, with chitchat about family, the movie business, guy stuff. I told him about filching my dad's cigars as a kid and he told me about having his first smoke with Maria's father in Hyannis Port. Our get-together was arranged by Adam Mendelsohn, Schwarzenegger's new communications director, who thought it was time for us to get to know each other a little better.

But I had a butterfly or two.

I have not gone easy on the governor the last three years, roughing him up for his flip-flops and his photo-ops. I wondered if, at some point, the former Mr. Universe might lift me out of my chair and dangle me from the roof by my toes.

So I decided to jump right in and ask how he felt about my taking batting practice on him.

"I don't dwell on it," he insisted, leveling his gaze at me and blowing smoke.

Just the same, I suggested he get even by taking his best swings at me. Not necessary, the governor said. When I write what he considers a (rhymes with witty) column, he blames his staff, not me.

"I always say if Steve does not know what our true intentions are, obviously someone in our office has failed to get the message out there," Schwarzenegger speculated.

The governor said he doesn't consider himself a shoo-in for reelection despite polls that show him leading Democrat Phil Angelides. But my guess is that he really thinks things are breaking his way again after his disastrous special election last fall. He said he's learned from his early mistakes that he can't alienate the very people he ought to be working with to solve problems.

The governor said he probably wouldn't be running for reelection if he'd accomplished all his goals, although he took credit for helping turn the economy around, pumping up education funding with billions in new revenues, reforming workers' compensation and several other things. The job's far from done, said the gov. I'm not ready to jump on his bandwagon, but as he staked out his goals, he struck me as someone who has grown more thoughtful and seasoned as a politician.

Still, he has a lot to answer for. I told him that in my humble opinion, he took two great opportunities to Sacramento and dropped the ball on both.

The first was a chance to use his landslide mandate and moderate positions to lead from the middle, whipping the legislature's bickering, partisan do-nothings into shape. The second was to follow up on his campaign vow to get the money and special interests out of the politics game. He admitted he stumbled on bipartisanship after a relatively good start, but he flinched at my suggestion that he "really blew it" on getting money out of politics, making former governor Gray Davis look like a junior leaguer when it comes to bellying up to the special-interest trough.

I suggested that to save face, Schwarzenegger ought to endorse Proposition 89 or come up with some other meaningful campaign finance reform. Prop. 89 would finance public elections with a 0.2 percent increase in the corporate income tax rate, and Schwarzenegger said there's no way he's going to raise taxes, period, after working so hard to prevent companies from fleeing the state because of an unfriendly climate.

It would be nice if he were as concerned about sticking the rest of us—and our children—with the bill for his unprecedented borrowing binges. There's not much difference between raising taxes and sticking citizens with the bill for years of debt service, and to make it all the more outrageous, this is the man who promised to tear up the state's credit card.

But Schwarzenegger's bigger offense is the way he's constantly scavenged for donations and turned campaigns into record-setting fundraising contests, with most of the money funneled into TV ads that turn off voters and shame the political process.

"You're mistaking money and selling out," Schwarzenegger said. "You can have all the money in the world in politics, but if you sell out—if you take money and you do favors in return—that's where the evil is. The evil's not in the money."

It isn't? You've got the business community paying bazillions to get the ear of Schwarzenegger and the Republicans, and you've got unions matching them on the other side, working the Democrats. It's a public policy bidding war that never ends.

The governor insisted he's never been influenced by a donation, but as I tried to explain, his donors aren't writing checks for the fun of it. Besides, his record is fairly consistent with the wishes of developers, financial institutions, insurance companies, oil companies and other players, just as the Democrats always seem to come through for union bosses who throw money around like confetti.

I don't think I gained much ground with the governor, who insisted the far bigger problem in California is the way political districts are carved up to benefit the most partisan candidates. He's working on that, he said, and with the skills he's learned in the last two and a half years, he thinks he's got a chance to make it happen.

The conversation lasted for an hour, and so did the cigar, and the governor invited me up to Sacramento to continue the conversation. I told him I'd bring the smokes, and he said not to bother. He knows what he likes. OK then, I said, I'll pick up the tab here for the bottled water and the few snacks he ordered.

Schwarzenegger looked me square in the eye.

"It's about time," he said.

A Rocky Week
for the City Attorney

(June 13, 2007)

What a week. The incorrigible little mayor of Los Angeles has moved out of the mayoral manse, the news out of King-Harbor is reliably horrific, the Department of Water and Power has ripped off multiple public agencies to the tune of $220 million, Paris Hilton has found God and summer has appeared on the horizon. But for my money, L.A. City Attorney Rocky Delgadillo has them all beat.

My colleague Patrick McGreevy started things off by reporting on a matter involving Delgadillo's wife, Michelle, and her escapades behind the wheel. She got into an accident three years ago, couldn't prove she had insurance, had her license suspended for three years, then got cited a year later for a moving violation.

Why no proof of insurance on the first offense? Was it because she didn't have insurance? Why no ticket for not having a license on the second offense? And while we're on the subject, if her license was suspended, wouldn't it have been impossible to get insurance? That's how I understand the law, but I'm not a city attorney.

How inconvenient that this news broke just as Delgadillo was ripping Sheriff Lee Baca for springing Hilton so soon after she was locked up for driving on a suspended license, of all things.

And then came another little bombshell from McGreevy: A city-owned GMC Yukon assigned to Delgadillo was banged up in a 2004 accident. But for some reason his aides can't find a report that would have identified the driver, and sources told McGreevy that Delgadillo occasionally handed his wife the keys to the city SUV.

On Monday, Delgadillo refused to answer McGreevy's questions regarding another source who said the accident, which caused $2,120 worth of damage that the city paid for, occurred at Cedars-Sinai Medical Center. And it happened on a day when Delgadillo's wife allegedly was there for a medical appointment.

On Tuesday, Delgadillo dug himself in deeper when he took a pass on an interview request. Too bad. Among other things, I wanted to know why the city attorney needs to drive a gigantic smog factory, same model as the mayor, in a city with notoriously dirty air. And, if someone unauthorized was driving the Yukon assigned to Rocky, shouldn't he pay for repairs with his own money?

Rocky, are you reading this? You're the city attorney. Please tell us that your wife didn't smash up your city vehicle. And if she did, please tell us she at least had insurance and a valid driver's license. Otherwise, maybe Paris should make room for a new bunkmate.

Look, we all know Rocky is not short for rocket scientist, but surely you can do better, and if not, try lying. Blame it on Baca. Blame it on the DMV. Say you were framed. Say that the matter is being thoroughly investigated internally and that your wife is under house arrest until further notice, ankle bracelet and all.

Say that she was at Cedars-Sinai to treat chronic amnesia. Better yet, say you're the one with amnesia. You drove the SUV that day, banged it up and bumped your head. How else to explain why you let your wife drive a city vehicle?

As a last resort, consider telling the truth, which sometimes works even for attorneys. Tell us who was driving the car. Tell us whether that person, whoever she might be, had a license and insurance.

And tell us that after thinking it over, you'd like to cover the cost of that accident out of your own pocket.

Mr. Mayor: Shut Up,
Grow Up, Slow Down

(June 14, 2007)

Okay, let me be frank: I've made mistakes in my life, I'm still flawed, and there is something to be said for the line about the hypocrisy of sinners casting stones. But I can't help myself. Los Angeles mayor Antonio Villaraigosa's halfhearted mea culpa Monday about his broken marriage was a disaster. I've tried to give him a break, given my own past sins, but in the end I just can't let it go without commenting.

We all knew what we were getting with this guy. He's a man of insatiable appetites, and anyone who needs to be loved as much as Villaraigosa is setting himself up for big disappointments and even bigger mistakes. Mistakes like the news conference in which he said that he and his wife of 20 years were splitting up.

Just as I shouldn't have to tell City Attorney Rocky Delgadillo to speak up about the caper involving his wife and his smashed city vehicle, I shouldn't have to tell Villaraigosa to shut up about his broken marriage. But somebody has to.

It would have been far more graceful for Villaraigosa to leave things as they were, with the statement from his office last week confirming the breakup and asking the public to respect the family's privacy. But Villaraigosa can't help but indulge his own worst instincts. At his core, he's an insecure soul who believes there is no better place to hide his weaknesses than in front of a camera, where he can emphasize his strengths.

So instead of moving on with his new life and focusing on his job, while Corina and the kids stay behind in the awkward limbo of the mayoral manse, the mayor called a news conference for Monday, ostensibly to further explain himself.

Fine, if he intended to offer new insights or say something about the toll an all-consuming job can take on a marriage. But he said little beyond what was in the earlier press release, when he asked that "the media and the public respect our privacy through this period of transition."

You want privacy? Don't call a news conference. Otherwise it looks smarmy and self-serving, and yet another slight to your wife and children.

A few relatives, including two daughters from prior relationships, were present, which made the whole thing seem all the more like a surreal episode of *This Is Your Life.* What are we supposed to take from their attendance? That the mayor's not such a heel that he can't talk a few relatives into serving as props?

"I want you to know that I take responsibility for what is happening, and I feel a personal sense of failure about it, and that's all I'm prepared to say on this question," Villaraigosa said when asked if an affair caused the split.

Unless he has had an affair with someone who reports on City Hall, or he otherwise compromised the office of mayor, it probably is none of our business. But Villaraigosa said nothing to dispel the raging rumors, and Corina Villaraigosa filed for divorce the next day, citing irreconcilable differences.

I wouldn't bet on it, but maybe when it all sinks in, the mayor will wake up and realize it's time to tame his incorrigible, teenage ways and do at least one job right. The 15-hour days haven't done us, him or his family any good. He's spread so thin, all his major goals are unmet.

With a long trail of close friends and supporters who feel Villaraigosa betrayed them to advance his own cause, let's hope this latest failure, as he calls it, could finally bring the humility he so badly needs.

The Rocky Horror Show

(June 17, 2007)

Welcome, dear readers, to the Rocky Horror Show. This is Day Nine. That's how long it's been since we learned that the wife of Los Angeles City Attorney Rocky Delgadillo got a ticket in 2005 while driving with a suspended license. This news, dug up by my colleague Patrick McGreevy, was of note because Delgadillo was squawking about the release of Paris Hilton from jail, where she was doing time for driving with a suspended license. Then, on Tuesday, we learned that Delgadillo's city-owned GMC Yukon was banged up in 2004. No big deal there, except that McGreevy's sources leave the impression that Delgadillo might not have been behind the wheel. But his wife could have been.

What's that, you ask? Is the relative of an employee allowed under city regulations to drive a city car? That answer would be no.

Let's say, for the sake of discussion, that Michelle Delgadillo was indeed behind the wheel of her hubby's Yukon when it hit a wall. Did she have her license back at the time? Did she have insurance? Is she related to Mr. Magoo?

I'm sorry, but I have to ask these kinds of questions because her license had been suspended for failing to show proof of insurance, which is always bad policy, but especially for the wife of one of the top law enforcement officials in the city.

The repairs, paid for by the city, cost taxpayers $2,120.

So, as you can see, this story is like fine wine. It gets better with age. And for that, we owe a debt of gratitude to Mr. Delgadillo, who has kept it alive by refusing to answer questions from me or anyone else. I tried again Friday, sending along 10 questions that were ignored. And it's clear that Delgadillo is following none of my damage-control advice, which included the suggestion that he say his wife suffers from chronic amnesia. Or that he does.

The truth might have worked equally well. He could have laid out what really happened and said he was going to turn in the Yukon, commute by bus, wear sackcloth for a year and lock his wife in the house. Instead, Delgadillo spent the whole week ducking, but it seemed there was nowhere to hide. The Los Angeles Ethics Commission nailed Delgadillo with $11,450 in fines for violating campaign finance laws in an unconnected matter, and L.A. County District Attorney Steve Cooley accused Delgadillo of going soft on crime, charging criminals with misdemeanors instead of felonies to keep the prosecutions under his jurisdiction.

You know you're on a really bad streak when $11,450 in campaign finance fines is the best part of your week.

City Controller Laura Chick had some good advice for Delgadillo, not that there's been any evidence he would be interested in such a thing. "I think it would be in the best interest of all of us if the city attorney brought all the facts out into the open, answered questions, and if there were mistakes that were made, it would be better to know it outright," Chick said. That way, she added, we wouldn't "have to use public resources" to get to the bottom of it.

Does that mean that Chick is conducting an investigation? She wouldn't say. But there should be an investigation or two, and I'd like to suggest someone take a good hard look at Columbia Law School and investigate how Delgadillo graduated.

Chick does indeed have the authority to investigate, as does the city's Ethics Commission. And then, of course, I suppose the district attorney's office could get involved.

If someone lets an unauthorized person drive a city car, the car gets dinged, the city foots the bill and the city employee seems to have misplaced the report that would have identified the driver of the car, is that a crime?

Joe Scott of the district attorney's office said he couldn't answer my questions. Nobody, it seems, can answer my questions.

I mentioned my frustration to Delgadillo spokesman Nick Velasquez, who finally got back to me on Friday afternoon to say that Delgadillo will gladly meet with me and another reporter on Monday.

Monday?

It's a simple question, really. Who was driving the car? Doesn't seem to me that the answer could change over the weekend, but come to think of it, Monday is perfect. Monday is beautiful. I like a nice round number, and Monday is Day Ten of the Rocky Horror Show. Be sure to stay tuned.

At L.A. City Hall,
the Summer of Love

(July 4, 2007)

At Cal State Los Angeles on Tuesday, Jaime Regalado was fielding a steady stream of e-mails, almost all of them from women who've had it with the Don Juan who calls himself our mayor.

"They'll never vote for him again," Regalado, who runs the Pat Brown Institute of Public Affairs, said when I asked the gist of the messages about Antonio Villaraigosa. "They say he can't be committed to anything and stay the course."

I was getting my own flood of mail and decided to call a few of the mayor's critics. A financial consultant named Hugo was equally disturbed by the mayor's admission of a long-rumored affair with a Telemundo anchor/reporter.

"When he won the mayoral race, I went to church with him and saw him walking side by side with his wife," said Hugo, 32, who held back his last name because "it's a small town."

"So I personally think it's a big disappointment, and he hasn't just done it once. It's the second time, and I think it says something about his character."

Yeah, and the last time the mayor stepped out on his wife she was battling cancer. Talk about a character issue.

Sue DiSanto, a medical transcriptionist, felt let down even though she lives in Chino. As a Latina, she said, she had high hopes that Villaraigosa would distinguish himself as a politician and be a role model as a man.

"Thanks for showing that Hispanic women don't really count, once you don't need them anymore," DiSanto said in a comment aimed at the mayor.

And so it went Tuesday as a heat wave gripped Southern California and the hottest temperature in the nation was recorded at L.A. City Hall. The only thing that has saved City Attorney Rocky Delgadillo and Villaraigosa from combusting in the summer heat is that the spotlight conveniently keeps shifting from one scandal to another in the ongoing adventures of our very own Rocky and Bullwinkle show.

As for the mayor, there are many who say they don't care what he does in the dark, as long as he does his job. But he's been no champ in that regard, either. It's hard to get back on track when you're tripping over your own pants.

Regalado wondered if the mayor's "charmed life" has run its course. At a certain point, he said, the mayor's infidelities to his wife and to a long line of former political allies can't help but inflict some political damage.

As for the mayor's "other woman," there had long been rumors linking him to a certain "on-air talent." I'm no psychologist, but can anyone be surprised that a man who counts the number of cameras at press events fell for someone in television?

My own suspicions of the current affair were all but confirmed last week when I called a Villaraigosa spokesman and asked to chat with the mayor about the rampant rumors. If there was no truth to them, I said, I would gladly sit down with the mayor and give him a chance to set the record straight. The spokesman promised to check with the mayor and get back to me. I guess he forgot.

That's too bad, because I would like to have known if Villaraigosa intends to keep his name. The mayor used to be Tony Villar until blending his last name with that of his wife, Corina Raigosa. If he ends up marrying Mirthala Salinas, will he then become Villaraigosasalinas? Or Villarsalinas?

My vote would be for Villasalinas, with no "r," although I could be putting the cart ahead of the horse. There's no telling how serious Villaraigosa's latest relationship is, but if they do end up walking down the aisle, I can't imagine that Salinas would be content with a husband whose blended last name is a tribute to his ex-wife.

Come to think of it, given the mayor's track record and the number of female anchors in Los Angeles, I'd hold off on any more name changes for a while if I were in his shoes. I mean, he'd be better off just getting a tattoo.

As for Salinas, she did not exactly distinguish herself as a journalist when, after the mayor's split with his wife, she reported on-air for Telemundo that "the rumors were true"—there was indeed a "political scandal" at City Hall. But that's the least of her worries. She may be about to discover that life with the mayor is always a threesome, and it's impossible to love him as much as he loves himself.

Hot on the Mayor's Heels
in Texas

(March 4, 2008)

I was having trouble getting the mayor's attention in Los Angeles, so on Sunday I headed to where I figured he'd be a little more accessible. Over the last two months, Mayor Antonio Villaraigosa has been on Senator Hillary Clinton's presidential campaign trail more than a quarter of the time, as my colleague Duke Helfand reported: Iowa, New Hampshire, Nevada and, over the weekend, Texas. When I landed in Dallas, I called Clinton's local headquarters and was told I'd find our mayor at an event in Fort Worth. Driving west in my rental car, I had time to think about all the things I wanted to catch up on with Villaraigosa.

If we allow ever-denser development when there's no money for transit, isn't the gridlocked city doomed? What's the point of controlling the school board if you don't order it to get rid of a superintendent who rates a C-minus on his better days?

And then there's the matter of Clinton, who hasn't exactly been on a winning streak lately. Does he think Latinos will support an African American nominee if she goes down in flames?

All good stuff to talk about. But I get the sense that Villaraigosa has held a grudge since my columns last summer about his unspectacular record as mayor. Maybe I shouldn't have suggested that his secret romance with a TV personality was distracting him from his duties. But out here on the campaign trail, 1,200 miles from home, I thought we might get a chance to bury the hatchet and have a good chat.

Unfortunately, the mayor had already come and gone when I got to Fort Worth. A Clinton volunteer said if I hurried I might be able to catch him at Clinton's Dallas office, where he was scheduled to meet with precinct captains. I hit the gas and headed east to a little bungalow off the highway near downtown Dallas.

To be honest, I was a little surprised Villaraigosa didn't call off this latest trip. I know Clinton has relied on him to help turn out the critical Latino vote, but that horrific shooting at a South-Central bus stop near a school last week—of the eight victims, five were children—happened just two days before the mayor left town Friday. The bus shootings followed a recent string of mayhem, including the February 7 killing of SWAT officer Randal Simmons and the Avenues gang shootout in Glassell Park. Don't I recall the mayor saying that fixing the city's disjointed and ineffective handling of gangs would be a priority for him?

The house was full at Clinton headquarters, where roughly 150 precinct captains and others were getting caucus instructions. When that was done, a couple of local politicos made speeches about the "very special friends" they were about to introduce, meaning Anaheim congresswoman Loretta Sanchez and our very own traveling mayor.

Earlier, I'd had thoughts about jumping out from behind a bush to surprise Villaraigosa, but there were no plants in the room. I stood off to one side, listening to Sanchez talk about the cowboy boots she was sporting, and then she introduced Villaraigosa to nice applause.

I had wondered whether, when I finally got together with Villaraigosa, he would argue that he hasn't really been out of Los Angeles all that much. But I soon realized I had nothing to worry about. The mayor told the crowd he'd left Los Angeles to go to "Iowa four times, New Hampshire for five days." And people have wondered, he added, "why I went to Nevada as many times as I did." And the answer?

"This is the most important election of my lifetime," he said, and whether the issue is health insurance for children or getting out of Iraq, Hillary is the answer. "This is where the rubber hits the road, and you all are the rubber." Maybe it's a line better reserved for a rally at a Goodyear plant.

As he left the room, I leaned in to the mayor and said: "What's a poor Angeleno have to do to get an interview with you?"

The mayor was a little surprised, I'd say, but gracious enough. I told him I'd come a long way and wondered if we might get together later in the day. He and press secretary Matt Szabo said they had a few more events, but they took my number, saying they might be able to meet Sunday night. If it didn't work out, I said, I'd catch up with them on Monday. Villaraigosa said he might head to Houston or San Antonio if he didn't decide to go back home, and I agreed to go wherever I had to.

Szabo said he was taking vacation days to be in Texas with his boss. That's fine, but what about the two police officers who generally travel everywhere with Villaraigosa, whether he goes to Dodger Stadium or Texas? They're usually on the city dime, according to the LAPD, with taxpayers covering flights, hotels and food.

Here's a question: Has there been a threat against Villaraigosa by someone in Texas so that he needs two cops shadowing him every minute of the day?

As for the mayor's time in the Lone Star State, his staff says he is not there as part of his official duties. But as an elected official who has no prescribed vacation time, he is authorized under the City Charter to spend his time as he sees fit while earning city pay. Whether that is in the city's interest or his own is, of course, subject to debate.

Before the mayor went off to his next event—a private affair—I told Szabo I'd call him in a couple of hours if I didn't hear from him. Three hours later, about 7:30 p.m., I called and was told my shot at an interview wasn't looking too good. The mayor was still tied up, and exhausted, and he'd decided to catch the first plane back to Los Angeles on Monday morning. I told Szabo I'd hang around downtown and take my chances.

While circling downtown Dallas, I had my eyes open for the red Ford Expedition I'd seen the mayor in earlier, which, if I'm not mistaken, is even bigger than transit advisor Jaime de la Vega's Hummer. As luck would have it, I came upon the beast, parked next to a "No Parking Any Time" sign outside a swanky nightspot called Scene. Through the window of the bar I could see a crowd.

"Is there a party in there?" I asked the valet.

"Yes, there is," he said. I began to back up so I could park behind the mayor's SUV, but the valet told me there was no parking allowed. I guess you need connections.

A half-hour later I saw the mayor emerge from Scene and get into the SUV. I figured he was heading back to his hotel, and decided to follow him in case he was ready for our interview when he got back. The SUV took a strange route. It circled the downtown area for a while, as if the driver were lost, and then began heading out of town. I did my honest best to stay with him, but I lost the mayor about 10 or 15 minutes later in a residential area. An hour after that, Szabo called to say the mayor was having dinner with friends and couldn't do the interview. Maybe he'll have some free time back in Los Angeles, he added.

I looked for the mayor at the airport Monday morning, hoping to get on his plane, but I think he beat me out of town. If he was looking out the window during takeoff, expecting to see me running after him on the tarmac, he was disappointed. I'm really not that desperate.

Call me when you're ready, Mr. Mayor. I'll go just about anywhere.

Toss Me a Plum Post, Too, Governor

(January 25, 2009)

My application has arrived in the governor's office and my fingers are crossed. If things work out, I could be joining the Schwarzenegger team before you know it.

Sure, the newspaper gig has been fun for 35 years, but the business is a bit shaky these days, and President Obama did ask that we all consider public service. After watching the governor appoint termed-out legislators and other pals to six-figure salaries on various boards and commissions, some of which meet only once a month, I figured it was time for me to begin a second career.

I hope you don't think of me as a sellout. To be honest, my first instinct was to flog the governor for yet another in his long line of blatant hypocrisies. In addition to promising balanced budgets on time, and getting money out of politics, he pledged to abolish many of the state's 300-plus boards and commissions. His own review panel recommended abolishing 88 of them, including some of the same ones to which he's been making appointments.

I know there are those who think it's wrong that former legislators are getting plum jobs with little or no heavy lifting in the midst of a $41 billion budget shortfall, especially when the state's unemployment rate has soared to 9.3 percent. And it's true that, even as he's taken care of connected cronies, the governor has ordered 238,000 state employees to be furloughed two days each month or give up nine percent of their pay, with layoffs a possibility.

And there are some gripers out there, like Kathay Feng of California Common Cause, who told me, "It's not clear why, for once-a-month meetings, someone should be earning $132,000."

But come on, everybody's doing it. In recent weeks, as my colleague Patrick McGreevy has reported, former legislators Carole Migden of San Francisco, Greg Aghazarian of Stockton, Bonnie Garcia of Cathedral City and George Plescia of La Jolla have all hitched rides on Arnold's gravy trains. They'll be making $128,109 and up for saying "here" at monthly meetings of the Integrated Waste Management Board and the Unemployment Insurance Appeals Board.

And then there's former assemblywoman Nicole Parra (D-Hanford), who was appointed to a newly created post. She'll get $128,124 as director of the governor's Regional Development Initiatives. The announcement raised a stir when Parra didn't even seem to know what the job entailed and told reporters, "I'm 38 and could get a job anywhere, but I'm coming home to help the valley." I'm sure the valley is jumping for joy.

I have one question for the governor: Why not me? As Feng noted, "the people appointed to these positions do not reflect any particular expertise in the commission's purpose," so I'm perfect for the job—whatever it is.

I called one of the governor's flacks, Rachel Cameron, to offer my services. She didn't seem to immediately embrace the idea, so I told her the governor and I hit it off nicely when we shared a cigar a few years ago, and he promised a follow-up that's long overdue. Cameron suggested I go to the governor's website and fill out an application. As a self-starter, I was already halfway through that task.

By my calculation, the governor makes appointments to 15 or more boards and commissions that pay good salaries in addition to daily expenses. I'm not going to be picky about it, but I did list a preference on my application for some of the highest paying boards: Integrated Waste Management, Workers' Compensation Appeals, Unemployment Insurance Appeals, Occupational Safety & Health Appeals and Public Employment Relations.

My research revealed that some boards actually require you to do much more than simply show up at meetings. Let's hope I don't get stuck with one of those. But I'm no shirker. "Let it be known that I'm willing to serve on more than one board simultaneously," I wrote on my application.

For instance, if there are only 12 annual meetings of the Waste Management board, I don't see why I couldn't also find the time for twice-monthly meetings of the Gambling Control Commission. That would give me two six-figure salaries and leave plenty of free time for hiking, golfing, movie-going, whatever. Even a full-time job, if I were feeling particularly moti-vated.

Cameron asked, rather pointedly, if I was going to call legislative leaders Karen Bass in the Assembly and Darrell Steinberg in the Senate and apply for one of the many board and commission jobs they control. Absolutely, I replied. I know both of them and can only hope they'll give me serious consideration.

Legislative leaders, in fact, recently lined up waste management posts for former Assemblyman John Laird of Santa Cruz and termed-out Senator Sheila Kuehl of Los Angeles, and there are plenty more unnecessary jobs where those came from.

The Kuehl and Migden postings were announced by Waste Management board chairwoman Margo Reid Brown, the governor's former sched-uler, who said she was "extremely pleased" to give the news. Her good cheer is a bit puzzling when you consider that, according to spokeswoman Camer-on, Schwarzenegger still thinks the board should be abolished and its work taken over by the state Environmental Protection Agency.

Let's hope that doesn't happen. How would we know to recycle and reduce waste without these people holding a dozen meetings a year at a cost of millions? Besides, I've got some strong feelings about integrated waste management and think it's high time we got serious about segregated waste management as well.

As for chairwoman Brown, I'm hoping she can put her background as a scheduler to good use by scheduling a party for me when I get to Sacra-mento. I'd like her to invite former Schwarzenegger aide Richard Costigan, who gets roughly $40,000 for part-time work at the Personnel Board, and all the other Schwarzenegger minions who've been rotated in and out of cushy jobs. And I definitely want to meet Nicole Parra and ask if she's finally figured out what she was hired to do.

I hope I don't get tripped up by question No. 30 on the application, which asked if I'd ever written anything controversial. My answer: "I have on occasion written some things about Governor Schwarzenegger that I now regret."

Honest, Arnold. Come through for me here and your next cigar is on me.

"Spanky" Duvall's Conduct Is Grounds for a Good Thrashing

(September 13, 2009)

Let me begin by saying I'm not into spanking. If I suggested to my wife that we give it a try, I'm confident she would spank the side of my head with a frying pan.

So maybe I'm not the best person to judge Mike "Spanky" Duvall, the family values crusader from Yorba Linda. He's the unfortunate chap who resigned from the California Assembly last week after he was caught on camera boasting of his sexual conquests and peccadilloes, which include a mistress who wears panties the size of an eye patch.

"So I am getting into spanking her," Duvall told his colleague, Jeff Miller of Corona, while the two sat on the dais during a break at a hearing in Sacramento. They did not know the microphone was on. "Yeah, I like it….She goes, 'I know you like spanking me.' I said, 'Yeah, that's 'cause you're such a bad girl.'"

Not that I don't have my own fetishes. I like to fantasize, for instance, that while two legislators kibitz at an Appropriations Committee hearing in a state with crippling budget problems and a ridiculous load of unfinished business, the knuckleheads are talking about something other than spanking and underpants.

On the other hand, this does put California back on the map when it comes to political sex scandals. We'd kind of lost our way for a while after championship performances by San Francisco mayor Gavin Newsom and Los Angeles mayor Antonio Villaraigosa.

Of course, it was hard to compete with South Carolina governor Mark Sanford, whose long absences were explained by a sudden interest in the tango, and now he's telling us God wants him to stay in office. But if there's a reigning champ in the Dog House for Life competition, I say it's former North Carolina senator and White House hopeful John Edwards, who canoodled with his videographer while his wife battled breast cancer.

"Spanky" Duvall is a gamer, though. Boasting about sextracurricular activities at a government hearing is brazenly bad form, but doing so with a camera in the room puts you in the Stupid Human Hall of Fame. And to make matters worse, one of Duvall's concubines may be a lobbyist with Sempra Energy.

Sempra has spent $800,000 on lobbying the first half of this year, $2,800 of it on Duvall, who was vice chairman of an energy committee and took Sempra's side in four votes this year. So this isn't just a sex scandal. It's a window on Sacramento's notorious pay-to-play culture, and now we're left to wonder if a G-string can buy as much influence as a campaign check.

On the upside, California Common Cause president Kathay Feng said Duvall has brought a new kind of sexiness to the dull topic of political reform. She intends to call for legislation requiring that every contact between a lobbyist and a politician be recorded as to who, when, where and why. And she said the scandal is one more reason to re-draw gerrymandered districts, in which candidates are anointed by party extremists rather than truly elected by voters, giving them a sense of invincibility.

Caught with his pants down, so to speak, Duvall resigned on Wednesday. On Thursday, he said his resignation wasn't an admission of an affair. The guy gets dumber every day. I expected a Friday news conference in which he said God had asked him to fight for his job and open a halfway house for recovering spankers.

"Nobody here is defending him," one of the employees at Chili's in Yorba Linda told me Thursday night. Chili's, one of Duvall's hangouts, is near the Richard Nixon Library, and I wondered if Duvall had considered a televised speech in which he insists, "I am not a spanker."

The Chili's employee, who asked that I not use her name because she knows the family and feels sorry for Duvall's wife, said she found Duvall's Thursday backpedaling preposterous, given the assemblyman's recorded boasts.

"So I was 54 on June 14th, so for a month she was 19 years younger than me," Duvall said on the tape. "I said, 'Now you're getting old. I am going to have to trade you in,' and she goes, she is 36, she is 18 years younger than me. And so I keep teasing her, and she goes, 'I know you French men, you divide your age by two and add seven, and if you're older than that, you dump us....'"

He's such a bon vivant, maybe "Frenchy" Duvall works better than "Spanky" Duvall.

At the nearby Main Street Restaurant, owner Lynn Ruocco was in tears, wondering if Duvall had ruined her career along with his own. She said that before she knew the full extent of the fix Duvall was in, she had made complimentary remarks about him to the *Los Angeles Times*, arguing that he should not have resigned. Now she was being roasted by critics.

"Shame on you," said an e-mail Ruocco showed me on her computer.

"I will never eat at Main Street Restaurant again," said another.

"I'm not the devil," Ruocco protested, calling herself a pillar of the community. One of her customers backed that up and put the heat back on Duvall, where it belonged.

"The biggest problem I had was that he was bragging about it," said the customer.

"Absolutely stupid," Ruocco agreed. "He's stupid." Yes, I'd say the verdict is in.

But it's not yet clear why the tape, recorded in July by state television, was released only now or by whom. Potential replacement candidates were popping up so quickly, you had to wonder if one of them was involved. My personal favorite replacement would be Orange County supervisor Chris Norby, 59, who in July married a woman in her early 30s. As the *Orange County Register* reported: "It is the fourth marriage for the 4th District supervisor, who last year came under fire for claiming $340 for a weeklong stay at a hotel during the summer of 2007, when his previous marriage was on the rocks. That same week he was also found sleeping under a bush at the Old County Courthouse in Santa Ana." Look, nobody's perfect.

Too bad for Orange County taxpayers that the kinky adventures of Mr. Family Values will cost them as much as $440,000 for a special election to replace him. The least Duvall should do is raise that money himself.

How about a tell-all book, *Swinging Sacramento*, that blows the lid off the orgy? A spank-athon at the Orange County fairgrounds? A new line of lingerie—"Frenchy" Duvall's Eyepatch Panties?

Yes, I'm spanking him around pretty good. But he's been a bad boy.

Seeing What the RNC
Saw at Club Voyeur

(April 18, 2010)

Well, it just seemed to me that somebody had to go check out the Voyeur club in West Hollywood. Why? To assess the damage that may have been done to the Young Eagles wing of the GOP. So I asked West Hollywood city councilman Jeffrey Prang to accompany me to his town's latest sensation, where the themes are said to include lesbian bondage and sadomasochism. Naturally, the club has been even hotter since the news that the Young Eagles, a group of up-and-coming GOP donors, had dropped by Voyeur on January 31 after a meeting.

"They say it's lesbian eroticism designed to arouse straight men," Prang told me over cocktails before we went to the forbidden palace along with his husband, Ray Vizcarra.

If you missed the story, the Republican National Committee picked up the nearly $2,000 tab for the donors' visit. One RNC staffer has been fired over the embarrassing revelations, which have also fueled calls for the firing of RNC boss Michael Steele.

They get a late crowd at Voyeur. At 10:30, traffic cones were set up on Santa Monica Boulevard across from Los Tacos, and an army of valets and security guards was in place to handle the expected crush of people. It's amazing how much happens in L.A. after my bedtime.

Prang, for his part, offered his full support to any Republican officials who'd like to drop cash in West Hollywood, which he described as a well-managed bastion of fiscal responsibility. He said he'd like to market a "threat to family values" tour that includes stops at Voyeur, the Pleasure Chest, the Body Shop, Circus Books and the Pussycat to help the GOP document decadence in America.

"Absolutely, we want more Republicans," Prang said. "We're a big-tent city."

Not that he needs my input, but I'd add the nearby Beverly Hilton to the tour. That's where married Democratic presidential wannabe John Edwards met with his concubine, the mother of his love child.

At Voyeur, male and female patrons gathered at a velvet rope, most of them in their 20s and 30s. Thanks to Prang's clout, we were led to a back entrance and greeted by owners and brothers Art and Allan Davis. The concept of Voyeur, Art said, is to have women doing things "you want to look at, but you feel you shouldn't."

It was all a little difficult to describe for a family audience, but I'll try. A woman in a glass box was doing a fan dance, or maybe she was dusting, I'm not sure. A woman dressed like an angel, I think, was posing atop one bar and making slow, strange gestures, as if trying to tell someone her bodice was too tight.

"There's a girl in a swing," Art said, pointing to a performer suspended from the ceiling like a naughty caterpillar in a cocoon. "There'll be a girl in a net soon."

Two more women, wearing dominatrix outfits and holding opposite ends of a rope, were doing some kind of mating dance on a long, narrow stage near the entrance, seemingly oblivious to onlookers.

"It's high art that people have to conceptualize to get," said a masked performer named Mia, who also manages the performers. I was trying to do some conceptualizing but found Mia too distracting. She was falling out of an outfit she called "a bit of *Clockwork Orange*," with a top hat and cane, and she was soon slithering around on a stage.

"It's meant to stimulate and shock, to get you a little nervous," said Art, and I was in fact a bit nervous as I wondered what exactly to write on my expense report. Art said he wasn't even aware the Young Eagles had been in his club until the news broke later on. "Maybe we lightened up their spirits a little bit."

While I sipped a vodka and took it all in, Art told me he admired Senator John McCain and his wife, Cindy, as well. And he's very disappointed in President Obama. I couldn't tell whether he was serious or simply trying to drum up more Republican business. On stage, Mia was doing neat tricks with the cane.

"She's moving art," said Art. "You don't even notice that she's there." I noticed.

"This must be the lesbian bondage," Prang said as we moved into another room and watched the two women work the rope as if they were trying to invent an R-rated Olympic event.

Prang said that although many conservatives have been known to be a little uptight about homosexuality, some straight men seem to relax their views under certain conditions—such as when it involves naughty-looking vixens in slap leather and spike heels. I think he may be on to something.

As we took in the sights, several customers came through the door wearing dark blazers and khakis, looking like they'd arrived by yacht. Were the Young Eagles back? I tried talking to one of the guys, and a woman in a blazer as well, but they both blew me off. Prang's husband engaged the woman, who said they were on a business trip from New York. She later told me she wasn't a Republican, but she and her colleagues had to check out the place after reading about the GOP faux pas.

"It's actually pretty tame," she said. And in a way, it was. No nudity, no lap dances and no lesbian canoodling to speak of. I felt sorry for the Young Eagles, who probably wished they'd gone to an old-fashioned strip club.

Just before we left, we stopped at the main stage and watched a scantily clad woman methodically cloak another performer in plastic wrap, like she was a leftover chicken breast.

If they wanted to see art, the Republicans could have saved themselves a lot of trouble if they'd gone to the Getty instead.

WHY LIVE
ANYWHERE ELSE?

Staying Ahead of the Pack
with a Professional Passenger

(June 1, 2001)

The plan was to beat the traffic. The plan is always to beat the traffic. But I was running late Thursday, and there was no way to make it from East Hollywood to Lynwood and back in time for an appointment. Not in morning rush hour. But a thought occurred as I approached the Home Depot on Sunset and saw the usual loose knots of day laborers.

A colleague of mine, Peter Hong, had told me he once considered hiring someone to ride with him east from Monrovia on the Foothill Freeway, so he could zip along in the carpool lane. Perfect. I pulled into the Home Depot and my car was swarmed, and out of the crowd I picked David Ramos, 40.

Ramos, a drywall specialist, wanted $25 for two hours. They all want $25 for two hours, but you can cut a deal for half that. Ramos had a kind face, though, so I said OK.

Somewhere in the gulf between my Spanish and his English, Ramos got the idea he'd been hired to trim trees. As we turned onto the Hollywood Freeway headed south, and then the Harbor, he realized I had hired him to do nothing but sit there.

By his expression, my Guatemala-born passenger seemed to be thinking: What a country. Once we hit the diamond lane and breezed past an endless trail of unfortunate laggards, Ramos seemed to be settling comfortably into the job. A little music wouldn't be a bad idea, he said, and he sang along with the ballad on the radio as this great land of opportunity breezed by.

"Suave trabajo," Ramos said as we warped into the carpool lane on the 105 East. Smooth work indeed. We pulled into Lynwood in record time, I completed my errand, and we rocketed back like we'd just robbed a bank. You hit that elevated flyway on the northbound Harbor Freeway and you're skywalking over the palms, like something out of *Crouching Tiger, Hidden Dragon*. All you can do from on high is pity the gas-guzzlers growing ulcers down there in the backup, one poor fool per car.

"Bye-bye," Ramos said, very much into the spirit of things now. As we turboed toward the downtown skyline, he wondered if I might need him again later in the week. And that was when the light went on.

Sure I could use him. Thousands of people could use him. We've got the worst traffic in the nation and you'd think there were land mines in the HOV lanes the way people avoid carpools. Meanwhile, an estimated 25,000 desperate men gather each morning on roughly 125 corners in Southern California to beg for work.

We could save the ozone layer, ease traffic, and redistribute wealth with one stroke.

Now is the time to get it going, if you ask me. Another three million people will pour into L.A. County over the next 25 years, and by the most optimistic projections, roughly 14 of them will carpool.

Ramos said I'd find no shortage of day laborers who'd gladly take six or seven dollars an hour as professional passengers. "I'll do it all day for $60, if you want me for eight hours," he said.

By the hour or by the day, Ramos is onto something about the commuter psyche. People would rather hire a passenger than endure the inconvenience of making carpool arrangements with a neighbor or office mate. I haven't even mentioned the cultural exchange component.

The round-trip between Hollywood and Lynwood, which I feared would be two hours of hell, was a stress-free 45 minutes. With nothing but time on my hands, I offered to take Ramos to the restaurant of his choice for breakfast. So there we were at Carl's Jr. on Sunset, and Ramos filled me in on his life story. He and his wife came up from Guatemala five years ago, leaving their three children with his parents. His wife is a Beverly Hills live-in maid and makes about $250 a week. Ramos makes roughly the same, sometimes more, and they send half of everything home to support the family.

It's a hard life, but people like the Ramoses head north because people here will pay for anything. They've got someone to walk their dogs, dress

A Few Coors Lights
Might Blur the Truth

(June 29, 2001)

It was about 8:45 Thursday morning when I walked into the Hermosa Beach Police Department with two dozen Krispy Kreme doughnuts and a 12-pack of Coors Light.

In college, that was a typical breakfast. But in this case, I was conducting a scientific experiment to determine how many beers a man has to drink before he's legally hammered.

Roger Clinton, the ex-president's half brother, went on *Larry King Live* last week to talk about his legal problems, which include but are not limited to a DUI arrest in Hermosa. Clinton, who lives in Torrance and plays in a band, denied selling presidential pardons to friends. He also denied that he was driving under the influence in Hermosa on February 21, even though he flunked three blood-alcohol tests after being stopped for driving erratically.

"I had had about two beers," he told Larry King. "Two Coors Lights."

My first thought when anybody in trouble appears on *Larry King* is that they are guilty as sin, because no matter what you've been accused of, you know Larry will keep it cordial. Had Mussolini been a guest, King would have asked a question or two about the fascista thing, Mussolini's attorney would have cut him off, and after a commercial break and a call from Idaho, King would have asked Mussolini if the balsamic craze was just a fad.

Sergeant Paul Wolcott greeted me at the station house in Hermosa. At precisely nine a.m., as Wolcott and Sergeant Tom Thompson looked on, I cracked open my first beer and bit into a glazed doughnut. It felt kind of like a hillbilly picnic, but that was apropos. The Clinton clan did not grow up in Paris.

By a lucky coincidence, Roger Clinton and I each go about 205 pounds, so our alcohol tolerance might well be about the same. Our taste in refreshment is not, however. I'd have had him locked up for his choice of beer alone.

Around 9:45, I'd slugged back my second can, and it was time for my test.

At exactly 10 a.m., I blew into the same device Roger Clinton had used. You're under the influence if you blow a 0.08 percent, Wolcott says, and Clinton ran up a 0.10 on his first try. Mine came up 0.01.

Geez, this Roger Clinton is no Billy Carter. Two wimpy Coors Lights and he's in the tank, with 10 times the damage those same 24 ounces did to me. Unless, of course, he didn't tell Larry King the truth.

"Keep drinking," Sergeant Thompson said.

I had my third beer by 10:15, my fourth by 10:30. And a couple more doughnuts, too. They gave me my own desk to drink at, and Wolcott did some paperwork in the corner under a movie poster of John Wayne in *The Sands of Iwo Jima*. At one point, they took me outside for the field sobriety test that Roger Clinton flunked, calling it a "Jane Fonda" workout on *Larry King*. Touch your nose, walk a line. That kind of thing. I passed like a champ.

"How do you feel?" Wolcott asked.

"Great," I said. "I just can't believe I'm getting paid to do this."

While sipping my beer, I perused the *Los Angeles Times* and noticed that Roger Clinton was on page one again. Reporter Richard Serrano's story said congressional investigators have evidence suggesting Clinton might have pocketed $50,000 for trying to arrange clemency for a convicted heroin dealer from New Jersey. The dealer is related to the Gambino crime family, so let me state publicly that nothing personal is meant by this little beer-and-doughnut social. Investigators also claim to have found "a couple hundred grand" in travelers checks cashed by Clinton, which can only mean that his band is doing really, really well.

Mark Geragos, Clinton's attorney, assured me there was no truth to any of the pardon-peddling allegations. As for the DUI, he claims without explanation that the blood-alcohol tests were inaccurate, and that Hermosa police had no probable cause to arrest Clinton. They did so, he says, as a matter of "political profiling."

You might say it was a strain of political profiling that led to pardons for 47 people, including Roger Clinton, as one of President Clinton's last acts in office. Roger had a 1985 conviction for cocaine distribution wiped from his slate.

While I chugged beer, Wolcott reviewed the police report, and it seems that although Roger told a national television audience he'd had only two beers, he told Hermosa cops he'd had four or five.

"Go ahead and have five and we'll test you again," Wolcott told me.

The fifth went down like water. I took a deep breath and blew a 0.04. Five Coors Lights and I'm only halfway to jail.

When they brought Clinton into the station, they gave him two more tests on a more reliable machine. He blew a 0.08 the first time, a 0.09 the second. Kind of ironic that in 1998, President Clinton campaigned for lowering the legal limit to 0.08 in all 50 states, saying: "To people who disregard the lethal threat they pose...lowering the legal limit will send a strong message that our nation will not tolerate irresponsible acts that endanger our children and our nation."

I can't remember the last time I drank before lunch, but in Hermosa, I dusted a six-pack by 11:15 and they hooked me up to the same machine where Clinton blew his 0.08 and 0.09.

My first shot was 0.05, the second was 0.06.

Reality TV is all the rage, and I think we've got a concept here. Roger and me, a keg and a Breathalyzer. Have your people talk to mine, Larry.

Law and Odor

(May 25, 2003)

For anyone out there who thinks cops lack creativity when it comes to crime-fighting, I offer you the Skunk Squad of the Los Angeles County Sheriff's Department. Lieutenant Shaun Mathers and his special assignment unit in Compton kept seeing the same old problems—prostitution, drug dealing, arson, etc.—in abandoned buildings and other gathering places. They'd round up the bad guys night after night, but the perps were back in no time, and citizens kept screaming for the cops to do something.

In a brain-storming session, Lieutenant Mathers, Deputy Scott Gage and others got a wacky idea that seemed ridiculous at first—maybe they could drive loiterers away with an unpleasant odor. No one even took it seriously until Gage bought a few stink bombs in a novelty store, and curiosity led him and Mathers to the Internet to search for something even smellier.

If this sounds as if it could have been a plot from *Leave It to Beaver*, maybe it's because Lieutenant Mathers is the younger brother of that show's star, Jerry Mathers. Lieutenant Mathers reports that The Beav was quite amused by the story that follows.

Deputy Gage discovered something called Liquid Fence, an animal repellent that smelled like rotten garlic. The deputies ordered it by mail and tested it at crime scenes, but the odor faded too quickly to be effective. Next they ordered a repellent developed by scientists in New Zealand. It's called Skunk Shot, and crime-fighting may never be the same. Mathers' crew knew it was onto something when Deputy Gage's wife called him at work to say a package had arrived by mail. Mathers got on the phone and asked her to open it, then heard a horrified scream.

"It contaminated my whole garage," Gage says of the Skunk Shot, a synthetic gel that comes in a small tube and reeks of a skunk's best work.

The Skunk Squad decided to try the repellent in an abandoned, burned-out motel at 1510 South Long Beach Boulevard. During a two-week stretch in January and February, Mathers' crew had made 30 arrests there. On this particular visit, Mathers' unit arrested six people, including three who had been arrested in the same location the day before. After the perps were carted away, the deputies reached for the Skunk Shot and went to work.

"A small amount of the olfactory nuisance was placed on the armrests of two abandoned couches," Mathers wrote in a report. "The odor of the product became immediately apparent."

Three hours later, the Skunk Squad returned and found the dilapidated motel empty, a rare sight at the illicit late-night flophouse. The deputies went back again two hours later, and it was still evacuated. From Mathers' report: "It appears that, at least for that short time," Skunk Shot "was able to do what fences, gates and barbed wire," along with multiple arrests, "had been unable to do." The high command was impressed.

"If it's one less place you have to worry about," says Captain Cecil Rhambo (his real name), "it's worth it." Especially since deputies are at high risk when entering boarded-up properties in nearly total darkness.

Sheriff Lee Baca, a proponent of creative crime-fighting strategies, couldn't have been more pleased when I filled him in on the details of Mathers' operation.

"Crime, in and of itself, is a nasty odor," quipped the top cop. "We're in a time when people don't want to hear excuses, and if we can come up with ways to fix a problem—ways as ingenious as this—my hat is off" to Mathers, Gage and deputies Dan Drysol, Matt VanderHorck and Brad Molner.

Mathers has since moved on to a desk job at headquarters, but he rejoined his former crew one day last week and made me an honorary member of the Skunk Squad. Our first stop was at that abandoned motel on Long Beach Boulevard. This time Mathers and Gage rousted two squatters, one of whom was cleaning his crack pipe. Then Gage donned rubber gloves and smeared Skunk Shot, which looks like Vaseline, around the room.

In the interest of public service, I stood there as the odor permeated the place and clocked through my sinuses, at least until my eyes crossed and I was ready to gag. My mind reeled as I thought of all the places I'd like to dab this stuff. Gang hangouts. Drug corners. Hollywood pitch meetings.

"It's non-toxic, non-flammable, non-staining," Gage said, and neither the deputy nor the criminal gets hurt. "There's no down side to this." Except that Skunk Shot doesn't work as well in breezy, open areas. Even in tighter spots, it usually wears off in a couple of days.

In another unit at the motel, the Skunk Squad became engaged in a war against an industrious crew of squatters who fought back with air fresheners.

"We'd hit 'em with Skunk Shot, and they'd come back with Glade," Mathers reported.

A day or two after being driven away holding their noses, the squatters would return with all manner of auto air fresheners and aerosol cans, trying to overpower the skunk odor. Outside the unit, I found an empty can of Airwick, Country Berries scent. Hey, better to trade foul odors than speeding bullets.

"I wish I had paid a lot closer attention in chemistry class," says Mathers, who figures there must be a way to brew an even more offensive, longer-lasting odor.

After fouling the motel, my Skunk Squad partners and I rolled to a notorious underpass at Rosecrans and Tamarind. For months, deputies had made hundreds of arrests there to no avail. And then, a few months ago, they brought out their stinky new friend. On our arrival, no one was there.

"I credit Skunk Shot with cutting the crowd by as much as two-thirds here," said Gage, who has been buying the stuff online and paying out of his own pocket. It costs $12 a tube, and you can skunk about five locations per tube. Gage, going above and beyond the call, has already spent more than $100.

Unfortunately the odor isn't wretched enough to scare criminals straight. It just pushes them along. But it's more effective than relying on bureaucracy to clear abandoned properties, and it brings relief to neighbors, even if it comes at a cost.

When the Skunk Squad arrived at an abandoned apartment complex on Spring Street near Compton Boulevard, I went next door and talked to Marlon Terrell and Joe Manley.

"You get people doing their dope in there," said Terrell as deputies brought out three squatters in handcuffs. When I explained the place was being skunked by deputies, Manley said he'd rather smell a skunk than worry about having a bunch of freeloaders next door.

David Garcia, who lives on the other side of the apartments, said he's afraid squatters are going to burn the block down. After Deputy Gage applied Skunk Shot, I led Garcia in to have a whiff.

"Woahhh!" he wailed, reeling back on his heels. Garcia wanted to know where he could buy some Skunk Shot.

"Look what you've done," Mathers said to me. "Now we've got vigilante skunkers."

In the last stop on our shift, the Skunk Squad returned to the abandoned motel where the repellent had been applied two hours earlier. The place still reeked, and we found not a soul.

Crime doesn't sleep in the naked city. But it's on the run in Compton, and holding its nose.

Tipping the Karma Scales

(January 18, 2004)

My pal Mark Morocco and I were going fishing one day when he introduced me to the owners of a bait shop in the Marina del Rey harbor.

"How's business?" I asked one of the two.

"We're surviving," he said. "Thanks to the Buddhists."

I said I wasn't aware that Buddhists were big fishermen, and he said they don't fish at all. They buy the bait and set it free. Good karma. This could be why the Catholic Church has had so much trouble lately. Growing up, we made a point of eating fish every Friday instead of releasing it.

The bait shop boys said sometimes Buddhists arrive by caravan and clean out their entire stock, spending as much as a couple thousand dollars. They promised to call me the next time Buddhists showed up, but they didn't follow through and didn't return my calls either. I started going through the Yellow Pages, calling Buddhist temples at random, but nobody knew anything about any bait release.

It could be tough finding the right group, said my colleague, religion writer Teresa Watanabe. All of the world's 100 Buddhist sects are represented in Los Angeles, naturally, and they tend to be pretty splintered. Watanabe suggested calling Reverend Noriaki Ito at the Higashi Honganji Temple in Little Tokyo.

"They're not Japanese," Reverend Ito told me, "because if they were Japanese, I would know about it. They might be Vietnamese."

I made a few more calls but kept striking out, and was about to give up. In a last gasp, I went to Google on the Internet, typed in the words Buddhist, bait, and Marina del Rey, and got a hit. It was a newsletter on the www.santamonicakksg.org website. I printed out the nine-page report from the Karma Kagyu Study Group, which is affiliated with a Tibetan lama who lives in New York. On the very last page was the heading "Liberation of Beings." It said that once a month, the Buddhist study group meets at a Santa Monica pet shop to purchase and release insects, or at a bait shop in Marina del Rey to release fish.

Daniel Kane, one of the group leaders, invited me to attend a fish release at the Marina del Rey Sportfishing bait shop, across the harbor from the bait shop that never called me back. Before the ceremony, I called owner Rick Oefinger, who said he's been selling bait to various Buddhist sects for years.

"We charge Buddhists half-price, because they usually buy in volume," said Oefinger. He remembers the day a large group bought nearly $5,000 worth of bait and dumped it into the harbor. He said he never sells Buddhists all his bait, because he has to save some for his regular customers.

"I was born and raised Catholic," said Oefinger, who is often handed reading materials by his Buddhist customers, including a lone woman who comes once a month and sets $50 worth of bait free. "But I respect all religion, and I'd just like to thank the Buddhists for their business."

Kane, of the Santa Monica Tibetan group, arranged for a high lama to officiate at last Sunday's fish release ceremony. Venerable Wanchen Rinpoche, of the Maha Vajra Center in Hancock Park, led five monks wearing deep purple robes as they clasped hands in prayer and chanted over a bait pool next to a "Live Squid" sign.

Thirty-five followers joined in the chant—om mani padme hum, the mantra of compassion. They bowed heads and fingered prayer beads as thousands of sardines and anchovies added their own energy to the ceremony, swimming furiously in the bait pool. No fewer than $1,000 worth of them would soon be free, if only to face new perils.

After several minutes of prayer, the lama gave the word and his followers took turns dipping long-handled nets into the well. They grabbed hundreds of the tiny fish in each scoop, and released them into the harbor, the fish scattering in all directions. There were smiles all around, as Buddhists basked in the glow of good karma on a blissfully warm January afternoon.

"The real purpose is not just giving life," the high lama told me, "but to establish an enlightened connection to animals and all living beings." We could be reincarnated as bait fish, and the bait could be reincarnated as humans, the lama continued.

I suppose he could be right. But I'm stressed out enough about paying the mortgage much less worrying that in the next life I could end up as bait, or perhaps a pizza topping. And for some people, fish is food, and bait is how you catch it. When I noticed two guys nearby, fishing off the end of the pier, I asked the lama what he thought of it.

"With all due respect, I think it's ignorant," he said, explaining once again that all living things are sacred. So I asked if he was a vegetarian.

"I accept meat," he said, much to my surprise.

With all due respect, I said to the Venerable Rinpoche, "isn't that ignorant?"

He didn't have much of an answer for that, except to suggest we're all weaker than we'd like to admit.

Not to play devil's advocate, but it did cross my mind that those liberated sardines and anchovies would now be free to get eaten by bigger fish, or to indiscriminately attack and kill plankton, the staff of life for so many fish. You'd like to think a single act of kindness can change the world forever. But can we control our own destiny, I wondered, let alone anyone else's?

I decided to go see what the two fishermen had to say. A man named Andy smiled as he tinkered with his fishing pole, looking over his shoulder in the direction of the high lama.

"When they release all this bait, it attracts bigger fish," he said, explaining that, out of respect, he usually waits for the crowd to disperse before baiting up to go after some serious lunkers. "Halibut, sea bass, barracuda. It's always good fishing after the Buddhists leave."

Two kids who had attended the ceremony with their parents weren't about to let the fishermen get to them. "It just makes you feel good about yourself to set something free," said 10-year-old Gabriel Greenland of Brentwood.

It's about getting a second chance, said Allegra, his 12-year-old sister. "If I get captured," she added, "I hope Buddhists set me free."

Not Legal But Need
a License? No Sweat

(September 5, 2004)

You don't have to find the people selling fake documents on the street near MacArthur Park. They find you. Green cards, Social Security cards, birth certificates. You name it, they can print it. It's an open-air bazaar in the City of Angels, where the underground economy sizzles and salesmen known as micaderos spot you from half a block away.

I slowed down at a corner and two men approached my car, asking what I needed. I am a California-born gringo of European descent, and so I had to come up with something to make them think I wasn't an undercover cop. In Spanish, I said I was an undocumented Spaniard.

"De España," one guy said to the other.

I need a driver's license, I said.

Two hundred bucks, they said.

And how long would it take?

Thirty minutes.

I said I'd think about it.

A couple days later, I tried another guy who said he could get me a license for $90. He led me behind a truck that served as a shield. Police were all over the place, he explained as he considered my undocumented Spaniard story. He asked me to wait there a minute, then disappeared, never to return. I found another guy who quoted me a price of $300.

No way, I said. I could get one for $90.

OK, he said—$150.

Deal. But he wanted me to promise I wasn't a police officer.

I promised.

Curse the police, he insisted.

I cursed the police to his satisfaction and had the feeling I wasn't working with the swiftest blokes in criminal history. I gave them my photo, my ID information and a $20 deposit. It usually takes an hour, they said, but they'd try to rush it.

This activity is no secret in L.A. Underage teens have been buying fake IDs near MacArthur Park for years, but illegal immigrants make up the bulk of the customers in what police call a multi-million-dollar trade.

For me, this exposes the futility of the endless debate on issuing legal driver's licenses to illegal immigrants. Sure, some might take advantage of the chance to come clean. But many others will choose instead to avoid paying for their own background checks and car insurance and easily buy fake licenses. Or none at all.

Now that Governor Arnold Schwarzenegger has used the national pulpit to invite the entire world to move to the United States, the more useful debate is whether California can accommodate the anticipated population explosion. Good-paying jobs are so scarce, 500,000 people recently applied for 3,000 openings at the harbor. Maybe those who missed out could apply to help out the micaderos.

An hour went by at MacArthur Park, and I still had no license. I thought about running over to Langer's Deli for a hot pastrami on rye, but I didn't want to miss my connection, and I'm trying to drop a few pounds anyway. My guys kept an eye on the street and an eye on me, too, as I wandered around. I began to think I hadn't passed their test after all. Maybe they thought I was a cop, and the license would never arrive.

Captain Charles L. Beck of the LAPD's Rampart Division says police are in the midst of cracking down on the MacArthur Park trade with the help of several federal agencies. They include the FBI and Homeland Security, both of which are concerned about the possibility of terrorists getting their hands on fake documents. Two sellers were arrested last week, Beck said, and police shut down a "printing mill" about a month ago. He said there are several other mills within a few blocks of the park, all with sophisticated machinery churning out documents that look amazingly authentic.

"We've had homicides related to the competition," said the Rampart chief. "Because there's a lot of money involved, there are a lot of territorial disputes and things like that."

Police seem to have put a huge dent in the drug trade around the park, so it's a safe bet they'll have the same success with fake documents. But bogus papers, like drugs, will always find another venue.

Three hours after I'd placed my order, my contact leaped into action, crossing the street in the direction of a man walking south along the park. The man appeared to put something in a garbage can, and it was retrieved by my contact. My guy and another man walked into a nearby variety store, nodding for me to follow. They stayed 10 paces in front of me, turned down an aisle, and planted a tiny brown envelope behind some bottles of shampoo. I picked up the envelope and placed $130 in the same spot.

The license, which I've since destroyed, was a beautiful piece of work. A DMV check would prove the number was bogus, but it looked almost exactly like my real license, complete with seals and careful attention to the tiniest details. Best of all, I ended up a couple of years younger, and I lost nearly 50 pounds.

There was only one thing left to do. I went to Langer's for the pastrami on rye, and it was so good I almost wanted to call the police and turn myself in.

Tired Types Flip Upside Down
in This *Crash*

(May 13, 2005)

New Yorker critic David Denby raved. The *New York Post* called it "a thoughtful road trip well worth taking." Thanks, guys, but it's my town you're talking about. The subject is the movie *Crash*, which depicts a seething, carved-up Los Angeles in which racial hostility blows as hot as a wicked Santa Ana wind. Why is it that out-of-towners can't resist the chance to cheer the long-awaited Los Angeles apocalypse?

My curiosity piqued, I went to see *Crash* at the ArcLight in Hollywood, but I didn't go alone. I took two members of the Los Angeles County Commission on Human Relations. The commission, as its website describes it, is "dedicated to promoting positive race and human relations in an increasingly complex and multicultural county." My guests were civil rights attorneys Thomas Saenz, a Mexican American, and Kathay Feng, an Asian American.

We didn't arrive early enough to buy popcorn, but *Crash* isn't that kind of movie. It's a 90-minute lecture from director Paul Haggis on what alienated monsters we are, despite the goodness and commonality trapped inside. So the instinct is to reach for a stiff drink or a tranquilizer rather than a tub of popcorn.

In the very first scene, we get a car crash that erupts into a shouting match. In one vehicle is an Asian woman who blames the accident on the occupants of the other vehicle—two Los Angeles Police Department detectives. The Asian woman says something about applying the "blakes" instead of the "brakes." I kind of peeked over to see if Kathay Feng was flinching, but I couldn't tell in the dark. Oh, well, we'd have plenty of time to share notes after the movie.

One of the detectives, a Latina, mocks the Asian woman's language, then goes home for a roll with the black detective, who insults her with a crack about Latinos parking their cars on the lawn. To this point, though, the most offensive line isn't a slur—at least not to a human. It's the black detective's first thoughts after the car crash. He says that in "real cities" there's more human contact than there is in Los Angeles.

"I think we miss that sense of touch so much," he says, speaking metaphorically, "we crash into each other just to feel something."

Did I say tranquilizer? It's the stiff drink I need after all.

At the risk of committing my own generalization, I'm not sure there are many cops who, moments after being plowed into by another driver, would offer up a quiet meditation on the emptiness of the human heart. And as for the observation that people in L.A. get around by car, I think I already heard that somewhere.

But *Crash*, to be fair, does pull off a neat trick. The dialogue is clean, if abrasive, and many of the performances are sharp, so it actually looks like a smart movie tackling a tough subject. As it clumsily develops, however, you realize you're watching a puppet show.

A racist white cop molests a black woman during a bogus traffic stop, but later saves her from a burning car. A Latino locksmith who looks like a gangbanger turns out to be father of the year. Two black carjackers drag a "Chinaman" down the street on the undercarriage of their stolen car, but turn out to be witty philosophers with hearts of gold. The D.A.'s wife, an insufferable witch, insults the ethnic help until she tumbles down the stairs and realizes her only friend in the world is the Latina maid. A crazed Iranian tries to kill the Latino locksmith, whose cute little daughter steps into the line of fire, but the little girl survives because the Iranian unwittingly bought blanks from a racist gun shop owner. This near-miss, naturally, is a transformative moment for the nut-ball Iranian. And I almost forgot to mention that the little girl was wearing an imaginary protective cape given to her by the father of the year.

Exhausted? I was. And I haven't even mentioned the scene in which a saintly white cop, off duty, picks up one of the black carjackers, who is hitchhiking in the San Fernando Valley. The carjacker's a hockey fan, of course, turning another stereotype on its head, and he's just been out for some ice-skating between car thefts. But the good cop panics when the kid reaches into his pocket for his St. Christopher statue—I swear every word of this is true—thinking the kid is going for a gun. The good cop puts a bullet through the kid's chest and then hides the body, and the poor lad becomes the first black man ever to die for the love of hockey.

On our way out of the theater, Saenz patted Feng on the back and told her that his people made out better than hers. True enough, Feng agreed. The Asian characters were all either racists or criminals, except for the slaves set free by one of the black carjackers (irony, Hollywood-style).

In a city that's half Latino, Saenz said, the only two Latino characters in the movie are cardboard. There's the loyal maid and the "noble savage"— the misunderstood Latino with baggy pants, neck tattoos and a gentle soul. Feng guessed the movie was interested in saying bad people can have goodness in them, even if that's not exactly a revelation. And she gave the movie credit for being provocative.

"But what does it provoke you to think about?" she asked, unsure of the answer. You can't think much of anything, Saenz said, because with only a couple of exceptions in the movie, there's no social and historic context for the characters' suspicion and hatred.

"It's just images thrown onto a flat screen, with no depth," he said, even when stereotypes are exploded and hope rises in the dust of the blast.

After seeing the movie, I read where director Haggis told *L.A. Weekly* that *Crash*—inspired by his own experience as a carjacking victim in Los Angeles—is not about race. "It's about strangers, others. About how we love to divide ourselves.... We will always manufacture differences."

In another interview, Haggis said we became terrified of one another after September 11, 2001, further isolating ourselves from one another. Some of this may be true, but if there's anything new in it, *Crash* doesn't tell us what it might be. To the extent that the movie is about Los Angeles, yeah, we're sealed off from one another, existing behind gates and car windows. But we do sometimes hook up—at Griffith Park, the beach, the Third Street Promenade, Dodger Stadium, Ralph's, and at movie theaters. In my New York apartment building, seldom did a word pass between me and my neighbors as we rode the elevator shoulder to shoulder.

Yes, L.A.'s got bigots. Yes, it's a flawed experiment in modern living. Yes, it's divided by race and ethnicity, as is the rest of the world, and there's always a rumbling of trouble off in the distance. But on most days it works. Would millions of us have come here, from every corner of the world, if it didn't?

Malibu: How the Other Half Leases

(August 24, 2005)

I've got good news for those of you who haven't yet planned your summer beach vacation. The smart shopper can sunbathe like a celebrity because great rental deals are available for the taking on the majestic, world-famous shores of Malibu.

"This one ordinarily gets 55 to 70," Irene Dazzan-Palmer was telling me in the living room of a modern two-story that has the Pacific Ocean for a backyard. "No, put down 75."

When Dazzan-Palmer says 55, 70 and 75, she means thousands of dollars. Per month. But those are high-season numbers, and they start to fall in September. If you move quickly and play a little hardball, you might be able to grab Dazzan-Palmer's Malibu Colony listing for a mere $50,000 a month.

"This goes downstairs and takes you out to the beach on the Tom Hanks side," Dazzan-Palmer noted. See there? Fifty grand and you're tossing a football on the beach with Tom Hanks, unless he's in one of his other houses.

"I've gotten $120,000 in the colony," said Dazzan-Palmer. "I mean, I've gotten big numbers....But after Labor Day the prices come down. I have a house on Malibu Road where we're asking $50,000, and then it drops down to $40,000 and $30,000." How could I say no to a bargain like that?

My interest in a Malibu rental began while reading the real estate listings in the *Los Angeles Times*, a regular source of weekend entertainment at my house. I always feel better about myself when I see an overpriced $20 million house and wonder who would buy such a tacky place.

At the bottom of the sales listings for Malibu, there's often a rental or two in the $10,000-to-$40,000 range. I found that to be astounding enough, but then my colleague Ruth Ryon wrote about Sting and Pierce Brosnan renting out their places for more than $100,000, while Ted Danson and Mary Steenburgen get $80,000 a month. Could I really be happy, I wondered, in a rental that cost a mere $10,000?

I got hold of Lee LaPlante, a Coldwell Banker agent, who said it was definitely possible. She said she could put me in a charming little two-bedroom on the Pacific Coast Highway for $6,900 a month. At that price, though, you've got to wonder what kind of riffraff is running loose in the neighborhood.

When I get my place, I'm going the same route David Geffen did before he finally caved in under pressure from the California Coastal Commission and opened the gates. If anyone tries to set one toe on my beach, I'll have lawyers chasing them all the way home to Glendora. I don't care if it is public property, and I may bring in guards on three-wheelers—like so many high-rollers do—to patrol the perimeter.

LaPlante hooked me up with her colleague, Dazzan-Palmer, who invited me to see a $29,500 rental on Malibu Road before we visited the $55,000-to-$75,000 place in the colony. I arrived at the house before she did, and the chef/house manager gave me a quick tour. Unfortunately, the chef/house manager doesn't come with the house. She works for the guy who rented it for the summer and commutes by private jet to Las Vegas, where he owns several nightclubs. I should have been a nightclub owner. I'd say the house is quite nice, especially the in-law cottage with the second-floor ocean view. But swimmers beware. For $29,500, can't someone get all those rocks up off the beach?

Dazzan-Palmer finally arrived with the widow of a celebrity, and I'm sworn to secrecy as to her identity. The widow lives near Zuma Beach in Malibu but is having work done—on the house, not herself, I don't think—so she's interested in a rental on the beach. Not uncommon, says Dazzan-Palmer. Although renters come from all over the country and the world, many come from hillside houses in Malibu or from other parts of Los Angeles.

"They're from Beverly Hills, Brentwood....I've got one guy staying outside the colony gates, he's a grape grower from Palm Springs with a house in Beverly Hills."

But he decided to get his kids out of the horrible heat of Beverly Hills and rent a $55,000-a-month beach house. Geez, maybe I could get out of the horrible heat of Silver Lake and rent his place in Beverly Hills.

"We have over a dozen billionaires that live here now," Dazzan-Palmer said of Malibu. "People want to come here because of all the wealthy people here. It's like a little chic place, like a little Carmel. Around the country, people see that everybody's in Malibu, and they say, 'We're going, too.'"

I thought I overheard someone saying Jane Seymour once rented the $29,500 house, but the widow wasn't bowled over. Dazzan-Palmer suggested we all drive over to the other house.

"The colony is great," she said.

"The colony is so cool," said another agent.

"Follow me," Dazzan-Palmer said. "I'm in the Jaguar."

I'm in the Honda. Behind me, the widow is in a Range Rover the size of the Los Angeles Coliseum.

"Should we name-drop?" Dazzan-Palmer asked when we entered the house next to the Tom Hanks house, which is not far from the Mel Brooks house and the Jim Carrey house.

"Diana Ross stayed here. George Foreman. Tori Spelling."

I'm sworn to secrecy again, but one of those three called Dazzan-Palmer one night when she was home in her pajamas. Dazzan-Palmer picked up the phone and heard a very whiny "I can't work the 'ja-cooo-zy.'"

Dazzan-Palmer had to get dressed, drive all the way down from her 6,000-square-foot, two-story, white neoclassical next to the castle up on the hill—I should have been a real estate agent—and into the colony, where she knocked on the door, walked over to the Jacuzzi, pushed the button and said, "There, now it's on." I'll give you one clue: It wasn't George Foreman.

So, I asked Dazzan-Palmer, "Who owns this joint?"

"He invented the ear plug," she said, pointing at her ear.

He did what?

"You know when you walk into a noisy factory and you put those foam rubber things in your ears? That's him."

Doesn't it tick you off? Any dope could have come up with that thing, including me. I should have been an inventor.

S.Lo's on Top, But
It's the Wrong Game

(January 29, 2006)

I've had only one guiding principle in life, and here it is: It's always important to look your best. So when S.Lo saw the story on the sizzling new A-list Hollywood bar that keeps out the riffraff, your man-about-town couldn't get there fast enough.

"I'm looking for personal style; sophistication but playfulness," owner Amanda Scheer Demme told the *Los Angeles Times* in describing Teddy's at the Roosevelt Hotel, which follows her sensationally exclusive Tropicana Bar at the same hotel.

"It doesn't really matter how old you are, doesn't really matter what you do for a living," Demme elaborated in explaining who gets in and who doesn't. "You have to be at the top of your game in your own way, whatever that may be." Top of your game? It sounded like a personal invitation to S.Lo.

And so, while most of Los Angeles slept, I cruised under the bright lights of Hollywood Boulevard, eager to frolic in a playfully sophisticated way. The clock struck midnight—party time in my world—as I parked near Grauman's Chinese Theatre and headed across the boulevard. Ahead of me, a cluster of maybe 15 people waited on the sidewalk, craning to be noticed by ushers. You have to feel sorry for people like that, the second-string hobbits who flock to the rope but never get a chance to swing.

I'm guessing the paparazzi didn't see me coming, because none of them popped a flash. I sauntered in among the crowd and waited to be noticed in my black Levi's, maroon shirt and casual brown suede jacket, an understated ensemble that says, "Hello, I'm here, I need no introduction."

The usher, a prim pug wearing what looked like a *Star Trek* costume, for crying out loud, must have been nearsighted. He gave the crowd the once-over, missed the obvious, and slid back into the joint, leaving S.Lo out in the cold.

"What gives?" I asked two young women.

"We're not famous," said one.

Speak for yourself, sweetheart.

Most of the crowd was a tad younger than S.Lo. OK, more than a tad. I looked like the chaperon on the bus that brought them here. But style has no age, as the owner of Teddy's pointed out.

Some of the youngsters were dressed up, some dressed down. The exception was a couple of middle-aged blokes who looked like they'd taken in one too many Aerosmith concerts. I wished I'd worn jeans that were either tighter or baggier, because the scene didn't appear to be relaxed-fit. A different usher appeared, sized us up, and disappeared. Maybe it was my Rockports.

"You might get in if you had three young babes on your arm," one of the paparazzi suggested. I closed in on the two young women I'd spoken to earlier, but they discreetly moved away. Either they thought I'd hurt their chances of getting in, or they thought I was a pervert.

Three young guys from Australia approached and asked if I had any pointers.

"You've got to be on top of your game," I said. They suggested we hire a paparazzo and have him photograph us as we strode confidently up to the rope. It wasn't a bad idea, but they opted instead to go around back and see if they could sneak in.

The door to the hottest night life in town suddenly opened and an allegedly famous person exited. The paparazzi followed him down the street, showering the guy with light. Before I could ask who it was, another young caballero appeared out of nowhere and the paparazzi closed on him fast.

"Who was it?" I asked.

"Brandon Davis," I was told.

I nodded and then asked, "Who's Brandon Davis?"

I was told he was dating someone on *The O.C.* That's his claim to fame?

Give me a break. If that was the definition of a man on top of his game, maybe I was at the wrong bar.

The ushers reappeared, scanned the crowd and looked right through me again.

"I'm with David Heath," one young woman pleaded, offering up an unanswered prayer to the gatekeepers. Whoever David Heath is.

A guy pulled up in a chauffeur-driven Rolls; he got in. A guy pulled up in a limo a block long; he got in. P. Diddy was already inside, a paparazzo told me. And Penélope Cruz. A man who'd been at the rope longer than I had introduced himself.

"I'm S.Lo," I said, to no recognition from him. "I don't think these nitwits know who I am."

Suddenly, a flutter and a stir. Out of nowhere, a young man appeared, and the ushers couldn't raise the velvet rope fast enough to let him in.

"Steve-O, could we roll with you?" one of his drooling fans called out.

Hey, I'm the original Steve-O. Who was this guy? Given all the talk of style and sophistication, he had to be a real Hollywood player. In the *L.A. Times* story, a fashion consultant had said of Teddy's, "It's classy and it's always a high caliber of people."

"So who's Steve-O?" I asked a paparazzo.

"He was in *Jackass*," he said. "Not the movie, but *Jackass* the TV show." I've never needed a drink so badly.

Philip Seymour Hoffman showed up, and it was Open Sesame. Straight through the chutes he went, riding fame's vapor trail. Truman Capote on the heels of Mr. Jackass in the celluloid city.

I thought my luck might change if I switched Walk of Fame stars, so I moved from Irving Thalberg to Julio Iglesias. I even tried Hugh Hefner's star for a while.

"If you don't have a reservation," an usher told the crowd, "we can't help you out tonight." Nobody left. It was clear that people without reservations were getting in.

"Can't a guy get a drink around here?" I asked an usher. He shook his head.

"I'm S.Lo," I said, and he turned away.

Just then the three Australian kids tumbled out the front door of the hotel, 86'd by bouncers. Before I could ask them about the playful sophistication inside, they zipped away in a cab.

OK, so maybe the S.Lo image needs some freshening up. An eye patch, torn jeans, neck tattoo, shaved head, bevy of bimbos. The city is crawling with image consultants who get people ready for their close-ups, and one of them's got to have the answer.

Keep a seat warm for me, Teddy's, because I'll be back. I was Steve-O before that Jackass bellied up to his first bar.

Bicker, Bicker—and Belt It Out

(February 26, 2006)

Alexis Rivera had the whole deal set up for Mickey Champion, his star singer. Nice little gig at the Venetian in Vegas, fat paycheck for an hour's worth of work, a room at the Hard Rock Hotel. And what thanks did Rivera get for his efforts?

"I ain't #&*%@ goin' nowhere, honey."

She's shy of five feet tall but gives no ground. Mules shake their heads in disbelief. Champion is somewhere around 80, but good luck trying to nail down the Crenshaw resident's exact age. She is perfectly happy belting out blues, jazz, gospel and pop at the Living Room, Little Pedro's and Babe's & Ricky's. Other than that, don't mess with her, don't expect her to get on a plane, and don't ask questions.

Rivera is 28, lives in Echo Park and has a crazy job spying on hotels for other hotels, so they know which corporate groups are staying where. In his spare time, the music lover and former critic is Champion's manager. He does it for free because he saw her perform a few years ago and thought it was a crying shame that one of the greatest singers ever to walk the face of the Earth never got her due. Together they're a sight, laughing, bickering, scolding, making up. They're worse than married, and this little showdown over Vegas was typical. Rivera cajoled, praised, scolded and begged.

"Bring me some fish," Champion finally said by phone, which was promising.

Rivera went to the Crenshaw Fish Market, because it's got to be from there and nowhere else. He picked up some fried sole and French fries and ferried the bag of grease to her house. But it still wasn't a sure thing. She hemmed, she hawed.

Finally, she gave in.

Champion left the house in a blue sweater, clutching her fish and chips, the sequins of her black cap shining like the lights of the Vegas Strip. She takes a while to get from here to there and needed Rivera's arm to keep her steady. Rivera all but jumped for joy. He called to tell the band members—who were already halfway to Nevada on the chance she would come through—and they couldn't believe it. Vegas or bust, baby. The young Mr. Rivera is driving Miss Mickey.

"&#%$@!!! Don't get too close!" Champion snaps before we even hit Rancho Cucamonga.

"Mickey, I know how to drive." He takes one cell phone call after another. He's also the volunteer manager for two other bands.

"I wish you'd get off that phone," she whines when he hangs up. The phone rings again.

"Let me drive," she says, eye level with the glove box.

"You're not driving, OK?"

She announces that if they make it to Vegas alive, she will not be needing her hotel room because she's going to party all night. Rivera knows she's not kidding. He's seen the sun come up with her more than once and knows that only a fool tries to trade drinks with Mickey, whose latest CD is called "I Am Your Living Legend." The Living Legend bites into the fish.

"Mmmmmmm, hmmmmm, lord, honey." She likes the fish. But not the traffic.

"You told me you wouldn't fly," Rivera says.

"I didn't say that."

"Yes, you did."

"Lord have mercy."

"What?"

"Look at that old lady drivin'."

Rivera slows for a line of slow trucks, and Champion braces herself, grabbing on to the strap above the window as if she's going to do a pull-up.

"Pass them!" she barks.

"I can't pass."

"I didn't say I wouldn't fly."

But that's one explanation for why she never hit the big time. Barbara Morrison, a sensational jazz and blues singer and good friend, says Champion is world-class but wouldn't go to Europe when that was the thing to do. Still, she made her mark.

"I think the blues singers who are her age and younger copied her style," says Morrison, who met Mickey 35 years ago and marvels at Champion's "walkin' the floor" act, in which she travels a room, bellies up to a bar and even walks outside, singing with or without the microphone. Who needs it?

"She was a pistol then, just like she is now," Morrison says. "The queen of the scene."

Champion grew those great pipes in Louisiana, came west as a teen and got hitched to bandleader Roy Milton. She worked the legendary Central Avenue jazz clubs and shared bills with Count Basie, Dinah Washington, Sarah Vaughan and Billie Holiday. But she gave it up to raise a family and punch a clock in Los Angeles Unified school cafeterias. It wasn't until she retired about 15 years ago that she started showing up again regularly in local clubs.

When you talk to her, there isn't much talking. She gives you short bursts, the words slung like brickbats, and sometimes she pauses mid-sentence to wonder how she got there and where she was headed. But hand her a microphone and she's a young diva again, vamping, grinding, hiking her dress, her pipes knocking dust off the walls next door.

Is there still time for a breakout? Hard to say, and it's not even clear she's pining for one. She loves being loved, no mistake about it, but there's plenty of love in the small L.A. places where people know she's got the chops. Maybe Champion is doing this trip for Rivera and the half-broke band rather than herself. She does insist, after all, that the money be split evenly.

Vegas is three hours up the road. Sam Cooke is singing "A Change Is Gonna Come," and Mickey is holding on to the strap with both hands like it's a ride at Disneyland, telling Rivera he's going to kill us all.

"Mickey," he says, interrupting a phone call, "I know what I'm doing."

We stop at a terrible Herbst in Barstow and she's a kid on Christmas Day, making a haul. She walks every aisle, grabbing pork rinds, Cheetos, Cracker Jack, two strawberry sodas. Now she's zeroed in on a Smirnoff Ice and smiles like a thief when Rivera picks up an 18-pack of Miller Genuine Draft. Ten seconds later they're bickering in the potato chip aisle.

"I wanna get me some nachos," she says, looking straight up at Rivera, who is normal height but looks like he's on a ladder next to her.

"Mickey, you messed up my car last time."

"What you mean?"

"Don't you remember? You ate nachos and got it all over my car."

The relationship survives the trip, and Champion is dazzled by the Strip. She rolls into the Hard Rock Hotel and Casino and her other boyfriend, lead guitarist Johnny Moezzi, wraps his arms around her but still can't believe Rivera managed to talk her into coming.

Two hours later, Champion, Moezzi, drummer Gary "Dap" Gibson and bass player Carlos Reveles cruise into the Venetian's Tao Nightclub, a popular cross between a brothel and a set from *Raiders of the Lost Ark*. There's fake fog, strip-club music blasting over the speakers and a nearly naked woman in a bathtub dropping flower petals over her head. Champion asks for a drink, and Rivera could use a double. He's worried about the scene and the crowd, which swells to hundreds. He's wondering if they'll connect with something real and original, or if they'll look at Champion as some kind of novelty or, worse, an intrusion on their party.

The canned dance beat stops. Champion, standing unnoticed in the crowd, takes the microphone. The band sets her up with "Next Time You See Me," and Champion reaches to the depths of those bottomless lungs and almost knocks Tao's hundreds of Buddha stones off the walls.

> Next time you see me
> Things won't be the same.
> If it hurts you, darling,
> You only got yourself to blame.

One verse and she has them. People swarm in for a better look, clapping, swaying, dancing. As guitarist Moezzi would say, Champion delivers a soul injection straight into the heart of the beast. Halfway through the next cut, "At Last," Rivera looks like the biggest winner in Vegas. He stands just a few feet away from Champion, in case she needs to take his arm, and he is lip-syncing.

> You smiled
> And then the spell was cast.
> And here we are in heaven
> And you are mine at last.

Downtown Drug Hunt:
He Strolls, He Scores

(August 19, 2006)

I wanted to do my part, so late Friday afternoon in downtown Los Angeles, I went shopping for drugs. To hear the brass of the LAPD squawk lately, they can't crack down on skid row crime because a federal court decision protecting tent encampments has kept drug transactions hidden and users out of sight. Balderdash.

Yeah, there are lots of tents on skid row. Hundreds of them, and there's no question that the folks inside are not all singing campfire songs. There's prostitution and rampant drug activity behind those canvas zippers. But drug sales and drug use outside the tents are so blatant it's stunning. People light crack pipes and inject heroin without even looking over their shoulders. It's one big block party after another.

I see it every time I'm anywhere east of Spring Street between roughly 3rd and 8th Streets. The cops must need help if they can't see what's going on out there, sometimes within a couple of blocks of the Central Station. Maybe I could help direct them. At 4:30 p.m., I headed south on Spring Street. By 5:15, I had been solicited three times. I was also eyeballed several times by guys who didn't look as if they were just admiring the downtown architecture. I'm guessing some of them thought I was an undercover cop.

My first connection was at 7th and Spring, where a guy lingering on one corner crossed the street to check me out. He wasn't sure what to make of me, so he walked to 7th and Main and spoke to another guy who now walked toward me wearing a white towel over his shoulder. Lots of white towels on shoulders out there, as if waiters are coming by to explain the menu.

"What you need?" the young guy asked. He was about 20.

"I'm OK," I said, and I kept walking.

How did I know to go to that corner, you ask? Because almost every time I travel Spring or Main, I see dealers working. There aren't any tents there, but there's plenty of action, and sometimes I see runners heading between there and the heart of skid row to the east. I didn't even go to skid row on my shopping spree, because that would have been too easy. I've seen dealers brazenly counting money, and on Friday morning I saw a guy drive along San Julian Street, casually get out of his car, buy some crack, smoke it, get back in the car and drive away—and this was a block and a half from the police station.

When I hit Main, I turned north and was halfway between 6th and 5th when a guy about 30 years old asked if I wanted anything for my pipe. I wasn't carrying a pipe and he wasn't talking about Prince Albert in a can. There's such a blatant drug operation on this street, next to a parking garage, that they might as well put up signs. Yeah, I know police have to see a transaction in order to make an arrest, but let's beef up the undercover corps and get things cleaned up.

The LAPD claims it doesn't have the manpower, and that's a better argument than their tent lament, but still not an acceptable reason for inaction. If police quit making excuses, and the politicians get off the dime and start bringing in the supportive housing, rehab and mental health services that are so desperately needed, then law-abiding residents and merchants can be rid of this nightmare.

While I was telling my man that I didn't really want any drugs, he looked over my shoulder and yelled, "Long john." No, he wasn't selling underwear. A cop car was approaching, he was the lookout and I guess "long john" was the signal.

Officers Holbrook and Fischer really blew my undercover operation. Dealers scattered as the team pulled up and got out of their car. Officer Fischer asked a couple of women herding three small children what they were doing there, which I thought was a pretty good question. Everyone is "smoking rock" around here, Fischer said, and it didn't make the best playground, but the women showed no inclination to move on.

The officers told me they work Main between 3rd and 8th. Holbrook said it can be frustrating to break up one operation and have dealers just move over to the next block. I suggested having a cop on a bike ride in circles around every block. That would knock this thing down big-time, I said, but the officers told me they didn't have the resources and then said they weren't authorized to conduct interviews.

Hey, I'm not authorized to work narcotics, but the LAPD obviously needs help.

I worked my way back to 8th, then cut over to Spring again and came upon an aggressive dealer between 5th and 6th. This guy was somewhere between his late teens and early 20s, and he was actually waving me over. I asked if he had any crack. He shook his head no.

"What do you have?" I asked.

"Heroin," he said. Heroin? Geez, I might have had a five o'clock shadow and maybe I looked a little haggard at the end of a long work week, but did I look like a heroin addict?

"How much?" I asked.

"Fifty dollars," he said. Pretty steep. I decided to go home and crack a beer instead.

Memo to Police Chief Bill Bratton: I'm available if you need me.

Transit Boss' SUV Is
Too Big to Ignore

(January 21, 2007)

Questions about the Hummer would be off-limits. That's what the mayor's press secretary told me as we headed to a City Hall meeting with transportation chief Jaime de la Vega, whose vehicle of choice seems odd for a man in his position.

No way, I told Matt Szabo. How can I not ask about it? What de la Vega drives is a private matter, argued Szabo. No it isn't, I told him. It's now a public matter, and I don't know how Mayor Antonio Villaraigosa can have any faith in a transit chief who drives a two-ton monster in a city with notorious traffic and smog. It's like having a surgeon general who smokes unfiltered Camels while snacking on Cheetos.

I felt a little sorry for Szabo, a decent enough chap who had arranged the meeting after I complained that de la Vega didn't answer my calls. But not sorry enough to pull punches. What's with the Hummer? I asked as soon as we were seated in de la Vega's office. De la Vega gave me a cold stare, his lips sealed. Then he looked at Szabo, who said we were there to talk transportation. I asked about de la Vega's background and he dropped the mummy act, telling me he'd gotten a master's in urban planning from UCLA. He was also Mayor Dick Riordan's traffic chief and a member of the Metropolitan Transportation Authority board. So you'd think he'd know better.

I just can't get past it, I told de la Vega. A Hummer? And then I noticed a quote on his wall from Rosa Parks. "Every person must live their lives as a model for others." I read the quote to de la Vega, who clammed up again.

"Should we all drive Hummers?" I asked. Silence. Szabo, meanwhile, looked like he might have some kind of a breakdown. He argued that de la Vega's vehicle is not the largest in the Hummer line.

"It's smaller than a Yukon," he said. Wonderful. So is the Queen Mary.

The polar caps are melting, we are at war in the oil fields and Mr. Transit is driving a hog that says who cares? But for Szabo's sake, I changed the subject, asking de la Vega if he'd checked out all the great ideas on my Bottleneck Blog (latimes.com/bottleneck), where people are posting solutions to our traffic mess. He said he hadn't looked at it, which is his loss.

De la Vega said he's looking at everything from charging people to drive in congested areas to creating one-way thoroughfares to synchronizing every light in the city. But the larger plan is to "maintain a first-class bus system" and get the Exposition light-rail line going, extend the Gold Line to the San Gabriel Valley and the Eastside, take the Green Line to the airport and the Red Line to the sea.

Sounds lovely, except that the city doesn't have $27 billion sitting around, and even if it did, the mayor hasn't sold me on whether rail would be the best use of that money in a city where people go in a million different directions to get here and there. Even at that, it would take years to get any of those lines in place, and we've got a crisis now. De la Vega said the city is looking at twisting the governor's arm and turning up the heat on Washington as well as considering a sales tax or a bond.

"There is no magic wand," he said. Yeah, no kidding. There's not even a formal transit plan for the city to begin debating.

It would help, I told de la Vega and Szabo, if the mayor and other public officials stopped taking huge campaign checks from developers and rubber-stamping their projects until we get some of the transit in place.

Villaraigosa, if you ask me, is now testing the limits of big ambition. How much more might he have accomplished by now if he hadn't devoted so much time to a school takeover bid that so far has been a disaster? We didn't elect him to run the school district, and he already has a full plate with homelessness, housing and public safety. Before he takes on the schools, too, he should use his popularity and gift of gab to step up on traffic, which affects millions of people every day and is redefining our lives, wasting time, money and productivity. An uninspired City Council is asleep at the wheel on this issue, by the way, offering the mayor little or no help.

But it's Villaraigosa who should use his million-dollar smile to charm people out of their vehicles at least one day a week, encouraging them to use transit, bicycles, carpools and flexible work schedules. And given the depth of its problems, Los Angeles and the surrounding region ought to have the smartest and most enviro-friendly innovations in the world rather than having to read about what works in London or Bangkok, Argentina or Brazil.

I don't want to hear that it can't be done, and I can't think of a better way for City Hall to show it's serious than to have Villaraigosa take de la Vega's Hummer and ship it to the troops in Iraq, where it might come in handy. Or he could trade it to the governor for a bigger chunk of state transit funding. I told him if they can't work a deal, I'll be happy to drive his tank back to the dealer and trade it in on a nice Honda or something.

De la Vega didn't respond, but I could tell he was beginning to see the wisdom of unloading this thing. All right, I told him. We'll trade vehicles for a week. He can gradually warm to the idea of a car that's smaller than Half Dome, and I'll be high enough off the ground to get a better look at just how awful the traffic has become.

Hoping for a Free Meal?
Fat Chance

(April 29, 2007)

About 500 hungry readers, give or take, confidently lined up for last Sunday's food quiz and took their best shot at a free meal.

"See you for lunch," said a contestant calling himself "Leonard, the lawyer from Long Beach." Unfortunately, Leonard missed six of the eight questions. But he had company.

"I am looking forward to my lunch with you!" said Susan Pearson, who proceeded to blow the quiz entirely. She missed eight out of eight.

"Allow me to embarrass myself," said Diana Arnold, a professional dietitian.

Congratulations, Diana. You missed seven out of eight.

For those who missed it, I bought lunch at five well-known dining establishments and delivered the food to a lab for a nutritional breakdown. I decided on my own quiz after the news that 523 Californians had flunked a test comparing the healthiest and unhealthiest offerings at popular chain restaurants, with not a single contestant correctly answering all four questions.

I got the Double-Double burger and fries at In-N-Out, two carne asada tacos at Burrito King, the bacon chili cheese dog at Pink's, the pepperoni-and-cheese pizza at Wolfgang Puck Gourmet and the slippery shrimp (with rice and a fortune cookie) at Yang Chow. At the lab, they tossed each item into a blender and extracted oils to determine fat content. Then they incinerated samples in a 950-degree furnace and tested the resulting moisture and ash to determine protein, carbs and calories.

"There's no way to accurately guess," wrote Diana, the professional nutritionist, without knowing the portion size or cooking methods. In my book, Diana, any bona fide Southern Californian ought to be familiar with these dishes.

But clearly not familiar enough.

Anyone care to guess how many of our 500 contestants correctly answered all eight questions (the most and fewest calories, most and least fat, most and least protein, most and fewest carbs)? Looks like I'll be eating alone. In other words, ZEEEEE-RO! Everyone flunked. True confession: I missed three out of the eight myself, so don't feel bad.

And the correct answers? You might be more than a little surprised. Let's just say that if you're going to eat an order of slippery shrimp and rice, you might want to have 911 on your cell phone's speed dial. But before you sink into despair, I have unbelievably good news: Two carne asada tacos are practically health food.

"Excellent," said Julian Montoya, the Burrito King, when I phoned him with the results. "We use very lean beef and cut out all the fat, so I'm not surprised."

Those two tacos total just 407 calories and also rank lowest in fat grams (16) and carbs (22).

And the shrimp with rice? Let me start with the positive spin: Those delectable slippery buggers add up to 64 grams of protein, the most in the test. But an order carries a walloping 2,519 calories, with 96 grams of fat and 347 carbs. Counterintuitive, huh? Tacos, good. Shrimp, bad.

When I called William Sung, the genial host of Yang Chow, I withheld the details for a moment and asked which food item had the most calories. He guessed the pizza or the burger.

"And how many calories do you think are in the slippery shrimp?" I asked.

"Five hundred," he said. "I'm guessing. Five hundred, a thousand." Keep guessing, William.

When I told him, I think he fell over backward, possibly into a plate of slippery shrimp.

"What the heck is in that stuff?" I asked.

"Garlic, ginger, vegetable oil, sugar, vinegar."

And it's fried, right?

"Yes. We fry it," William said, as if he was confessing to a murder.

In William's defense, Diana the nutritionist was onto something when she mentioned portions. I didn't give readers the weight of each food item, but the lab listed the slippery shrimp and rice at 1,026 grams, or more than twice the weight of the burger and fries, which tipped the scales in second place at 405 grams. Even if you cut the shrimp portion in half, though, it would still have more calories than the burger. I guess this means I'll have to take several people along next time I get a craving for slippery shrimp.

Here's another surprise from the lab: If you took equal 100-gram portions of each item, which do you think would have the most calories? Paging Wolfgang Puck.

The pizza at your gourmet express (280 calories for roughly one-fourth of a small pizza) beat out the 100-gram portions from In-N-Out (260 calories), the Pink's bacon chili cheese dog (247) and the shrimp (246). If anyone's looking for one more excuse to go Mexican, a 100-gram portion of the carne asada tacos had the most protein (19 grams) and the least fat, carbs and calories. Of course, I didn't order the refried beans.

"Oh, nice," said Burrito King's Montoya. "Thank you very much for calling."

Although there was no winner, I do want to announce two awards. The first, for cheeriest contestant, goes to a reader named Claudia.

"I'm not going to participate in your little contest," she wrote. "I would like to put in my two cents worth, as a physician and nutrition expert. None, I repeat NONE of these lunches comes even close to being healthy. Why would any person even risk eating at any of these horrid places....No wonder everywhere I look I see fat people!" Are you available for parties, Claudia?

And the award for most ambitious contestant goes to Annie Lin. Lin did the most extensive investigation, consulting 11 websites for nutritional information.

"You'll find attached a spreadsheet detailing how our calculations were made," said Annie. So how'd she do? Got all eight answers wrong. Your consolation prize, Annie, is a free lunch. Get back to me right away.

(Quiz answers: 1. Most calories and fewest: shrimp, 2,519, and tacos, 407. 2. Most fat and least, in grams: shrimp, 96.85, and tacos, 16.48. 3. Most protein and least, in grams: shrimp, 64.13, and hot dog, 29.3. 4. Most carbs and fewest, in grams: shrimp, 347.81, and tacos, 22.79.)

Three Million Dollars Doesn't Buy What It Used to

(November 7, 2007)

Sabrina Gordon-Gilardian grew up in the San Fernando Valley with her heart set on living in one place, and one place only. (Two clues: Swimming pools. Movie stars.) In February, it finally happened.

"I spent three million dollars to live in Beverly Hills 90210. To be the crème de la crème of society. I am supposed to be at the pinnacle here," she wrote to me.

But little did she know that paradise could be hell.

In April, wildfires came too close for comfort. In July, she read about the burglary ring hitting the homes of the rich and famous in Beverly Hills and surroundings. But the toughest blow of all came last month, when coyotes ate her miniature beagle, Lucy.

"I am miserable living here and did not get what I bargained for," Gordon-Gilardian wrote, asking if I could help.

I drove as fast as the law allows to the Gordon-Gilardian home between Coldwater and Benedict Canyons, just under Mulholland Drive. Gordon-Gilardian led me out back, where a nanny watched her two young boys, one of whom drives a miniature battery-operated Cadillac Escalade.

Gordon-Gilardian, 31, pointed up a steep embankment to the place where the vicious predators came through. She and her husband were just back from a weekend at the Morongo Casino, heard a yelp and made the horrifying discovery.

"That was my angel dog," she said, telling me the pocket-size beagle cost $2,000 at Pet Love in the Beverly Center five years ago. For $2,000, you'd think you could get a full-size beagle. Not only did they lose their dog, but now they've had to drop $5,000 more on an electric fence to keep the coyotes from making off with the kids.

I quickly assessed the situation and observed that Gordon-Gilardian's property line abuts a wilderness canyon where, it can be assumed, some wild animals might be living. Did that possibility ever cross her mind? Sure, she said. She'd have no problem seeing the occasional deer.

"But we didn't know coyotes lived here."

While we were talking, Sabrina got a cell phone call from her husband, who trades with China in the import-export business. She told him I was on the case and she hoped some good would come of it. When she called the city of Beverly Hills for help, she claims to have gotten the run-around and was told animal control officers might or might not come. When Sabrina asked the fire department about clearing the brush next to her property, she reportedly was told it was her concern.

"That's city property," she said, suggesting the city should be clearing the brush and trapping and removing coyotes. I told her as diplomatically as possible that in my experience, cities don't tend to have teams of animal trappers on the payroll. They tend to see coyotes as part of the deal.

"Not in Beverly Hills," she said. "I didn't move to Pacoima. I was told by the realtor at Sotheby's that this was going to be my dream life." Fair criticism. I've certainly never met a real estate agent who says, "It's got Italian granite, a luxurious swimming pool and wild predators."

There will be some readers, I warned Gordon-Gilardian, who might say that we humans have invaded the coyotes' habitat rather than the reverse.

"I thought about that," she said. "But that doesn't give them the right to viciously maul my dog and pull her organs out. I paid three million dollars for this. I paid three million dollars." Yeah, but three million dollars ain't what it used to be.

Britney lives up there, Gordon-Gilardian said, pointing. And Paris up there.

Talk about wildlife.

"Everybody lives in Beverly Hills." And her closer neighbors include Gary Collins and Alana Stewart.

Alana Stewart?

"Rod Stewart's ex," Sabrina replied. "She had a talk show." I'm so out of it.

"Now they're robbing Sherry Lansing and all the celebrities who live in the hills of Beverly Hills," she said. "And I hear that a gardener said there's a mountain lion out here. If there's a mountain lion here, why isn't the city trying to catch it? I should have bought something in the flats, on the other side of Neiman Marcus."

I suggested Gordon-Gilardian consider hiring a game tracker to patrol her perimeter. Angelenos hire people for practically everything else, so why not that?

Before leaving, I promised to call Beverly Hills mayor Jimmy Delshad, give him her name and address, and see if he could be of any assistance. Delshad got back to me quickly and said he was sorry to hear about Lucy the beagle, but he had even worse news for Gordon-Gilardian. I called to break it to her.

"You don't live in Beverly Hills," I said. There was a brief moment of silence on the other end.

But the zip is 90210, Gordon-Gilardian said. And on her mail "the city is Beverly Hills." But as Mayor Delshad explained, lots of people get their mail delivered by the Beverly Hills Post Office but don't live in the city limits.

"You live in Los Angeles," I told Sabrina Gordon-Gilardian. I figured that was enough of a blow, so I didn't tell her there's only one wild animal control officer for the entire city of Los Angeles and he's so swamped with calls, he seldom leaves the office.

But I told Sabrina she could solve a lot of problems by selling the house and moving into Beverly Hills proper. Far as I know, there have been no coyote sightings anywhere near the Neiman Marcus.

Gay Pair Sing New Tune
on Marriage

(June 18, 2008)

On occasion and for no particular reason, I break into song. But my crooning has been considerably less enjoyable for me and my family since we met Jamie Offenbach, a Juilliard-trained opera singer who often marches into our house in mid-performance. Just the other night, Jamie and my wife and daughter were singing "The Sun'll Come Out Tomorrow" with full-blown Broadway bravado, drowning out my feeble attempts to do backup. I can't do Ricky Ricardo, let alone Ethel Merman.

Jamie and his partner, Stuart Zwagil, an executive for an entertainment and documentary production company, have been our pals since my wife, Alison, and I bought our Silver Lake house from them seven years ago.

I'm bringing up the boys, as Alison calls them, because of California's gay and lesbian marriage revolution. Before the state Supreme Court ruling cleared the way, Jamie and Stuart maintained they had no desire to get married. They'd been together happily for 24 years, they said, and didn't need anyone's validation.

I took them at their word, so imagine my surprise when, during a cookout at our house, they announced plans to get hitched sometime this summer. What changed their minds?

Actually, nothing changed. As Stuart described it, their earlier nonchalance about marriage grew out of not wanting to get their hopes up about something that wasn't possible. So until the Supreme Court justices began throwing rice last month, they didn't talk much about tying the knot. But that didn't stop them from thinking about it.

Jamie said that at dozens of weddings for straight friends over the years, he was painfully envious. "That'll never be me," he thought each time, feeling like a second-class citizen. Stuart, meanwhile, said he always wanted to be married because he so admired his parents' deep, loving commitment.

"Oh my God," Stuart told a friend 24 years ago when he first spotted Jamie in Baltimore. "He is the most beautiful man I've ever seen."

Jamie, meanwhile, nervously told a co-worker: "I just bumped into a guy I know I will be with for the rest of my life." And what'd the co-worker say?

"She said, 'That's what you said two weeks ago,'" upon seeing another hunk.

But three weeks later, Jamie and Stuart moved in together and they've never parted. They say love at first sight, and monogamy, may have saved their lives, because AIDS was just beginning to claim many of their friends. Over the years they avoided places in the country where knuckle-draggers are the dominant class, they embraced the freedom of Los Angeles, and they celebrated the gay movement's small steps forward as nothing less than civil rights victories. And now they can finally stop living in sin.

It's a sweet story, no doubt about it. But there's enough vinegar in the mix to keep it interesting. As any couple knows—gay or straight—nobody gets through a day without a grievance or two. One reason my wife and I are such pals with Jamie and Stuart is because we're very much alike. Loving, yes, but not afraid to speak our minds.

In the case of Jamie and Stuart, there's a Felix and Oscar thing going on. Jamie has spasms over a crumb on the counter. Stuart doesn't like that Jamie is keeping count. (Separate toothpaste tubes are essential to keeping the whole thing from unraveling.) The other day Stuart was rushing out to an important meeting and left a wooden spoon in the sink after eating a cup of yogurt. Jamie saw the spoon, feared damage to the wood finish, and e-mailed the offending party.

"Are you purposely trying to drive me crazy?"

Stuart quickly shot back: "Yes. I am trying to slowly drive you crazy."

Then there are the scuff marks on the floor. "He wears his little boots, little go-go cowboy boots," Jamie snarked. "He's in front of the mirror for 15 minutes doing his hair. Then he comes back out to read his e-mail. Then back to do his hair for 15 minutes. By the time he leaves there's a trail of black marks. Either take the boots off or clean the marks. I am not his mother."

My advice? Jamie has to let go of the wooden spoons. Stuart, who's in his 40s after all, has to give up the cowboy boots. Little compromises like these, while difficult, are much less painful than the fees charged by divorce attorneys. But I'm not sure how they'll resolve the problem of Stuart getting home late from work and then, rather than "focus on us," as Jamie puts it, keeps checking office e-mail on his Blackberry, which Jamie calls his Crackberry. I have a feeling, though, that the boys—who've been together twice as long as my wife and I—are going to make it just fine as Mr. and Mr.

After a few playful barbs, they were dancing in the foyer of their Hollywood Hills home where I visited them Monday night (Stuart had the boots off). Pouring on the schmaltz, they were singing the tune they jokingly called their wedding song:

> Always and forever
> Each moment with you
> Is just like a dream to me
> That somehow came true.

L.A.'s Hitchhike Rating:
Two Thumbs Down

(August 24, 2008)

All I was trying to do was catch a lift at City Hall. I was an innocent man, hoping for one small act of human kindness in the cold, cruel city. And it almost got me arrested.

"That's illegal," a uniformed cop barked, trying to run me from the parking lot exit where I was thumbing for a ride.

What's illegal about it? I asked.

"You can't hitchhike here," he insisted. He had a real mouth on him for a City Hall General Services Department cop with a nice shiny badge but no gun. "It's illegal." What?

After decades of horrible land-use and transit planning by legions of public officials, someone should have been thanking me for trying to take one more car off the massively congested streets. Instead, Barney Fife was ready to have me locked up.

I'd been hoping to catch the eye of Jaime de la Vega, the creativity-challenged deputy mayor for transportation under Mayor Antonio Villaraigosa. Surely he'd have plenty of room for me in his big honking Hummer, and I could ask what he's done for us lately besides chug around town at 12 miles to the gallon. But there was no sign of de la Vega, and one driver after another left the City Hall garage without giving me more than a glance. Even Councilman Bill Rosendahl pulled out of the lot, shot me a quick look and hit the gas. I thought he was a better man than that. And then Officer

George Ebroyan came marching over to run me off, pulling out his little black book to show me hitchhiking is illegal. There it is, he said. Section 21957 of the vehicle code.

"No person shall stand in a roadway for the purpose of soliciting a ride from the driver of any vehicle."

"I'm not in the roadway," I said. "I'm on the sidewalk" Ebroyan insisted it was still illegal.

"You're just trying to make us look bad," he said, and then he went to make a call. "I owe you an apology," he said when he came back, finally convinced I was a law-abiding citizen. I didn't want an apology. I wanted a ride.

Tami Abdollah was right. She's a tough young reporter at the *Los Angeles Times* who was worked into a lather one day because she couldn't get a ride to the office. She'd dropped her car off for repairs and tried to hitchhike to work, but one driver after another blew right past her.

What is it with L.A.? Tami asked. She's hitchhiked all over the world, no problem. Lots of cities even encourage hitchers to use established pickup stations.

But in the city of a million single-occupant cars, many of them big enough to cart soccer teams, poor Tami kept striking out.

Three or four decades ago, a lot of us thought nothing of thumbing it. Sure, it can be dangerous to pick up a hitchhiker, and maybe even more dangerous to be picked up. I'm not suggesting that everyone take a risk and begin thumbing it to work tomorrow, but how could things have changed so much?

The day after I struck out downtown, I went to 26th and Colorado in Santa Monica and tried again. Why there? Because that's the epicenter of one of the worst urban planning disasters in all of Southern California. The Water Garden complex and other humongous offices provide thousands of jobs, but public officials utterly failed to make sure there was enough additional transit to avoid the crippling gridlock. So did that mean that commuters would take pity on an old graybeard who was trying to buck the trend? Nope. One lone driver after another cruised under the palms and right past me and my weary thumb. BMW convertibles. Mercedes shimmering like black pearls. Escalades lumbering like painted tanks.

I got down on my knees, pleading. Nothing. Would I have to throw myself in front of a car?

My editor had one more bright idea. After striking out in West L.A., I went to an art supply store for some poster board and a marker, then stationed myself at the southbound entrance to the 405 on Ventura Boulevard with my sign: PICK ME UP—CARPOOL LANE MUCH FASTER. To help emphasize the point, I stood next to a sign that said Carpool Vanpool Info, Call (213) 380-RIDE.

What is hitchhiking, after all, but a form of carpooling? Why can't we have neighborhood pickup stations where, once a week, you leave the car at home and catch a ride with a neighbor? Given the flat terrain and great weather, why don't we have more bike paths like the great cities of the world, and why can't the long-abandoned Expo right-of-way be developed for cyclists?

Because any creative solution would take a little imagination and political leadership, and we're more likely to find large gold nuggets in the Los Angeles River than we are to have public officials who work together to solve our transit needs. In the latest act of cowardice and double-speak, some of the L.A. County supervisors are on the fence about a proposed half-cent sales tax increase to pay for billions in transit projects.

After 20 minutes of developing lung disease near the onramp, I was losing hope of catching a ride on Ventura Boulevard, and half expecting to be arrested for trying. Then a gray Honda Accord pulled over.

"Where you headed?" asked the driver. I had to think fast.

"Santa Monica," I said.

The middle-aged driver smiled. He was headed there to pick up his daughter. So I climbed in and we were on our way.

I know what you're thinking. What kind of irresponsible person picks up a hitchhiker? Richard Sarradet was his name. And his profession? Come on, what city do we live in? Sarradet played attorney Howard Lansing on *General Hospital* and was in *Knots Landing, Quincy, Simon & Simon, The Bionic Wom*an and *The Waltons*, to name a few. Now 62, he's a special education teacher and heads the drama and history departments at Westview School in West Los Angeles. So why did he pick me up?

"I guess because you just, you looked OK," Sarradet said, "and I didn't think you were a risk."

Sarradet said he grew up hitchhiking and still occasionally picks up hitchhikers, though he wouldn't have taken a chance if his daughter were in the car. Not everyone can afford a car and insurance, he reasoned, and there isn't enough public transportation, so every once in a while he'll pull over and take a chance. One rider, a woman, turned out to be a hooker, so he dropped her off. Several times, he had to explain to male riders that he was not interested in a business transaction. And now he'd really hit rock bottom, picking up a guy cruising for a column.

"It's interesting to see who you run into," he said, "and you catch a flavor of somebody else's life." Exactly.

We had a nice conversation on our drive, and I may even get another column out of it. Sarradet told me about his exhausting fight against state bureaucracy to become credentialed for a job he's been doing for years. When his cell phone rang, Sarradet told the caller he'd picked up a hitchhiker who claimed to be not an ax murderer, but a columnist. The caller wondered if that was safe.

"I'm lookin' for the ax in his back pocket," Sarradet replied.

Caught Between Heaven and Hull

(September 10, 2008)

Before I try to sell you the opportunity of a lifetime, some truth in advertising: They say the two happiest days in the life of a boat owner are the day he buys the boat and the day he sells it. You be the judge.

Six years ago, three partners and I set out from the Alamitos Marina in Long Beach on a 22-foot sailboat we had bought for $800, or $200 apiece. It was no yacht, in other words. And we didn't even make it to the breakwater before oil began gushing down the shaft and the motor froze. Rather than do the sensible thing, which would have been to sink the boat and swim to shore, we got towed back to port and bought a new motor that cost exactly twice what we had just paid for the boat. Smart boys, no?

A year later, having learned not a whit, the same four musketeers decided to upgrade to a boat named *Interlude*, which cost us $1,100 apiece. We were departing Alamitos on yet another maiden voyage when I observed, with great pride, that the motor was pleasingly quiet. With good reason. It had shut off, and we were soon drifting uncontrollably toward a bona fide yacht. One of my mates practically lost a leg fending us off, and now we were floating backward toward the concrete wall at Joe's Crab Shack, providing great entertainment for Sunday diners. With no time to spare, we got the motor started and averted disaster.

Why risk such embarrassment with every voyage, and why stay in the game when a replacement part the size of a safety pin costs the same as air-fare to Hawaii?

Because I have a thing for salt air and open sea. The love affair began when I was a boy in the San Francisco Bay Area, and summer vacations were in Santa Cruz and Monterey. I knew I wanted to live close to the water someday, and my favorite thing about greater Los Angeles is that someone had the good sense to put it between mountain and sea.

We've sailed Santa Monica Bay, floated down to Redondo Beach for lunch, and crossed the channel to the quiet side of Catalina, where the water is turquoise and the land virtually unspoiled. We've seen schools of dolphins along the way, and always envied the folks who live the quiet life in the tiny beach town of Two Harbors.

It's also fascinating to watch the world's economy at work off the coast. Oil tankers cruise past us with high-priced crude, and container ships steam in from Asia packed with answers to the U.S. demand for cheap goods. One of these years, I'm going to visit a toy factory in China and follow the ship-ment across the sea and onto the trucks at the port, writing about all the lives along the route.

One of my mates on *Interlude* loves the marine life so much he bought a second boat all his own from a former reporter. Its name is *Newsboy*. But slip fees have been spiking in Marina del Rey, which used to be more of a playground for the middle-class in the days of aerospace and manufactur-ing. Now it's being rebuilt for the gleaming yachts of the super-wealthy. To save money, we decided to sell *Interlude* and all go in together on *Newsboy*.

First we offered the old boat cheap to friends, urging them to grab it before the rush. No takers. Then we tried Craigslist, listing the boat at $2,500, and noting that it was more than a boat—it was waterfront real estate. *Interlude* sleeps four, some of them comfortably. And how else can a person get waterfront property—a flotel, if you will—for a monthly slip fee of $345?

A dozen people answered the ad, and we even scheduled an "open boat" to show it to prospective buyers. But nobody came. So we decided, with heavy hearts, to give the boat away. And struck out again.

Has anyone around here looked at a map lately? That blue stuff is an ocean, and yet we couldn't give away a perfectly good boat. Sure, it needed a little work, but nothing major. We tried the Sea Scouts, who used to gladly take donated vessels. But the slow economy has hit the boat world hard, and the scouts have more than they can use.

Finally a Wilmington salvager named Jack Shubin expressed interest. We thought we had him hooked, but then we talked again. A boat is a tough sell nowadays, he reminded us. He might be reduced to dismantling the keel and selling the ballast, and the price of lead was falling. But sure, he'd come see *Interlude*, although it was going to cost him a small fortune just to gas up his truck.

When he arrived, Shubin looked us over real good, sizing us up. He had grease under his fingernails, a face of red leather and a dust bowl voice. Crooks, women and the economy had done him in, he said, spinning his tales of junkyard philosophy. He knew he had us. He might be persuaded to take the boat, he announced, if the price was right. But we had a different view of who should pay whom.

Great negotiators that we are, we got him down to $100, forked it over, and said goodbye to *Interlude*. But I couldn't quite let go, and so I headed out to see Shubin one day last week. I drove down past the Valero refinery, a trash collection center and an auto demo yard. His lady came out of a double-wide trailer. A welder played ranchero music. Boat and vehicle parts were strewn from here to west Texas.

In the middle of the yard, *Interlude* was held aloft, dangling from a hoist like a lost orphan at a Rust Belt boat show. No takers yet.

"I just wanted to see our boat again," I told him.

"I thought it was my boat now," he said.

Indeed it is, and so last weekend we headed for Two Harbors in *Newsboy*. The hull was gouged by a mooring buoy, the dinghy sprung a leak and took on water with us aboard, and we nearly got decapitated when the motor surged and sent us speeding toward the blades of a raised propeller.

Ah, the sailing life.

A Bleacher of Girthly Delights

(June 3, 2009)

On Monday night, I went to the Ravine to see if the recession was driving more fans into the right-field bleachers, where a ticket comes with a promise: All you can eat, no questions asked. Think about it. You can fast all day, pig out at the ballgame and not have to eat the next day.

On Monday, the Dodgers were playing the Arizona Diamondbacks, who aren't exactly a big draw. But even on a slow night, roughly 850 diehards feasted on baseball and enough hot dogs, nachos, peanuts, popcorn and soda to feed the California National Guard.

Purchased in advance, a ticket to the All-You-Can-Eat Pavilion costs $25. If you were to buy an advance ticket to the left-field bleachers, you'd pay $11, but one hot dog, peanuts and a soft drink would have you up around $25. So the smart shopper heads for right field. Dodger spokesman Josh Rawitch said that although total Dodger attendance is up one percent this year, it's up six percent in the All-You-Can-Eat Pavilion.

"We were just talking about this, and I think the recession might have something to do with it," said Eddie Vidana, usher captain, who has seen more sell-outs this year in right field.

As the game was getting under way Monday, I spotted Robert Ruiz, Juan Avalos and Steve Martinez, who all work at the Porterville Developmental Center north of Bakersfield. They were eating like they'd been sentenced to death and were going for broke on their last meal. Ruiz had polished off two hot dogs, nachos, a bag of popcorn, a soda and a water by the first inning. Avalos was keeping pace with two hot dogs, two nachos and a soda. Martinez was on his third hot dog and had a tray with four sodas on it, all for himself. L.A. is more than three hours from Porterville, the buddies said, but the endless supply of food makes the long trip worthwhile, even with a $15 parking fee.

"The last time we came, he called in sick the next day," Ruiz said of Avalos, but they couldn't agree on whether it was four hot dogs or six that did the damage.

On the field, meanwhile, Dodger slugger Andre Ethier wound up and tossed a souvenir warmup ball into the bleachers between innings. It floated up like a big scoop of ice cream and landed in the grateful hands of Avalos.

"All you can eat, and a baseball too!" he exclaimed.

To be honest, though, these guys were pikers. Several rows down, Daniel Tzec, a Pomona housekeeper, had eaten six hot dogs and one order of nachos by the second inning. He also had quaffed three beers, which cost extra, unlike sodas or water. Tzec looked like he was running out of gas, but he insisted otherwise.

"It's just a little rest," he said, and he may not have been kidding. Four more dogs, on very short leashes, were cradled next to him on a cardboard tray.

As I talked to Tzec, I began questioning my support for universal healthcare. Do I really want to take on the burden of medical care for someone who's inclined to eat six hot dogs in two innings? According to the Farmer John website, a Dodger Dog has 240 calories, 200 of them from fat, as well as more sodium than the Salton Sea. Do you get a souvenir defibrillator with your 10th dog?

One of the ushers told me she'd seen people eat themselves sick in right field, and when the ballgames are over, fans have been known to smuggle more peanuts and hot dogs past security and out of the stadium. There's no way to prevent it, one guard said, so they don't even try.

Despite my rush to judgment, I must say there's something exhilarating about the idea of living without self-control or the desire to develop any. When I saw Paul Galle lift his girth off the bleachers and head under the stands for refills, I noticed that he was smiling like a thief, as if he couldn't believe the Dodgers and Levy Restaurants, the stadium concessionaire, were foolish enough to let him plow through their buffet of saturated fat to his heart's content. He said he was still hungry after two nachos, one popcorn, two bags of peanuts and eight hot dogs.

Eight hot dogs?

"Actually that's four double dogs," said Galle, who's in his 30s. And what exactly is a double dog?

Galle, a schoolteacher from Chino Hills, explained that he gets the maximum allowable four hot dogs on each trip to the concession stand, then throws away two of the buns and stuffs the extra dogs into the remaining buns. With less bread, he's able to eat more meat. Galle has it down to a science at the condiment station, where he nimbly makes the dog transfer, tosses spare buns, and loads up with ketchup, mustard and relish.

"That's unfortunate," he said as one bun split under the weight of two dogs, and he substituted a backup bun. By the way, his ticket to this little orgy had cost him just $17.50 on eBay.

"I don't know if that's a recession-buster, but it's a great deal and an awesome value," said Galle, who said he weighs 320 pounds but tries not to think about it. "I wouldn't weigh myself for a week after coming to Dodger Stadium," he said. "I'm not a glutton." Yes, he admitted, he feasts on life, lives in the moment and offers no apologies.

"I'm very existentialist," he said. "I was a philosophy major."

Galle's father, the much slimmer Richard, told me Paul had recently shed 25 pounds to get in shape for an Alaskan cruise in July. They're going with two friends and decided they couldn't all fit into one cabin, so they reserved two. Richard said his son is a good-hearted guy, but he needs to do something about his insatiable appetite.

"All he can say is 'Oink,'" said the father.

"Thanks, Dad," said the philosopher, who ate 12 hot dogs (or six double dogs, I should say) before calling it quits by the seventh inning.

The Dodgers lost, by the way, 3-2. But out in right field, that was beside the point.

A Reaganite Rejects the Ranting

(September 20, 2009)

The Republican California political guru who crafted four success-ful Ronald Reagan campaigns, two for governor and two for president, does not watch Fox News or its conservative bobblehead pundits. Why not?

Fox News has an agenda, 82-year-old Stuart Spencer said over breakfast in Palm Desert, where he and his wife make their home. The same is true of MSNBC, he added. One goes right and the other goes left, and Spencer doesn't see why those interested in educating themselves on matters of national importance would turn to either for reliable information.

Glenn Beck? Spencer can't watch the maudlin Fox host, who blubbers over the destruction of the nation by a president he calls a racist.

Keith Olbermann of MSNBC? Spencer wants reason, not rants. He wants substance, not smirks. He has no interest in watching one side lob grenades at the other in nightly warfare that further divides the nation along cultural and political lines.

It annoys him that Fox can't admit that Sarah Palin was a cynical and preposterous choice as a VP candidate ("she just wasn't qualified"), and MSNBC can't admit that President Obama is too reliant on government cures or that he's tall on rhetoric and short on details. Spencer said the last time he appeared on *Hardball* with motormouth Chris Matthews, the host asked a question and then interrupted before Spencer uttered two sentences. So he's scratched that show, too.

Spencer, who estimates he ran 400 political campaigns in his career, said he reads the *L.A. Times* and the *Desert Sun*, and sometimes adds the *Wall Street Journal* or *New York Times* to the daily mix.

"If I watch TV news, it's usually CNN," Spencer said. "Not that they don't have their own agenda. Or I'll watch the Jim Lehrer show for something more solid."

I knew I could count on Spencer for a good dose of common sense, and that's why I drove out to see him. It's always been clear to me that while most Americans are somewhat reasonable, a good 10 to 15 percent of partisans at either end of the spectrum are out of their minds. But the wackos are wackier than ever.

First it was scary people on the left who insisted 9/11 was an inside job, and now the right is carrying that flag. Then we've got those who go on believing Obama is a Muslim or a communist when he's not busy being a racist. Such craziness might die quietly, except that there's around-the-clock punditry and Internet delirium to fuel the paranoia, and the daily national conversation is framed at the fringes. Instead of talking about healthcare, we talk about the congressman who interrupted Obama's speech on healthcare to call him a liar.

It's hard, Spencer said, to pinpoint exactly where we went off the rails. There have always been cultural and social changes in the nation, and over time the differences of various regions became more pronounced. House Speaker Newt Gingrich and cohorts exploited that when they tried to commandeer the policy agenda by acing out Democrats, Spencer said, and he thinks current House Speaker Nancy Pelosi is doing the same to Republicans.

I asked Spencer if part of the problem is the growing influence of money, which makes politicians more beholden to special interests and therefore more divided. Maybe, he said, but money was always a factor in politics. Today there's also a different kind of money in play: the fortunes that TV and radio broadcasts make by having gasbag commentators fan the flames day and night. It's more than a little interesting that Spencer has such contempt for the media megastars who often invoke the name of his former boss as their supreme being.

"When I had a place in Oregon, I'd drive 25 minutes and [Rush] Limbaugh would be on three different stations," Spencer said. "I couldn't get rid of the son of a bitch." Acquaintances would ask Spencer about Limbaugh's brilliant observations, and Spencer would politely say he never listened. His astonished pals, knowing how close he was to the Gipper, would demand to know why not.

"Because he's an ass," Spencer would say, only he added a second syllable.

Reagan was himself at times a divisive and hypocritical leader whose debacles, including the Iran-Contra scandal, have been obscured by years of myth-making. But he was civil to his political foes and built lasting relationships, political and social, with the Kennedys, among others. He worked closely with Senator Ted Kennedy on budget matters and international disarmament, and with Soviet leader Mikhail Gorbachev on the end of the Cold War. The tenor was different then, Spencer said, recalling that on Thursday nights, Reagan invited Democrat Tip O'Neill, the House speaker, to the White House for hours of storytelling and problem-solving.

It was a time when you sat down with your political counterparts and tried to find common ground. If the other guy got the best of you, you would look him in the eye and say, "OK, you win. But I'm going to get you next time."

In Sacramento, Spencer said, "you could fight all day and then go have a cocktail with the other side at night." His fix for California's intractable budget mess would begin with redrawing legislative districts.

"The first thing I used to tell a candidate was that he had to fit his district," Spencer said, but the districts are now drawn to be safely to the right or safely to the left, so moderates never get out of the blocks and Democrats and Republicans can't agree on the time of day.

Ordinarily, a plate of pancakes puts me in a good mood. But Spencer was in an even better mood than I was as we finished our breakfast.

"I'm Irish and I'm an optimist," he said.

In his lifetime, Spencer has seen inventions and advances he never could have imagined, and he still likes to think anything is possible. The TV and radio pundits he loathes are capitalizing in part on national dissatisfaction with political leadership, and that just might lead to better representation. Spencer's not ready to put money on it. But he's not giving up hope.

"It's all cyclical in politics," he remarked, and then he headed home.

With his TV and radio turned off, and no computer skills to speak of, Spencer has an easier time than the rest of us believing that better days are just down the road.

KEEP THEM IN YOUR PRAYERS

A Billboard Landmark
in a Cultural Wasteland

(June 21, 2002)

Careful readers might have noticed two stories this week that were unrelated but undoubtedly linked. One was about the demise of hell. It explained how Sunday preachers are watering down their warnings of pitchforks and lakes of fire, partly to avoid scaring parishioners away from the collection plate. The other story concerns a West Los Angeles billboard promoting a new CD from Death Row Records. It depicts a cartoon character on a toilet with his pants down, and under the commode is a tough-guy boast containing a four-letter word for poo. Obviously, hell was there for a reason.

The billboard is at Wilshire Boulevard and San Vicente, which puts it in City Councilman Jack Weiss' district. When I griped about it this week, Weiss said he shared my view, but wondered how we got so old so fast. Weren't we among those who defended controversial pop figures like Lenny Bruce and Jim Morrison, and giggled over a puritan obsession with obscenity? Yes, I said. But this is about pop culture in a death spiral, dragging all of us down with it. Weiss agreed again, but worried that if we make too much of the billboard, we might play into the hands of its creators. Maybe so. But what's the cost of doing nothing?

"You sound like Dan Quayle giving his Murphy Brown speech," Weiss said, referring to the former vice president's attack on an unmarried TV mom. Are standards really lower than ever? Weiss wondered. And who are the arbiters of obscenity and taste?

Until further notice, I am. I'm the guy, after all, who wrote about the promotion for the *Bernie Mac Show*, which Fox aired during the World Series. In that promo, you may recall, Mac was seated on the can.

There's actually something honest about this trend. Given what the pop culture factory cranks out, particularly in Hollywood, there's a goodly amount that makes me want to reach for a plunger.

Let's get a group shot the next time Hollywood lays an egg. Actors, writers, directors, producers, studio chiefs. Instead of the usual over-the-top billboard ad, let's put them all up there on a giant commode. And then why not do the same with the eight million billboards for TV news teams, whose hairdos alone violate several of my own obscenity standards? And why do we need 12 million billboards for strip joints with names like Spearmint Rhino? What in the world is with that name, anyway? Do they trot out naked pachyderms?

I'm convinced there are no standards in Southern California for visual clutter. Certainly not at Wilshire and San Vicente, where the first person I ran into on Tuesday was Patsy Garcia. She looked at the billboard and said: "I can't believe it's still up there. I work in an ad agency, and we all said the same thing. We didn't think you could use [that] word on a billboard."

Garcia took me up to the 10th-floor offices of D'Arcy, Masius, Benton & Bowles, where many of the windows offer a bird's-eye view of the pinhead on the toilet.

"It's the lowest common denominator principle," said Kevin Yarbrough, an ad manager who finds himself ever more vigilant as he tries to protect his two kids from the steady advance of the crass and profane.

Scott Anderholt, an account manager who takes his three daughters to the Agoura Bible Fellowship, has the worst deal of all. The billboard practically fills his office window, making it seem as if he's in the bathroom with this joker. He gets to work in the morning, and that guy's on the can. He comes back from lunch, and the guy's still on the can. It's the longest bathroom visit since Elvis died on the throne.

And looking beyond the billboard offers no relief to the churchgoing Anderholt. Rising over the top of it is the House of Hustler, with "Flynt Publications" emblazoned across the building in Satan's own script.

"I ignore it as much as possible," Anderholt said. "And the good thing is that I'm facing west, so when the sun starts to set, I close the blinds and can't see any of it." He looked out the window again.

"The TV culture is now on billboards," Anderholt lamented, adding that his 15-year-old daughter is rebelling against her parents with all her might, and wants to see R-rated films, as her friends do. Good luck, Dad.

I put in a call to Death Row Records, by the way, which had no comment. Instead, they referred me to a publicist who had no comment. It seems to me someone in the operation is expendable. Meanwhile, neighbors circulated a petition calling for the billboard to come down. Councilman Weiss was investigating whether the thing violates decency standards, and whether Death Row even had permission to put it up.

Readers of my World Series column wrote to tell me *Bernie Mac* really was a pretty good show, for which I'd like to congratulate everyone involved. Others wrote to tell me what a schoolmarm I was, while still others called me a dope for having been shocked to discover that pop culture is circling the drain.

Allow me to clarify. I wasn't shocked by the TV promo, and I'm not shocked by the billboard. If this stuff were shocking, it might actually have some social value.

The crime is that it's obvious, unoriginal, crass, crude and vapid, and it can have no impact other than to diminish civility and lower the national IQ.

Eternal damnation got a bad rap if you ask me. Is it too late to bring back hell?

The Posse Is Headed
in the Wrong Direction

(April 1, 2005)

Except for the fact that the posse is headed in the wrong direction, you can't really blame the cowboys riding to the border near Tombstone, Arizona to git them durned e-leegles. Los Angeles will have subways to the beach before the United States gets its goofy immigration policy straightened out, so I can understand the frustration of the group that calls itself the Minuteman Project.

The ringleaders, who include a retired Orange County accountant, were expecting several hundred volunteers—some of them armed—to saddle up and seal the Arizona-Mexico border today. If you happen to be in the area, give wide berth to anyone who looks like a cast member from *F-Troop*, and do not wear a straw hat or carry a jug of water, because you could be shot dead.

I don't know if the Minutemen gave it any thought, but I'd have asked Pat Buchanan to get everyone's adrenaline pumping by firing a few rounds into the air and yelling, "Lock and load!"

My call to the Minutemen, who were using the Arizona office of the *Tombstone Tumbleweed* on Toughnut Street (I swear it's all true), was not returned. But the Minuteman website had a nifty slogan at the top of the screen: "Americans doing the job Congress won't do." Right on target. So why not saddle up and ride to D.C.?

"This represents a general tendency to demonize the immigrant," said Harry Pachon of the Tomas Rivera Policy Institute. He spoke to me during a break at a downtown Los Angeles conference on immigration. As I've said before, it's fair to ask hard questions about the impact of illegal immigration. Can we afford to pick up the healthcare tab? Can we afford to educate every child who crosses the border? Last year, a Fullerton printer asked me how she could keep paying living wages and health benefits to her employees when competitors were hiring illegals at minimum wage and no benefits.

Fair questions, all. But how can anyone blame immigrants for leaving corrupt and economically inept countries to come here? They wouldn't risk their lives, hungry for work, if we weren't hungry to hire them with a wink and a nod, if not give them driver's licenses.

Look, I don't want to break up the party now that those amateur cowboys are on the job, guarding a border that will always be impossible to seal unless we stand agents shoulder to shoulder along its 2,000-mile length. But as I said, the posse went the wrong way.

It should ride to Wal-Mart, which hired illegal immigrants to clean the floors.

It should ride to the poultry farms that have hired illegals to cut costs and boost profits. It should ride to Wells Fargo and other banks that are happy to cash in on the fat business of opening accounts for illegals. It should ride to the farms where U.S. ranchers get taxpayer subsidies that help drive Mexican farmers out of business and north across the border. And it should ride to Washington, D.C., where Congress sees a few thousand dead border crossers as a small price to pay for an endless supply of dirt-cheap labor.

A compromise immigration bill won't be easy to work out, but it's long past due. It would offer some form of legalization, safe passage that puts an end to smuggling, and a crackdown on employers and immigrants who don't play by the rules.

One last thought: While the Minutemen ride to the border, Harry Pachon asked, are their children being watched by nannies without papers?

The Cardinal Is
First-Class Pope Material

(April 6, 2005)

I wasn't going to say anything until a reader noticed the same thing I did in a story about Los Angeles Cardinal Roger Mahony. His Eminence, flying to Rome in the Pope's final hours, was stretched out rather comfortably in first class.

"I know that it's a little early to be nitpicking about these things," said a reader named Carol. "I thought at some point...you might want to do a column about this, because I think it's just shameful."

In the photograph Carol is referring to, Mahony was sitting with his flack, Tod Tamberg. The cardinal, with his eyes closed and rosary beads in his hands, has his comfy seat tilted so far back that he appears to be crushing the woman in the row behind him. This may be a bit presumptuous of me, but I think it's only fair to ask the obvious question: Where would Jesus sit?

You don't have to have spent your formative years in Catholic school, as I did, to know that—if he hadn't walked across the Atlantic—Jesus would have flown coach.

Generally speaking, it's always better for a man of the cloth to sit with his flock than with his flack.

On the other hand, now that the church is in transition with the death of Pope John Paul II, maybe it's high time for a pope who sees himself as a first-class kind of a guy. Mahony is one of 117 cardinals from around the world who, in choosing a successor, will chart a new course for an institution often criticized for being out of touch with its own followers.

Mahony may be reluctant to suggest it himself, but what the church really needs is the man Pope John Paul II referred to as "Hollywood," and I'm more than happy to sing his praises if it boosts his chances of moving to the Vatican. That's right, I'm backing Cardinal Mahony as the next pope.

Let me explain. Even though I often disagreed with Pope John Paul II, I respected him for having been unapologetically steadfast in his conservative views on abortion, homosexuality, birth control and divorce. The man believed what he believed, and he stuck to his principles rather than bend with the political breezes.

But church attendance is down, the number of priests is dwindling, Catholic schools are closing, anti-gay teachings have brought cries of hypocrisy, and millions of people died of AIDS and starvation while the pope preached against condoms.

Besides that, you can't get an annulment unless you're Frank Sinatra or former Los Angeles mayor Dick Riordan.

The church needs to realize it's in trouble. Big trouble. I heard on the radio that Ireland, a longtime priest factory, now has to import padres because the home-grown variety is drying up. What the church needs, more than ever, is a politically progressive, media-smart leader who can aggressively market the institution even as he keeps a tight lid on its darkest secrets. Mahony was born for this job.

As for the progressive part, Mahony has been more open-minded than many high-ranking church officials on the subject of homosexuality and on marriage for priests. On the way to Rome, he spoke of a push for a less centralized church. I e-mailed Mahony flack Tamberg, by the way, to ask about flying first-class, Mahony's reform ideas and his chances of becoming pope, but I got no response. He may have been busy lining up votes for His Eminence.

As for marketing genius, Mahony has no peer. He single-handedly brought the Rog Mahal into being, raising a whopping $200 million that might otherwise have gone to schools and social services for the poor. Mahony sold crypts under the altar at the Cathedral of Our Lady of the Angels for up to $50,000 apiece, hawked paving stones for $5,000, peddled wine under the cathedral's name—and accomplished all of this while managing one of the biggest church scandals in modern history. The most amazing thing about the scandal, in fact, is that Mahony continues to pass himself off as a national sex abuse reformer, even as he zealously stonewalls investigators trying to get to the bottom of cases involving priests accused of molesting young boys.

Alleged victims have pleaded and prosecutors have screamed for the cardinal to open up his files on accused priests. So have attorneys handling the 544 civil claims pending against the archdiocese. Mahony shuts out their cries, and yet he endures, head high.

He's Teflon. He's Hollywood. He's first-class. Could we call ourselves good Christians if we didn't share him with the world?

A Corner Where L.A.
Hits Rock Bottom

(October 17, 2005)

A few hours after a homeless guy named Virgil died of an overdose in the portable toilet, the blue plastic outhouse at 6th and San Julian Streets was back in business. Not as a toilet, but as a house of prostitution. Five portable toilets stand at that corner in the darkened heart of skid row. T.J. says she sometimes has a customer in each of them—a john in every john—and scurries from one to the next, taking care of business.

"I run this corner," says the stocky 52-year-old woman, whose initials stand for Thick and Juicy. "I'm the madam, and those are the cathouses."

T.J., who keeps her wardrobe in one of the outhouses and changes every few hours, is wearing a sheer red top, nothing underneath, and skin-tight black pants. She's bummed a Newport and has it to her lips, but can't find a light. As she speaks, a rat skitters up from the sewer and through a grate, past a discarded brassiere, a smooshed apple and an empty bag of Fritos. Rats run into, under and around the portable toilets with a brazen sense of entitlement, as comfortable as house pets.

Sights like this are common on L.A.'s skid row, a rock-bottom depository and national embarrassment. A place where disease, abuse, crime and hard-luck misery are on public display and have been for years, conveniently out of sight and mind for most Angelenos. No matter how many times I go in, I come out shocked all over again.

A couple walk past the 6th and San Julian toilets now, pulling shirts up over their noses to block the stench. At times, the toilets are actually used for their intended purpose, and the unspeakable odor that envelops the corner is toxic enough to buckle your legs. This is not the only place on skid row where business thrives in Porta-Potties. Prostitution, drug dealing and drug abuse are common in toilets across the eastern flank of downtown. The outhouses were put here to keep people from defecating on the street. Instead they provide a hiding place for crime, and urine still runs in the gutters.

"I've seen one prostitute and three guys in a Porta-Potty," says Los Angeles Police Department captain Andy Smith. "That's a record. Four people. I don't even want to think about what was going on in there."

The usual, no doubt. A cheap trick, a quick hit. The prostitutes aren't generally working for food or shelter, both of which are available, says Smith. They're working for drugs, and skid row is the bottom of the barrel for prostitutes—a cursed landscape that makes the darkest corners of Hollywood look glamorous by comparison.

"They're getting from five to ten dollars for oral sex," Smith says. "They'll brag that they're getting more, but when one of our undercover officers goes in, it's always five or ten."

Five dollars buys a crack rock, and if you doubt the power of that drug, you only have to look at what the prostitutes will do to get it. Anyone who passes the Porta-Potties at 6th and San Julian knows what's going on. It doesn't take a detective. On a balmy night, I watch from a distance at first, moving in closer when a distress call emits from one of the stalls.

Now a thin young woman in a slinky dress is trying to wrestle someone out of the portable toilet. The woman turns to me and a photographer and pleads for us to go get help. A passerby peeks into the toilet and says the woman in distress appears to have overdone it with crack. "It makes you hyperventilate like that," he says.

The person in trouble, it turns out, is T.J., who later swears to me she wasn't high; she was having a nervous breakdown. The slender young woman trying to yank her out of the portable toilet by her arm is her friend T.T. It stands for Tall and Tiny. When the door opens, T.J. is wearing nothing but black underclothes. She's sitting on the lap of a man perched on the toilet, and the man's arms are wrapped around her in a bear hug. He's apparently trying to calm her down.

"She needs help!" T.T. orders, her torn corduroy dress slipping down to where it barely covers her. I dial 911, but when paramedics arrive, T.J. has cooled off and moved into the toilet where she keeps her wardrobe. She tells them she's OK, and the paramedics leave, counting themselves lucky they didn't have to venture into an outhouse crawling with rats.

"T.J. lost her brother a while back, and her friend died here today," says T.T., who walks with a horrible limp, swinging sharp elbows to throw her emaciated body left and right. She claims she destroyed her hip playing basketball, an injury that ended her dream of a scholarship, and there wasn't much to fall back on in her broken family. She came west from New York, quickly hit the skids, and landed on this corner four or five years ago.

"Death is part of it," T.T. says of the scene out here, which she describes as *"Escape from New York* without Kurt Russell." She's 24 but looks younger, with hair dyed the color of Sunny Delight and teeth white as powdered cocaine. With no warning, she suddenly loses the street-tough pose, and her body slacks as she cries big wet tears for the nine-year-old daughter she never sees.

"I never even had an ID," she says, ashamed of herself. It's as if she doesn't exist. T.J., whom she calls Mama, seems to be the closest thing she's got to family here. "She don't want me to die like this," T.T. says.

We cross the street to get away from the distraction of steady business. T.T. stops and leans against a wall outside the Midnight Mission. She sees a family approaching. "Kids!" T.T. yells for all to hear, down the street and around the corner.

That's so anyone smoking crack or shooting up will take cover, says T.T.'s friend Molly. You've got to watch out for the kids, so they don't see too much out here.

When T.T. walks away, Molly talks about the working girls on skid row who are known as strawberries. What's that? I ask. That's what they call girls who turn tricks for the price of a rock, Molly says. Some of the girls don't just do business in those toilets, she says. They live in them. Molly tells me she doesn't need to be here because she lives "in a castle" in Monrovia. Then why is she here? Because everything you need is here, she says. "I'm a heroin addict."

Before midnight, T.J. emerges from her outhouse wearing the see-through top and a snappy black brim. She's flashing seven rings, a bracelet and a necklace.

Not a good day, she says. Virgil, the guy who OD'd earlier, was a good friend. Some of the men are just lonely, she says, and she takes them into the toilets to cheer them up, listen to their stories or share a smoke.

"I'm not a prostitute," she claims, playing coy. "I give God's word in there 99.9 percent of the time. Of course, there are those occasions…" And on those occasions, her portable toilet serves as "the head office" of her bustling enterprise, T.J. tells me. T.T. is second in command, she adds, because "she thinks like me."

What do you do if the johns get rough? I ask. She yells out "Daddy," T.J. says, and a big bouncer comes hauling up San Julian Street, where, generally speaking, heroin addicts encamp on one side of the street and crack addicts on the other. T.J. also has gangbangers watching her back, she claims. Not that she needs cover. Some call her Little Miss Tyson, she boasts. It all began five years ago, by her accounting. She drove out from Ohio with a beau who got drunk, the rotten snake, and dumped her on skid row, never to be seen again. T.J. did what she had to. She's a survivor, a pro. She runs this corner.

T.J.'s chief associate is now limping into the street and calling out to a regular as he walks by. "Hey, baby," T.T. sings, trying to lure him into her lair.

At least two of the toilets are in action, with someone bumping the inside walls of the one next to T.J.'s. A middle-aged gent is taking a young woman by the hand now and leading her into another toilet.

"That's my daughter," T.J. says proudly.

Your real daughter?

"No, that's what I call my girls."

I ask T.J. if it's true she lives in the outhouse. No way, she says. She's got an apartment in Inglewood. But sure, if it's late or she's tired, she stays in the portable toilet. Maybe 15 days out of a month, she sleeps in there. Why not? She's got a pillow in there and all the comforts, she says, letting me poke my head in for a tour.

"This is my closet," she says, pointing out some clothes and a hanger on one wall. "That's my library over there." I see two books, including a Bible. She's even got a stereo, and T.J. flips it on to show off the wrap-around sound. The rats don't bother her, T.J. says. Sometimes they'll pop in as if they're her roommates. "They're cute," she says.

How does she sleep in such tight quarters? I ask.

You pile the clothes over the toilet for bedding, T.J. says, and then curl up sideways. Or you roll onto your back, prop your feet up on the wall and close your eyes.

Home sweet home.

Here's What You Get
for a Few Coins

(November 12, 2006)

I was making my way back from Hemet, where I had just met with the family of a soldier killed in Iraq, when I thought about my colleague Doug Smith. Smith, an *L.A. Times* scribe for 36 years, was on his third volunteer tour of duty reporting from Iraq. I know it's tough on his wife, Jackie, when he's away, so I called her at the Smith home in Pasadena to check in.

Jackie had just gotten off the phone with Doug, and there was nervous relief in her voice. He had been out of touch for a while, embedded with American troops. As it turned out, he'd been riding in an armored vehicle when the troops he was with came under fire. They were OK, Smith reassured his wife, and he'd be home soon.

I suggested we chain Doug to his desk next time he puts his hand up for combat duty. Jackie liked the idea, but she knew it wouldn't fly. She understands why her husband keeps returning to Iraq. There's no glory in it and no hazardous duty pay, but there's something more elemental.

"He thinks it's important for someone to be there and tell the story," she said.

I share this because newspapers do a lousy job of telling you what you get for two quarters on weekdays and a buck-fifty on Sunday. The *L.A. Times'* latest ad, in which prospective customers pause at a news rack and peer at the paper but can't seem to figure out whether to buy it, is so bad that whoever created it should be locked out of the building.

A good ad would tell you that Smith is under fire in Iraq, that T.J. Simers may soon come to blows with a Dodger or Laker, that Robin Abcarian's takes on local culture and celebrity are smart and sassy, that Dan Neil is on the Santa Monica Freeway test-driving another car, that George Skelton has explained everything on the California ballot with clarity and nary a hint of partisanship and that the coupons alone will cover the cost of dinner.

As you might have heard, the newspaper industry is struggling to figure out how to maintain readership and ad revenue as the business shifts to the Internet. And yet the geniuses who run the industry are loath to kick even five percent of their still-robust profits into telling you why you ought to buy a paper or check one out online.

The *Los Angeles Times* is my seventh newspaper. Before this job, I traveled around the country writing a column for *Time* magazine, and I read lots of newspapers. Trust me, we have one of the best in the country. My boss at *Time* advised me not to take the job here. The *L.A. Times* has hurdles like no other publication, he warned, because not only are there 88 towns in L.A. County alone, but if you asked 100 people to design a paper to fit their own needs, you'd get 100 different plans.

I took the job for that reason. I wanted the challenge of trying to connect in a sprawling polyglot metropolis that's unconventional, ever-evolving and defiantly resistant to simple definitions. Though a newspaper can't be all things to all people, The *L.A. Times* searches out stories of universal local appeal and tries to craft national and international coverage to regional interests.

We can still do better in many ways. We should have developed the website more quickly. We need to connect in creative ways with more readers, and fast.

Unfortunately, greatness and ambition don't come on the cheap, something newspaper owners don't seem to get. In my five and a half years here, two publishers and two editors who believed staff cuts were bad for business were pushed off the roof.

Those of us who are still here have a message for the brain trust in Chicago— or for any of the local billionaires itching to buy the joint: Even the most old-school curmudgeons among us know we've got to learn new tricks and do more with less if the newspaper business is going to thrive again. But the bones of this operation are still pretty strong, and severing limbs won't do the journalism or the bottom line any good.

I work in an office that's neat as a landfill, poorly lighted and so cramped that reporters and editors can hear one another breathe. Ken Weiss works near me, a local native who, along with Usha McFarling and Rick Loomis, spent long days and nights—more than a year—reporting a groundbreaking series on the decline of the world's oceans.

I'm a few feet away from Charlie Ornstein and Tracy Weber, who barely took a breath after their exposé of King/Drew Medical Center before moving on to an alarming series on organ transplants. And they share a work area with Cara Mia DiMassa, who has owned the story of downtown L.A.'s changing face. I feel like a laggard when I see Joel Rubin and Howard Blume rush in from interviews and call out to each other as they coordinate daily stories on the revolutionary changes in the Los Angeles Unified School District.

Whether it's Ron Brownstein on the president, Kim Murphy on Russia, Megan Stack covering the war in Lebanon or Iraq, Stephanie Simon reporting religion and culture with scrupulous neutrality, Jason Felch and Ralph Frammolino getting inside the disastrously run Getty Museum, David Zucchino following wounded soldiers back home from Afghanistan and Iraq, Patt Morrison slicing and dicing, Bob Pool filing sublime snapshots of the city, Tom Hamburger and Peter Wallsten breaking political stories in Washington or Bill Plaschke digging for a local sports angle no one else thought of, there is personality and purpose in every edition, and it costs less than a cup of joe. I don't know anyone at the *Times* who doesn't consider it a privilege to come into your kitchens each morning with news from around the corner and around the world.

Getting back to Doug Smith, he got home safely from his latest storytelling in Iraq and immediately returned to work on a local investigative project. He is the son, by the way, of the late *L.A. Times* columnist Jack Smith. In his own quiet and dignified way, Doug has built a career as distinguished as that of his famous father, unwaveringly loyal to the story, to tradition and, most important, to you.

A Free Crypt
from Cardinal Mahony?

(February 18, 2007)

Journalists are not allowed to accept gifts from the people they write about, but I'm thinking of making an exception in the case of Los Angeles' Cardinal Roger M. Mahony. Mahony recently gave a tour of the Cathedral of Our Lady of the Angels to my editor and publisher. In the mausoleum under the altar, where crypts are available for purchase, the cardinal offered my bosses a deal. He said he'd provide a final resting place, free of charge, if they promised to put me in it. Imagine that. Me, lurking in the bowels of the Rog Mahal, into eternity.

My editor said this friendly chat took place in the vicinity of Gregory Peck's crypt, which sounds like a pretty good neighborhood to me. Besides, with crypts near the altar going for as much as a few hundred thousand dollars, this could save my survivors a small fortune. It wasn't clear whether I would get a crypt or a mere cremation niche, but my guess is the latter. Something tells me Mahony would like to have my cremains in the basement, perhaps as soon as Ash Wednesday this week. In case it escaped your notice, I've written a column or two about his handling of the priest molestation scandal and the district attorney's harangues about "a pattern of obstruction."

Giving him the benefit of the doubt, I have decided to assume His Eminence was extending an olive branch when he mentioned my demise. After all, he was inviting me to spend eternity in his home. So I called Tod

Tamberg, the archdiocese's director of media relations, to see if the cardinal wouldn't mind personally escorting me to see my final resting place. I also had an idea I wanted to pitch to Mahony—an idea that might just save both our souls.

Sorry, Tamberg said. He's out of town. No problem. I waited awhile, then e-mailed a second request. I was welcome to come on up and conduct my own tour, Tamberg said, asking if I'd ever been to the cathedral. Of course I had, I told him.

"On occasion, I like to go up there and pray for the cardinal."

Tamberg responded with a gift basket that included two bottles of wine and a tour book. Nice, but I didn't want a consolation prize. I was holding out for Mahony.

I also informed Tamberg that I had intended to return the gift basket, but some scoundrel in my office had stolen the wine. It was no surprise, really. Half the people in my business are lily-livered social misfits, and they're the good half.

"Too bad about the mysterious demise of the wine," Tamberg responded, "but given the daily occurrence of bad news coming from the *Times,* I'm not surprised that one of your colleagues may have found comfort in hitting the sauce—even if that reduced them to stealing it from such a fine fellow as yourself."

Did I detect a note of sarcasm?

"Since your focus is on the material and not the spiritual resting place, your request seems to me to be inappropriate and is declined," he said, adding that there was no such thing as a free crypt. That's not just un-Christian, it's bad PR.

I had been planning to honor Lent by going 40 days without a single swipe at the cardinal. And that would be quite a sacrifice, especially since *Deliver Us from Evil,* the documentary in which a pedophile priest criticizes Mahony for protecting the molester instead of his victims, could win an Oscar next Sunday. But clearly, Tamberg intended to keep me in some kind of purgatory, and I'd have to find a way to hook up with his boss on my own.

Truth be told, I had an agenda. So last week I trekked up the hill and checked the plaza and the cathedral. There was no sign of Mahony. Such a shame. I think he would have liked my proposition. Ash Wednesday is a day of penitence for sinners. It kicks off the season of Lent, which ends with the resurrection on Easter. I was going to suggest that if Mahony celebrates

Mass that day, he should inspire his flock to help save the hundreds of souls who sleep on the pavement not far from St. Vibiana's, which was abandoned when the cardinal moved into his new $189 million home.

Look, I was never a perfect student in Catholic school. But I recall a thing or two about the Christian duty of looking after the neediest amongst us. And if I've learned anything in the last two years, it's that this city has a lot of need. It's time for Mahony to lead his army of Christian soldiers down the hill and into the service of their fellow men. I know from experience that one person can make a difference in someone's life. I'd even volunteer, selflessly, to make some introductions. Especially if there's a free crypt in it for me.

It was a bit strange, I must admit, descending the stairs to the room where I'll take the Big Sleep. But if there is an afterlife, the lighting is perfect down there, with a nice golden glow on Spanish limestone. I found Gregory Peck's crypt and wanted to put a "reserved" sticker on the next one over.

And should I meet our maker before Mahony does, it'll be nice to know I'll still be able to keep an eye on him.

A Deposition That Is
an Eye-Opener

(June 20, 2010)

I've said many times that Cardinal Roger Mahony should stop resisting the release of church documents in the sex abuse scandal. But after a Mahony deposition in a molestation case was made public by the courts last week at the request of the *Los Angeles Times*, I can see why the cardinal has fought to keep things under wraps.

The deposition involved former priest Michael Baker, who is now serving a 10-year sentence for molestation. After he confessed to Mahony in 1986 that he had molested two boys, Mahony sent him to one of the drive-through "treatment" centers used by the church back then. After that, the archdiocese shuffled Baker around to different parishes—some with elementary schools.

Despite reports that Baker continued to have contact with minors in violation of church orders, the archdiocese did nothing to stop the priest, who went on to molest other kids. You can see why this one troubles Mahony. But is he troubled about the suffering of the victims or the reflection on him? Consider this exchange between the cardinal and attorney John Manly, who was representing one of Baker's many victims:

Manly: I mean, you would agree with me that the first thing any priest should do...when you learn that a priest has molested a child is call the police, right?

Mahony: Not necessarily.

It's not a difficult question. A child is abused; that's a crime, so you call the police and rush to the aid of the minor, right? Not Mahony. And despite admitting mistakes, he continues to blame his failure on the times, the circumstances, the procedures that were in place. He'd have you think that 1986 was 100 years ago, and the terms of moral responsibility were different. When he's asked the same question again by the disbelieving lawyer, his answer begins:

> "If you want to review the suspected child abuse form, you'll see that the very top little section of the form says name of mandated reporter, title of mandated reporter..."

It goes on like that, with Mahony suggesting the form couldn't be filled out because the names of the victims and their parents were not known. So he didn't call the police and he didn't call the parish where Baker was living to warn of other potential victims.

Manly: I take it at that point you instructed your staff to try and find the kids?

Mahony: No, I did not.

Huh? You know that children have been horribly violated by one of your priests, and you don't move heaven and earth to find them and get them help? The cardinal said he didn't know their names and was under the impression they might be illegal immigrants who had returned to Mexico. So couldn't he have demanded that Baker tell him their names and where to find them?

"It's not hard to find boys like this," says attorney Lynne Cadigan, who in 2000 negotiated a $1.3 million settlement for two brothers she believes to have been those very victims.

In his deposition, Mahony said Baker admitted to one or two instances of "touching" the boys. But in Mahony's 2004 report to parishioners on the sex abuse scandal, he said Baker indicated there was a "relationship" with the boys from 1978 to 1985, beginning when they were five and seven.

"It's utterly ridiculous for him to say, 'I couldn't find them,'" Cadigan said of Mahony. "He didn't want to find them." In fact, Cadigan said, the boys' mother worked at the parish where they were molested. Baker knew that, and continued molesting the boys for years, according to Cadigan, in Los Angeles, Mexico and Arizona.

In his deposition, Mahony said he established a sexual abuse advisory council in 1992 to use as a sounding board on such cases. The man he put in charge was someone he'd known from Catholic social events: L.A. County Superior Court Judge Richard Byrne. In his own deposition last October, Byrne—now retired from his job as presiding judge—sounded like a Mahony clone. Even in cases in which he thought a crime had been committed, Byrne said he didn't believe anyone on the advisory council ever called police.

Manly: I mean, did that ever even cross your mind?

Byrne: No....But I did assume that whatever needed to be done was being done. I had that belief in the archdiocese and the system.

Unfortunately, such faith didn't do the victims any good. And pardon me, but if the cardinal wanted expert advice on whether crimes had been committed, he should have gone to the police or the district attorney, not to handpicked loyalists with no authority.

When I asked to speak to Mahony about his deposition last week, one of his attorneys said I hadn't been fair to the cardinal in the past, that I'd focused on his mistakes without mentioning "how those mistakes led to a complete reformation of how child abuse allegations were handled by the archdiocese."

Thanks for the advice, but my duty isn't to the cardinal. It's to the victims of sexual abuse and to ferreting out the truth about an institution that was putting its own image before their welfare. As for the archdiocese's reformation, is there any reason to believe that without lawsuits, media pressure and the threat of criminal prosecution, there would have been any changes at all? And would there have been the $660 million payout in 2007, when the archdiocese settled 500 cases of clergy sex abuse?

As we saw again last week, the cardinal is a man who, even when he admits mistakes, doesn't seem capable of taking full responsibility for the consequences of them. He's still trying to construct the image he'd rather be remembered by, and with each attempt it slips further away.

AROUND THE CORNER AND THE WORLD

Amid the Ruins, a Separate Piece

(September 15, 2001)

"**Look at this.** Just look at this," Vincent Bury said as he aimed his cab toward the smoke. "That used to be a beautiful view of the towers, but I'm going to tell you something. You see all these people out here? Everybody helping out in whatever way they can? They tried to break us up, but this city's never been more unified."

Vincent Bury drove slower than any cabby has ever driven in New York, loving his wounded city. The heavens thundered with an advancing storm, and flashes of lightning illuminated American flags that hung from fire escapes. A few poor souls wandered the streets like ghosts, photos of missing loved ones taped to shirts or strung around their necks. They were consoled by people they did not know and would never see again.

"Look at this," Vincent Bury said again, his heart full. He turned a corner at 15th Street and 11th Avenue to find a group of teenagers cheering. "Thank you Thank you Thank you," said the signs they held. They were spending the night at the intersection to greet rescue workers who came up for air after digging with their hands for hours. Digging for miracles. Ambulances lined the streets, waiting for a call.

On a normal night, Vincent Bury would have been driven off the road by angry motorists leaning on horns. But they passed politely, letting him mourn in his own time. He calls himself the last white native New York cabby, and he is different in another way, too. Instead of ramming fenders and bumpers, like you're supposed to do to let off steam, he meditates.

"The inner self never dies," he said, and he was sure something good was going to come of this tragedy. "Where to now?" he asked.

"A Hundredth and Riverside. The fireman's memorial."

Bury parked on Riverside and got out of the car with a camera. He said that in his 49 years, he had never seen the fireman's memorial and its twin statues of Courage and Duty. He wanted to take the memory home to Brooklyn with him.

A little earlier in the evening, an advertising man named John Avery had left his Upper West Side apartment to walk his poodle Gracie. Avery had been in a state of shock over the attack on New York, but the shock was becoming sadness and anger. A co-worker lost her husband in one of the towers, and it was hitting Avery in a way it hadn't until then. He was thinking, too, about the estimated 300 firefighters believed to have died under the rubble of what used to be an American symbol.

Three hundred.

Avery walked two blocks to the memorial that has stood since 1913. Firefighters never hesitate, he was thinking as Gracie tugged on the leash. They take chances with their own lives to save others, and there is a striking gallantry about them. The bravery, the bond, the cut of the uniform.

On this night, candles had been left at the memorial, and they flickered in the breeze of the coming storm. Bouquets were laid about, and some well-wishers had written anonymous notes of thanks and sympathy. "The whole world is a very narrow bridge," said one. "Words can not express our sorrow," said another. Avery's eyes filled, and anger floated just beneath the sadness. President Bush and the rest of America have to have the guts to root out terrorists wherever they are, he said, his voice deepening.

"We must go after the terrorists and anyone who harbors or finances them. It's not about revenge; it's about protection. If we don't do it, this can happen again. But if it's about revenge, we've sunk to the morality of the terrorists." The storm had moved across the Hudson, bringing with it a drenching rain that sent John Avery and Gracie the poodle home.

Vincent Bury took a picture of the memorial, which has the following inscription: "To the men of the Fire Department of the City of New York, who died at the call of duty. Soldiers in a war that never ends."

Bury drove away at funeral speed, in touch with both the living and the dead. It rained like everyone was crying all at once, and it seemed to me that New York had never been more beautiful.

No Telling Where a War
in Iraq May Take Us

(September 29, 2002)

Forget what you've heard. National polls, some of which suggest 70 percent of Americans support a war against Iraq, are not to be trusted. Roughly 75 percent of my readers are opposed, and that many people can't be wrong. Twice now I've raised questions about the wisdom of such an undertaking, and several hundred people have backed me up. So who's out of step? Us, or Washington?

I was going to suggest that we reinstate the draft, and see if the thought of sending their own children and grandchildren into battle makes lawmakers slow the drumbeat. But a growing number of people in Congress have come out of hibernation and are finally asking why President Bush is in such a hurry. They're also wondering if we have any idea what we're getting into.

Good question, and for an answer, I checked with USC professor Richard Dekmejian. He's an authority on international terrorism, Islamic fundamentalism and Middle East politics. Dekmejian, for the record, is no fan of Saddam Hussein, who has never been shy about slaughtering anyone who doesn't bow before him. In a 1985 book called *Islam in Revolution*, Dekmejian wrote about the murder of a Shiite holy man by Saddam's forces, and he was invited by Hussein's emissaries to visit Iraq and hear Saddam's version of history, an offer he declined.

The best-case outcome of U.S. intervention, Dekmejian would agree, is the one put forth by President Bush. Saddam Hussein is destroyed, his weapons program dismantled, and democracy takes root in Iraq and beyond, spreading love and happiness throughout the Middle East. There is, unfortunately, a better chance that a blind pig will snort a truffle in Baghdad and open a chocolate shop. Things could go terribly wrong very quickly, says Dekmejian. He thinks it would be much smarter to continue containing Iraq and limiting Hussein's access to atomic weapons than to stir more madness.

"If Saddam sees that this is his end, he might just as well use whatever he has, not only against Israel, but American troops," Dekmejian says. "When that happens, do the Israelis attack back, and do they use atomic weapons? I don't know, but one has to remember that the man in charge of Israel can be dangerous, too. Not as dangerous as Saddam, of course. And this could escalate the entire Arab-Israeli conflict."

If chaos reigns, he says, it's not a stretch to imagine India and Pakistan following America's lead on preemptive strikes and going to war over Kashmir. A war that could well go nuclear. But let's, for the moment, push aside the specter of the United States pulling the trigger that starts World War III. Let's assume we accomplish the first objective and blow Saddam Hussein into the next century.

What then?

No telling, says Dekmejian. But one distinct possibility is chaos. "And the human cost will be enormous."

Imagine Los Angeles if you were to get rid of all official authority and turn the city over to the Crips and Bloods. That's what we'd be looking at in Iraq, only worse, and American troops would be caught in the middle of it. The Crips in this case are the Shiites, and the Bloods are the Sunnis, who currently rule the country. They don't much like each other, and it'll be a race to see who gets to the Sunnis first—the Shiites or the equally vengeful Kurds, who have been gassed, and persecuted for years, by Saddam's people.

I happen to have spent some time in Iraq's Kurdish reaches, and I can tell you firsthand that they don't even get along with each other. And one faction has been particularly close to Iran, which arguably is more dangerous than Iraq, and could conceivably get drawn into this mess. If so, Dekmejian says, Russia could follow. Given the long, complex histories of these conflicts, and the depth of hatred that exists, Dekmejian has a neat summary of any expectation for democracy to triumph in Iraq: "It's completely insane."

"First of all," Dekmejian explains, "you need some precedent for democracy, some cultural inclination and homogeneity, and the fellows opposing Saddam don't even run their own organizations democratically.

"We'll need a massive military force to occupy the place and keep people from killing each other, so it will mean a long-term commitment financially and militarily."

And that, believe it or not, could be the least of our concerns. Bombing Iraq could work wonders for the recruiting efforts of the world's anti-American terrorist organizations, says Dekmejian, who fears the radicalization of untold thousands of Muslims.

"For a variety of reasons that have to do with U.S. foreign policy and our support of authoritarian regimes in that part of the world, the countries of Islam are at a mass level of anger and fury," he says. "Attacking another Arab country in this atmosphere of hostility is the wrong thing to do, and it's going to contribute to terrorism rather than detract from it. I expect the blowback to occur across the world."

Blowback, of course, is another word for September 11. Shall we take another poll now?

Killed in Iraq—He's Not
a Statistic, But a Son

(July 27, 2003)

Yes, there were lots of other things the San Fernando Valley woman could have talked about regarding the war in Iraq. But this wasn't the time for politics.

On this day, Jane Bright was a mother, just a mother who wanted to talk about her son. Evan Ashcraft was killed last week. He was 24 and an Army sergeant in the 101st Airborne Division. When his mother invited me to visit with her, she had only one purpose. She wanted to honor her boy, and to put a human face to the daily tally of casualties.

"I don't want them to be just numbers," said Bright, human resources director for a North Hollywood aerospace company. "This anguish is unspeakable, and another family goes through it every day. We're not speaking enough about the losses."

Evan Ashcraft's 23-year-old wife, Ashley, was staying with her dad in Castaic when word came Thursday at dawn. The Army messenger was in tears before even delivering the news. Upstairs, Ashley knew it without hearing a word.

"I was on the floor, screaming," she said. "I didn't want to let them tell me."

Ashcraft was one of three American soldiers killed in an ambush near Mosul in northern Iraq. He might have been part of the mission that claimed the lives of Saddam Hussein's sons, but the family just doesn't know the details yet. They believe Evan was killed by a rocket-propelled grenade.

Every day, Jane Bright would read news accounts from Iraq and breathe a sigh of relief if her son's division was somewhere other than in the middle of firefights that continue with no end in sight, despite early claims of victory. She had reservations about the war from the start, and she had closely followed the debate about whether the world had been misled regarding the justification for combat. But she loved and supported her son without qualification, and losing him makes the politics entirely irrelevant.

Nothing matters except that he's gone. Nothing matters except that his wife, Ashley, had just finished school and was going to be a teacher. Nothing matters except that Evan, who played classical piano, was going to go to college before becoming a cop like his father-in-law, LAPD sergeant Loren Farell, and then have children with Ashley.

"There's still so much of his energy. It's important not to just let him die," says Bright, and so she tells the story of the life he planned. Bright got the phone call from her ex-husband. "He said, 'I hate to be the one to tell you this.' I couldn't even fathom Evan being killed." Now the entire family, including Evan's little brother Drew, 17, is gathered in Castaic. The Army rep who delivered the grim news has returned to discuss arrangements for the shipping of Evan's body back home, and Bright excuses herself to listen in. When she leaves the kitchen, her husband, Jim Bright, speaks up.

"I think it's normal to say, 'OK, I lost a son. Was this for a good cause?' But what Jane is saying is that she lost a son, and people need to know he was not a number. He was someone to be honored and remembered. She and I both believe it transcends political consideration. Kids are dying, and that is what it is. Kids are dying."

He was top-notch, Bright says of her son when she returns. "Absolutely top-notch, like so many of these kids who are fighting over there. It's important that we tell their story, because they need our support."

Evan had been cited last April for rescuing two wounded soldiers. The El Camino Real High School grad had told his family that, if anything happened to him, he wanted them to throw a party, not a wake.

"We're going to do it," Bright said. "We're going to celebrate his life."

Before going to Iraq, Evan told his mother he was aware of her reservations about the war. She told him it didn't matter; she'd do what a mother does. She'd love him. She'd believe in him. And she'd support him and his fellow soldiers 100 percent.

"He believed in what he was doing, and I told him, 'Go do your job. Do what you were trained to do. And come home safe.'"

The Town That
NAFTA Sent North

(June 18, 2004)

San Juan Atenco, Mexico—Pay a visit to this hilltop farm town with the pretty little church in the plaza, a state official had suggested, and I would discover something was missing. Half the population.

Where'd they go? I asked.

Los Angeles, he said.

I figured he was exaggerating. He wasn't.

"Si, un mitad," said the first person I met in San Juan's quiet, nearly evacuated central plaza. Yes, one half.

The official population of San Juan Atenco, four hours south of Mexico City, is 6,000. But the only work here is in the cornfields, and locally grown corn is worth next to nothing. In the country that introduced corn to the world, campesinos can't compete with cheap U.S. imports. So they go north, or they go hungry.

The San Juan mayor told me as much as 70 percent of the money in town is sent home by displaced sons in Los Angeles. I was also told that the church, a gleaming white beacon in a town that's rough around the edges, was lovingly restored with money sent back from L.A.

Unfortunately, the padre wasn't around the first time I knocked, so I began exploring the town, asking people if they had relatives in Los Angeles. Many said yes. Others said, "No, in Culver City," or, "No, in San Fernando."

"In the fields here, I made six dollars a day," said Misael Gomez, 23, who recently returned home from several months in Santa Monica, where he worked as a gardener. "In the United States, I made six dollars an hour."

Six bucks an hour was so attractive, he gladly paid $250 for a plane ticket from Mexico City to Tijuana, and then worked eight months in Santa Monica to pay off a $2,500 ransom to the coyote who led him across the border. Gomez missed home, though. He returned after a year to be with his wife. Together they were dismantling the little stand where they sell fresh-squeezed orange and carrot juice in the plaza near the church. Gomez showed me a box with the day's receipts. Forty pesos, about four dollars. Not much, he sighed. But better than what he'd make in the sun-blasted cornfields these days.

The Mexican government deserves much of the blame for that. Farmers get no price supports and scant government aid. Bank credit is nonexistent, so farmers work the fields with primitive tools and no tractors. But if Mexican ineptitude has staggered the campesinos, American policy has delivered the knockout punch. The U.S. government paid more than $34 billion in subsidies to American corn growers between 1995 and 2002, according to the Environmental Working Group. An estimated 1.3 million Mexican farm jobs have been lost since the beginning of free trade in 1994, according to a Carnegie Endowment report. They couldn't compete with American farmers propped up with U.S. tax dollars doled out by vote-chasing politicians.

Just beyond San Juan's town center, I found farmers with wives and children in tow, heading in from the cornfields on horse-drawn wagons after a day of hard labor. Two sisters, Silvia, seven, and Anaseli, six, had been kept out of school that day to help plow fields with 15-year-old big sister Barbarita, who had to quit school in the third grade. They were riding home with their father, Hipolito Casiano Atilano, and their mother, Manuela. I asked the youngest sisters what they liked better, school or work?

"La escuela!" they shouted in unison.

If the girls don't help work the farm, said their father, the family won't eat. They used to eat some and sell some of what they grow on the seven acres they work as sharecroppers. But Casiano said the price of the maiz that is used to make tortillas has dropped to 16 cents a kilo because of all the cheap foreign corn on the market, some of it genetically modified.

The situation is so bleak that Casiano's two sons, 17 and 24, headed north to work as gardeners in L.A.'s San Fernando Valley. The boys used to send money back home, but even with 12-hour workdays in the United States, they have trouble paying their own bills. There's suffering, said their mother, on both sides of the border.

Another farmer pulled up with his whole family aboard a creaky old wagon, and the same story was repeated. At 16 cents, Joaquin Urbina said, do you realize how many kilos of corn you have to sell to buy a pair of shoes? Urbina said his eldest son, 28, is a gardener in L.A. I asked one of Urbina's daughters, a girl of about 12, what it's like growing up in a town where all the young men have disappeared.

"It's fine that they go," she said, "because they send money."

The story is as old as the world. It's the story of families torn apart in the name of survival, the poor crossing oceans, climbing fences, running for their lives. From San Juan Atenco, it's clear why millions head north, trading history and culture for food and opportunity. Next week, many of those new Angelenos will head home to celebrate the feast of San Juan Bautista. Sometimes there's a long line of vehicles returning to town, one man told me, many of them with California plates.

When I got back up to the central plaza, an elderly gent named Edgardo was in the church bell tower, tugging at a rope. The chimes carried across the plaza, over the rooftops and into the cornfields under a metallic sky. Edgardo took me into the church after climbing down, proud to show it off. Inside the ornate, impeccably maintained house of worship was a plaque honoring everyone who helped in the rebuilding between 1993 and 1998. Special mention was given to those who sent money from Los Angeles, where half the town of San Juan Atenco sleeps.

Kovic Asks If Vietnam
Taught Us Anything

(September 19, 2004)

Ron Kovic comes toward me in his wheelchair before the doors of the elevator close. He reaches for my hand and squeezes hard. "Come on," he says, and we slip into the third-floor Redondo Beach apartment where he's been painting, writing, suffering through another war. Kovic's home is strikingly neat, as if this is his way of bringing order to the world. His canvas paintings hang from the walls like Polaroids of disturbed dreams. They hang next to photos of him with Oliver Stone and Tom Cruise, who played Kovic in the movie based on his searing, angry and sorrowful book, *Born on the Fourth of July*.

Kovic, with clipped white beard and wire-rim glasses, apologizes for not answering my first call a couple of weeks ago. He was holed up here, in mourning and rebellion, as the three-year anniversary of September 11 rolled around about the same time the toll of dead American soldiers in Iraq hit 1,000.

"What did we learn from Vietnam?" Kovic asks.

It all comes back to that. Kovic, 58, was shot on a Vietnam battlefield 36 years ago, and he has been paralyzed from the chest down ever since. When he gets into his hand-controlled vehicle and drives to a war protest, when he shifts his body onto his bed at night and closes his eyes, he has to believe his sacrifice has advanced the cause of peace. I don't have the heart to tell him we aren't conditioned to learn from mistakes, but he already knows it.

"The president says the terrorists hate us because we're free," Kovic says, bristling at the simplification. Let's go get the terrorists, he says. But let's admit there's a backlash against decades of hypocritical U.S. foreign policy based on economic self-interest, and let's admit this country has bedded a long line of despots.

"People forget that we supported Saddam Hussein to begin with," Kovic says. "What's been missing after September 11 is a national dialogue about all of this." It's missing in the presidential campaign, too.

"Democracy is loud, it's angry, it's spirited, it's passionate," Kovic says. "I love this country and care about the safety of every American, and for our future security, we have to talk about what happened, and why, and go on from there."

Kovic is writing a book on the subject. He's also writing a fresh preface for the re-release of *Born on the Fourth of July*, drawing on current events.

"When I first heard it was 1,000 dead in Iraq, I went online and looked at the faces," he had told me earlier by phone. "I scrolled down and looked at as many of them as I could, and I saw the same young faces I saw from my days in the service."

He saw himself, too. The gung-ho New York kid who was born on Independence Day, dreamed of playing for the Yankees and couldn't wait to enlist with the Marines. If you were strong, you answered the call without question.

You believed. You believed everything they told you until you were surrounded by the screams of young men without faces or limbs, and it was only then that none of the justifications added up. Iraq, 40 years later, has raised Kovic's ghosts.

"People say, 'Yeah, I support the war, I support the president, I think we should be in Iraq.' Do they really know what it's like to be there? To be hit by a bullet? To live with your wounds for the rest of your life? Do they have any idea what parents go through?"

Kovic leans forward, eyes burning.

"Will these people who support the war be there when these soldiers come home? Will they be there on lonely nights five years later, 10 years, 20 years later? Will they be there when they're homeless because their lives have been ruined, or they're in prison because they were never able to adjust?

"I'm glad President Bush didn't have to suffer the way some of us did. I'm glad he didn't get shot and end up in a wheelchair and suffer all the awful consequences. I know what it means. I've been on the battlefield fighting for my life when another Marine came up to save my life and was killed.

"I know what it means to come home to a government that isn't prepared for all the wounded. I saw paraplegics and quadriplegics. I remember it, I can smell it and I will never forget it.

"This is a war we should never have fought to begin with, and it's becoming a catastrophe and a mirror image of Vietnam. Another guerrilla war, another senseless quagmire....It can only make us greater targets of terror, and it can only harm the soul of America."

Kovic takes off frequently on these flights of rage, then almost seems to pull himself back. Don't get him wrong, he tells me. He's not a cynic, because he can't afford to be.

"I feel a lot of energy," he says. "This is a great challenge." He looks down toward frail bent legs, smiles and adds: "How can I turn this into something wonderful? Victorious? It's important for me not to be a victim. Dignity over despair is what I tell myself. Dignity over despair."

Kovic takes me on a tour of his apartment. In the dining room is an abstract scrawl that might be called a self-portrait for its sadness and hope. "Look to the sky," say the painted words, "when the tears of life are driving you wild."

Kovic leads me out and toward the elevator. He asks about my wife and daughter and says he's always wanted to get married, but hasn't found the right girl yet. Out front, he is on the porch as I walk away, thanking me for coming. I get into my car and open *Born on the Fourth of July* to the first page:

> I am the living death
> The memorial day on wheels
> I am your yankee doodle dandy
> Your john wayne come home
> Your fourth of july firecracker
> Exploding in the grave.

After Katrina, Betting on a Break

(September 5, 2005)

"**I've been cryin'** for a week," a red-eyed Gail Plank from eastern Texas said as she played the 25-cent Sizzling 7 slot machines in Lake Charles on Sunday morning and drew hard on a Doral cigarette.

"I have family that's still lost."

Plank insisted she wasn't really in the mood to yank slots after the Gulf states tested their luck against Katrina and lost big. But she gambles so often, she was invited to participate in the Lazy Labor Day Slot Tournament at Harrah's Casino & Hotel, so she figured why not? If she wins, Plank said, Hurricane Katrina evacuees are in luck.

"I'm giving it all to the Red Cross."

I had seen the riverboat out of the corner of my eye as I sped toward the center of the disaster zone and drove right past it before realizing it was a casino.

Who, I wondered, would be throwing money away in a casino when thousands of Gulf shore residents have lost their lives, their homes and their jobs? When the Big One hits Los Angeles and one-story houses suddenly become split-levels, will we all meet up around a poker table in the City of Commerce?

Doubling back to Harrah's, I figured maybe the place was being used as a staging or rest area for rescue crews, even though Lake Charles is two hours from the worst of the damage.

But I was wrong, of course.

Down the long corridor I walked, past the food court, past the "Come on Down" one-million-dollar giveaway promotion and down the ramp to two riverboat gambling halls: *Pride of Lake Charles* and *Star of Lake Charles*. I went with the *Pride*, and although it was sparsely populated, it was filling up fast with gamblers, not rescue workers. To back up her claim that all winnings would go to the Red Cross, Gail Plank called out to her friend.

"Ain't that right, Tony?"

Tony Aguilar, who paints houses in Houston, seemed irritated by the interference. He was concentrating on his own 25-cent slot, but sauntered over when he lost again. Yes, he confirmed, Plank said something about giving money to the Red Cross. So I had to ask them. Why not just send a donation instead of taking a chance at a casino?

"Good question," said Tony, who wore a cowboy hat and puffed on a Winston. Apparently it's a state law in Louisiana that you're not allowed inside a casino unless you smoke.

"I have a gambling problem," he confessed, "as opposed to an alcohol problem."

"We're both recovering," explained Plank, who works in the ceramic tile business. But they've still got their vices.

Even if they lose, Aguilar said, the money is going to a good cause, because Harrah's lost two casinos to Katrina and is paying severance packages to its staff. Dropping a paycheck at the slots would be practically like making a charitable donation.

Melanie Dunse, a cocktail waitress on the *Pride of Lake Charles*, appreciated the sentiment.

"The first couple of days after the storm hit, I was a little surprised people were in here gambling," she confessed. But she and other employees are kicking a portion of their tips into a relief fund, so they're thankful that business is picking up.

By early afternoon at Harrah's, hundreds of gamblers roamed the *Pride* and the *Star*, each of which has three floors of wall-to-wall gaming. One bald gnome was slumped in front of the dollar slots, pounding the "Bet One Credit" button over and over again, losing a buck each time. When I asked about Hurricane Katrina, he ignored me. Bet One Credit. Bet One Credit. Bet One Credit.

Not far away, I noticed another man whose body language said "losing streak." He was wearing a shirt that read, "I Got Out of Bed for This?"

"Oh, I'm losing all right," Ralph Moten said as a slot machine ate his quarters. "Down $100 already." Yeah, that is a lot.

"I lost my house," he went on. "Lost everything."

You lost what?

"Lost my house."

To the hurricane?

Yes, he said, hitting the "Bet One Credit" button again.

Moten said he left his four-bedroom home in Metairie, close to the New Orleans boundary, just before the hurricane hit. Neighbors who stayed behind have told him the whole area is underwater, including much of his house. Moten and 11 other family members, including seven grandchildren, made their way to Lake Charles and met a cop who escorted them to a shelter at the local civic center.

It's all been a bit too much to handle, said Moten, 56, a former welder who is on disability after a serious car accident several years ago. He has no idea how badly damaged his house is or when he'll be able to return, and his bed is now a narrow cot in a crammed, noisy auditorium, where he tosses all night but can't really turn.

"I had to get out of there," he said. "It's too much stress and too depressing, and one little baby cried all night."

One of the other evacuees said he'd been to the casino for a little relief, and Moten found himself out back of the civic auditorium, looking across the lake at the casino.

"You can see the riverboats from there," he said in his own defense. "I had a $10 Harrah's coupon in my pocket, so I had to come."

Moten didn't tell any of the relatives what he was up to. "I just said I'm going for a ride." Now he wondered if he should quit while he still had enough money to buy lunch. Then again, he was way overdue for a change of luck. It's all a roll of the dice, Moten knows all too well. Who loses his house in a hurricane, who wins a million bucks at a casino. A roll of the dice.

I saw him a half hour later, way up on the third floor of the *Pride*. The casino was mobbed by then, and he was playing the one-cent slots, still waiting for that lucky break.

A Barbaric End to a Barbaric Life

(December 14, 2005)

In an odd way, the most disturbing thing about watching a man die by lethal injection is how discreetly death creeps into the room. No sudden jolt, no snapping of the neck at the end of a rope, no severed head. The inmate gets a shot, he closes his eyes, he sleeps.

The room where Stanley Tookie Williams was killed Tuesday morning is set up like a theater, with neat rows of spectators sitting or standing on risers to view the execution. Late Monday night, as one of 39 witnesses, I was ushered past dozens of guards and prison officials and into the viewing area a few feet from the octagonal death chamber.

Before us in the stuffy little auditorium, the curtains were opened, Williams was led in by guards, and the midnight show began—a dark, sinister, medieval drama in an archaic prison. San Quentin.

Never having witnessed an execution, I had tossed my name into the ring of potential spectators in order to see precisely what we're all a party to in a state that sanctions capital punishment. And now here I was, watching the clinical, calculated procedure used by the state of California to kill a man.

I watched the executioners struggle to tap a vein, digging into Williams' arms for minutes that seemed like hours. He was calm, if exasperated by the delay. Splayed out on his back and secured with tape and restraints, he lifted his head to study our faces, and he mouthed goodbyes to supporters who shared these close quarters with the relatives of his victims. There was no apparent sign of suffering on Williams' part when the lethal injection did its duty. He lay motionless for several minutes before he was declared dead and the curtains were closed, show over.

"The state of California just killed an innocent man," three of his supporters shouted in unison. That struck me as an insult to the families of Williams' victims. Of all the things Williams might have been, he wasn't innocent, and watching him die made me feel no differently about the man. His victims, all four of them, were shotgunned as if it were a cheap thrill for Williams. And as one of the first Crips, he started something that destroyed everything in its path, bringing genocide to neighborhoods on top of all the other problems.

Williams was a tough guy in prison, too, spending years in solitary confinement for his mayhem behind bars before he took a different tack. His anti-gang books and speeches from death row were great gestures, but the Nobel Peace Prize nominations were preposterous, and the marketing of Williams as a hero was offensive. If he were truly redeemed, he would have taken responsibility for the murders, he would have rejected the duplicitous code of honor among those who refuse to tell what they know, and his dying words would have been a call for the dismantling of the gang he started.

Those who tried to cast Williams as a martyr, including the usual Hollywood rabble, once again picked the wrong man to carry the banner against the death penalty. They made a cause of Tookie Williams as others have done with Mumia Abu Jamal, the Philadelphia cop killer and death row inmate whose claim of innocence is pure fiction, despite the celebrity bestowed on him.

And yet, watching Williams put to death Tuesday morning by agents of the government—his execution sanctioned in a country where godliness and virtue are synonymous, even as torture and execution are defended—made me all the more certain that capital punishment is barbaric.

Though I don't question Williams' guilt, no one can dispute that across America, class, race and money figure prominently in the circumstances of crime and the quality of legal defense. Since 1973, in fact, 122 death row inmates have been exonerated or granted new hearings. A better poster child for abolishing the death penalty is No. 123, whoever that might be.

Twelve U.S. states no longer use capital punishment, and the possibility of a mistake is one of the reasons 40 countries have abolished the death penalty since 1990, including Mexico, Bosnia-Herzegovina and Senegal. In 2004, the United States followed only China, Iran and Vietnam in the number of executions.

Coming down the death row pike in California is a violent killer named Horace Edwards Kelly, whose wicked crimes are not in question. But he has been diagnosed as severely mentally ill, if not retarded, and was virtually tortured as a child. Should we feel just as good about killing Kelly as we're supposed to feel about killing Williams? Will the premeditated and clinical execution of a feeble-minded man make us more civilized, more humane or any safer? Is life in a cage not enough to satisfy our puritanical beliefs or lust for blood?

Apparently not. Modern as we are, we still live by the law of an eye for an eye—as long as it doesn't get too messy. The needle is perfect. He closes his eyes, he's gone. It's much easier to handle that way. Not just for the person put to death, but for us.

Like a Third-World Country

(August 16, 2009)

"Do you want to see the tooth?" Dr. Mehrdad Makhani asked me Friday morning at the free clinic being staged inside Inglewood's Fabulous Forum. "Come. I'll show you." Jenny McLean, 36, opened her mouth and Makhani aimed a little flashlight in there. "You see here?" he said. The area around a back tooth was red and swollen, and McLean's eyes were teary with discomfort. She'd endured the pain for more than a year because she's had neither insurance nor the money for a dentist since losing her job as a social worker. It was a story repeated hundreds of times last week at the Forum, where a nonprofit called Remote Area Medical (RAM) had brought in volunteers to treat legions of the uninsured.

"Here, look at this," said Makhani, pointing to a second tooth that would have to be extracted and yet another that needed a root canal. Makhani pointed me to another dentist. "Talk to him. He's worked in Brazil." That would be Joseph Chamberlain, a Westwood dentist who said he's done charity work in Brazil, but not in conditions like this.

"They have a nice system of public hospitals and clinics," he said.

But don't patients have to wait for treatment?

"Yes," Chamberlain said. "But not like this. Not for a year."

Stan Brock, who founded RAM in 1985 to bring medical care to Third-World countries, told me that in 1992 he began getting requests to do the same work in the United States.

"The people we're seeing here have teeth as bad as the people in the Upper Amazon," said Brock, who used to tangle with wild beasts on *Mutual of Omaha's Wild Kingdom.* It would be nice if we could send Brock to the nation's capital and have him grab the vipers and hyenas by their necks until they work out a healthcare reform plan. But Brock has a better idea: The nation's leaders should instead come spend a day at one of his clinics and learn a thing or two. He pulled out a chart showing that at his last medical jamboree, in Virginia, volunteer dentists performed 4,304 tooth extractions in two days, among various other medical procedures.

"President Obama was just down the road somewhere a couple days later, talking about healthcare," Brock said. "I think it would have been a lot more interesting if he came to our clinic."

Eugene Taw, an ear, nose and throat specialist with the Buddhist Tzu Chi Free Clinic in Alhambra, was one of many Forum volunteers who has worked in other parts of the world. Yes, he said, there are far too many parallels between the uninsured in the United States and the residents of impoverished Third-World nations. At the Forum, his patients included a diabetic amputee who had not been able to buy his medicine for months, a retiree who couldn't afford an X-ray for a lung problem, and a 30ish female diabetic with a kidney ailment so serious that Taw called for an ambulance to take her to a hospital.

"This is great for helping people in need," Taw said of the Forum clinic. "But it's not a good way to do healthcare."

Diabetes and hypertension require regular maintenance, Taw said, rather than occasional urgent trips to an emergency room after the patient deteriorates and the treatment is more expensive. By some estimates, Taw said, 85 percent of the estimated 47 million uninsured Americans are members of working families. So why not divide the cost of their health insurance evenly among employer, employee and the government?

Taw said he'd seen the Friday headline in the *Los Angeles Times* about the latest cut in California's Healthy Families Program budget, which means nearly 670,000 children could lose medical coverage by next June. A disaster in the making, he said. Yes, and Brock told me the biggest difference between the Third World and the United States is that in our country, children have had far greater access to doctors.

The huge turnout each day at the Forum made it clear that although Southern California has quite a few free medical and dental clinics, there aren't enough to handle the demand. Among those waiting patiently for help was Walter Samwel, a 70-year-old Vietnam vet from Gardena who has been putting off a root canal for two years. I asked Samwel why he didn't go to the VA and he said they're swamped with recently returning vets, and more severe dental problems take priority. He had arranged time off from his part-time job as a maintenance man at a Long Beach senior center to come to the Forum, but this was his third attempt to get help. The first two days, his number was too high, and the dental clinic shut down before he was called.

Would his Medicare cover the dental work?

No, he said. There's lots it doesn't cover.

There's something shamefully wrong, I told him, when a man who served his country overseas for seven years can't get basic dental care.

"This is true," Samwel said, "but nobody wants to hear it."

Across the Forum, Adrienne Teeguarden was waiting for her first eye exam in two and a half years. Since her layoff as a clothes designer, she's been working as a part-time nanny and can't afford health insurance or glasses.

Greg Pearl, an optometrist who has done medical relief in Mexico and South America for Volunteer Optometric Services to Humanity, said it's outrageous that vision and dental care are not in most U.S. insurance plans and are rarely part of any conversation on healthcare reform. When I asked him about differences in the patients he sees overseas and in clinics such as the one at the Forum, he had a quick answer.

"Here, the patients speak English."

I can't say I was surprised by the spectacle at the Forum, but with each of two visits, I knew I was witnessing the perfect distillation of an unconscionable societal failure. Whether the answer includes the public option Obama has pitched, or the clampdown on obscene insurance company profits proposed by a doctor friend of mine in a recent *L.A.Times* article, a civil society has no excuse for not finding a better way.

"I don't have the answers," said Makhani, the dentist who insisted I look closely at his patient's ailing mouth. "I'm not a politician. But I have people here with infected teeth, gums, abscesses. I saw a lady bus driver who lost

The Captives Put on a Show

(March 3, 2010)

The whale and dolphin shows I saw at SeaWorld in San Diego a couple of years ago with my wife and daughter weren't just good, they were spectacular. I think that's one reason they gave me the creeps. The more amazing the stunts were, with super-intelligent mammals performing circus tricks for us humans, the dumber I felt. I had subjected my daughter to a contrived spectacle just a mile from the natural wonders of the open sea. Did I really want her to think that wild animals exist for our amusement, or that it's OK to ride a killer whale as if it were a pony? Soon after, I talked about it with my cousin, a marine biologist. The general rationalization by marine parks, he said, is that the shows raise public interest in the mammals and enhance conservation efforts.

Those claims strike me as dubious after the death last week of an Orlando SeaWorld trainer who was grabbed by her ponytail and slain by a killer whale before an audience. The same killer whale had been involved in two other deaths, and orca shows were temporarily halted in Orlando and San Diego. Now officials are investigating the death and prior incidents in Orlando, even as the shows have resumed and crowds have returned.

"We stand very strongly behind the fact, and our surveys bear this out, that people are coming here and gaining a greater appreciation for these animals and the ocean environments they live in," said Dave Koontz, a San

Diego SeaWorld spokesman. "The fact that they have an opportunity to see these animals in person makes a huge difference," he says.

But aren't they seeing something artificial?

"We don't feel that there's anything about it that's artificial at all," Koontz told me. I don't think he was kidding.

Look, I'd agree that many of the exhibits at the San Diego marine park are legitimate educational tools—although if you want to really learn something about sea creatures, you're far better off going to the Aquarium of the Pacific in Long Beach or the Monterey Bay Aquarium. But the big draws at parks like those in the SeaWorld chain, which was just bought for $2.7 billion, are the killer whale and dolphin shows.

It's not about education, it's about big business, says Ric O'Barry, who you may have seen in *The Cove*, the Oscar-nominated documentary that exposed the secret slaughter of thousands of dolphins in Japan—and how a few of the most beautiful mammals are spared and sold to marine parks.

"It's a form of bad education," O'Barry says of theme park shows. "There's no connection between conservation and stupid dolphin tricks."

O'Barry traveled a long way to get to that point of view. He caught and trained the dolphins used on the TV show *Flipper*, and he has been credited with training one of the first killer whales used in a show.

"I was as ignorant as I could be for as long as could be, and I was making a lot of money," says O'Barry, who told me he used to lug a television down to the docks "so Flipper could watch himself on TV on Friday nights at 7:30."

O'Barry says he eventually learned enough about the mammals, which depend on sound waves to navigate, to know they were suffering in captivity, subjected to unnatural confines and bombarded by noise for the sake of human entertainment. He believes that one of the dolphins used in *Flipper* committed suicide by refusing to come up for air.

"I got tired of being a professional liar," O'Barry says. "You have to lie about education and research."

If you go to the San Diego Zoo, he said, you'll note that a snake at least has a relatively natural habitat. "There's some grass and tree limbs, and he can climb under rocks to get away from the public. If you go to SeaWorld and put your head under the water and look around, there's a concrete box," O'Barry says.

Gwen Goodmanlowe, a marine biology lecturer at Cal State Long Beach, says there is some legitimate research at SeaWorld. "But I don't think there's enough to counteract the captivity," she adds, arguing that killer whales can travel hundreds of miles daily in the ocean. She thinks it's cruel to confine them to small enclosures.

J. William Gibson, author of *A Reenchanted World: The Quest for a New Kinship with Nature,* says he thinks O'Barry's evolution and my own regret about taking my daughter to SeaWorld are part of a movement toward a human relationship with nature that's more harmonious and less dominating. To put it another way, Gibson says watching captive whales and dolphins perform is "not a good way for us to express our appreciation of wild animals."

If you want a more natural experience than, say, Dine with Shamu, hook up with Heal the Bay for a whale-watching adventure on Santa Monica Bay. Or go to the beach and wait for the dolphins to come by.

For me, seeing them in their element is an unbeatable show filled with mystery and wonder, and admission is free.

GRACE NOTES

A Bright Future Bought with
Hard Work and Tacos

(May 30, 2003)

I am a man of simple pleasures, one of which is driving around Southern California with the windows down, searching for restaurants that throw off the right scent.

Several years ago, on Pico just east of Bundy in West L.A., I swerved to a stop after passing Talpa. I may not know much, but I know how a proper Mexican restaurant is supposed to smell from the street, and this one had the right look, too. Very little money had been sunk into the exterior design. Inside, the joint was just as unpretentious. Formica table tops, artificial plants, a mural of rural Mexico.

I headed for the bar and ordered a fat burrito and a cold beer from a man named Andres Martinez. The Dodgers were on TV, a warm summer breeze was blowing in through the back alley, and I felt like a dog having its belly scratched.

I don't get to Talpa often enough. But in bits and pieces for several years, usually during Dodger games, Andres has been telling me a story. It began when I told him I had lived in Philadelphia.

"Oh," Andres said. "My daughter is in Philadelphia. She's in medical school."

He was obviously a proud papa, but his modesty kept him from gloating. Over time, I picked up on the fact that he and his wife, Guillermina, were both working at Talpa to keep up with the cost of tuition. On another visit, Andres, who has a sixth-grade education, told me his daughter was just about done with law school at Loyola.

"I thought she was going to be a doctor," I said.

"That's the other daughter," Andres told me. "This one's going to be a lawyer."

He and his wife, who didn't finish high school, were paying for that, too, on the proceeds from this little hole-in-the-wall restaurant. A doctor and a lawyer, I thought. That's a lot of tacos.

"At $1.95 a taco?" Andres said. "Yes, that's a lot of tacos."

Last week, with the Dodgers on TV and summer finally beginning to come around, I went back to Talpa. Andres was busy at the bar, so I talked to Guillermina first. She and her two sisters—Nelly and Evie—have run Talpa with Andres for 30 years. Was it true, I asked Guillermina, that she and Andres had already paid off all the loans for law school and medical school? Yes, she said. As soon as the girls were born, they started putting away $10 a week, upping the ante as business improved.

"When they were both in college," she said, "Andres and I worked seven days a week for five straight years."

I don't have to tell you why. It's the familiar story of immigrants wanting a better life for their children. Andres, who was born in Jalisco, Mexico, worked at Casa Escobar on Pico as a young man. In 1963, he used to stop by another Pico Boulevard restaurant, called Reboso, before work and buy a cup of coffee. He had a crush on the waitress.

"Coffee was 15 cents, and he always left a dollar," says Guillermina, who was from Zacatecas, Mexico.

It took Andres two months of big tips to get up the nerve to ask her out. They went to see *Cleopatra* on their first date and got married two years later, saving up to buy Talpa at about the time Maritza and Cynthia were born. The girls both went to St. Joan of Arc, followed by Notre Dame Academy, with Maritza going to UCLA as an undergrad and Cynthia to Georgetown.

"We believed always in education," says Andres. "We believed that if you don't have it, you don't have a chance in this country."

The girls were often at the restaurant, but their parents wouldn't let them work there. They told them their only job was to pay attention in school.

"I wasn't allowed to come home with Bs," says Maritza, 32, an ob-gyn in her last year of residency at Abington Memorial Hospital near Philadelphia.

"A-minuses were OK, but they weren't really satisfied. They wanted us to never suffer or struggle like they did when they first came to this country."

Cynthia, 30, works for a big law firm in downtown Los Angeles. "We wouldn't be where we are without them," she said. "It's as simple as that."

Andres said he and his wife finally paid off the student loans a few years ago.

"It feels very good to make that last payment," he said. Going to his daughters' graduations felt even better.

"What happened to my kids is a real big thing," he said. "When I went to Philadelphia for my first daughter's graduation, and they announced her name, I cried. I was just a little guy from a small town in Mexico, San Gaspar de Los Reyes, Jalisco."

Andres is 65 now, and with all the bills paid, I wondered if he and Guillermina would finally give themselves a break and sell Talpa. Maybe, he said, because although he loves his family of regular customers, 30 years is a long hustle. But on the other hand, there's no rush to retire. Cynthia has a child now, Andres said, and he and Guillermina are expecting big things for little Lucia, who is eight months old.

"We've started a college fund for her," he said.

A Busboy Remembers
Bobby Kennedy

(June 1, 2003)

When you write stories for three decades, occasionally someone asks if you had a favorite. I never did until five years ago, when I met Juan Romero. An editor at *Life* magazine had asked if I remembered the busboy who knelt at Bobby Kennedy's side on June 5, 1968, when he was shot at the Ambassador Hotel in Los Angeles. Of course I remembered. The photos of that skinny kid in the angelic white service coat, cradling Kennedy, were searing.

Go find him, said the editor.

Romero wasn't hard to track down. I found him doing hard labor in San Jose, his strong hands calloused by years of toil for a paving company. But 30 years after the assassination, he was still haunted by that night, and talking about it was not one of his favorite things to do. We went out for a couple of beers, and Romero began squirming and twisting himself up. When he finally found a way to let it out, it was for his own sake as much as mine.

Thursday marks the 35th anniversary of the Kennedy assassination, so last week, I went to visit Romero again in San Jose. The father of four, now 53, was pouring concrete under a merciless sun. When he got off duty, we went out for a cold one, just like last time, and Juan Romero revisited the day that has shaped his life. It was Juan's stepfather, an Ambassador waiter, who got him the job. Juan, whose family moved to Los Angeles from Mexico when he was 10, had been flirting with trouble in his East L.A. neighborhood, and his stepdad's solution was to get him off the streets.

"I wore black pants and a white shirt to Hollenbeck Junior High every day," says Juan, who caught the bus for the Ambassador after school. The routine continued when he moved on to Roosevelt High. Juan worked room service and met scads of celebrities in the Ambassador's glory days, but for him, the arrival of presidential candidate Bobby Kennedy during the 1968 California primary topped the charts.

Juan remembered photos of John F. Kennedy on the walls of homes in Mexico—"next to the Pope and the crucifix"—and he knew Bobby Kennedy had championed the cause of California farm workers. "Bobby rolled up his sleeves and walked with them," Juan says.

When Kennedy checked into the Ambassador and called for room service, Juan, then 17, cut a deal with the busboy who drew the job. Juan would retrieve all the other guy's trays that night in return for the Kennedy job.

"He wouldn't do it," Juan remembers of his stubborn colleague. "So I said, 'All right. I'll pay you too.'"

A Kennedy assistant answered the door of the Presidential Suite, and Juan, his eyes wide, pushed the food cart into the room and found himself standing next to Kennedy.

"He shook my hand as hard as anyone had ever shaken it," Juan says. "I walked out of there 20 feet tall, thinking, 'I'm not just a busboy, I'm a human being.' He made me feel that way."

The next night, Kennedy won the California primary. He made his victory speech at the Ambassador and headed through the kitchen to escape the crush of people, but there was a crowd in there, too. Juan, who wanted to congratulate him, used his skinny frame to knife through the pressed bodies. This man was going to be the next president, Juan thought, and he wanted to see if he could shake his hand once more.

"People were six and seven deep," Juan says, but he got close enough to stick out his hand. As Kennedy grabbed it, Juan heard a bang and felt a flash of heat against his face. Sirhan Sirhan, the assassin, had fired from just off Juan's shoulder.

"I thought it was firecrackers at first, or a joke in bad taste," says Juan, but then he saw Kennedy sprawled on the floor and knelt to help him up. "He was looking up at the ceiling, and I thought he'd banged his head. I asked, 'Are you OK? Can you get up?' One eye, his left eye, was twitching, and one leg was shaking."

Juan slipped a hand under the back of Kennedy's head to lift him and felt warm blood spilling through his fingers. "People were screaming, 'Oh my God, not another Dallas!'"

Ethel Kennedy knelt down at her husband's side and pushed Juan away. Juan looked on, angry and stunned, fingering the rosary beads in his pocket.

"When I was in trouble, I would always go and pray to God to make my stepfather forget what I'd done, or to keep me out of trouble the next time. I asked Ethel if I could give Bobby the rosary beads, and she didn't stop me. She didn't say anything. I pressed them into his hand but they wouldn't stay because he couldn't grip them, so I tried wrapping them around his thumb. When they were wheeling him away, I saw the rosary beads still hanging off his hand."

Juan was taken to the Rampart police station and questioned about what he saw and what he knew. He was released, still trembling, headed for home, and went to school the next day. It was at Roosevelt High that he saw Kennedy's blood under his fingernails, and decided not to wash his hands.

"Then the mail started coming to the hotel," Juan says. "Sacks and sacks of mail. You couldn't believe the amount of it." Most of it was supportive, addressed to the anonymous busboy. It was a kind of celebrity Juan never asked for or wanted, and he grew apprehensive about hotel guests asking to see him. He also heard from a handful of lunatics asking why he didn't take the bullet himself, or telling him Kennedy would still be alive if he hadn't stopped to shake Juan's hand.

Juan left Los Angeles for Santa Barbara. He returned briefly to the Ambassador, but was finally driven away by ghosts. He worked at a hotel in Wyoming, then relocated to San Jose and married. He settled comfortably into family life but lived with the cruel, nagging conviction that he'd been thrown into the path of history for a reason, and he hadn't been up to the challenge. Juan was convinced he was supposed to find a way to express the hope Kennedy represented for him, but he couldn't find the words.

During the debate over California's Proposition 187, he felt that people were taking one look at his brown skin and figuring him for a freeloader. He wanted to scream that the ballot initiative was proof we needed another Kennedy, but he couldn't find a stage. And that was just fine, because to remember that day in 1968, Juan ended up doing something more elegant and true. He took the faith expressed in that first handshake from Kennedy and honored the memory by working hard, providing for his family and living a life of tolerance and good deeds.

He doesn't always get it right. Juan's wife tells him he does so many odd jobs for others, it often comes at the expense of time with the family. Maybe so, but Juan has to help those he can. And he has to keep moving, hurrying from one job to another like a man being chased. Especially around this time of year.

"For words to come out of my mouth that express how I really feel is so hard," Juan says, his eyes filling. "After years and years and years to think about what to say about that night, I can't figure out anything that does justice."

I tell him, once again, that he has said all the right things.

The Right to Die
Is a Personal Matter

(March 23, 2005)

I'm praying, I'm begging, I'm even offering money. If by some unexpected turn I end up hospitalized in a vegetative state with virtually no chance of recovery, please kill me. I'm hereby putting out a contract on myself, offering $1,000, a pair of field-level Dodger tickets and my bowling trophy to the first person who storms the hospital and sends me into the Great Beyond.

Pull the plug. Put a pillow over my head. Make me watch Bill O'Reilly. Whatever it takes. (Note to doctors: Feel free to harvest any of my organs that might keep someone else alive, although I'd steer clear of the liver.) I'm asking for reader assistance in case nobody believes my wife when she says I authorized her to yank my feeding tube.

I don't want the courts, Congress, the President of the United States or anyone who goes around waving photos of aborted fetuses to decide what's morally appropriate for me. Don't get me wrong. Abortion is a tragedy, and so is the act of pulling the plug on a brain-damaged human being.

I'm not suggesting the Florida case of Terri Schiavo isn't a can of worms, legally and morally, with her husband and parents in disagreement about whether the brain-damaged woman's feeding tube should have been removed. In fact, I'm with those who argue it's cruel to let Schiavo slowly starve while we all stand around on national death watch. If the decision is that she has a right to die, why aren't we evolved enough to make it happen as quickly and humanely as possible?

The Schiavo case stands as a reminder to get my own living will in order. If I can't tell the difference between my baby daughter and a bag of groceries, God forbid, and if my only movements and expressions are random and involuntary, I'd rather not hang around, thank you.

Start the cyanide drip. Better yet, make it a lethal dose of tequila. In lieu of flowers, send a donation to the Hemlock Society, or whatever they call it now.

I just saw the movie *The Sea Inside*, in which an alert and intelligent quadriplegic begs family, friends and the Spanish government to let him die. His loved ones are all conflicted for obvious reasons. How could they deliver a lethal blow to a man with so much grace and wit that women still keep falling in love with him?

He doesn't advocate his choice for other disabled people, the quadriplegic says. To each his own. But he has decided, after being immobile for 27 years following a diving accident, that he would rather die with dignity than continue suffering with the memories of a full and active life. He also insists that no one but he should have the right to determine his fate. No judge, no government, no religion has a monopoly on virtue. The quadriplegic finally tells an admirer there is only one way she can prove her love for him. Amen.

Dying doesn't scare me as much as the idea of staring past the people I live for. Look, if I'm in bad shape but there's a realistic chance I might one day be up and around, by all means, do everything possible to save me, and don't be afraid to overbill Blue Cross. But if I were no more alert than a cucumber, the last thing I'd want is for my family to stand vigil day after day, month after month, year after year, as nurses change my bedpan every few hours.

I appreciate life too much to have them sacrifice theirs.

Violinist Has the World
on Two Strings

(April 17, 2005)

Nathaniel was shy in our first encounter a few months ago, if not a little wary. He took a step back when I approached to say I liked the way his violin music turned the clatter around downtown L.A.'s Pershing Square into an urban symphony. "Oh, thank you very much," he said politely, apologizing for his appearance. He had gone through a couple of recent setbacks, Nathaniel said, but he intended to be whole again soon and playing at a higher level. Next time I saw him, he had relocated to the mouth of the 2nd Street tunnel near Hill Street.

"Well, first of all, it's beautiful here," said Nathaniel, 54, who told me he had been diagnosed many years ago with schizophrenia. "And right there is the Los Angeles Times building. New York, Cleveland, Los Angeles. All I have to do is look up at that building and I know where I am."

Nathaniel had an orange shopping cart that contained all of his belongings, including a huge plastic water gun, a single black boot and his violin case. We were practically in the shadow of the new Disney Concert Hall, and although Nathaniel said he wasn't sure where it was, he had written the following on the side of his shopping cart: "Little Walt Disney Concert Hall—Beethoven."

Nathaniel plays classical music, some of it recognizable to me, some of it not. One day, I asked if he could play jazz, and he tucked the violin under his chin, closed his eyes in anticipation of the ecstasy that music brings him and began to play "Summertime." He doesn't always hit every note, but it's abundantly clear that Nathaniel has been a student of music for many years.

"That was Ernest Bloch," he casually told me after one piece, spelling out Ernest and then Bloch. "Opus 18, No. 1." I was more than a little impressed, especially when it occurred to me that Nathaniel's grimy, smudged violin was missing two of the four strings.

"Yeah," he said, frustration rising in his brown eyes. "This one's gone, that one's gone and this little guy's almost out of commission. You see where it's coming apart right here?" Playing with two strings wasn't that hard, he said, because he began his music education in the Cleveland public schools, where the instruments were often a challenge. "If you got one with one or two strings," he said, "you were happy to have it."

I noticed an empty bag from Studio City Music in Nathaniel's violin case and gave the store a call to ask if they had a homeless customer. "Black man?" asked Hans Benning, a violin maker. "We do have a guy who plays with a badly beaten-up fiddle. He comes here every so often. He's very kind, very gentle and very proper. He's a delight." I told Benning his name is Nathaniel Anthony Ayers, and he seems to know a thing or two about music.

"Yes, he does," Benning said. "He talks about the Beethoven sonatas and then slips back into another world." The reason he used to hang around Pershing Square, Nathaniel told me, was so he could study the Beethoven statue for inspiration.

"I've never seen anything in my life that great," he said. "I'm flabbergasted by that statue because I can't imagine how he's there. I don't know how God is operating."

When I asked more about his training, Nathaniel told me he had gone to Ohio University and Ohio State University. He also said he'd played many times at the Aspen Music Festival, and he'd gone to Juilliard for two years in the early '70s.

Juilliard? I asked.

"I was there for a couple of years," he said, as if it were nothing.

While waiting for a callback from Juilliard, I called Motter's Music House in Lyndhurst, Ohio. Nathaniel told me he had bought many instruments there over the years, including the Glaesel violin he now owns.

"He's an outstanding player," said Ron Guzzo, a manager at Motter's.

He saw a lot of Nathaniel over a span of 20 years, because Nathaniel's instruments were often stolen from him on the streets. He would work at a Wendy's or shovel snow to save up for another.

"As I understand it, he was at Juilliard and got sick, so he came back home. He'd sit out in our parking lot on a nice day playing the cello, and we'd wonder where the heck that was coming from. It was Tony," Guzzo said, using Nathaniel's nickname.

Cello? Yes, it turns out Nathaniel started on the bass, switched to cello and has never had any training on the violin. He switched to the latter after ending up on the streets, because it fits more neatly into his shopping cart. Everything he had told me about his life was checking out, so I figured Juilliard must be for real, too.

Sure enough. Nathaniel Anthony Ayers, who sleeps on the streets of the city, takes his meals at the Midnight Mission and plays a two-string violin, attended the acclaimed New York City music school on a scholarship. Nathaniel told me a bass player named Homer Mensch was one of his mentors at Juilliard. Mensch, 91, is still teaching, and he immediately recalled Nathaniel.

"He had the talent, that was for sure," said Mensch, who remembered that Nathaniel had suddenly disappeared, never to return. I told him Nathaniel's illness had begun while he was at Juilliard and he was now a homeless violinist in downtown L.A. "Give him my very best," said Mensch. "I would certainly like to hear from him."

Nathaniel has memorized the phone numbers of the people who inspired him. To recall the numbers, he writes them in mid-air with his index finger. One day he gave me the home phone number of Harry Barnoff, a bass player and former teacher who recently retired after 46 years with the Cleveland Orchestra. Barnoff was in tears at the memory of Nathaniel.

"Please," Barnoff pleaded, "you have got to go tell him how much I think of him and that I still remember what a wonderful musician he was." Barnoff says Nathaniel was a bit of a slacker when he was in junior high and taking lessons at the Cleveland Music School Settlement. But with encouragement, Nathaniel set the highest possible goals for himself.

"During the riots, he was in the music building, practicing. He really worked at it and got to where he knew I had gone to Juilliard, and he wanted to go, too....Next thing I knew, he got a scholarship."

Nathaniel had the potential to play with any of the major orchestras in the United States, Barnoff said. He tried to help Nathaniel through his most difficult times, offering him work around his house and taking Nathaniel's calls from mental hospitals and the streets. Nathaniel was often in a state of distress, Barnoff says of his former student, until they began talking about music. And then everything was right with the world. "He once sent me a card saying he would give his left hand for me," Barnoff recalled.

I got hold of Nathaniel's sister, Jennifer Ayers-Moore, at her home in Fayetteville, Georgia. She was relieved to hear that her older brother is OK but disturbed to know he's on the streets—again. He was never the same after he got back from New York, Ayers-Moore said, and he has been in and out of hospitals and group homes for three decades. Time after time, he has tested the patience of the people who love him.

"It got to the point where he didn't want to talk to anybody and didn't want to be in reality. I couldn't watch the movie *A Beautiful Mind* because every stitch of it reminded me of Nathaniel."

As do so many schizophrenics, Ayers-Moore says, her brother would improve with medication but then refuse to take it and slip back into his tortured world. "It was very difficult for my mother, because he would curse her out, call her names, threaten her. When we went to visit her in the nursing home on her birthday, she looked at me and said, 'I miss Tony.' He was her pride and joy, and she did everything she possibly could to help him."

Nathaniel talks often of his mother, expressing his love in his own way.

"She was a beautician," he said. "That's beauty. And music is beauty, so I guess that's why I started playing." Nathaniel came west after his mother's death five years ago. He hooked up with his estranged father and other relatives but soon found the streets.

"It's an absolute dream here, and I notice that everyone is smiling," Nathaniel said at 2nd and Hill, where he sometimes steps into the tunnel to hear the echo of his violin. "The sun is out all day, and the nights are cool and serene."

Nathaniel often takes a rock and scrawls names on the sidewalk. "Oh, those," he said. "A lot of those are the names of my classmates at Juilliard."

One day I asked about his hopes and dreams. "Oh, that's easy," he said. "I need to get these other two strings, but I don't have the money right now." He had no use for a house, he said, or a car or anything else. "All I want is to play music, and the crisis I'm having is right here," Nathaniel said, pointing to the missing strings and calling out the names of Itzhak Perlman and Jascha Heifetz, as if the renowned violinists might hear his plea and send along the strings.

Nathaniel refused to accept money from me or freebies from Studio City Music. I suggested he go back to Pershing Square, where passersby often dropped money in his violin case, but it didn't seem logical to him. When I brought him a new set of strings from Studio City Music, I had to insist that he not pay me for them. He had trouble attaching the strings because his violin is in such bad shape. But by the next day, he had jury-rigged them and was happy to give me a show at his Little Walt Disney Concert Hall.

I had invited two staffers from Lamp Community, a service agency for homeless, mentally ill men and women. Maybe they could get his trust, I figured, and determine whether they could help him at some point. But as Nathaniel began to play, I doubted there was anyone or anything that could deliver the same peace that music brings him. He was in his sanctuary, eyes half-mast in tribute to the masters.

As cars roared by and trash flew off a dump truck, Nathaniel was oblivious. He played a Mendelssohn concerto, a Beethoven concerto and the Brahms double concerto for violin and cello, his bow gliding effortlessly as it sliced through the madness.

A Twilight Concerto
for Rats and Cello

(May 29, 2005)

I know only part of his story. I know him playing the cello on a dairy crate in the morning sun, suspended somewhere between boy genius and lost traveler.

But where does he go after dark? For answers, I've come to skid row in downtown Los Angeles to spend the evening with Nathaniel Anthony Ayers. The sun has dropped behind glittering skyscrapers, and hardened creatures roam the streets.

Strung-out prostitutes strut their way down trashed sidewalks. Fallen drunks are sprawled like bodies in the desert. Dozens of human forms disappear under piles of rags and casket-shaped cardboard boxes. Predators and hustlers lurk at the edges, tossing glances sharp as knives. Sewer smells mix in with the stench of urine, rotting food and unending stress.

No sign of Nathaniel yet on Los Angeles Street. This is his spot, he has told me. We were to meet at dusk. But dusk comes and goes. More than a dozen people have staked out their spots and turned in for the night. I wonder if he's decided to spend the night elsewhere. Nathaniel told me earlier about a savage beating that happened around here the other night. He didn't see the assault, but he saw the results.

"The guy's bones were rearranged in his face. I don't know why you'd beat a person like that. It makes no sense."

As I wait, a San Fernando Valley ministry serves chicken dinners to a long line of takers. Then the volunteers form a circle, call me to join hands with them and bow their heads in prayer. When the missionaries leave, a dazed blond woman caked in filth dials 911 on a pay phone. Sirens echo off concrete as two fire rescue crews approach.

"It's my heart," she tells the rescue crew, and the chief tells me they respond to calls like this repeatedly, night after night. The woman is loaded into a van and taken to the hospital.

I'm beginning to give up hope on Nathaniel when, around nine o'clock, I see the familiar orange shopping cart approach from a block away. Everything he owns after half a century is in that basket. The violin he bought in Cleveland is in there, along with the violin and cello donated to him by a reader from the Inland Empire.

Nathaniel has stopped under an apartment building, where live rock music is pouring out a second-floor window.

"You like the music?" I ask.

"You call that music?" Nathaniel responds.

He's classically trained. Boy wonder in Cleveland. Scholarship to Juilliard. And then 30 years of voices, demons, unexplainable outbursts, mental hospitals, antipsychotic drugs, missed opportunities and tormented, heartbroken, worn-out relatives.

Two dead palm fronds rise from the front of his basket, Jesus entering Jerusalem. At the rear, two sticks form an X. They are slid into the slots of a Ford hubcap, and Nathaniel has painted "Beethoven" on one and "Brahms" on the other.

Nathaniel rolls the cart down to his spot in front of a locked-down storefront.

"I know these guys," he says, pointing to half a dozen sprawled men who don't acknowledge his arrival. Nathaniel tells me that if a fight breaks out, he knows whom to count on, whom to run from, where to hide.

"Straight down that street is the police department," Nathaniel says. His survival skills are sharp after years on the streets, but he moves warily at times, and feels for the sawed-off wooden chair leg attached to his belt and hidden under a sweater tied around his waist. He remembers how that man looked after the horrible beating. Maybe it was a drug deal, he says, or a hustle gone bad.

"Did they have to beat him like that?" he asks.

I ask Nathaniel if he ever thinks about sleeping on safer streets, or cleaning up a bit and getting an apartment somewhere. No, he says. This is his turf.

"I'd rather die where I know my way around. I'm out here breathing fresh air, and I'm not trapped in some apartment, cooped up and unheard of."

This is exactly what's so frustrating about Nathaniel. He can sound so sensible, even eloquent. But his irrational choices reveal the depth of his mental illness. Nathaniel takes a cloth strap and lashes his shopping cart to the metal door of the storefront. Then he unpacks for the night, a ritual he performs while telling me the meaning of his music and his life.

"My vision—I hate to admit it—but I'm going to have to do what Mozart did, and die. My vision is to stay in good with God and not worry about far-off stuff, just get across the street safely and be thankful. Honor thy mother and father, don't be disrespectful to people, be good, and maybe the music will take care of itself." Not five feet away, a young, ashen-faced man slumps down and lights a crack pipe.

Helicopters chop up the night, an amputee rolls by in a wheelchair and Nathaniel chases away cockroaches the size of Volkswagens.

"My god doesn't have a special name," Nathaniel says without my asking. "Beethoven could be my god."

He'd been to the library earlier in the day looking for sheet music, carrying a list of the pieces he wants. A Brahms double concerto. Tchaikovsky's Variations on a Rococo Theme for cello and orchestra. Mendelssohn's Third and Fourth Symphonies. Sibelius' Symphony No. 2. Strauss' Don Quixote. He couldn't find them, but was thrilled to come away with Camille Saint-Saens' Concerto for Violoncello.

"There's something like 18 or 19 notes in a single pickup," he says with a child's awe. "It's very pleasing that Saint-Saens had all those ideas and was fast enough to get this all down." Out comes a whisk broom and Nathaniel, perhaps the most compulsively neat person I've ever met, sweeps the sidewalk where he intends to sleep. "Have to get all this nasty business out of here," he says. He's particularly disgusted by cigarette butts. The job done, he turns to me. "Welcome to my humble abode." Then Nathaniel reaches into the bottom of his cart and offers me a can of Shasta Tiki Punch soda.

"Care for a drink?"

I notice my name written in the center of a clock on which he's replaced the broken hands with a plastic fork and spoon. "You work for the *Times*," he explains, "and this is a timepiece." Out of the basket comes the cello, which he cradles as if it were his child, kneeling down and placing it gently against the wall.

"I'd go to war to defend it," he says. Next comes the violin, which goes on top of the cello, followed by several layers of blankets and then a tarp.

"Gotta protect those guys," Nathaniel says. Now he brings out the violin he bought several years ago in Cleveland at Motter's Music House.

"I use it for my pillow," he says, placing the encased violin on the ground against the wheels of his cart. He pulls the "Beethoven" stick out of the Ford hubcap and sets it upright against the cart.

"When the rodents come," he explains, "this guy takes care of them." I ask if he beats the rats.

"No, you tap it on the ground, like this. It scares them away." How about when you're sleeping? I ask. Instead of answering, he quotes Shakespeare.

"To be or not to be; that is the question...." I stand back, smiling.

Nathaniel gestures theatrically with a gloved hand, his shoulders riding the rhythm of the words. He forgets not a word, and his accent is pitch-perfect. It's Richard Burton's *Hamlet* in an exclusive skid row performance.

"For in that sleep of death what dreams may come when we have shuffled off this mortal coil...."

A piercing human howl rises from somewhere unknown. Next to us, a rail-thin man scratches maniacally, as if his skin were crawling with bugs. Salvagers come jangling through the streets, plucking away bottles and cans. Before bed, Nathaniel recites the Our Father, head bowed, then opens his eyes to see prostitutes trespassing on his prayers.

"I think these children of God are going to be OK," Nathaniel says. "They're going to sleep and dream, like human beings do."

A rat the size of a meatloaf has arrived on the scene, darting up out of the storm drain and heading toward us in search of food. Nathaniel taps the Beethoven stick and the beast retreats. Should I be more assertive, I wonder, in trying to steer Nathaniel out of skid row and into a residential program? Wouldn't a little arm-twisting be more humane than leaving him here on the streets, where decades of horrendous public policy have created a colony of lost souls?

As he prepares his bed, Nathaniel plays the gracious host and offers me his dairy crate.

"You can rest on there and put your head against the cart," he says.

Before he crawls under the covers, he has a comment. "I love to think about musicians," he says. "I can imagine Mozart or Beethoven sitting in a room up there with the light on. They hunger and thirst like we do. It's angelic." He sounds exhausted, but has one last thing to say.

"I hope you rest well, Mr. Lopez. I hope the whole world rests well."

From Skid Row to Disney Hall

(October 9, 2005)

Nathaniel was in a panic over what to wear. "I can't wear these grubby things," he said, taking stock of clothes that bore the stain of the streets. "I've washed them over and over, and that's the best I seem to be able to do."

For months, Nathaniel Anthony Ayers had been excited about an invitation to see the Los Angeles Philharmonic in action at Disney Hall. "The anticipation is horrible," he told me a week before the designated day. He'd started showering daily at a shelter, he said, to gussy himself up as much as possible.

Nathaniel was a music student more than 30 years ago at the prestigious Juilliard School when he suffered a breakdown. Today, as he continues to battle the schizophrenia that landed him on skid row, music is one of the few things that inspires and consoles him. He plays violin and cello for hours each day in downtown Los Angeles, lifting his instruments out of an orange shopping cart on which he has written: "Little Walt Disney Concert Hall—Beethoven."

Thursday was the big day. Nathaniel had decided it would be best to attend a rehearsal rather than a concert, because he didn't want to make a scene—a homeless man in the company of well-heeled Angelenos. He was particularly excited because the orchestra would be rehearsing Beethoven.

Nathaniel finally decided on fresh-washed burgundy sweatpants, a black T-shirt, a blue cardigan and white sneakers. He tied a red sweater around his waist and parted his hair in the middle, pasting it down neatly. But something was still bothering him Thursday morning before we left skid row. Nathaniel was talking to himself more than usual, spouting something about how a cockroach doesn't give orders to a thoroughbred. He refused to leave his cart at a shelter, as arranged, insisting on hauling it to my office parking lot, a 30-minute trek guaranteed to put us behind schedule.

I drove to my office to make the arrangements and then waited, fearing he'd get distracted and lose track of time. But just as I was writing him off, Nathaniel appeared in the distance, lugging his cart west on 2nd Street. He parked it in the garage, pulled out his violin and headed jauntily toward Disney Hall like a student on his way to school. At 2nd and Hill, where Nathaniel often plays against the clatter and percussion of incessant traffic, I mentioned that Itzhak Perlman would perform at Disney Hall later this month.

"Oh, my God," Nathaniel enthused. "He's like molten lava on violin."

The angry man I had seen on skid row continued to soften as we approached Disney Hall, the Frank Gehry creation Nathaniel referred to as an iron butterfly. The mysteries of his illness are so profound that I still find it impossible to reconcile the poetry with the madness. This is a man I've heard many times carry on incoherent conversations with someone who isn't there, only to then rhapsodize on the structure of a Mozart composition.

When he reached 1st and Grand, Nathaniel studied the performance schedule outside the hall, awed at the thought of the world's greatest musicians playing a mere two blocks from where he takes a bow and "saws away," as he calls it.

Adam Crane, the Los Angeles Philharmonic's director of public relations and an amateur cellist, greeted Nathaniel as if he were a visiting dignitary, handing him a copy of Gehry's book on Disney Hall. Crane reminded Nathaniel that the orchestra would be rehearsing Beethoven's Third Symphony.

"The Eroica," Nathaniel said, asking if they would play each movement, and delighted that they would. Crane asked Nathaniel when he had last set foot in a concert hall. Nathaniel laughed bashfully.

"I haven't been in a concert hall in four billion years," he said. Crane, who had read about Nathaniel's rise from Cleveland's public school music program and his ultimate fall, gave him a VIP tour. "We're right behind the stage right now," Crane said in the bowels of the auditorium.

"It's like a dream," Nathaniel said. "I don't know if this is a dream or purgatory."

A voice came over the P.A. system as we entered a long hallway, which Nathaniel said reminded him of the announcements in a Cleveland mental hospital.

Nathaniel asked about famed cellist Yo-Yo Ma, intrigued to know if he was a regular guy. Crane said he seemed quite nice indeed. Nathaniel also threw out the names of the conductors he remembered from his days at Juilliard: James Conlon, Lorin Maazel and Herbert von Karajan, no longer seeming like the man who an hour earlier had delivered a skid row rumination on cockroaches.

"Do you know Dvořák's Cello Concerto?" Nathaniel asked.

"It's one of my favorites," Crane said. He told Nathaniel he had a Czechoslovakian cello made in 1875. Nathaniel was impressed.

"I don't wanna mess with it," he said. "I don't even want to look at it. I'll just wear dark glasses."

It was almost as if he were a student again, joshing with a classmate. Was Nathaniel being sly, fishing for an invitation to have a go at Crane's cello? If so, it worked. And when Crane offered, Nathaniel didn't hesitate. He sat in Crane's office tuning up, the PR man marveling at the sharpness of Nathaniel's ear. And then he played, without the bow at first, picking the strings with his right hand. It was Bach's Cello Suite No. 1: Prelude. Several Philharmonic staffers heard the music and wandered over, peering in to see a man of the streets, tattered and elegant, close his eyes and drift into ecstasy.

Nathaniel was still floating as we made our way toward the hall, where the orchestra was gathering. "Stage Level Door 1," read the sign in front of us.

"Are you ready?" Crane asked.

Yes, he was ready, and he was certainly impressed by the hall—a stunning monument to his sustaining passion. But it was the musicians who drew his eye, the hallowed messengers of the gods he worships.

A cellist named Peter Snyder came over to say hello to Nathaniel, whom he had read about. Nathaniel mentioned a resemblance to Hungarian-born cellist Janos Starker and marveled at Snyder's 33-year career with the orchestra. Snyder returned the compliment, mentioning Nathaniel's own record of survival on the streets.

"I just want to play," Nathaniel said. "I'll live underneath a rock."

Nathaniel took a seat front and center in the orchestra tier for a rehearsal that would amount to a private concert.

"They look so happy," he said as the musicians tuned. "I would be happy, too, if I was going to play the Third Symphony, especially with good players. You look over at the next player and say, 'Wow.'"

On most days, Nathaniel goes to Pershing Square to study the Beethoven statue for inspiration. On this day, he leaned into me during the first movement and whispered that Beethoven was with us in Disney Hall.

"He's in the room," Nathaniel said later as the funeral march began, a low, creeping dirge. "If his spirit was in the room, it would be somewhere around there. Do you see the conductor? That's Beethoven. He will interpret Beethoven. He is Beethoven."

Nathaniel listened intently, a student at times, an unabashed fan at others. He nodded, swayed, giggled with joy, and now and then conducted the orchestra with an imaginary baton. The Third Symphony is charged with thunderous bursts that collapse in tender reflection and then rage again, the song of Nathaniel's life.

"They are flawless, flawless, flawless players," he whispered in unabashed awe. "Every single note is there. There's not any nonsense. Of course, this is a world-renowned orchestra."

When the rehearsal ended, Nathaniel had one word for the triumph he had witnessed.

"Bravo."

Yes, he said, he'd be delighted to meet the conductor. Esa-Pekka Salonen graciously accepted Nathaniel's compliments and gave him an autograph.

Nathaniel also chatted up Ben Hong, assistant principal cellist, on the genius of Beethoven and the physical and emotional challenges of the Third Symphony.

As it turned out, there had been no need for me to worry about how Nathaniel would handle the day or whether he would be troubled by the sight of people living a life that once seemed within his reach. He was gracious and self-assured, a perfect gentleman.

I now know, after several months of trying to coax him toward a safer and more productive life, that Nathaniel won't be saved any time soon. The man who was back in his element at the concert hall on the hill is also comfortable sleeping on skid row, where he chases away rats with a stick on which he has scrawled Beethoven's name.

But Nathaniel has his own idea of salvation, and he removed it now from the violin case he had been carrying. He stood near the stage after the musicians had left and tuned his instrument. Then Nathaniel Anthony Ayers, in the concert of his life, tucked the violin under his chin and played Disney Hall.

Behind Each Letter, a Life

(November 27, 2005)

For 60 of his 84 years, Frank Ramirez has lived on West Broadway in San Gabriel, just past the old mission in the center of the historic district. I drove there Friday morning to answer, in person, a letter he had written to me. Sometimes it feels as though I'm losing ground in responding to readers who write or call. On the holiday weekend, it seemed appropriate to offer all those people both an apology and a thank-you, as well as to highlight one of many who took the time to write.

In Ramirez's letter, which I drew randomly from a box, he told me a few things about himself. He fought under General George S. Patton and was wounded in the Battle of the Bulge on Christmas Eve in 1944. He ran Panchito's restaurant in San Gabriel for 37 years and won "hundreds of awards!" And he was very disturbed by the tales of suffering in my series on downtown L.A.'s skid row.

"Hoping to hear from you," he wrote in longhand on lined paper, signing his letter "Sinceramente, Frank W. Ramirez."

Ramirez answered the door of the little GI stucco home he bought after World War II, offered a big handshake and a bigger smile, and led me directly to the kitchen table where he spends hours a day writing letters and organizing the history of his life. Queenie the cat and Baby Dolly the Chihuahua were at his feet, along with stacks of folders and envelopes.

He showed me a copy of the letter he had written to me, but it wasn't a photocopy. Ramirez doesn't have a computer or a copy or fax machine. When he writes a letter to the President of the United States to complain about the rising cost of medical care for people on fixed incomes, or a letter to anyone else for that matter, Ramirez then pens a second copy for his personal files.

"That's why it takes up so much time," said Margaret, his wife of 66 years. "It's late sometimes when I go to bed, and he's still here writing."

They met on Olvera Street, by the way, a couple of local kids, born and raised. "He was clean and not fancy," Margaret said when I asked how Frank managed to sweep her off her feet. "I didn't trust boys. They'd say, 'Prove how much you love me,' but they didn't know who they were dealing with."

Sixty-six years, five children, 12 grandchildren and seven great-grand-children later, they're still happy to be together.

"Never argue," Ramirez advised me out of his wife's presence. "That's the key, because nobody ever wins an argument."

Every time he made a point, Ramirez gently grabbed my arm or poked me, his warm and expressive brown eyes peering over the tops of gold-rimmed specs. He said he couldn't wait to show me the history of his life in photos, then he squeezed my arm and led me into his den. The first thing to catch my eye was the large glass case with Ramirez's Purple Heart and other medals, along with news clippings about the war.

"Patton would come up to the front lines, and he could speak Spanish," Ramirez told me. "You know, he was from here in San Gabriel."

The Battle of the Bulge was one of the bloodiest confrontations of World War II, with 19,000 Americans killed while countering Hitler's last-ditch attempt to turn back the Allied advance. Ramirez, fighting with the 5th Infantry Division, remembers the freezing cold as well as thoughts of his wife and two children back home in L.A.

"The Germans had us pinned down with machine guns," Ramirez said, crouching to show his position and tapping me on the arm to make sure I was paying attention. He's diabetic and walks with a stoop, but is in pretty good shape otherwise. "I didn't even know I'd been shot. One of the guys tells me, 'Hey, Frank, you're bleeding.'" It was a minor wound to his fore-arm, but enough to get him shipped to Paris and then England for treatment. When he got back to the front lines, the war was just about over.

A Cal-Vet loan got Ramirez into the house, which had a sticker price of

$10,000. He worked with his brother George at Alhambra Patio for years, and then, with no experience and going on nothing more than a whim, he opened Panchito's in 1956.

"My father was a stonemason and he always told me, 'Whatever you do in life, do it your best,' and that's what I did," Ramirez said, showing me photos of the restaurant where he worked 14-hour days and was known to generations of loyal customers as "Mr. Panchito," the genial gent in traditional Mexican garb.

"You should have tasted the beef. It was aged for two to four days and marinated in a blend of 18 ingredients. We were known for our steaks."

He became known as a guy who could be tapped to join service groups like the Kiwanis and serve on this commission or that. He was also known to write checks and lead fundraisers for everything from muscular dystrophy to Salesian schools. Ramirez admired President Kennedy and, in particular, Ronald Reagan, who as governor appointed Ramirez to the commission of the El Pueblo de Los Angeles State Historical Monument.

"I think he's a very proud man," Cindy Morales said of her father. "He really does love that feeling of giving."

At one time Ramirez had 60 restaurant employees, but rising overhead costs hit hard, and Ramirez said business slumped when the Asian population of San Gabriel grew and the white population decreased. Panchito's, which closed in 1993, is now a Chinese restaurant. Back when he was trying to keep Panchito's open, Ramirez borrowed against his home, and now, 60 years after moving in, he owes more than $100,000 on the house he bought for $10,000. After paying the monthly mortgage, there's not much left of the $2,000 Social Security check, but even at that, he still makes donations to his favorite causes.

"He's a giver," said Margaret Ramirez, seated near a plaque that reads, The Lord is my shepherd, I shall not want. "Money is important," she added, casting an eye around a room that could maybe use some fresh paint. "But it's not our God."

"You know what I think?" Ramirez interjected, telling me he doesn't think there are enough rehab programs and other services for the skid row population he wrote to me about. "I'd like to donate $10. If everybody else in Los Angeles did the same thing, don't you think that could make a big difference?"

He led me out back to the garage, where he keeps more memories stowed. His backyard has an arbor covered with a grapevine snipped from his restaurant, a vine that originated at the San Gabriel Mission, established in 1771. Ramirez didn't have big plans for the rest of the day, but in the house, I noticed he had already penned four more pages of a follow-up letter to me. It was filled with more memories, the story of a small garden, well-kept.

"That's part of history," Ramirez said, "and if I don't write it down, it's gone."

Looking for an End to Her Skid

(May 7, 2006)

Six days a week at seven in the morning, a gray Dodge Neon pulls up to a bluff overlooking the beach in Playa del Rey. The driver, a bespectacled 71-year-old woman named Lee Sevilla, is accompanied by her shaggy dog, Sandy. The two of them have lived in a car for more than eight years. She never would have imagined it, said the silver-haired Sevilla. She was a wife and mother with a pretty normal life until a divorce and a couple of bad breaks put her on the street. It seemed like a temporary setback at the time, but the weeks became months and the months continue to drag on.

Sevilla sleeps in nearby El Segundo, where she pulls up to the same parking spot beside a public ball field each night and settles in. At dawn she uses the restroom at the nearby Chevron station, then buys a cup of coffee and drives to Playa. It boosts her spirits, she explained, to start each day with a million-dollar ocean view.

"It's wonderful," she said, looking out over Dockweiler State Beach, near the edge of LAX. "If it's clear I can see from Malibu to Palos Verdes, and sometimes Catalina. You can see the dolphins from up here, too."

The one day she's not there is Sunday. That's when she pulls her church clothes off the hanger in the back seat of the Neon, goes to services at the Crystal Cathedral in Garden Grove, then splurges on a $45 room at a Motel 6 in Santa Ana. Don't tell anyone, but she sneaks in a hot plate to cook spaghetti, her one big meal of the week. As for the Crystal Cathedral, "I'm not overly religious," Sevilla said. "But I do depend on Him more lately." Three days before I met her, in fact, she opened her journal one morning on the sea bluff, took pen in hand and addressed a note skyward.

"You know, God, I'm getting too old for this," she wrote. "It's getting harder and harder, and I can't seem to get out of this rut."

When a reader in Playa del Rey suggested I track down Sevilla, I thought I'd find yet another L.A. story of hard luck in the shadow of conspicuous riches. But this one stands out: a great-grandmother who worked her whole life, avoids trips to the doctor because she can't afford the Medicare deductibles and has to sleep with a foot on the brake.

Sevilla is from Long Beach but moved to Chicago with her husband. When the marriage came apart in the late 1960s, she raised her three kids by working as an interior designer. She returned to California in 1989, following two of her children, but found it difficult to get decent pay for honest work. She wondered if her age—mid-50s at the time—was beginning to weigh against her. A daughter took her in, but the apartment was cramped and Sevilla felt uncomfortable about imposing. When the daughter got married, Sevilla packed her bags, determined to make it on her own and confident that she would.

"It's my responsibility to take care of myself," she said, but that was easier said than done. She found part-time jobs, but with a developing heart condition, she couldn't be on her feet for more than a few hours at a time. For a while, she ended up sacked out at her son's place in Irvine. But he had been in a terrible car accident, suffered brain damage and felt horribly depressed about the burden he'd become.

On Christmas Eve in 1998, Sevilla asked her son to accompany her to church, but he wasn't feeling up to it. The next day, he went off by himself, put a gun to his head and took his life. He was 40. That's when Sevilla found herself living in the car, wounded, distraught, scared. She couldn't believe the depth of her fall, nor could she handle the dismissive stares from people who wondered what kind of loser ends up living in a beat-up Mercury with 300,000 miles on it. Just hang in there, she told herself. Another week, maybe a month.

"I thought it was temporary. But it just keeps going."

The situation is awful, said her daughter, who still lives in the same cramped apartment in El Segundo. But her mother won't accept help, except for occasional loans, and is stubbornly determined to fix her own problems.

"I worry about her sleeping in that car," her daughter said. "I think about her all the time."

Six months ago, Sevilla answered an ad in the *El Segundo Herald* for a part-time receptionist. She showed up for her interview at the small, home-based company that refinishes bathroom countertops and furnishings, and got the job on the spot. "It pays $10 an hour, which is really pretty good," she said. "And I love the people." Her employers don't know, by the way, that she has lived in the Neon for three years, having moved up from the Mercury. But the job is only 16 hours a week, and Sevilla clears less than $600 a month. Combined with her $480 Social Security check, it's not enough to get her into an apartment.

"If I could figure out how to make another $500 a month, I think I'll be fine. But you just do the best you can. I think a lot of people don't realize how close they are to being like this. You lose one or two paychecks and it can happen quickly."

Sevilla went to a shelter once but it wasn't for her, and she doesn't care to venture to skid row in downtown Los Angeles, where most of the homeless services are. Nor does she care to take a bed that could go to a woman with young children, even if some kind of transitional housing opened up. Her options are further limited because of Sandy, but there is no way she is ditching the Lhasa-terrier mix she picked up at the pound 10 years ago. "I don't know if I would have gotten through this without her," she said.

To look at Sevilla, you'd never guess she lives in a four-door economy car. Her shoulder-length hair has a nice wave and her clothes don't look like they were pulled out of the trunk. Over lunch at Café Milan in Playa del Rey, she wore a teal-colored El Segundo T-shirt and looked nearly a decade younger than 71. "I do keep myself clean and neat," she said. It's a matter of pride, she told me. She wants to project a look that says: This is not going to get the best of me.

When she leaves the beach each morning, Sevilla goes back to the Chevron station and gives herself a quick sponge bath in the restroom before work. It's not the greatest setup, but when she gets to the Motel 6 on Sunday and steps into the shower, it's like being at a spa.

"I'll tell you something: There are a lot of people out there living in their cars," Sevilla said. It's no wonder, she adds, when you look at the price of a one-bedroom apartment, let alone a house.

"I just don't understand how we can go to Iraq and build up that country, but not be able to figure out how to get homeless people off the streets or build affordable housing."

Still, Sevilla is sure that she's one break away from getting a place of her own. About 10 years ago, she answered a lifelong dream, got a student loan and took a few art classes at UCLA. "I discovered I've got a gift," she said, proudly showing me her pencil sketches of wildlife and domestic animals. "If only I could figure out how to make something happen with it now. I seem to be in a rut there too."

After she gets off work, Sevilla motors over to the El Segundo Public Library on Main Street to work on her drawings. Employees and patrons were so impressed, they began bringing in photos for her to sketch, and she's good enough to command $60 for a print. For an additional $20, she'll make 12 postcards on handsome stock, using her laptop as a print shop.

"She's an amazing woman, and so talented," said Roz Templin, a library assistant who, along with a colleague by the name of Kimberlee Carter, is trying to arrange an exhibit of Sevilla's work at the library. Templin said she can identify with Sevilla's financial problems. She works two part-time jobs herself, helps cover the bill at her mother's assisted-living home and wishes her pay went up as often as her rent. "To be honest," Templin said, "I'm living paycheck to paycheck myself."

After the library, Sevilla generally drives a few blocks to the area between the park and the gas station. The other day, she had a Post-it sticker on the console of her Neon. "Ice," it said, reminding her to reload the Igloo she dips into at night to make a sandwich for dinner. She eats at the park, then drives to the Rite-Aid parking lot and plugs in a five-inch TV powered by the car battery. The reception is better at the drugstore, where she watches the local news, followed by the nightly news, and then scans the *L.A. Times*. She said her heart filled when she read that my friend Nathaniel, who lived on the streets of downtown Los Angeles for years, had moved into an apartment. "Good for him," Sevilla said.

And that's the thing, she added. Every time she gets down, she thinks about all the people who are worse off. She's not mentally ill, she's not hooked on drugs or alcohol. At least she's got a car and a few bucks. It will get better, she tells herself. It will get better. And El Segundo isn't a bad place to be if you're homeless. She feels safe, she told me, and looked after. "I feel like a member of the community."

Sevilla makes one last trip to the Chevron before turning in, then drives to her spot and rearranges the car, clearing enough space to recline. She says goodnight to Sandy and then says a prayer of thanks. Thanks for getting us through another day, she says, and then she drifts to sleep under a blanket of ocean air.

As Lovers of Music, "We're Brothers"

(October 29, 2006)

All last week, Nathaniel Anthony Ayers wore a T-shirt with Yo-Yo Ma's name scrawled on it, along with the date and location of the concert: October 27, Disney Hall.

We had tickets for that concert, and he couldn't wait. Los Angeles Philharmonic publicist Adam Crane had put in a request for Ma, the world-renowned cellist, to meet with Ayers after the performance. No guarantees, but maybe. Either way, just watching Ma play would make for a special night for Ayers. Thirty-five years ago, he and Ma were young talents whose paths crossed briefly, when neither could have imagined the life that awaited.

The story begins February 4, 1970, when Ayers, a restless 19-year-old, filled out and sent an application to the Juilliard School. As a freshman, he was doing very well in the music program at Ohio University, but he wanted a stiffer challenge.

The application, which I recently pulled from the school's archives on a trip to New York, asked Ayers to list his father's address. "Unknown," he answered in black pen. His father had been out of the picture for nearly a decade, and Ayers had been raised by his mother, who ran a Cleveland beauty salon. Asked about his sources of financial support, he answered: "Small portion from the Cleveland Scholarship Program Inc." Please list below the music you plan to play at your entrance exam audition, the application instructed.

Dragonetti Concerto in A, the young Mr. Ayers wrote, along with the first movement of the Eccles Bass Sonata, unaccompanied.

To his surprise, Juilliard called almost instantly, and he flew "student standby" to New York. Then he stood before three professors with his string bass, reached inside for all he had and nailed the audition. Ayers was offered a full scholarship and was told to finish up his freshman year of college and then catch a plane to the Aspen Music Festival, a sort of summer school for music students. Aspen was a success, but also a little intimidating. The talent started at great and went up from there. Still, Ayers proved he could play, and it was a confident young man who settled into New York in the autumn of 1970 to study under Homer Mensch, a longtime bassist with the New York Philharmonic.

"This was Homer's room right here," Joe Russo, a former classmate, told me as he led me on a tour of Juilliard. Russo and Ayers were both in awe of the rich sound Mensch could coax out of the bass and overwhelmed by the intense pressure and competition at Juilliard.

"You were constantly comparing yourself to other musicians," Russo, now a conductor and composer in Connecticut, told me as we walked past the dozens of practice rooms on the fourth floor. I looked into one, a windowless space the size of a prison cell, a place to test your limits in airless solitude. Russo said that when students walked down the dim, stifling hall, they could faintly hear classmates practicing in the bunkers. If someone was better than you on the same instrument, it could be a motivator or it could break you. Once, Russo said, he was walking to class on the third floor when he heard a bassist practicing in an audition room. That had to be Mr. Mensch, he thought. What a gorgeous sound. "But when I opened the door, it was Nathaniel."

Ayers wowed teachers, as well. "A very musical performance and a most promising talent," one jury member wrote of Ayers' final exam audition at the end of the first year at Juilliard, giving him an A+.

The following year, Ayers often bumped into a fellow student with a strange name who was thought to be from another universe. Yo-Yo Ma. For a brief time, they played in the same Juilliard orchestra, although Ayers didn't think of Ma as a peer. Ma, though four years younger, was way out there on his own, a jaw-dropping talent. He was even a notch above another superstar cellist: Ayers' roommate Eugene Moye.

Moye would go on to great success as a soloist and orchestral performer in New York. Ma would become an icon. And Ayers? Even before he left Juilliard, his future was disintegrating. Classmates began to notice increasingly hostile and strange behavior from him, and some grew tired of his tirades about racist white America. Russo thought it must be Ayers' way of dealing with the pressure, which he assumed was even greater for Nathaniel, as one of the only African American students at Juilliard.

In reality, it was the beginning of a breakdown. In his third year at Juilliard, just a few months after more raves from teachers at his year-end audition, Ayers began hearing voices and getting wildly confused, suspicious and frightened. One night, he started speaking incoherently and took off his clothes in the apartment of a classmate. The friend called the police, and Ayers was taken by ambulance to Bellevue Hospital. Soon after, he left Juilliard for good.

In the 33 years since then, many of them spent living on the streets of Cleveland and Los Angeles, Ayers has often wondered about his former classmates, holding onto a connection to them through the music he continued playing. When I met him early in 2005, he played with purpose and joy each day near the Beethoven statue in Pershing Square, even though his violin was missing two strings.

Some of you may recall that for many months he resisted my efforts to talk him indoors. Then, early this year, he finally agreed to take an apartment, and he's been there ever since. On Easter, he came to my house for brunch and played the violin, cello and piano, recited Shakespeare and Herman Hesse, sang in Italian, spoke French and had a grand time. When we went to a Dodgers game over the summer, he was out of his seat cheering half the time, having abandoned his hometown Indians.

Other days a chemical change comes over him and the darkness never lifts. He can be verbally abusive and menacing, he doesn't care to see a doctor let alone consider medication, he objects to being called schizophrenic and it seems as though the roller coaster ride will never end.

Our relationship is deeper than ever, more demanding, more exasperating and more rewarding. When it gets exhausting, I remind myself that he's come a long way from two violin strings and a shopping cart, thanks in great part to the staff at Lamp, the mental health agency that has made a life and a home for him.

On Friday, Mr. Ayers—we've agreed to call each other mister, since he refuses to call me by my first name—was playing "Joy to the World" on his new trumpet at Lamp Safe Haven, which is near his apartment. Not everyone at Lamp is thrilled that Mr. Ayers has taken up a brass instrument, especially since the bugling is not always quite on key.

"Joy to the World" didn't sound half bad, though. I waited for it to end before reminding Ayers that I'd be by in a few hours to pick him up for Disney Hall. I also told him the good news. Yo-Yo Ma had sent word that he'd gladly receive Mr. Ayers after the concert.

When I arrived, he had cleaned up well and was wearing a Rite Aid polo shirt on which he had written my name and "Mr. Ma" with a black pen. He wore a red and blue necktie and leather jacket, and his hair was parted in the middle. Before going to Disney Hall, I drove him over to Lamp Village to check out something that's been in the works for months. Lamp is clearing space for a music studio, and the artist in residence will be Mr. Ayers. He's going to teach, take lessons, rhapsodize about the Beethoven statue in Pershing Square and, if I had to guess, recite Shakespeare there on occasion. "This is really going to be something," Mr. Ayers said as he checked out the space and told me he couldn't wait to set up shop.

He talked about it all the way to Disney Hall, where we were greeted by Ben Hong, first assistant principal cellist with the Los Angeles Philharmonic and another former Juilliard student. Mr. Ayers had met Hong before, at one of several concerts he has now attended, so they spoke of music like old pals.

The concert featured just two musicians, Ma and pianist Emanuel Ax. "There he is," Ayers said when they took the stage to warm applause. "Mr. Yo-Yo Ma." The program was all Beethoven, except for a Mendelssohn encore, and Ayers followed along in a book of Beethoven compositions he had brought with him, running his finger over the notes. He also nudged me several times and whispered for me to take notice of Ma's bowing technique. "Bravo," he called after each piece. He laughed with delight at times, and by concert's end, he was of the opinion that it had all come off brilliantly.

Ben Hong led us backstage, and as we waited for Ma, Mr. Ayers was nervous, giddy and chattering like a kid. But not for long. Suddenly, Ma was in the room, grabbing Mr. Ayers' hand. "You're an amazing player," Mr. Ayers said bashfully.

"Did you like it?" Ma said. "I know you like Beethoven." Ma heard Ayers call him "Mr. Ma" and saw the name printed on the Rite Aid shirt. "First of all," he said, "I'm Yo-Yo. Not Mr. Ma." I could have told him to forget it, but I didn't want to intrude.

"I remember your hands from Juilliard," Ayers said, examining them again as if trying to decode the magic.

It wasn't clear whether Ma remembered his old classmate, but that wasn't important to Mr. Ayers. He told Ma of several specific Ma performances he recalled from their youth, and of bumping into him around school. Ma reached around Mr. Ayers and pulled him close. "I just want to tell you," Ma said through a bear hug, "what it means to meet you. To meet somebody who really, really loves music. We're brothers."

In a rare moment, Mr. Ayers was practically speechless. Especially after Ma had one of his cellos brought in and told Mr. Ayers to go ahead and play it while he went off to greet some other fans. Mr. Ayers held the cello in position but was frozen. "This," he said, awed and bewildered, "is Yo-Yo Ma's cello." He stood there a few moments before fiddling just a bit and brightening at the deep and beautiful tone.

It was not easy to get him out of Disney Hall after that. He talked music with Hong, lingered in the hall, struck up a conversation with Emanuel Ax and admired photos of L.A. Philharmonic members, specifically the mug of his teacher, cellist Peter Snyder. He would have used his Beethoven sheet music as a pillow and slept on stage if I had let him.

Thinking back on his trajectory 35 years ago, before the fall, it's hard not to wonder what might have been for Mr. Ayers. But he has little time for self-pity or regret. With several good instruments to play and a studio about to open, he's got work ahead of him. Whatever's been lost, and however isolating his long struggle has been, the music never left him.

Getting Paid
to Act Her Age: 97

(December 17, 2006)

Every couple of months my friend Mae Laborde checks in to let me know how her acting career is going. She's in a tough racket, to say the least, but Mae is definitely a working actress, with a steady flow of jobs in commercials, TV shows and film. Not bad for someone who just broke into the business four years ago, at the age of 93.

"Listen to this, honey," Mae said the other day on the phone. "I've just had a call to go to a studio near Hollywood. It's for some kind of TV show, I think, and I didn't even have to audition for this one. They just called and said I had the job. Not bad, huh?"

She'll be A-list by the time she hits 100, I swear it.

I'd been telling Mae I wanted to see her in action, and this seemed like the perfect opportunity. So I headed over to The Lot, the old Samuel Goldwyn Studio on Formosa Avenue, where *Some Like It Hot* and *West Side Story* were filmed. Mae, who lives in Santa Monica, was filling out her contract when I arrived at Stage 7. The job involved a promo for HBO's *Real Time with Bill Maher*, and Mae said she wasn't quite sure what "promo" meant.

It's a commercial, I explained, asking if she'd ever heard of Bill Maher.

"Oh, yes," she said, "back when he was on the regular channels."

You mean ABC? I asked.

Sounds right, said Mae, who was disappointed to hear the promo was for HBO. "I don't get cable, honey. It's too expensive." Mae and I were neighbors years ago when I lived in Santa Monica. A widow, she was long retired from her jobs as a sales clerk at Henshey's department store in Santa Monica and as a bookkeeper for *The Lawrence Welk Show*. She used to barrel around the neighborhood in an Oldsmobile Delta 88, and at four-foot-ten, barely able to see over the dash, she looked like she was piloting a PT boat. I wrote a column four years ago about Mae's skills behind the wheel, as well as her tea leaf parties and dancing exploits, and an agent called to sign her up.

"I have more fun representing her than any other client," said Sherri Spillane. "If she doesn't hear from me for a few days, she calls and says, 'I haven't heard from you, and I want to go out on another audition.'"

Alicia Alexander, the production manager on the Maher promo, was surprised to hear that Mae, now 97, only recently took up acting.

"We all just assumed she was old Hollywood," said Alexander, who told me Mae arrived at Stage 7 and promptly announced that she doesn't generally require much makeup and rarely needs wardrobe.

"My driver has a bag with my clothes," Mae said, referring not to a limo driver, but to Pearl Soledad, Mae's caretaker since she took a fall several months ago and had to give up driving.

Alexander began sharing Mae's story with other crew members. "She started acting in her 90s, she's been on *MADtv* and *Spike Feresten*, she's got her SAG card and her AFTRA card," Alexander said, referring to the acting guilds. "I know people who would give their eyeteeth to get into SAG."

Mae has taped five episodes of the Feresten show, a cable talk show that hasn't hit the air yet. On *MADtv*, she played an elderly Vanna White. She's also done *Blue Collar TV*, played a cheerleader on an ESPN awards show, just finished a Ben Stiller movie not yet released and made commercials for Sears, Lexus, Chase Bank and Tyco.

"When we did the Lexus commercial, someone on the set asked me what kind of transportation I used when I was young," Mae said. "I told them my father had a horse and buggy."

She wasn't kidding.

"I just got another check in the mail for JP Morgan/Chase Bank," Mae said, telling me that commercial work really helps out with the bills, because every time they run, she gets a little something in the mail. Mae didn't have to audition for the Bill Maher promo, because casting director Kirkland Moody, who went through dozens of photos of grandmotherly actresses, came across Mae and called off the search.

"Check out Mae!" he wrote in an e-mail to Alexander, the production manager. Sure enough, Mae's head shot is a winner. She's a central casting granny, with a smile that says she just crocheted a scarf and took some fresh Toll House cookies out of the oven.

On Stage 7, Mae watched other actors do their thing while awaiting her call. The Maher promo, scheduled to air next year, is a series of over-the-top skits on American politics and greed—an Enron executive standing in a shower of money, an elephant wrestling a donkey, an elderly woman with no health insurance (that's our gal Mae).

"This is more interesting than sitting at home," Mae said as she watched the action, waiting for her moment in the lights.

Wardrobe artist Jane Mannfolk took Mae into the dressing room and returned with her in a cotton house dress and cardigan. "It's so different when you deal with real people instead of celebrities," Mannfolk said with a smile. Yeah, but I noticed that Mae borrowed the arm of a crew member to help her move around the stage several times.

"Too drafty here," she kept saying. Can a personal trainer and private chef be far behind?

"Next up is the grim reaper and my little old lady in the wheelchair," called a crewman.

In real life, Mae uses a cane, not a wheelchair, and she'd like to think the grim reaper won't be visiting any time soon, but she said she's not super-stitious. She climbed into the chair and was wheeled across the stage to director Sammy Silver.

He thanked her for coming and explained that without speaking a word, she'd have to convey a range of emotions having to do with government skimping on elder care. She'd hoist a sign that said, "NO insurance!" and go from happiness and sunshine to being annoyed and disgusted. In the next scene, Silver said, death would stalk her. "You're very grandmotherly, filled with contentment. And then you'll be seeing the grim reaper putting a hand on your shoulder. I think you can have fun with it. You can play it any way you want."

The stage was buzzing as Mae pulled off the first scene like a pro. It took several takes to get camera angles and frames just right, and during a break, Mae asked Silver why she hadn't been asked to audition.

"We saw you and said, 'She's the one,'" Silver told Mae, who looked like she might be thinking about asking for a couple of points on the back end of the deal.

As they started up again, the grim reaper approached Mae and handed her a bouquet of flowers. She looked up and smiled as if he were a trusted friend, then grew puzzled and ultimately suspicious as he wheeled her away. Mae was so smooth, and slyly comical, she had the whole crew in stitches.

"Her timing is exquisite," said Alexander. "It's not like she just [mugs] the expression. She turns into it just right, so it looks real."

After a clean final take and a "Cut" from the director, Mae interrupted the clatter of applause to ask Silver if that was OK. "Yes," said the director, who was beaming. "As a matter of fact, it's really great."

Ms. Laborde was then chauffeured home to her beach cottage, where the actress hoped to catch some beauty rest before Hollywood's next call.

At 20, He's Made It Big

(January 27, 2008)

He's how old? Twenty was the answer. And he's a violinist in the Los Angeles Philharmonic? Yes. He nailed his audition last spring at the age of 19, beating out hundreds of applicants who had far more experience.

So went my conversation with the orchestra's publicist on the subject of Robert Vijay Gupta, who has seven months to go before conductor Esa-Pekka Salonen can legally buy him a beer after a concert.

I bumped into Gupta at Walt Disney Concert Hall recently and said hello, but didn't know anything about him until that conversation with the publicist. I asked Gupta if we could get together, and he invited me to his home, just west of the 405.

Before going to see him, I looked up his biography, which made me consider throwing myself in front of a moving truck.

The New York native graduated from college with a pre-med biology degree at 17. He graduated from Yale with a master's in music at 19. In his spare time as an aspiring neuroscientist, he did laboratory research at Harvard and two other colleges, studying Parkinson's, spinal cord regeneration and the effects of pollution on the brain.

I wasn't sure whether I wanted to interview him, clone him or strangle him. But I was definitely curious to find out how he got where he is, and whether there were any universal lessons in the story of his success. Gupta greeted me at his condo with a polite "Welcome, Mr. Lopez." This is not a young man who's likely to cross paths with Lindsay Lohan on the club circuit. He's got poise and humility, and his eyes are dark reservoirs of maturity.

The musician poured me a cup of coffee and said his father would be with us shortly. It's a safe assumption that Gupta is the only member of the orchestra who needed a parent with him to get settled. The elder Gupta, who has managed his New York travel agency by phone while helping his son set up a home, had to cosign on the condo loan since Robert had no credit record.

"You have to be 25 to rent a car," Robert added, so his father also had to ferry him to rehearsals and concerts until he found time to buy a car. The next youngest member of the orchestra is 28, and publicist Adam Crane said he has so far been unable to find a younger musician in a major orchestra anywhere in the country.

For dinner, if the Guptas are not scoping out a new hole-in-the-wall restaurant as they explore their adopted city, father and son try their hand at cooking Indian food. This involves the occasional frantic call to Robert's mother, Chandana, for advice. An accountant, Mrs. Gupta is busy raising Robert's younger brother, Akshar, a classical pianist and biochemistry major who, of course, will graduate from college in May at the age of 17. So what gives with this family?

Mr. and Mrs. Gupta, both born in Kolkata, formerly known as Calcutta, raised their boys to hit the books and work toward good-paying jobs in medicine, law or business. Music was supposed to help round them out, not get in the way of the important stuff.

"My parents tell me I liked to dance to music when I was three or four," Robert said. His father, Vivek, came in from another room to clarify the matter in scientific terms.

"He was a weird child."

Mr. Gupta recalls tuning the television to *Tom and Jerry* cartoons and watching Robert flip to New York Philharmonic concerts on PBS. Piano lessons followed, then violin.

"I was completely infatuated," Robert said.

Breezing through the Suzuki method, he completed in two years what normally takes eight or ten. At the ripe old age of six, he stunned his parents when he aced an audition for the pre-college program at the Juilliard School in New York City, which became his music lab for the next seven years.

But Vivek Gupta doesn't want people to get the wrong idea. "I hate it when people call him a child prodigy," he said. His son didn't play like an angel the first time he picked up the violin. It was years of devotion that got Robert where he is, thanks in large part to the sacrifices of Mrs. Gupta. She drove her son to and from schools and music lessons while he did his homework in the car. Robert performed as a young solo phenom in Israel, India, Europe and Japan. Even Oprah Winfrey had to have him. In school, the cherubic lad skipped a grade because of how advanced he was, but got picked on and occasionally beaten up for being such a young whiz.

"People in high school were like wolves," Robert said, so he doubled up on courses with a tutor and finished his high school graduation requirements two years early. Then, simultaneously, he was a full-time student at the Manhattan School of Music in Harlem and at Mount St. Mary College before transferring to Marist College.

Yeah, I know. It begins sounding like one of those stories where children experience everything in life but childhood. Except that Robert never felt that way. "I loved every second of it," he said.

When I asked how he could excel as both an artist and a scientist, he leaped at the question as if it were a pizza fresh out of the oven.

"I have a theory," he said, telling me he believes that music training at an early age—when there are more neurons in the brain—enhances the band of fibers that connects the two hemispheres of the brain. Get to know Mozart's 4th Violin Concerto, in other words, and Einstein's quantum theory of light might make a little more sense. You listening, parents? Get the kids some piano lessons.

Robert said that as far back as he could remember, music for him was "exhilaration, joy, complete release." But he also believed that immersing himself in science, history and philosophy would make him a better violinist. "To be an artist, you have to know something outside your instrument," he said. "You have to be a human."

After collecting his master's from Yale in May, it was time to figure out what to do next. Rather than rush off to medical school or go for an MBA, Robert thought he'd take time to reflect while doing some freelance soloing. Might as well have told his parents he wanted to work at a car wash.

"His mother wanted him to become a doctor and so did I," said Vivek Gupta, who had always thought music would be something Robert did on the side, to take a break from his real job. "We thought he was wasting his time."

But Robert had developed a mind of his own, and a friend told him the L.A. Phil had openings for two violinists. Interesting, he thought. He'd counted on a career as a soloist, but believed an orchestral job would be more challenging and useful at this stage of his development. He'd have to interpret the conductor, take a cue from the section leader, work in tandem with his stand partner, and still produce an original sound. Honestly, though, Robert figured he had a better chance of jumping off a chair and landing on the moon than getting hired in Los Angeles, which he believes is supplanting New York as the music center with all the buzz. But long odds could work to his advantage, he theorized. It would free him to play without pressure. "I wanted to not think about the result."

Of the 332 musicians who applied for two violin positions, 111 were invited to audition. In the first round of trials, Gupta's strategy worked well enough to move him into Day Two. And then it worked again. For most of the performances, musicians played behind a screen, so judges evaluated only the sound and not the person. But in his final two performances, Robert was face to face with conductor Esa-Pekka Salonen.

In the first of those sessions, Gupta felt like he'd faint from lack of food. But someone rescued him with a snack, and so he was in front of Salonen one last time, with the conductor asking him to play Mendelssohn's Midsummer Night's Dream.

Gupta dug down once more, trying not just to play the piece, but to feel and interpret it. If his boldness cost him the job, so be it. By the end of the night, Salonen had made his decision. Gupta and David Chernyavsky were the winners, and Gupta would be invited back the following week for tryouts with the full orchestra. After just three concerts, Gupta was called to the conductor's office.

"I'm very honored to offer you the position," Salonen said. "Will you accept?"

"Absolutely," Gupta said.

Here's what Salonen told me about why he hired a 19-year-old kid for his world-class orchestra. "I was struck not only by the sheer quality of Robert's playing, but also by the boldness and confidence of it, which is kind of rare at that stage....Many people who come to audition are trying to play it safe...and it's playing that...is quite often not very interesting."

I wondered, though, if Salonen might be worried that he would show up to work one night and see an empty seat in the orchestra because Gupta had gone off to run Cedars-Sinai Medical Center.

"In a sense," Salonen said of Gupta's far-ranging interests, "this made me even more confident about his future in music, because very clearly Robert is not playing violin in the L.A. Philharmonic for any other reason than his love of music."

In concert at Disney Hall, Gupta appears to have settled in comfortably but lost none of the exuberance. After a recent performance of Beethoven's 4th, he stood Boy Scout proud, basking in warm waves of applause. Last week, he passed his first season of probation with unanimous support from his colleagues.

"He's really a joy to be around," whatever the topic of conversation, said principal concertmaster Martin Chalifour, who finds Gupta's music "enlightened" and "aesthetically beautiful."

Gupta said he looks forward to the occasional solo opportunity, playing chamber music, and perhaps competing one day for a higher position in the orchestra. When he's off duty, he studies literature and science on his own.

Is there still a chance he'll be a doctor one day?

"My wife and I gave up," Vivek Gupta said. "Whatever he decides will be fine. And without music, he would go crazy."

Mortality and That Gift
We Call Time

(June 15, 2008)

Readers send me handwritten letters, and lots of e-mails, too, about a cruel reality none of us wants to think about: our inescapable mortality. I hear about sick children and about adults of all ages suffering from catastrophic illness or the effects of injuries. Nothing stops the steady flow of mail, which continues through the months and through the years like chapters of an endless story we'll all be a part of one day.

I don't usually turn these into columns unless someone is fighting a health insurance company for a chance to stay alive. But maybe I should, because the letters often contain life lessons, soul-searching discoveries and a grace that is humbling.

All of this comes to mind for a very personal reason. I didn't write a Sunday column last week because I was at a Redwood City hospital, waiting nervously with my parents while a doctor performed brain surgery on my sister, Debbie. I don't know if it's really true that bad news comes in bunches, but my father had seized up a week earlier, on his 80th birthday, and was diagnosed with a mini-stroke. He was still in the hospital when my sister, who had been having severe headaches, got the results of an MRI that revealed her brain tumor.

My sister is only 57, and her son is scheduled to be shipped to Iraq later this year with the Marines. She was due a break when she went in for that MRI, not that fairness is anything but a concept. Two years ago, she was diagnosed with ovarian cancer, the disease known as the silent killer because it's often very advanced when symptoms first show up and is likely to recur even when initial treatment seems successful. The surgery, chemotherapy and radiation were all grueling, but she made it through with great courage and her usual sense of humor. And now this.

Was the tumor unrelated, maybe even benign? Possibly. Had it metastasized from the ovarian cancer, which would mean it was malignant? Possibly.

I marvel at the strength people find to handle these challenges. My sister laughed and joked at dinner the night before the surgery, and even on the gurney the next morning as we rode with her in the elevator on the way to surgery. She said she'd bargained with God for at least five years when ovarian cancer was first diagnosed, and she was still counting on him honoring the agreement. I gave her the agnostic nod, squeezed her hand and told her I loved her. While my sister was in surgery, I paced, drank coffee and in the end had to jot down some thoughts. This is part of the post I sent to the *Times'* L.A. Now blog:

"Human suffering—whether it's Chinese children crushed by an earthquake, masses killed by a cyclone in Myanmar, or my poor sister having a tumor dug out of her brain while my parents try to pray away the worst-case scenario—makes me less rather than more inclined to believe in anything but mortality."

So I didn't take my sister a holy book, but I did take her one that might provide a different kind of hope. At the Book Expo in Los Angeles, they were giving away advance copies of a book called *Anticancer: A New Way of Life*, by David Servan-Schreiber. It's not the sort of title this cynic would generally pick up, but my sister's situation made the decision for me. Besides, though we spend billions trying to cure cancer, we're still in the Dark Ages when it comes to understanding the causes, so I wanted to see what this guy had to say about it.

The author, a French-born psychiatrist and professor at the University of Pittsburgh School of Medicine, was diagnosed with a brain tumor and then a recurrence, so he set out to research everything that is known, anywhere in the world, about cancer and what causes it. Then he drastically changed his life.

Did it help? He wrote the book 14 years after his diagnosis.

Servan-Schreiber is careful not to give false hope. Who gets cancer and who survives can be random events. But he makes a compelling argument that cancer rates are higher in the U.S. than elsewhere because of our exposure to toxins in everything from plastics to deodorant, and because of the use of pesticides and feed grain additives. Then there's the typical Western diet: not enough fruits and vegetables and too much refined sugar, white flour and the omega-6 fatty acids found in vegetable oils and animal fats, which Servan-Schreiber calls fertilizer for cancer cells.

When the surgery was done, my sister's doctor had good and bad news. The golf ball-size tumor was removed without complication. But it was a malignant spread of the ovarian cancer. Since then my sister has cried and prayed and found new resolve. There will be radiation and maybe chemotherapy, too. She's on Chapter Four of the book and is determined to put herself at the long end of the survival curve. I believe she'll pull it off.

I spoke to her surgeon the other day and ran Servan-Schreiber's anti-cancer ideas past her, wondering if she'd dismiss them. She didn't. In fact, she said she encouraged patients to embrace the idea of nutritional and lifestyle approaches to fighting cancer and other diseases, along with conventional medicine. "I absolutely believe that," she said, adding that sugar can fuel the growth of cancer cells.

For all of us, time is a gift, and my sister has me thinking about how I spend the moments in a day. Each time we speak I feel blessed, and lucky to know her strength and love.

Cancer?
Ask Plenty of Questions

(September 7, 2008)

When I first wrote about my sister's health problems earlier this year, a Cedars-Sinai doctor I know called to ask if he could help in any way. Actually, I said, I'd appreciate a referral to a good oncologist. What's happened since then is a cautionary tale for anyone who gets sick.

My sister Debbie, 57, was diagnosed with ovarian cancer about two and a half years ago. She lives in Northern California, where we both were raised, and she got excellent care from her managed-care provider. I'm withholding the name of the provider because when I spoke with doctors there, it was as a concerned brother rather than a journalist. A large tumor was surgically removed from my sister's abdomen. Then she underwent grueling bouts of chemotherapy and radiation, and began her recovery. Just when she was feeling herself again, she got more terrible news. In June, an MRI revealed a brain tumor the size of a golf ball. The doctors said it was possible the tumor was benign, unconnected to her previous cancer. Surgical removal showed otherwise. My sister's growth was a carcinoma. Her ovarian cancer had metastasized.

When Debbie was well enough to visit her oncologist, he strongly recommended she undergo whole-brain radiation over other treatments, so she resigned herself to the procedure. Meanwhile, I began doing a little research.

The median survival rate for someone who has surgery followed by whole-brain radiation, according to one often-quoted study, is 23 months. I also learned there can be significant side effects from whole-brain radiation, including memory, hearing and vision loss. I found the news so grim that I withheld it from my sister until she'd regained some strength. She had said, by the way, that her doctor had led her to believe that side effects from whole-brain radiation are often minimal and don't show up for years.

In the meantime, I called the doctor recommended by my friend at Cedars. When she heard the details of my sister's case, the doctor, one of the nation's leading specialists in women's cancers, strongly recommended that we get a second opinion—because from what I was describing, whole-brain radiation might not be necessary. She also disagreed on another point, saying side effects from the procedure were not uncommon, often immediate and potentially severe. In similar cases, she recommended gamma-knife radiation for her patients, a more localized treatment that doesn't kill anywhere near as many healthy cells. If the cancer returned, as it often does, that would be the time for whole-brain radiation, she said.

I called my sister with the news and she decided to hold off on a decision. Meanwhile, I spoke to two more prominent oncologists who backed the doctor from Cedars-Sinai, one of them emphatically. He said the approach recommended to my sister was old-school medicine. My sister's oncologist disagreed. If she wanted the gamma knife, he told me, he'd support it. But it would require an out-of-network referral, because his hospital didn't have the equipment.

"If she were my sister, I'd recommend whole-brain radiation," he said, insisting that the procedure was the best way to ward off any recurrence for the longest period of time.

He's a doctor; I'm not. Should I stay out of it? Not a chance.

I called the experts I'd spoken to earlier with more specific information about the cell structure of my sister's surgically removed tumor. Based on what I was telling them, they stuck with the gamma knife recommendation, and my sister's own research had led to the same conclusion. So what was going on? Was the managed-care doctor's recommendation based on good medicine and familiar protocol, or on the company's aversion to out-of-network expenses?

I got the names of specialists at the UC San Francisco Medical Center, and my sister's oncologist agreed to send her there for a second opinion. The referral process was maddening, and my sister found battling the bureaucracy almost as tough as trying to recover from brain surgery. In the end, a team of UCSF doctors barely considered whole-brain radiation. Their recommendation? Gamma knife surgery.

I began wondering about all the people who might have undergone whole-brain radiation, and had their quality of life diminished, because they weren't told enough about other options. And how many thousands of times does that happen with other illnesses?

My sister had the advantage of a hell-raising brother who's accustomed to rattling cages and demanding answers. And I was lucky enough to know a doctor who gave me entree. But Jamie Court of Consumer Watchdog advises all patients to ask tough questions of their doctors.

"If the best treatment isn't in the HMO network," he said, "the patient may never hear about it. Even if it's the most likely way to save their life." To learn more about your right to a second medical opinion, Court suggested visiting www.calpatientguide.org. Mike Bidart, a Claremont lawyer, has represented several clients who were denied gamma knife treatment. He said he's won out-of-court settlements in each case, but only after tough fights.

There's no doubt that cost is a consideration in medicine, said Art Caplan, a medical ethicist at the University of Pennsylvania. And it should be, of course. We can't all expect to get referrals for every treatment available, while at the same time screaming about the high cost of healthcare. But Caplan added that it's a doctor's duty to lay out in detail all the known options for a patient with a deadly disease.

My sister underwent gamma knife surgery three weeks ago at UCSF and is doing well, volunteering in her spare time to raise money for cancer research. Her managed-care provider has said it will pick up at least part of the bill this time, but perhaps not if she needs surgery again. She knows, as we all do, that the cancer may return. But she's strong and willing to keep fighting, whether the foe is cancer, an HMO or both.

Cancer Can't Dim
a Passion for the Cause

(September 17, 2008)

Dorothy Green was trying to be polite, but the founder of Heal the Bay made it quite clear that she wasn't terribly interested in talking about the things I had come to discuss in her Westwood home.

Death? "It's part of living," she said, flicking away the question.

Her legacy? "I don't look back, only forward."

Her deteriorating condition? "It's interesting that cancer is what you want to talk about."

Now 79, Green has beaten her grim prognosis by years. But the melanoma first diagnosed 30 years ago metastasized to the brain six years ago, and she's now been told there's no way to stop the rapid spread of the disease. She's in hospice care now, a bit wobbly on her feet and wearing a smart-looking cap to keep warm.

"I hope it happens sooner than later," she said of her demise. "It's so hard getting one thought put with another now."

You're not afraid? "I'm scared for the whole world, for the Earth. Not for me."

To those who know her, this is classic Dorothy.

"She tells me we have to keep talking about these issues because it's what keeps her alive—her passion to do what's right for California," said Carolee Krieger.

Krieger and Green co-founded the California Water Impact Network, a nonprofit devoted to educating Californians about what they see as environmentally destructive water mismanagement in California, with public officials caving to the desires of big agriculture. Though Green is clearly addled by painkillers and exhausted by her fight with cancer, so much so that she often pauses mid-sentence to steal the strength to continue, she immediately interrupted me when I mentioned California's water shortage. "There is no water shortage," she said sharply.

Not that anyone should run out and plant a 40-acre lawn, she cautioned. We waste far too much water as it is. But there's no water hog like agriculture, she said.

"Big agriculture uses 80 percent of the developed water in the state," she said, calling their conservation measures abysmal. "And almost half the agriculture in the state is for low-value, water-intensive crops like cotton, rice, alfalfa."

The siphoning of such huge amounts of water for agriculture is destroying the ecosystem in the Sacramento-San Joaquin River Delta, she argues. And the boondoggle is made possible by the lackeys on the state Water Resources Control Board. She gave the Governor Schwarzenegger-appointed board members lousy grades for their two main duties: managing water supplies and managing water quality.

But in Dorothy Green's book, they aren't the only culprits. More than once during my visit, she blamed the media for not hammering away at the story and helping light a fire under the aloof and detached general public. As for the latter:

"They turn on the tap and water comes out," she said, and that's all the average Californian cares to know about water issues. If she weren't still fighting the fight, Green told me, she doesn't know what else she'd be doing.

"This year, she had her spleen and kidney removed and showed up at our board meeting five days later," said Mark Gold, executive director of Heal the Bay. "She has been the most influential water activist in California in the last 30 years."

Green's life is a lesson in reinvention. All that activism lay dormant as she raised a family with a husband who was in real estate. But after the kids were out of the house, she filled the void by volunteering for one cause after another, beginning with programs related to the needs of her own mentally challenged child. She later campaigned for Proposition 20, which led to the creation of the California Coastal Commission. Her outrage over the lack of restrictions on sewage treatment and discharge into the ocean led to community organizing in her living room, followed by the creation of Heal the Bay and the watershed councils for the San Gabriel and Los Angeles rivers.

I assumed a person of her background might choose to have her ashes scattered over a bay she has helped heal. But Green shook her head, calling herself more traditional than that. "Bury me in the soil," she said with a devil-may-care grin. "Worms crawl in, worms crawl out."

I asked Green if she thought it was easier to face death having made a great contribution to society and knowing she's left a lasting mark. That's not something she'd given much thought to, she said, as if such rumination would be a waste of precious time. "It's been a good life. A very rewarding life," she admitted.

She regrets that she won't be around to see three-year-old granddaughter Tara grow up, and she regrets all the unfinished business. But she's not finished just yet. She and Krieger were scheduled to meet today and strategize on fundraising for California Water Impact Network. I promised Green I would direct readers to the website, so they could educate themselves on the issues she's passionate about.

So please, dear readers, take a look at www.C-Win.org. Or spend a few minutes at www.healthebay.org.

You might get angry; you might even get involved. And Dorothy Green's great legacy, in spite of her modesty, will only grow.

Caught Between
Love and the Law

(September 28, 2008)

Jimmy Wheeler, 84, is out on bail. The charge? Attempting to kill his wife. I stopped by his daughter's house in Carpinteria and he greeted me at the front door, ready to talk about what he intended as an act of mercy. Wheeler shook my hand and led me to the dining room table. A pleasant smile was fixed on his tanned, lined face, but he was dabbing at his eyes. And then he lost it on the first question.

I asked how he met his wife, Betty, whom he calls Beckie. He sobbed, his chest heaved and then he began his story. They were students at UCLA, he said, his memories still fresh. He never saw her on campus, though. The first time he laid eyes on her was at the beach in Santa Monica. She was with friends, but they were invisible to Jimmy.

"She was cute, she was smart, she was happy," he said. "And she had a nice shape."

Wheeler drove a Model A station wagon painted UCLA blue and gold, and Beckie agreed to ride back to campus with this lanky young poli-sci major. He looked a little like Jimmy Stewart, with piercing blue eyes. They were married two years later, at the height of World War II. Soon he was off to fly bombing missions over Europe. After the war, he finished school at Oregon State and got a graduate degree from Stanford. Jimmy then found work as a petroleum engineer, and he and Beckie raised a son and daughter in Carpinteria.

This is a love story, of course. The attempted murder notwithstanding. It's a story many of us find familiar in one way or another, particularly we boomers with ailing parents. I couldn't stop thinking about—and talking about—my own parents as Mr. Wheeler and I chatted. A hundred times in the last year, my siblings and I have wondered whether we're intruding too much, or not enough, into our parents' lives. Is it time to insist on home care? Should we insist it's time to surrender driver's licenses? We're much better at the questions than the answers.

Wheeler and his wife have been married 64 years, and they've enjoyed what he called "a wonderful life." But Beckie, 85, has Alzheimer's. Jimmy Wheeler took good care of his wife, stealing all that he could from what was left of normal. They kept traveling, one of their great joys, until her illness made that impossible. Until quite recently, he and Beckie could be seen walking down the street to the beach, holding hands like young lovers. But Beckie was fading into solitude, the world around her a growing mystery, and then finally Jimmy was a stranger to her.

"She wakes up in the morning and doesn't know who the guy in bed with her is," Wheeler told me with wet eyes, capturing perfectly the horror of watching a loved one disappear into a fog. In a way it's crueler than death itself, because there's no moving on for the survivor. There is only this ghost, a constant reflection of love and loss.

"Are you OK?" Jimmy's son-in-law, Stan Scrivner, asked him one morning when he came to the door in obvious distress.

"No," Wheeler said. "Beckie's gone." Scrivner asked what he meant.

"She's gone," Wheeler repeated. "She doesn't recognize me anymore."

Wheeler couldn't bear to see her like that, and eventually he came up with a plan. "She said she wanted to be with Jesus," he said. "I just wanted to be with her."

Although Wheeler has pleaded not guilty, the basic details of what happened next aren't in dispute. One night earlier this month, he reportedly turned on the gas burners in the house.

"It was Romeo and Juliet," Scrivner said. Except that it didn't work.

Plan B, authorities said, was to run a hose through a window and into the house from the exhaust pipe on Wheeler's '99 Olds. Wheeler wrote a suicide note and included instructions for cremation of the bodies. He left a check to cover the cost. He advised loved ones on how to handle his estate, says his attorney Steve Balash, cautioning them to be careful about probate lawyers who charge too much.

The exhaust might have done the trick, but a neighbor saw what was up and called police. Jimmy Wheeler ended up behind bars, charged with attempted murder and elder abuse. He slept on a mattress on the floor of the overcrowded Santa Barbara County Jail. A county prosecutor called Wheeler a threat to himself, his wife and the neighborhood. Superior Court Judge George Eskin listened to that argument but at a recent bail hearing he said the case called for "compassion and understanding."

"I am aware of the tragedy of Alzheimer's," Eskin told me by phone. He noted that unlike other countries and the state of Oregon, California has not embraced legalized options—including assisted suicide—for people nearing the end. Eskin allowed Wheeler's release on $100,000 bail pending a preliminary hearing on October 8, and ordered him to be supervised and undergo grief counseling.

"He's not going to do her in," Eskin reasoned, so the judge's emphasis was on making sure Wheeler gets help to see if "he can find the strength to go on."

Even if California had passed a death with dignity bill (the bill has failed three times, with strong opposition from doctors and organized religion), the Wheeler scenario wouldn't have come into play. The proposed bill, patterned after the one in Oregon, would have required a terminally ill patient to be of sound mind and to self-administer the lethal drug. Alzheimer's is not considered a terminal illness, and Beckie was in no shape to make the decision to end her life.

"Somehow they have to figure out how to create a new area of law that's about compassion and mercy," said Jeff Wheeler, Jimmy and Beckie's son. With good reason, he finds it incomprehensible that his father is being treated like a common criminal, prosecuted the same way as, say, a spurned boyfriend who gets a revolver and goes gunning for his girlfriend's new love interest.

After three swings and misses, Assembly members Lloyd Levine and Patty Berg have given up on a death with dignity bill in California. But they now have one before the governor that would require doctors to give terminally ill patients information on all their options, including hospice care and sedation. Let's hope Governor Schwarzenegger signs it. But still it would be a far cry from what they've got in Oregon, and Californians might go on using bridges, guns, toxic cocktails and underground suicide options. Or they might make botched and bungled attempts like Jimmy Wheeler's.

Kathryn Tucker, a lawyer with Compassion & Choices, says that patients in Oregon can sign an "advance directive" stipulating that in cases of progressive dementia, they would want no steps taken to keep them alive. Here in California, we've got the prospect of an 84-year-old grandfather going to jail if a jury finds that he tried to lie down beside his wife and die with her. Sure, you could argue he had no right to decide for his wife whether she should go on living. But prosecuting him aggressively and sending him to prison would be a miscarriage of justice and a waste of tax dollars.

"I'm trying not to think about that possibility," Wheeler told me. I asked if he had considered taking his wife to a nursing home—she's in one now—instead of trying to die at her side.

"My sister is in one of those convalescent homes," Wheeler said. "Those people are just passing the time of day, not knowing what's going on. That's no kind of life." And what would he want to happen to him, I wondered, if he were as sick as his wife?

"I'd want to be gone," Jimmy Wheeler said. I understand completely.

If I ever get to where I don't recognize the people I care about, I wouldn't want to hang around. And I'd be grateful to any friend or family member who helps me move on. I'd consider it an act of love.

Serenade in the Key of Glee

(July 12, 2009)

He was so eager to make the trip, he called several times to make sure
it hadn't been canceled.

"Mr. Lopez, is the pickup still at nine a.m?"

"Yes, Mr. Ayers. I'll see you in the morning."

When I pulled up, he was standing on the sidewalk playing a skid row
reveille on his trumpet. He had a small overnight bag and five more instruments—cello, violin, French horn, clarinet and flute, meaning he had made
the difficult decision to leave several other instruments home.

We stowed the gear in the station wagon and caught Interstate 5 for the
long haul north. My friend Nathaniel Anthony Ayers, who had never been
to San Francisco, was scheduled to be honored by the National Alliance on
Mental Illness. Flying was out of the question because he has no photo ID.
I've never looked forward to that monotonous stretch of I-5, but for better
or worse, Mr. Ayers was likely to liven things up. Sometimes he can get a tad
claustrophobic or edgy, and being trapped in a car for six hours might take
its toll. In other words, I had no idea what to expect. But nothing soothes
Mr. Ayers' soul like music, so I tuned the radio to classical KUSC-FM as we
left Los Angeles. Mr. Ayers sat in wonder, squinting as if searching for a way
to describe Chopin's Piano Concerto No. 1, Opus 11.

"That's the sound of a child's heart," he said. He listened a little longer
and added, "That's what God looks like."

Up and over the Tejon Pass we cruised, Mr. Ayers marveling at the majesty of open spaces. As we descended the Grapevine and hit the floor of the great valley, he was reminded of Texas, Colorado and his home state of Ohio. The turnoff for the little farm town of Arvin streaked by, and he said he wouldn't mind living in the area.

"It's nice and clean here," he said. "You get back to skid row and it's filled with debris."

We passed fields of corn and big rigs carrying mounds of tomatoes, and the open road ahead disappeared into the horizon. Mr. Ayers, as I had long known, is the world's worst back-seat driver. He's a white-knuckler, bolting forward frequently to brace himself against the dash.

"Mr. Lopez, we're going to be killed," he said as a lumbering truck pulled in front of us.

I plugged in a CD to calm his nerves. Tchaikovsky's Serenade for Strings. Mr. Ayers, who studied at Juilliard before his dreams came unraveled, once told me he practiced that piece while standing in the window of his New York City apartment, watching the falling snow. As he listened now, he recalled his first romance in Cleveland.

"Donna," he said with a sigh. "My heart was messed up for a long time. Somebody else got her."

We stopped for gas and food near Buttonwillow. When I came out of the restroom, Mr. Ayers was playing French horn in the parking lot, wearing a military jacket and a red Kangol cap with "Obama" on it. This drew a few curious glances from am/pm mini-mart customers.

I piled back in, a smile on my face, and Mr. Ayers blew his horn for the next 50 miles from the cramped quarters of the passenger seat, the window down and the warm valley air pouring through the car. With soft, mellifluous bursts from Mr. Ayers, the Central Valley had a classical soundtrack now, and the long dusty drive wasn't so monotonous. When he finally rested his lungs, I put on Jacqueline du Pré, Mr. Ayers' favorite cellist.

"That is really, really soulful playing," he said of the striking blond musician who died at 42. "Do you see what she's saying? It's a recitation of Shakespeare."

As du Pré worked her way through the Bach unaccompanied cello suites, Mr. Ayers gazed upon the rolling terrain and remarked, "The grass is the color of her hair."

Just after three p.m, San Francisco Bay came into view, the landscape as surreal as ever, and Mr. Ayers was dazzled by the sight of Alcatraz and the Golden Gate Bridge. We crossed the bay and were met in the lobby of the Hilton Towers by his sister, Jennifer, who has built a foundation in Mr. Ayers' name. But there was little time for him to catch up with her. It was as if a rock star had arrived, and Mr. Ayers was mobbed by admirers who were attending NAMI's annual convention.

NAMI is a national organization dedicated to improving the lives of those affected by mental illness. Though Mr. Ayers has many challenges ahead, the story of his long journey—from psychiatric hospitals to the streets to supportive housing at Lamp Community—has given hope to many. They wanted to thank him, hug him, pose for pictures and get his autograph, and Mr. Ayers was all too happy to oblige.

That evening, he performed on cello and violin for a crowd of several hundred. I've never seen Mr. Ayers happier than he was when a roar broke out as he was given an award for his courage and spirit, and for sharing a story that has helped decrease the stigma.

When the celebration was done, Mr. Ayers linked up with a young pianist named Will, who has a story similar to his own. They adjourned to the lobby of the Hilton Towers and jammed into the wee hours. The lights of San Francisco twinkled through the windows behind them as the musicians found a way past the labels, limitations and isolation they've known, rescued once again by the music.

On the ride back home, Mr. Ayers switched to trumpet and blew hard enough to be heard by the cows at Harris Ranch. He thought aloud about moving to San Francisco but then said he'd miss Los Angeles, and besides, there were so many homeless people in the Tenderloin district.

"It's depressing," he said, as if the illusion of a magical place, without pain or suffering, had been shattered.

We were about to climb the Grapevine when Mr. Ayers began dreaming about recording a CD. We decided that if it happens, he should do nine cuts and play a different instrument on each one, like a baseball player who fields a different position every inning of a game. The CD would be called "Putting on Ayers," we decided, and before we knew it, we were home.

Riding Out a Wave of Tragedy

(July 19, 2009)

It's another beautiful day in paradise and I'm out on the ocean, riding waves with a former national surfing champion and onetime prostitute who's about to join a seminary. Go ahead, try to name one other state where I could have written that sentence.

"Terrific!" yells Mary Setterholm, my instructor, who forgives my every wipeout and cheers when I finally ride a wave all the way to shore. Setterholm, who now runs a Santa Monica surfing school, won the U.S. Women's title in 1972, at age 17. And you're not going to believe where her trophy is.

On Cardinal Roger M. Mahony's desk.

Where do I even begin? Perhaps with the e-mail from Ann Hayman, a minister at Brentwood Presbyterian, who remembered that I once wrote about a skid row prostitute who lived in a Porta-Potty but later turned her life around. Hayman, who worked with prostitutes for 28 years, had someone she wanted me to meet.

So I drove to Brentwood to meet Hayman and Setterholm. Over coffee—and the next day at the beach—Setterholm spun a tale both tragic and triumphant.

As a young child, Setterholm told me, she was physically and sexually abused repeatedly by a baby-sitter, and then beginning in seventh grade, she was molested for years by a now-deceased priest from her Catholic church in Westwood. When her family moved to the Huntington Beach area, Setterholm found herself drawn to the sea. There was honesty and security in the rhythm of the waves, but the ride to the shore was fraught with danger.

She routinely hitchhiked, and the men who picked her up—some of them regulars—took detours on the way to the beach. Setterholm was too damaged and confused to stop their advances, so she built a reality in which by charging them she established an illusion of control and even normalcy. It was simple economics. Survival.

"I was so used to perverted behavior by men, I didn't know that what I was doing fit into the context of prostitution," she said.

On the water, she was a fearless acrobat, but on the shore, she kept making all the wrong moves. She got married way too young, to the wrong guy, of course, and had five children before she had learned to take care of herself. When the marriage bombed, she returned to prostitution.

This pattern of self-destruction came as no surprise to a Catholic nun who helped Setterholm find her way past buried secrets, paralyzing hatred and self-loathing. "I know many victims who try to work it out by getting into serial relationships," said Sister Sheila McNiff, and it appeared to her that Setterholm had done precisely that, digging herself in deeper all the while.

McNiff was the victim assistance coordinator for the Los Angeles Archdiocese, serving under Mahony as the church began dealing with its scandalous history. She first heard from Setterholm in 2002, when the surf queen called to tell of the abuse she'd suffered 30 years prior.

"I asked her, 'Where can I meet you?'" McNiff recalled. "She said, 'At the beach.'"

It wasn't long before nun and surfer had formed a mutual admiration society. Setterholm wasn't looking for a financial settlement with the institution that had betrayed her. She wanted to finally look into the eyes of church leaders, tell them what she'd been through, and pray that she'd be healed.

"She had a very strong sense of trying to be a reconciler," said McNiff, who worked with Setterholm to arrange "apology" Masses for victims. McNiff also helped arrange a meeting with Mahony at the Cathedral of Our Lady of the Angels, and Setterholm had a lot to tell the good cardinal. That he needed to do less moralizing and more listening. That many victims can't feel safe again in a church. That it was difficult for her to face him, but impossible to survive without doing so.

"She told him her story and the cardinal apologized," said McNiff, who was in tears and could see that the cardinal was deeply moved as well. Setterholm volunteered to pass a message from the cardinal to other victims.

"Tell them it is not their fault," she recalls him saying. Setterholm held hands with the cardinal and prayed with him. And, as a gesture of reconciliation, she gave him one of her most prized possessions. The trophy from her surfing championship.

"He said he would keep it on his desk," McNiff recalled.

Setterholm has become something of a missionary since that encounter, reaching out to working women and street dwellers and bringing some of them into her own home in Hermosa Beach. With McNiff and Hayman serving as mentors, she formed Serenity Sisters, a support group to help recovering prostitutes. And she runs Surf Bus, a program that brings hundreds of inner-city children to the beach each summer to learn how to surf.

McNiff persuaded Setterholm to go back to school, and she graduated from Loyola Marymount last spring with a degree in theology. Next month, she'll begin the master of divinity program at New York's Union Theological Seminary, which is affiliated with Columbia University. She was accepted by the school despite an application that included this entry under the "Work Experience" category: "Prostitution, Independent street/sex worker, 1970-76 and 1992-11/3/2002."

In certain denominations, a graduate degree would mean that Setterholm had gone from prostitute to priest. She said she doesn't care about the title. She just wants to return to L.A. and run a ministry devoted to rescuing lost souls. She'll never give up the surfing life, though, or working to turn more people onto the sport. Speaking of which, McNiff recalled one more thing Setterholm said to Mahony that day at the cathedral.

"She offered him surfing lessons at some point."

And what did the cardinal say?

"He did not commit himself," said McNiff.

Come to the beach, Your Eminence, and we'll hang 10 together. There's nothing as pure and cleansing as the ocean. Mary Setterholm is a great teacher, and every wave is like another baptism.

A Quiet Success Story in L.A.

(December 2, 2009)

On weekday evenings, a white van circles the neighborhood of Lafayette Park west of downtown Los Angeles. The driver, William Correa, is killing time. Sometimes, instead of motoring, Correa goes to the library for a couple of hours and reads or watches movies. Other times he goes shopping or has a snack to hold him over until dinner. At 6:30, the waiting is over. He picks up his two sons at HOLA, or Heart of Los Angeles—a nonprofit after-school program—and drives them home to Paramount.

Recently I met Juan, the eldest son, a lean and handsome young man of 15. I was on a tour of HOLA when someone introduced us. He was quiet, polite, painfully shy. Later, I was told that he used to live in the neighborhood and began attending HOLA four or five years ago. Juan got hooked, especially on the art program, and the HOLA staff got hooked on him.

"He's so quiet, but there's an intensity," said Dan McCleary, an accomplished artist who has exhibited extensively and is one of Juan's teachers at HOLA. "And he's phenomenal for his age."

When Juan was about to leave middle school, McCleary suggested he apply to his own alma mater, the private Catholic boys school Loyola High. Juan wasn't sure he could measure up, or perhaps it was something else that gave him pause. His parents are Colombian immigrants, and William Correa's salary as a religious aide at St. Emydius in Lynwood, where he helps parishioners prepare for sacraments, was modest, as was that of his wife, who works as a secretary at the church. Only in a dream could they come up with the tuition to a fine private high school.

McCleary wasn't about to give up. Though his own art career had been quite successful, he had never felt entirely fulfilled by it. The young energy and talent at HOLA had reawakened something in him, and he was eager to go to bat for Juan.

"I see myself in his quietness," McCleary said.

McCleary called Loyola to talk up the boy, and he asked the principal to consider a scholarship for him. It worked, with a catch. The school didn't offer a full scholarship. Juan would still have to pay $3,000, and his family still couldn't cover it. That's when the staff at HOLA got creative.

HOLA is a place where the kids inspire the adults as much as the reverse. Walk the campus with Tony Brown, the executive director, and he'll introduce the kid who made it to UCLA, the one who's on his way to UC Santa Barbara, the guy from Sudan who worked out his problems at HOLA as a kid and volunteers as an adult.

The staff was determined to get Juan into Loyola, so they asked him to hurry up and start drawing and painting, because his work was good enough to sell. Juan does striking, intricate pencil drawings of people, animals and nature scenes. He quickly completed 30 works of art, which were purchased by volunteers, employees and visitors at $100 apiece.

The $3,000 got Juan into Loyola. He's now in his sophomore year there, and talking about one day trying for Loyola University, or perhaps Stanford, which he visited recently with McCleary for an art show. The idea of becoming an artist burns in him, but knowing it will be tough to make a living that way, he wants to study graphic design, too.

"Dan encourages everybody to do their best," Juan told me late one afternoon in the bright and airy HOLA art studio. "But he helped me a lot, mostly with drawing. He's an artist, but he's also a mentor."

Juan knows that getting to HOLA day after day has created a hardship for his father. Before Loyola, Juan went to school in the Lynwood parish where his father works. His father would drive him to school in the morning, go to work, then drive him to HOLA in the afternoon. Even after the rent was raised on their apartment and they were forced to move in with relatives in Palmdale, the family wouldn't give up on HOLA. But it meant leaving home at 4:30 a.m. and getting back to Palmdale at eight p.m. The routine was so grueling that they moved last summer to Paramount, which is closer, but still a slog. Mr. Correa drives Juan to Loyola in the morning, goes back to work in Lynwood, then drives his younger son to HOLA in the afternoon and has two or three hours to kill as he waits for both sons.

This kind of sacrifice by parents, McCleary says, is the under-told story of the L.A. inner city, a place where the sensational and the tragic are more likely to make the evening news. "Juan was living in the middle of gang-land," McCleary said, but he is typical of the many kids from good and decent families. His story is a quiet one, as quiet as Juan himself, and there is no high drama in his father's daily routine. There is only pride and work and yearning.

On my second visit with Juan, we waited in the parking lot for his father to pull up. Just past 6:30, he appeared. I shook William Correa's hand and asked him why he endures this grueling daily routine.

"Because my mother and father gave me an opportunity to go to an excellent school in Colombia," he said. "So I give to Juan and his other brother the same opportunity. I want them to do better than I have."

"Hello, Nathaniel":
Obama Welcomes Mr. Ayers to D.C.

(July 28, 2010)

In those early days after we met five and a half years ago, when Nathaniel Ayers slept on the streets of skid row, he was a dreamer. He'd play a two-string violin at the feet of the Beethoven statue and imagine a day when he would figure out how to get the two missing strings, or a day when he might visit a concert hall or play well enough to draw an audience. But he never would have guessed that one day he'd be invited to the White House to meet the president and to perform at a celebration commemorating the 20th anniversary of the Americans with Disabilities Act.

"It's the most incredible thing I ever could have imagined," Mr. Ayers said a few weeks ago on hearing of the invitation through his sister, Jennifer. To be honest, I had misgivings about the trip. I tend to err on the side of being overprotective and shielding my friend from stressful situations. Despite remarkable progress, he is still at the mercy of unpredictable storms like those that knocked him out of the Juilliard School of Music nearly 40 years ago with a diagnosis of schizophrenia.

But the dreamer already had the scene in his head—Mr. Ayers goes to Washington. And he made a passionate appeal to our friendship, asking me please to be there with him. OK, I said. But Mr. Ayers needed a new set of duds for his big day, so Bobby Witbeck, a longtime Ayers family friend, took him to a Hollywood Suit Outlet. Mr. Ayers knew exactly what he wanted, and when I later asked why he got a white suit, white shoes, white bowtie and white derby, I already knew the answer.

"Because it's the White House," he said.

And so it was that on Monday, a warm and sunny day that followed a pounding storm, Mr. Ayers found himself in the diplomatic meeting room at the White House in a splendid vanilla-colored outfit, a nylon hair wrap under his derby, waiting to meet the first African American President of the United States.

"Mr. Ayers, " I said, nudging him across from a portrait of George Washington. "You're in the White House."

"I can't believe it," he said.

"What are you going to say to the president?" I asked.

"I'm going to tell him to have a good day and a blessed presidency," said Mr. Ayers, who had written Obama's name on his trumpet case and, to top off his outfit, was wearing garden gloves with the fingers cut out.

Soon afterward, Mr. Ayers was called in for a private moment and a photograph with Obama. When he returned, he was beaming.

"I'm flabbergasted," he said. He said the president had greeted him with, "Hello, Nathaniel."

To which Mr. Ayers said: "The President of the United States of America. Praise the Lord!"

Outside, on the back lawn of the White House, about 300 government officials and others had assembled to hear a speech by Obama and performances by Patti LaBelle and Mr. Ayers, who would be accompanied by his buddy and former Juilliard classmate Joseph Russo. In the crowd were many pioneers in the fight for the rights of those who had known rejection, discrimination and stigma because of all manner of disabilities. There's still progress to be made, particularly for those with mental illness, and there are still critical shortages of supportive housing and rehabilitation. But this was a day of celebration.

"It's a great day," said Alan Toy, a Los Angeles civil rights activist and disabled actor. He had been in the same spot 20 years ago for the signing of the disabilities act by President George H.W. Bush, a law mandating access and employment rights.

After a few speeches, the big moment arrived. My heart rose when Mr. Ayers was introduced and emerged from the back door of the White House in his dandy suit, walking under the Seal of the President of the

United States. I was nervous because I knew he felt the pressure, and I was proud, because he'd come so far and represented the hope of so many. I had informed the White House staff that you're not always sure what you'll get musically from Mr. Ayers other than passion, but the White House had taken a risk. Mr. Ayers was to be included, not left at the gate. Kareem Dale, a special advisor to the president, had told me this would be an audience that knew and respected perseverance. Dale himself is blind.

Maybe it was the sweltering heat, or the pressure, but Mr. Ayers couldn't seem to get his fiddle tuned, and as the moments dragged on, it was unclear whether he would proceed. Mr. Russo, on piano, and the audience, waited patiently. I, meanwhile, was practically hyperventilating, and pulling for my friend.

Finally, he found a groove, and the audience swayed, Mr. Ayers lifting spirits with his music. He switched to trumpet after a few minutes, and although he would later say it wasn't one of his better performances, Mr. Ayers' very presence at the event—his journey from skid row to the White House—was a triumph his audience understood and applauded. "Yes, we can," Obama later said in rallying the crowd to continue the fight for equal opportunity.

After the speech, Mr. Ayers shook hands with Obama again and darted in and out of the White House as if he were a resident. On the back lawn, he accepted congratulations and posed for pictures. Russo said he had never been more inspired by his buddy Nathaniel Ayers, saying his performance was perfect for the event. He struggled, Russo said, but he soldiered on.

When we got back to skid row Tuesday, the White House seemed a million miles away. As I dropped Mr. Ayers off at his apartment, I asked how he would ever top his trip to D.C. He had an answer.

"Do you think we can go to Rome and meet with the pope?"